Organizational Behavior:
Experiences and Cases

FOURTH EDITION

by Dorothy Marcic
Czechoslovak Management Center and
Prague School of Economics

WEST PUBLISHING COMPANY
MINNEAPOLIS/ST. PAUL   NEW YORK   LOS ANGELES   SAN FRANCISCO

WEST'S COMMITMENT TO THE ENVIRONMENT

In 1906, West Publishing Company began recycling materials left over from the production of books. This began a tradition of efficient and responsible use of resources. Today, up to 95% of our legal books and 70% of our college texts and school texts are printed on recycled, acid-free stock. West also recycles nearly 22 million pounds of scrap paper annually—the equivalent of 181,717 trees. Since the 1960s, West has devised ways to capture and recycle waste inks, solvents, oils, and vapors created in the printing process. We also recycle plastics of all kinds, wood, glass, corrugated cardboard, and batteries, and have eliminated the use of Styrofoam book packaging. We at West are proud of the longevity and the scope of our commitment to the environment.

Production, Prepress, Printing and Binding by West Publishing Company.

Table of Contents

Introduction

Written for the introductory organizational behavior course, this fourth edition has been significantly revised. Nearly 20 of the exercises and cases are new. Added are topics on learning organizations, path-goal leadership, resume-writing skills, gender differences in communication, protected classes discrimination, the new management paradigm, and integrative cases. Also, quite a number of new exercises emphasize management skill development. Organizational Behavior (OB) is a discipline which has both theoretical and practical elements. Most OB textbooks do a decent job of developing the theoretical foundation, but many have less emphasis on the practical aspects. This book was designed to fill that gap. It has been developed with the following assumptions:

1. Learning can be interesting and fun. It does not have to be painful or boring.

2. Most theories of learning place application at a higher level than intellectual understanding. (Imagine a statistics course where you learned theories but never worked on any problems.)

3. Organizational Behavior is particularly suited to learning through application by the use of experiential exercises.

4. Most OB instructors can incorporate some types of experiential exercises into their courses, depending on their own interests and inclinations.

5. A person who has a better understanding of herself and how groups function will make a better manager because she will be more aware of her own resources and how to utilize them effectively.

In order to provide a diversity of experiences, the following types were used:

1. Group or individual activities
2. Diagnostic instruments
3. Role-plays
4. Case studies

Because some teachers prefer group activities, while others use more role-plays, the attempt was made to cover all four areas. In addition, the exercises range from very simple to more complex, so that seasoned as well as newer experiential exercise users can find ones they are comfortable with. The instructor's manual has a difficulty grid which helps instructors gauge how complex the exercise is before it is tried. There are other grids in the instructor's manual, as well: one which shows related topics of each exercise, and another one which shows the compatibility of this book's topics with that of many of the major OB textbooks.

Times given for each exercise are sometimes variable (this is shown as the "+" sign after the number of minutes) and can be done in the minimum time for shorter classes or with more time in longer classes.

Another difference is that some of the exercises use "real-world" examples, while others use the university or the classroom as a focus for studying organizations and groups. This second type was chosen also because undergraduate students can usually relate quite easily to managerial and organizational issues on campus or in the classroom. However, one change in this edition is the addition of more "real-life" examples to satisfy the needs of older, more experienced students.

Many OB textbooks and exercises deal with mainly cognitive issues and ignore or gloss over the affective or emotional. Craig Lundberg gave a presentation on this at an Organizational Behavior Teaching Conference. A general feeling of the more than 50 participants was that there indeed was a lack of affective material in texts and that this ought to be corrected. An article on "Dealing with Emotions in the Classroom," in the instructor's manual, addresses this topic more thoroughly.

At that same OBTC meeting, several of us spent two hours with Robert Tannenbaum discussing the importance of helping students to understand themselves better. Tannenbaum feels OB professors have generally been negligent in giving students direction in terms of knowing who they are, where they would "fit" best and, therefore, how to live and work more productively. Some of the exercises in this book are designed to overcome this deficiency.

A final note is given on how students should "use" experiential exercises. To gain maximum benefit, keep the following points in mind:

1. Try to take the exercises seriously. If you take them as jokes, you will not learn much.

2. If you have a disagreement with one instructor or part of an instrument, try not to let that overtake the potential learning. Do not lose sight of the bigger goal of learning about yourself as a potential manager and learning about organizations.

3. Even if you do not understand why you have to do something, still try to get into the exercise; otherwise you probably will not learn from it.

4. Take responsibility for your own learning. The teacher is a facilitator and you need to be an important part of the learning model.

And finally, remember – learning can be fun and at times unsettling. One of my professors used to say, "It's good when you are confused, because it shows you are learning."

Contributors to This Edition

So many people have given tremendous support and assistance for the fourth edition. My editor, Esther Craig, was always willing to give a helping hand and her positive attitude smoothed over many a bumpy road. Further, John Szilagyi at West was most supportive. Don Hellriegel, John Slocum, and Dick Woodman gave invaluable time and effort in the first, second, and third editions.

In addition, numerous colleagues provided useful and productive feedback, including Gadi Harel of Technion University (who laughed me through several exercises), Peter Vaill of George Washington University, Howie Schwartz of Oakland University, Andre Delbecq of Santa Clara University, Ken Murrell of the University of Western Florida, Steven Birkland of Metropolitan State University, Minnesota, Bob Marx of the University of Massachusetts, Larry Miller of The Miller Consulting Group, and my dear sister, Janet Mittelsteadt. This fourth edition was done while I was a Fulbright Scholar at the Czechoslovak Management Center and the Prague School of Economics, and I was helped a great deal by both institutions. Colleagues at the Czechoslovak Management Center helped a great deal during the long period of getting this book done. Former dean Bill Pendergast offered support and assistance, while Carol Pendergast gave ideas and emotional support. Michal Cakrt, who has become one of my closest colleagues, taught me many things about OB in a cross-cultural setting. Current dean Jo Olson has given support as well, especially at the stressful ending time. Other colleagues who were there and I am grateful to are Rudolf Galik, Jaroslav Jirasek, Marie Pribova, Elena Ockova, Jana Matesova, Juraj Koman, Charles Sabatos, and Dagmar Glaukofova. Similarly, at the Prague School of Economics I was given assistance by Ivan Novy and Eva Jarosova. Finally, I cannot forget the love and support of friends who cheered me through the difficult and the fun times. They include Diane Cabolt Garga, Elaine McCreary, Margaret Clayton, Roberta Law, Heidi Grebacher, Ivan Sterzl, George Starcher, Floyd Tucker, Jeff Mondschein, Barbara Gorski, Debby and Bob Rosenfeld, Michael Winger-Bearskin, Marketa Glancova, and Maja Curhova.

Several OB faculty members reviewed the third edition and offered worthwhile suggestions during the revision process. Special appreciation goes to Barbara McIntosh of the University of Vermont, David M. Leuser of Plymouth State College, Sally Dresdow of Asbury College, David Leland of Red River Community College, Joseph Seltzer of La Salle University, Marianne Benieris of California State University at Long Beach, Joy V. Peluchette of University of Southern Indiana, and Joy Benson of Sangamon State University.

Huge thanks go to those who offered hours and hours of their time working on the (at times) overwhelming support tasks. Patrick Uram was there for months filling in the cracks and keeping track of details, the most crucial and challenging being permissions, and he never lost his wonderfully cheerful attitude. Victoria Murphy was there for support and helpful assistance. A great deal of time, energy, and patience was given by Martha Pinder who labored over the difficult task of layout and design of the text, and thankfully added some wonderful creativity to the book.

And lastly, thanks to my family: to my sister, Janet Mittelsteadt, and to my three daughters, Roxanne, Solange, and Elizabeth, who became used to playing around me at home as I pounded away on the computer. Their love and support carried me through many a rough day.

To my sister, Janet,
my best friend and my biggest cheerleader

Chapter 1

Introduction to Organizational Behavior

1. Assumptions About People and Organizations[1]

Purpose:
To develop an awareness of Organizational Behavior issues.

Group Size:
Three to six members.

Time Required:
25-50 minutes.

➡ Introduction

Before beginning this course and learning more about people and how they function and relate within organizations, it may be helpful to explore your own assumptions about what are effective behaviors for managers. In other words, what types of things can make an organization and its people more productive, more satisfied.

The following inventory contains some statements, some of which people say embody "common sense." You will get a chance to see how "common" your common sense is within your class.

---

[1] Adapted from Robert Weinberg and Walter Nord, "Coping with 'It's All Common Sense,'" *Exchange: The Organizational Behavior Teaching Journal,* 7, no. 2 (1982), pp. 29-32. Used with permission.

Exercise Schedule

		Unit Time	*Total Time*
1.	**Complete inventory**	**5-10 min**	**5-10 min**

Students complete inventory independently.

		Unit Time	*Total Time*
2.	**Small groups**	**10-20 min**	**15-30 min**

Small groups discuss what they think the correct answers are. Optional: If you have a copy of the course syllabus, indicate which chapter you think each course session would be covered in.

		Unit Time	*Total Time*
3.	**Class discussion**	**10-20 min**	**25-50 min**

Instructor leads a class discussion on the issues raised by the inventory.

Introductory Inventory

Below are 20 sets of ideas about organizational behavior. For each set, indicate whether you think "a" or "b" is most accurate.

1. a. A supervisor is well advised to treat, as much as possible, all members of his/her group exactly the same way.
   b. A supervisor is well advised to adjust his/her behavior according to the unique characteristics of his/her group.

2. a. Generally speaking, individual motivation is greatest if the person has set goals for himself/herself that are *difficult* to achieve.
   b. Generally speaking, individual motivation is greatest if the person has set goals for himself/herself that are *easy* to achieve.

3. a. A major reason why organizations are not as productive as they could be these days is that managers are too concerned with managing the work group rather than the individual.
   b. A major reason why organizations are not as productive as they could be these days is that managers are too concerned with managing the individual rather than the work group.

4. a. Supervisors who, sometime prior to becoming a supervisor, have performed the job of the people they are currently supervising are apt to be more effective supervisors than those who have never performed that particular job.
   b. Supervisors who, sometime prior to becoming a supervisor, have performed the job of the people they are currently supervising are apt to be less effective supervisors than those who have never performed that particular job.

5. a. On almost every matter relevant to the work, managers are well advised to be completely honest and open with their subordinates.
   b. There are very few matters in the work place where managers are well advised to be completely honest and open with their subordinates.

6. a. One's need for power is a better predictor of managerial advancement than one's motivation to do the work well.
   b. One's motivation to do the work well is a better predictor of managerial advancement than one's need for power.

7. a. When people fail at something, they should try harder next time.
   b. When people fail at something, they should try quitting.

8. a. Performing well as a manager depends most on how much education a person has.
   b. Performing well as a manager depends most on how much experience a person has.

9. a. The most effective leaders are those who give more emphasis to getting the work done than they do to relating to people.
   b. The most effective leaders are those who give more emphasis to relating to people than they do to getting the work done.

Introductory Inventory (cont'd)

10. a. It is very important for a leader to "stick to his/her guns."
    b. It is not very important for a leader to "stick to his/her guns."

11. a. Pay is the most important factor in determining how hard people work.
    b. The nature of the task people are doing is the most important factor in determining how hard people work.

12. a. Pay is the most important factor in determining how satisfied people are at work.
    b. The nature of the task people are doing is the most important factor in determining how satisfied people are at work.

13. a. Generally speaking, it is correct to say that a person's attitudes cause his/her behavior.
    b. Generally speaking, it is correct to say that a person's attitudes are primarily rationalizations for his/her behavior.

14. a. Satisfied workers produce more than workers who are not satisfied.
    b. Satisfied workers produce no more than workers who are not satisfied.

15. a. The notion that most semi-skilled workers desire work that is interesting and meaningful is most likely incorrect.
    b. The notion that most semi-skilled workers desire work that is interesting and meaningful is most likely correct.

16. a. People welcome change for the better.
    b. Even if change is for the better, people will resist it.

17. a. Leaders are born, not made.
    b. Leaders are made, not born.

18. a. Groups make better decisions than individuals.
    b. Individuals make better decisions than groups.

19. a. The statement "A manager's authority needs to be commensurate with his/her responsibility" is, practically speaking, a very meaningful statement.
    b. The statement "A manager's authority needs to be commensurate with his/her responsibility" is, practically speaking, a basically meaningless statement.

20. a. A major reason for the relative decline in North American productivity is that the division of labor and job specialization have gone too far.
    b. A major reason for the relative decline in North American productivity is that the division of labor and job specialization have not been carried far enough.

2. My Absolute Worst Job (or Boss): An Icebreaker[1]

Purpose:
To become acquainted with one another.

Group Size:
Any number of dyads.

Time Required:
35 minutes.

Exercise Schedule

		Unit Time	*Total Time*
1.	**Write answers**	**5 min**	**5 min**

The instructor will tell you whether to fill out the questionnaire on your job or your boss, on the following pages.

2.	**Individuals share**	**5 min**	**10 min**

Find someone you don't know and share your responses.

3.	**Dyads share**	**10 min**	**20 min**

Get together with another dyad (preferably new people). Partner "A" of one dyad introduces "B" to the other dyad, then "B" introduces "A." The same process is followed by the other dyad. The introduction should follow this format: *"This is Mary Cullen. Her very worst job was sewing buttons in a clothing factory and she disliked it because... She would rather be a financial analyst."*

4.	**Quartets share (optional)**	**10 min**	

Each group of four meets another quartet and gets introduced, as before.

5.	**Number of people in categories**	**5 min**	**25 min**

The instructor asks for a show of hands on the number of people whose worst jobs (or bosses) fit into the following categories:

a. Factory	e. Professional
b. Restaurant	f. Health care
c. Manual labor	g. Phone sales or communications
d. Driving or delivery	h. Other

[1] © 1988 by Dorothy Marcic. All rights reserved. Thanks to Georgann Bohlig-Nirva for sparking the original idea.

6. Group responses   **5 min**   **30 min**

Instructor gathers data from each group on worst jobs and asks groups to answer the following questions:

   a. What are any common characteristics of the worst jobs in your group?

   b. How did your co-workers feel about their jobs?

   c. What happens to morale and productivity when a worker hates the job?

   d. What was the difference in your own morale/productivity in your worst job versus a job you really enjoyed?

   e. Why do organizations continue to allow unpleasant working conditions to exist?

For Boss Option, do same as above, substituting "boss" for "job."

7. Group discussion   **5 min**   **35 min**

The instructor leads a group discussion on Questions a-e above.

Questionnaires

Option A – Job

a. What was the worst job you ever had? Describe:

   (1) The type of work you did

   (2) Your boss

   (3) What made the job so bad?

   (4) The organization and its policies

   (5) Your co-workers

b. What is your dream job?

Option B – Boss

a. What was your worst boss like?

   (1) Task-oriented or people-oriented?

   (2) Ability to listen

   (3) Loyalty of workers to boss

b. Compare this to your best boss.

3. A Socialization Exercise: Learning the Ropes in an Experiential Course[1]

Purpose:
To explore student expectations about experiential learning.

Group Size:
Any number of groups of four to five members.

Time Required:
45 minutes.

Preparation Required:
Steps 1-2 (Part A) should be completed before class (or allow more time).

Related Topics:
Learning

Exercise Schedule

Part A – Inventory

1. **Complete the inventory on the following page (pre-class)**

[1] Adapted with permission from Patricia Sanders and John N. Yanouzas from *Exchange*, Vol. 8(4), 1983, pp. 29-34.

Experiential Socialization Index

Below you are asked to indicate how much you agree with several statements describing students' behavior, attitudes, and beliefs related to learning in classroom activities. Please respond to all items individually. Do not make ties between statements. Use the following scale for reference:

Strongly Disagree (SD) 1	Disagree (D) 2	Mildly Disagree (MD) 3	Neutral (N) 4	Mildly Agree (MA) 5	Agree (A) 6	Strongly Agree (SA) 7

As a student in this class, my role is to...

1. accept personal responsibility for becoming involved in learning experiences.   1 2 3 4 5 6 7

2. be willing to participate actively in classroom analysis of learning activities.   1 2 3 4 5 6 7

3. accept affective (feeling) learning as an important source of learning.   1 2 3 4 5 6 7

4. recognize the importance of integrating cognitive (thinking) learning.   1 2 3 4 5 6 7

5. be willing to engage in self-assessment.   1 2 3 4 5 6 7

6. be willing to learn from my classmates.   1 2 3 4 5 6 7

7. be willing to make connections between classroom experiences and cognitive content.   1 2 3 4 5 6 7

8. be willing to learn from observing my own behaviors and the behaviors of others.   1 2 3 4 5 6 7

9. believe that information learned will be useful in the future.   1 2 3 4 5 6 7

10. accept the instructor's authority to conduct the class.   1 2 3 4 5 6 7

11. complete assignments and readings prior to class.   1 2 3 4 5 6 7

12. maintain a formal student/teacher relationship.   1 2 3 4 5 6 7

13. be willing to come to class on time.   1 2 3 4 5 6 7

14. be willing to do extra work when needed.   1 2 3 4 5 6 7

15. accept the instructor's authority to make decisions about the relevance of course content and assignments.   1 2 3 4 5 6 7

16. contribute to maintaining a structured classroom atmosphere.   1 2 3 4 5 6 7

17. believe neatness on assignments is important.   1 2 3 4 5 6 7

18. be willing to share with others personal strengths and weaknesses.   1 2 3 4 5 6 7

	Unit Time	*Total Time*
2. Collect data	**10 min**	**10 min**

The instructor passes out data collection forms to fill in the responses to the index. Based on this, the instructor prepares class medians for the 18 items.

Items 1-9:   pivotal norms

Items 10-18:   peripheral norms

	Unit Time	*Total Time*
3. Socialization Matrix	**10 min**	**20 min**

Task: Plot your score on the matrix below and answer the two questions at the end of this section.

Socialization Matrix

Peripheral Norm Acceptance

(63) High	Playing the game	Conformity
Med.		
Peri.		
(9) Low	Rebellion	Creative individualism

Low (9)   Med. Piv.   High (63)

Pivotal Norm Acceptance

Conceptual Model. The ESI is based on Schein's (1968) model of socialization. According to Schein, not all organizational values and norms are equally important for the organization. Some are pivotal in importance, while others are only peripheral for membership in the organization. Pivotal norms represent those behaviors which are central and necessary for productive membership in the organization. As applied to experiential learning, pivotal norms of learning would include:

(1) the locus of responsibility for learning must be shared between student and instructor;

(2) affective as well as cognitive processes are involved in learning;

(3) learning goals include transference of knowledge as well as development of skills and attitudes;

(4) the student must be an active participant in the learning process (Bowen, 1980).

If the pivotal norms are to be accepted, the instructor must actively seek to enhance their value through appropriate socialization.

Peripheral norms are those behaviors which are not absolutely necessary to embrace for group membership, but are peripherally related to group goals and productivity. The peripheral norms of experiential learning include values such as being punctual; completing assignments neatly; willingness to do optional work; and accepting the authority of the instructor. These are not absolutely necessary for the attainment of learning in the experiential method but can contribute towards learning.

Questions

1. How does your score differ from others in class, and from class norms? Were you surprised with the results?

2. Do you agree or disagree with your socialization type?

Part B – Group Discussion

	Unit Time	Total Time
1. Small group	**20 min**	**30 min**

Form groups of four to five members and discuss scores as well as answers to the above two questions.

Each group is to generate a list of issues and questions related to their expectations of the course and prepare a summary to report. Some guidelines are:

a. What are the instructor and student roles in this course?

b. Do you agree or disagree with the pivotal and peripheral norms indicated on the ESI? Why or why not? What could you add to this list?

c. What should students expect from this course?

d. What resources do students have to offer?

e. What does the instructor expect from students?

f. What is the hoped-for outcome of the course?

g. What application does the concept of organizational socialization have for membership in a work organization?

2. Presentations	**10 min**	**40 min**

Each group presents summaries to whole class.

Reference

Schein, E.H. "Organizational Socialization and the Profession of Management," *Industrial Management Review*, Vol. 9, 1968, pp. 1-26.

4. The Tinkertoys Exercise[1]

Purpose:
1. As an icebreaker.
2. To examine issues of group dynamics and leadership.

Group Size:
Any number of groups of three to eight members.

Time Required:
35 minutes.

Materials:
One box of Tinkertoys for each group.

Object:
To build the tallest self-supporting structure with the contents of one box of Tinkertoys.

Exercise Schedule

		Unit Time	Total Time
1.	**Each group gets Tinkertoys**	**20 min**	**20 min**

The first step is planning. Groups have 20 minutes to plan. No assembly is allowed during this time. Pieces may be looked at, but not even trial assembly of two parts is allowed. At the end of 20 minutes, pieces go back in the box.

		Unit Time	Total Time
2.	**Construction phase**	*only 40 seconds*	
3.	**Groups view other towers**	**4 min**	**25 min**
4.	**Instructor leads discussion**	**10 min**	**35 min**

    a. How did groups plan?

    b. Did a leader emerge?

    c. How were conflicts resolved?

    d. What behaviors emerged during construction?

---

[1] Adapted from *Organizations and People* by J.B. Ritchie and Paul Thompson (St. Paul: West Publishing, 1984), p. 56. Used with permission. "Tinkertoys" is a registered trademark of the Questor Corp.

Chapter 2
Personality and Attitudes

5. Red and Blue Instrument[1]

Purpose:
1. To build a simple awareness of your personal attitude framework in comparison with others.
2. To acquire an understanding of self; that is, how does the way we see the world affect our attitudes, our perceptions of others, and, thus, our management styles.

Time Required:
20-30 minutes or more.

Exercise Schedule

1. **Pre-class**
    Individuals take and score the quiz.

		Unit Time	Total Time
2.	**Small groups discuss (optional)**	15 min	

Instructor will divide the class into groups to interpret and discuss results.

3. **Class discussion**   20-30 min   20-30 min
    Instructor will lead class discussion about interpreting the results of the quiz, and their application to management issues.

_____

[1]Adapted from RSAP (Runner Studies of Attitude Patterns). © Communication Materials Center, Wyncote, PA, USA.

RED

Y	N	Do you feel that your best work is the result of inspiration rather than planning?
Y	N	Do you find that your most satisfying ideas come to you when you are not thinking of anything in particular?
Y	N	Does your enthusiasm sometimes blind your "better judgment?"
Y	N	Is it important to you to have periods of quiet solitude, when your mind can freely receive whatever comes into it?
Y	N	Are some of your happiest hours spent in fields of impersonal and abstract thought?
Y	N	Do you question many things that other people seem to regard as established facts?
Y	N	Do you have some ideas you keep trying to develop even though other people say they are unworkable?
Y	N	Are you discontented unless you have ample opportunity to work out new ways of doing things?
Y	N	Do you like best to work in spurts of activity rather than to follow a planned program?
Y	N	Do you get so absorbed in your projects that you are inclined to be absent-minded about other matters?
Y	N	After you have solved a problem to your own satisfaction, are you inclined to lose interest in it?
Y	N	On a job, is it important to you to feel free to develop your ideas?
Y	N	Do you sometimes devote yourself to developing an idea even though you know it has little chance of success?
Y	N	Do you tend to lose interest in an idea when it no longer presents new problems?
Y	N	Are you inclined to be so impatient to get results that you neglect orderly procedures?
Y	N	In general, do you decide for yourself whether or not you will conform to a social custom?
Y	N	Is it difficult for you to apply yourself to a task unless you are personally interested in it?
Y	N	Do you dislike being given advice unless you ask for it?
Y	N	When you have made up your mind to do something, are you likely to be quite stubborn about it?
Y	N	Even in intimate relationships, do you try to avoid becoming dependent on the other person or letting that person become dependent on you?

BLUE

Y	N	Are you quite particular about getting the details of a project worked out ahead of time?
Y	N	For your personal affairs, do you maintain careful records and accurate accounts?
Y	N	Do you make the most of your purchases within a strict budget?
Y	N	Do you give careful attention to preparing yourself for possible emergencies?
Y	N	For your free time, do you usually make plans ahead rather than do things on the spur of the moment?
Y	N	Insofar as possible, do you make it a regular practice to schedule your time for each day's activities?
Y	N	Do you make it a point to make a place for everything and to keep everything in its place?
Y	N	Do you have definite rules by which you judge proper conduct in other people?
Y	N	Do you believe there are certain general rules and beliefs which no one in our society has a right to question?
Y	N	Does it irritate you when subordinates fail to show proper respect for their superiors?
Y	N	Do you disapprove of people in responsible positions who do not conduct themselves with special dignity?
Y	N	Do you believe that one of the best ways to judge a person is to know the groups to which he or she belongs?
Y	N	Do you prefer to know a person's background before accepting him/her as a personal friend?
Y	N	Do you believe everyone has a proper place in society and should behave accordingly?
Y	N	Are you careful not to assume people are trustworthy until they have proven themselves so?
Y	N	Are you careful not to lend money to anyone unless you can be sure it will be paid back?
Y	N	Do you believe that for most people, fear of punishment is the best prevention against wrong-doing?
Y	N	Are you inclined to be a little suspicious of people's motives?
Y	N	Are you quite cautious in your dealings with strangers?
Y	N	Do you feel that most people will sometimes deliberately misrepresent the facts if they have something to gain by doing so?

6. Personality Assessment: Jung's Typology[1]

Purpose:
To determine personality according to Jung's Personality Typology.

Time Required:
15-20 minutes to complete and score inventory.

Introduction

Your personality is what you are. You have similarities to and differences from other people. The differences measured here are not better or worse, merely different. Complete and score the inventory below to find out your personality type. Then look in the Appendix to learn what it means.

Personality Inventory

For each item, circle either "a" or "b." If you feel both "a" and "b" are true, decide which one is more like you, even if it is only slightly more true.

1.   I would rather
     a. Solve a new and complicated problem
     b. Work on something I have done before

2.   I like to
     a. Work alone in a quiet place
     b. Be where "the action" is

3.   I want a boss who
     a. Establishes and applies criteria in decisions
     b. Considers individual needs and makes exceptions

4.   When I work on a project, I
     a. Like to finish it and get some closure
     b. Often leave it open for possible change

5.   When making a decision, the most important considerations are
     a. Rational thoughts, ideas and data
     b. People's feelings and values

6.   On a project, I tend to
      a. Think it over and over before deciding how to proceed
      b. Start working on it right away, thinking about it as I go along

7.   When working on a project, I prefer to
      a. Maintain as much control as possible
      b. Explore various options

8.   In my work, I prefer to
      a. Work on several projects at a time, and learn as much
         as possible about each one
      b. Have one project which is challenging and keeps me busy

9.   I often
      a. Make lists and plans whenever I start something and
         may hate to seriously alter my plans
      b. Avoid plans and just let things progress as I work on them

10.   When discussing a problem with colleagues, it is easy for me
      a. To see "the big picture"
      b. To grasp the specifics of the situation

11.   When the phone rings in my office or at home, I usually
      a. Consider it an interruption
      b. Don't mind answering it

12.   Which word describes you better?
      a. Analytical
      b. Empathetic

13.   When I am working on an assignment, I tend to
      a. Work steadily and consistently
      b. Work in bursts of energy with "down time" in between

14.   When I listen to someone talk on a subject, I usually try to
      a. Relate it to my own experience and see if it fits
      b. Assess and analyze the message

15.   When I come up with new ideas, I generally
      a. "Go for it"
      b. Like to contemplate the ideas some more

16.   When working on a project, I prefer to
      a. Narrow the scope so it is clearly defined
      b. Broaden the scope to include related aspects

Personality Inventory (cont'd)

17. When I read something, I usually
    a. Confine my thoughts to what is written there
    b. Read between the lines and relate the words to other ideas

18. When I have to make a decision in a hurry, I often
    a. Feel uncomfortable and wish I had more information
    b. Am able to do so with available data

19. In a meeting, I tend to
    a. Continue formulating my ideas as I talk about them
    b. Only speak out after I have carefully thought the issue through

20. In work, I prefer spending a great deal of time on issues of
    a. Ideas
    b. People

21. In meetings, I am most often annoyed with people who
    a. Come up with many sketchy ideas
    b. Lengthen meetings with many practical details

22. Are you a
    a. Morning person?
    b. Night owl?

23. What is your style in preparing for a meeting?
    a. I am willing to go in and be responsive
    b. I like to be fully prepared and usually sketch an outline of the meeting

24. In a meeting, would you prefer for people to
    a. Display a fuller range of emotions
    b. Be more task oriented

25. I would rather work for an organization where
    a. My job was intellectually stimulating
    b. I was committed to its goals and mission

26. On weekends, I tend to
    a. Plan what I will do
    b. Just see what happens and decide as I go along

27. I am more
    a. Outgoing
    b. Contemplative

28. I would rather work for a boss who is
    a. Full of new ideas
    b. Practical

In the following, choose the word in each pair that appeals to you more:

29. a. Social   b. Theoretical

30. a. Ingenuity   b. Practicality

31. a. Organized   b. Adaptable

32. a. Active   b. Concentration

Scoring Key

Count one point for each item listed below which you circled in the inventory.

Score For I	Score For E	Score For S	Score For N
2a	2b	1b	1a
6a	6b	10b	10a
11a	11b	13a	13b
15b	15a	16a	16b
19b	19a	17a	17b
22a	22b	21a	21b
27b	27a	28b	28a
32b	32a	30b	30a

Totals ____   ____   ____   ____

Circle the one with more points:
I or E
(If tied on I/E, don't count #11)

Circle the one with more points:
S or N
(If tied on S/N, don't count #16)

Score For T	Score For F	Score For J	Score For P
3a	3b	4a	4b
5a	5b	7a	7b
12a	12b	8b	8a
14b	14a	9a	9b
20a	20b	18b	18a
24b	24a	23b	23a
25a	25b	26a	26b
29b	29a	31a	31b

Total ____   ____   ____   ____

Circle the one with more points:
T or F
(If tied on T/F, don't count #24)

Circle the one with more points:
J or P
(If tied on J/P, don't count #23)

Your Score Is: I or E _____   S or N _____   T or F _____   J or P _____

Exercise Options

Option 1: Most Important Feature of an Ideal Job (30 minutes)

Purpose:
To relate research findings about the most important features in an ideal job to the participants' responses and personality types.

		Unit Time	*Total Time*
1.	**Small groups** In personality-similar groups, discuss "What's the Most Important Feature of an Ideal Job?"	10 min	10 min
2.	**Comparisons** Compare the responses with other groups.	15 min	25 min
3.	**Closing** See "What's the Most Important Feature of an Ideal Job?" in the Appendix.	5 min	30 min

Option 2: Like and Do Well (30 minutes or more, depending on number of groups)

Purpose:
To analyze aspects of a job which are not liked and are not done well.

		Unit Time	Total Time
1.	**Complete the Like and Do Well Grid (pre-class)**		
2.	**Small groups** In personality-similar groups, discuss your answers.	15 min	15 min
3.	**Comparisons** Compare with other groups.	15 min	30 min

Like and Do Well Grid

Things I like and I do well:	Things I like but do not do well:
Things I do not like but do well:	Things I do not like and I do not do well:

7. Locus of Control[1]

Purpose:
To measure Locus of Control.

Group Size:
Any number.

Time Required:
15-20 minutes to complete and score inventory.

Related Topics:
Motivation

Locus of Control Inventory

Directions: Answer the following questions. There are no right or wrong answers. Don't take too much time answering any one question, but do try to answer them all.

One of your concerns during the test may be, "What should I do if I can answer both yes and no to a question?" It's not unusual for that to happen. If it does, think about whether your answer is just a little more one way than the other. For example, if you'd assign a weighting of 51 percent to "yes" and assign 49 percent to "no," mark the answer "yes." Try to pick one or the other response for all questions and try not to leave any blanks.

Put "Y" to indicate Yes and "N" to indicate No.

____ 1. Do you believe that most problems will solve themselves if you just don't fool with them?

____ 2. Do you believe that you can stop yourself from catching a cold?

____ 3. Are some people just born lucky?

____ 4. Most of the time do you feel that getting good grades means a great deal to you?

____ 5. Are you often blamed for things that just aren't your fault?

____ 6. Do you believe that if somebody studies hard, he or she can pass any subject?

____ 7. Do you feel that most of the time it doesn't pay to try hard because things never turn out right anyway?

---

[1]By Stephen Nowicki Jr. and B. Strickland in *The Mind Test* by Rita Aero and Elliott Weiner. New York: William Morrow, 1981, pp. 20-23. Used with permission.

Locus of Control Inventory (cont'd)

____ 8.   Do you feel that if things start out well in the morning it's going to be a good day no matter what you do?

____ 9.   Do you feel that most of the time parents listen to what their children have to say?

____ 10.   Do you believe that wishing can make good things happen?

____ 11.   When you get punished does it usually seem it's for no good reason?

____ 12.   Most of the time do you find it hard to change a friend's opinion?

____ 13.   Do you think that cheering, more than luck, helps a team to win?

____ 14.   Did you feel that it was nearly impossible to change your parents' minds about anything?

____ 15.   Do you believe that parents should allow children to make most of their own decisions?

____ 16.   Do you feel that when you do something wrong there's very little you can do to make it right?

____ 17.   Do you believe that most people are just born good at sports?

____ 18.   Are most people your age stronger than you are?

____ 19.   Do you feel that one of the best ways to handle most problems is just not to think about them?

____ 20.   Do you feel that you have a lot of choice in deciding your friends?

____ 21.   If you find a four-leaf clover, do you believe that it might bring you good luck?

____ 22.   Did you often feel that doing your homework had much to do with what kind of grades you got?

____ 23.   Do you feel that when a person your age is angry at you, there's little you can do to stop him or her?

____ 24.   Have you ever had a good-luck charm?

____ 25.   Do you believe people like you based on how you act?

____ 26.   Did your parents usually help you if you asked them to?

____ 27.   Have you felt that when people were angry with you it was usually for no reason at all?

____ 28.   Most of the time, do you feel that you can change what might happen tomorrow by what you do today?

____ 29.   Do you believe that when bad things are going to happen, they are just going to happen no matter what you try to do to stop them?

____ 30.   Do you think that people can get their own way if they just keep trying?

____ 31.   Most of the time do you find it useless to try to get your own way at home?

	31.	Most of the time do you find it useless to try to get your own way at home?
___	32.	Do you feel that good things happen because of hard work?
___	33.	Do you feel that when somebody your age wants to be your enemy there's little you can do to change matters?
___	34.	Do you feel that it's easy to get friends to do what you want them to do?
___	35.	Do you usually feel that you have little to say about what you eat at home?
___	36.	Do you feel that when someone doesn't like you there's little you can do about it?
___	37.	Do you usually feel that it was almost useless to try in school because most other children were just plain smarter than you were?
___	38.	Do you believe that planning ahead makes things turn out better?
___	39.	Most of the time, do you feel that you have little to say about your family plans?
___	40.	Do you think it's better to be smart than to be lucky?

Scoring the Scale

Using the scoring key below, compare your answers with the previous pages. Give yourself one point each time your answer agrees with the keyed answer. Your score is the total number of agreements between your answers and the ones on the key.

1. Yes _____	21. Yes _____
2. No _____	22. No _____
3. Yes _____	23. Yes _____
4. No _____	24. Yes _____
5. Yes _____	25. No _____
6. No _____	26. No _____
7. Yes _____	27. Yes _____
8. Yes _____	28. No _____
9. No _____	29. Yes _____
10. Yes _____	30. No _____
11. Yes _____	31. Yes _____
12. Yes _____	32. No _____
13. No _____	33. Yes _____
14. Yes _____	34. No _____
15. No _____	35. Yes _____
16. Yes _____	36. Yes _____
17. Yes _____	37. Yes _____
18. Yes _____	38. No _____
19. Yes _____	39. Yes _____
20. No _____	40. No _____ **TOTAL SCORE** _____

Interpreting Your Score

Low Scorers (0-8) – Scores of zero to eight represent the range for about one third of the people taking the test. As a low scorer, you probably see life as a game of skill rather than chance. You most likely believe that you have a lot of control over what happens to you, good or bad. With that view, internal locus of control people tend to take the initiative in everything from job-related activities to relationships and sex. You are probably described by others as vigilant in getting things done, aware of what's going on around you, and willing to spend energy in working for specific goals. You would probably find it quite frustrating to sit back and let others take care of you, since you stressed on the test that you like to have your life in your own hands.

Although taking control of your life is seen as the "best way to be," psychologists caution that it has its own set of difficulties. Someone who is responsible for his or her own successes is also responsible for failures. So if you scored strong in this direction, be prepared for the downs as well as the ups.

Average Scorers (9-16) – Since you've answered some of the questions in each direction, internal and external control beliefs for you may be situation-specific. You may look at one situation – work, for example – and believe that your rewards are externally determined, that no matter what you do you can't get ahead. In another situation, love perhaps, you may see your fate as resting entirely in your own hands. You will find it helpful to review the questions and group them into those you answered in the internal direction and those you answered in the external direction. Any similarities in the kinds of situations within one of those groups? If so, some time spent thinking about what it is in those situations that makes you feel as though the control is or is not in your hands can help you better understand yourself.

High Scorers (17-40) – Scores in this range represent the external control end of the scale. Only about 15 percent of the people taking the test score 17 or higher. As a high scorer, you're saying that you see life generally more as a game of chance than as one where your skills make a difference.

There are, however, many different reasons for any individual to score in the external control direction. For example, psychologists have found that people in many minority and disadvantaged groups tend to score in the external direction. One recent suggestion for such scores is that people in these groups perceive their life situations realistically. In general, blacks, women, and lower-socioeconomic-class individuals really do have more restrictions on their own successes – fewer job options, lower pay, less opportunity for advancement – in many cases no matter what they do or don't do. An internal locus of control belief in such situations would be quite unrealistic and inappropriate. Thus your own high external control score could be a realistic perception of your current life circumstances.

On the other hand, your score may represent a strong belief in luck or superstition and a concurrent feeling of helplessness in controlling your life. Research studies have shown a relationship between unrealistic external control beliefs and problems like anxiety, depression, low self-concept, and poor physical health.

Only you can decide exactly how much of your external belief system is accurate and how much of it is inappropriate given your life situation. If any of the emotional and/or physical problems listed do fit your view of your own life, professional help is definitely called for and is very likely to produce positive results. But you'll have to take the initiative and make the first major move to regain control – or the belief of control – over your own life.

About the Scale

Do you believe in luck? Is it something like luck or chance or the actions of others that determines what happens to you? Or do you see the direction of your life determined by your own actions? These two views represent the extremes of a personality concept labeled "locus of control." This concept is concerned with whether an individual believes in an internal or an external control of his life.

In 1954, psychologist Julian Rotter was supervising Dr. E. Jerry Phares as he conducted therapy with a single, 23-year-old man in a Veterans Administration hygiene clinic. As therapy moved along, Drs. Rotter and Phares noted that Karl's (not his real name) problems were not of the common variety — at least not common to the Freudian understanding used in therapy before and during the 1950s. In recalling the therapy, Dr. Phares writes, "It gradually dawned on the clinician that Karl did not perceive any causal relationship between his behavior and the occurrence of rewards. He attributed such occurrences to luck or other factors over which he had no control. Once the clinician realized this, Karl's behavior made sense."

Over the next 12 years, Drs. Phares and Rotter jointly and separately pursued the concept labeled "locus of control." Dr. Rotter culminated this work in 1966 by publishing the first Locus of Control Scale. That test attempted to measure how we perceive the relationship between our own actions and the consequences of those actions. Dr. Rotter felt that we learn from past life experiences whether to believe that our rewards and punishments depend on our own actions or on those of people around us.

After hundreds of research studies investigating Rotter's test and the locus of control concept, psychologists Stephen Nowicki Jr. and B. Strickland developed a related but significantly different test. With the publishing of their scale, Drs. Nowicki and Strickland attempted to deal with certain criticisms that had been leveled at Rotter's test and, in addition, made it possible to measure locus of control in children. In 1974, Dr. Nowicki and a colleague, Dr. Marshall Duke, revised the earlier Nowicki-Strickland scale into the adult test we have included here.

Chapter 3
Perception and Attribution

8. Interpersonal Perception Exercise

Purpose:
To compare your perception of yourself with others' perceptions of you.

Group Size:
Any number of groups of four to five members.

Time Required:
30 minutes.

➤➤ **Introduction**

We often do not get a chance to know how other people see us. This exercise is designed to have you look at yourself in a different light and to find out how others see you, using the same categories.

Exercise Schedule

		Unit Time	Total Time
1.	**Introduction**	**10 min**	**10 min**

Form groups of four to five members. Each member fills out Interpersonal Perception Sheet 1.

2.   **Small groups**   **20 min**   **30 min**

Share your perceptions with the other group members. Person 1 tells how she/he sees herself/himself and, in turn, all other group members tell how they see that person. Person 2 repeats the same procedure, followed by all other group members (until everyone has had a turn). While perceptions are being shared within the group, members should fill out Interpersonal Perception Sheet 2.

Interpersonal Perception Sheet 1

My Perceptions

Type Person Description	Self Perception	How you perceive Person #1	How you perceive Person #2	How you perceive Person #3	How you perceive Person #4
One-sentence description					
Animal					
Type of music (e.g., jazz, rock, classical)					
Song					
Movie or TV star					

Interpersonal Perception Sheet 2

Others' Perceptions of Me*

Type Person Description	Person #1	Person #2	Person #3	Person #4
One-sentence description				
Animal				
Type of music (e.g., jazz, rock, classical)				
Song				
Movie or TV star				

*You may wish to use this space to record others' perceptions of you as members begin to share their matrices in the second part of this exercise.

9. Attribution Theory: A Case of Personality?[1]

Purpose
1. To examine interpersonal perception issues.
2. To apply attribution theory.

Group Size
Up to ten groups of four to six members.

Time Required
50 minutes or more.

Exercise Schedule

1.   Preparation (pre-class)

a. Read the case study and determine who is more responsible for Naomi's dilemma.

b. Rank order characters according to directions at the end of the case.

c. Write a brief response to each of the discussion questions.

	Unit Time	Total Time
2. Group discussion	**25 min**	**25 min**

Mixed-sex groups of four to six members discuss rankings and responses to questions, trying to achieve consensus. Select a spokesperson to present to the class.

3. Reports	**25+ min**	**50+ min**

The instructor will post the rankings on the board as each group presents its report (maximum for each group = 2 minutes). Pay attention to the different interpretations and assumptions made by different individuals and groups to the common set of facts.

4. Class discussion (optional)	**20 min**

The instructor will lead a discussion on the following questions: (to be answered before class)

a. Is this a problem of personality or something else? If it is something else, please explain.

b. What legal recourse, if any, might Naomi have?

c. If Gretchen were not hired, and the position were instead given to Naomi, would Gretchen have any legal recourse? Explain.

d. How could this type of problem be avoided in the future?

[1]© 1991 by David M. Leuser, Ph.D., Plymouth State College of the University System of New Hampshire. All rights reserved.

Case Study: _____

A Case of Personality?

Naomi graduated in 1991 with a B.S. in marketing (*summa cum laude*) from the Massachusetts Institute of Technology. In spite of persistent efforts, she was still unemployed in November. In desperation she responded to an ad in the Boston Globe placed by HotSpeck Minerals from western Texas. There were two openings, one as secretary in the marketing department. The other, which she applied for, was for an administrative assistant to the vice-president, and the job required "an involvement in creative strategy and graphic design with substantial responsibility and opportunity to travel." Within a week she received a call from Louise, the employee relations clerk at HotSpeck, who indicated the VP for marketing was impressed and wanted to interview her. She was told, however, that HotSpeck's policy required applicants to demonstrate serious interest by paying their own expenses.

HotSpeck Minerals was located in an isolated area and employed 320 people, mostly men as miners. About 30 support personnel were women, though, who lived in the women's dormitory. There were 25 management and staff positions, six of which were filled by women, who lived in company apartments. Most employees worked 10-hour days and then commuted to their homes for three-day weekends.

Naomi waited outside Ernest Jordan's office for the VP of Marketing to interview her. She overheard him laughing and talking, evidently about mining, for he said he hoped to get a strike this time.

As Mr. Jordan walked towards her and she introduced herself, Naomi saw his face fall and asked if something was wrong.

> "Oh, nothing. Just thought Ivy League gals **looked different**, that's all."

"Oh, nothing," came the reply. "Just thought Ivy League gals looked different, that's all. But no matter, we can find work for you. You type?"

"Of course! I have competence in word processing, spreadsheet and database analysis, and statistical and market research skills. I'm particularly interested in your need for graphic design skills. There was an article in *Western Business* about your upcoming campaign to communicate the cost-effectiveness of your new refining process to potential customers. I think I could..."

"Now hold on there, little lady," said Mr. Jordan as he told her all he needed for now was a secretary at $10 an hour, with free meals in the dining hall and a free apartment. After being pressed, he even agreed to pay moving expenses, since they were "all family" out there.

Promotion Material?

Naomi had a difficult time at first, for the work was boring and the place was isolated. She was not interested in visiting the bar where most of the men hung out, nor in watching the many video movies available. Instead, she stayed in her apartment and read or prepared for work. After all, Mr. Jordan had told her it was possible for her to get promoted to administrative assistant if she "worked out right."

Even though her secretarial evaluations were glowing at the three- and six-month points, Mr. Jordan said she needed to improve her attitude, to try to fit in more and socialize with the others. She did try to be friendly, but she was still called "Miss Stuck-up" by the women. The men on staff either ignored her or made off-color comments. Mr. Jordan told her to ignore them, for "boys will be boys."

Finally Naomi went to Mr. Peter Evans, a relatively new VP for Human Resources, who seemed to be the only man she could relate to. Unfortunately, Mr. Evans didn't seem to be in the "management club," but Naomi thought she would try anyway. He told her he would look into the matter and agreed there were some problems which needed to be addressed. Two weeks later Mr. Evans left the company abruptly. "Family problems," she was told.

During the seventh month, Mr. Jordan asked Naomi to take care of travel arrangements (at company expense) for Gretchen Steubbins, who would be interviewing for the administrative assistant position. Naomi felt uncomfortable, even betrayed, but she knew better than to question Mr. Jordan.

Naomi decided to discuss it with Louise, the employee relations clerk and the only woman Naomi could talk to. Louise commuted weekly to her family home. Naomi asked her why she didn't move to the city and get a real job which would double her salary. Louise replied her husband and kids liked the area. And Naomi found out the reason Louise wore the tight jeans was that the "boys like it that way." Another piece of information was that Gretchen had been discovered at the recent trade show, where she had been a floor model with a machinery supplier.

When Gretchen's resume arrived, Naomi was not impressed. She had only nine months' experience in "product promotion." She took nearly six years to complete a B.A. in theater arts from some unknown college. Her accomplishments included homecoming queen, sorority president, and winner of a beauty contest. Her special skills included being personable and eager to please. Naomi was furious, for she saw no marketing background. Still, she kept her anger to herself.

The next Friday morning Gretchen herself arrived. Naomi did not fail to notice she looked like a beauty contest winner and had an enormous smile, which was almost matched by the grin on Mr. Jordan's face as he escorted her into his office and closed the door. Two hours later he informed Naomi that they would be gone the rest of the day on a tour of the facilities.

The Critical Incident

Monday morning Mr. Jordan instructed Naomi to process the paperwork to hire Gretchen as administrative assistant at an annual salary of $35,000. Naomi exploded in anger and demanded to know why she was not promoted to the position, given her obvious qualifications and outstanding performance to date.

"Mr. Jordan, you know I can fly circles around this Gretchen girl. I demand to be given a chance at the job."

"Well, Naomi, dear. This outburst just adds to the evidence that you don't belong here. I have seen how unhappy you are with our company, and as of today I am relieving you of your duties. Louise will process your papers and you will be given four weeks severance pay."

Later Louise helped Naomi pack and chided her, telling her she never seemed to care what anyone at HotSpeck wanted or liked. She always wanted things her way, rather than "going with the flow" and putting up with some corny, but necessary, behaviors. That's life here, she told Naomi.

"That's a bunch of you know what!" screamed Naomi. "All the men here are sexist pigs. Hey, I'm talking sex discrimination and that's illegal. I demand to know what *you* are going to do about it."

> "That's a bunch of you know what!" **screamed** Naomi.

Louise sadly told her there wasn't much she could do. "Except one thing. Give you some advice. Forget this lawsuit thing and get on with your life. Nobody but you thinks there's a problem here."

Directions: Rank order the characters in the story in terms of their degree of responsibility for Naomi's current dilemma. Assign number "1" to the most responsible person and "5" to the least responsible, and so on. Also, list your reasons for the rankings you gave to each person, specifying assumptions made which were derived from specific facts in the case.

	Rankings	Reasons
Ernest Jordan, VP for Marketing		
Peter Evans, VP for Human Resources		
Louise Landis, Employee Relations		
Naomi Pidgeon, Secretary – Marketing		
Gretchen Steubbins, Administrative Assistant		

Discussion Questions

1. Why did Mr. Jordan hire Naomi?

2. Why did Mr. Jordan fire Naomi?

3. Why didn't Naomi fit in with the "company family"?

4. Why did Mr. Jordan hire Gretchen?

5. Who was more qualified for the administrative assistant job? Why?

6. Should/could Naomi trust Louise? Why or why not?

7. What should the company do with Gretchen? Why?

8. What should the company do with Naomi? Why?

9. What should Naomi do now? Why?

Chapter 4
Individual and Group Problem-Solving Styles

10. Boyberik: A Problem-Solving Exercise[1]

Purpose:
To explore methods of solving problems.

Group Size:
Any number of groups of five to eight members.

Time Required:
35-50 minutes.

☐ Background

The new country of Boyberik has requested help from the World Bank to develop its economic system. One project approved is to develop a reasonable pricing system for its products, in order for it to compete in the global marketplace. The main industry in Boyberik produces bubkes of high quality. In Boyberik, bubkes are made of bunches of gaggles. Paper currency is called bani-bani, while the four types of coins are groshen, mezuma, penizay, and fluce.

Instructions

Your task is to determine the price each bubke should sell for. The instructor will give each group a set of cards with information on each one. You are allowed to tell other group members what your cards say, but you cannot *show* the cards to anyone else.

Exercise Schedule

		Unit Time	*Total Time*
1.	**Introduction**	**5 min**	**5 min**

Instructor gives instructions and divides class into groups of five to eight members. Instructor may assign observers for each group. Each group goes to a different part of the room, after which the instructor gives a set of cards to each group. One person in the group "deals" the cards out to each person, trying to give an equal amount (or near equal) to each member. Members may not show cards to anyone else, but may share information orally. Cards should not leave "owners'" hands during play.

2.	**Problem-solving**	**15-20 min**	**20-25 min**

Each group tries to solve the problem of what the price of each bubke should be.

3.	**Solution**	**5 min**	**25-30 min**

Instructor announces solutions to the groups.

4.	**Debrief**	**10-20 min**	**35-50 min**

Observers give feedback. This can be done either within individual groups, after which there will be a general discussion, or there can be general feedback given in the whole group.

11. Executive Etiquette[1]

Purpose:
To discuss issues of social relations in business.

Group Size:
Any number of groups of five to eight members.

Time Required:
10-40 minutes or more.

Preparation Required:
Read the seven letters and answer the questions.

Related Topics:
Women in Management (#1, #2, #3, #7), Conflict Management (#6), Leadership (#2), Dynamics Within Groups (#4), Interpersonal Perception (#1), Interpersonal Communication (#5, #6), Organization Culture and Norms (#2, #7)

☐ Background

Our mythical businessperson, Mr./Ms. Fast-Tracker, has a plethora of etiquette problems. In order to get intelligent advice, Fast-Tracker has written to Prudence Trueheart, the quintessence of knowledge in social interactions.

Exercise Schedule

1. **Preparation (pre-class)**
    Read the seven letters and answer questions after each one. The instructor may assign one letter at a time in different class sessions.

2. **Discuss letters for 5-30 minutes, depending on number of letters discussed**
    For one or more letters, groups discuss questions and etiquette/social interaction issues.

3. **Correct answers**   **5-10 min**
    Instructor reads aloud Miss Trueheart's responses for appropriate letters and conducts a class discussion.

---

[1]Adapted by Jack Brittain and Sim B. Sitkin and reprinted with permission of Scribner, an imprint of Simon & Schuster, from *Miss Manners' Guide to Excruciatingly Correct Behavior* by Judith Martin. © 1979, 1980, 1981, 1982 by United Features Syndicates, Inc. Copyright on original material by Jack Brittain and Sim B. Sitkin.

Letters

Dear Miss Trueheart:

I am a young, single, female executive. I work for the regional office of a major bank, and must occasionally travel to our corporate office in New York to work on a deal. My problem is this: a friend from work recently bumped into a woman from the New York office while on vacation. The woman asked my friend if she knew me, and then inquired about a "rumor" she heard in New York. Apparently the "gossip" in New York is that I had a torrid affair with a married man with whom I worked on a deal. This rumor is supposedly widely circulated, much to my embarrassment. There was no affair.

My friend rose to my defense and quickly denied the rumor, but I doubt it had any impact. What should I do? Ignore it and assume that if my managers hear the rumor, they know me well enough to ignore it? I am also concerned that my hard-earned professional image will be damaged in the eyes of Senior Management in New York. Do you have any advice?

> *Sincerely,*
> *Fast-Tracker*

Questions

1. Given what we know about how people make social judgments, what advice would you offer in this situation? Should Fast-Tracker go around denying the affair to anyone who will listen?

2. What steps can Fast-Tracker take to influence the boss's perceptions of what occurred? How can the discussion be managed so that the boss will be guided toward a positive attribution?

3. How important is behavior in this situation? Why?

4. How does the behavior we exhibit "enact" our reality in this situation?

Dear Miss Trueheart:

I am an unmarried businesswoman. I am occasionally invited out to dinner with out-of-town executives and their local managers. I am leery of these situations and have turned down all such invitations, but know my male counterparts have sometimes come away from the table with valuable information that can be used to the company's and their benefit.

How should I act as the only female member of a dinner party? Should I invite a date to accompany me to such a dinner in order to retain respectability and keep weird ideas out of the head of some gentleman who is half smacked by the time the salad is served? What should I wear to such an event – a business suit or dinner dress? Should I meet the gentleman at the restaurant, or allow him to pick me up at home? When I travel out of town on business, am I expected to invite my hosts out to dinner? This problem is easier, because then I could invite their wives as well.

Your advice on this matter is going to be appreciated – not only by me, but by our managers, who are chary of allowing their female subordinates enough rein to become involved in such situations.

> *Sincerely,*
> *Fast-Tracker*

Questions

1. What does this person's dilemma tell us about how people understand social situations?
2. What is the difference between a business and a social situation?
    How do we know if we are in one or the other?
3. What factors can this executive control in influencing the behavior of her dinner guests?
4. Can a manager learn anything about influencing employees' behavior from this situation?

Dear Miss Trueheart:

The event that has created a permanent state of embarrassment for me happened several months ago at a semiformal Christmas party. Please confirm whether my behavior was so atrocious that my career is ruined and I must look forward to spending the rest of my days without stock options.

My date and I were introduced to Mr. and Mrs. CEO in this way: "Mr. Fast-Tracker..." – at which time I extended my hand – "...and Miss Holstein." Mr. CEO ignored my hand and turned to the lady with me. My open hand was left hanging in midair for what seemed like an eternity before it fell, shaky but unshaken, to my side. I have been confounded ever since, and so unraveled that I have taken refuge in the company of accountants, where good manners are irrelevant as long as one is suitably dressed.

Does a man not offer a handshake until after his female companion has been introduced and/or shaken the hands of the party to whom they are being introduced? Am I a bumbler, or did I just have the misfortune of running into an arrogant stick-in-the-mud? My habit has always been to extend my hand immediately upon being introduced.

> *Sincerely,*
> *Fast-Tracker*

Questions

1. What is this social ritual all about?
    What is the relationship between rules of etiquette and the concept of norms?
2. How important is "normatively correct" behavior for business success? Why?

Dear Miss Trueheart:

I recently took over as local manager for a national service firm. The local newspaper was doing a feature on women in business, and asked if I would submit to an interview on the "life-style" my husband and I share. A pleasant and seemingly professional young woman came to my house for tea one afternoon, and we chatted for some time about many things, including her social life. We got quite friendly and I even considered including her in our social circle. You can imagine my horror when I saw that she had violated the spirit of the visit by printing everything I said, even those things which look insulting to friends and associates in print.

It is true, as she said when I complained to her boss, that I had not specified that anything was "off the record." I did not think I needed to, because I assumed she had the good sense to know what was proper for her article and what was not. I was not, after all, holding a press conference: I was acting as a hostess in my own home. I wish you would say something about this particular form of rudeness. I personally plan to avoid the press in the future, rather than expose myself to such public inspection.

> *Sincerely,*
> *Fast-Tracker*

Questions

1. What are the boundary differences in friendships and working relationships?

2. What expectations of loyalty are there with friends and in professional relationships?

3. Give examples of problems you have encountered when professional and personal boundaries were blurred.

Dear Miss Trueheart:

I trust that Miss Trueheart will not find this inquiry too indelicate to comment on. I am a successful young MBA who is fortunate enought to have an exceptionally well-qualified administrative assistant. She has performed her job brilliantly, and contributed a great deal to my own rapid climb up the corporate ladder. As a result of working closely together over the past year, my feelings of appreciation and respect for her are now, I detect, taking on romantic characteristics. As I have not expressed these feelings I have no idea if she shares them, and am not experienced enough in such matters to "read" any subtle indications on her part.

What, if anything, should I do, and how should it be done? The options I see are business-as-usual, frank revelation and discussion, or gradual encouragement of her to indicate her feelings. I am not a seducer, and do not wish to lose my assistant as a result of some foolish action on my part. Also, I am married. Would Miss Trueheart please suggest what she thinks I ought to do, and how I ought to do it?

> *Sincerely,*
> *Fast-Tracker*

Questions

1. What are the advantages/disadvantages for both Fast-Tracker and the administrative assistant of "getting involved?"

2. Does it make a difference in such an involvement if one or both are married?

3. How can romantic feelings at work be managed?

4. What should a manager do when two workers are "involved?"

Dear Miss Trueheart

I fear I have inadvertently insulted a co-worker. I offer no excuses: I behaved badly. How might I go about making amends?

> *Sincerely,*
> *Fast-Tracker*

Questions

1. In normal office conflicts and snafu, how are problems often resolved when one person goofs up?

2. Is it better to smooth over problems or directly apologize?

Dear Miss Trueheart

I want to be fair and responsible, but there are some things I cannot get used to about the "new manners." Specifically, I am embarrassed when a woman I am lunching with grabs the check. Some of them do this quite aggressively. My company is perfectly willing to pay for any business lunches I consider necessary, and my lunch partner does me no favor by making a show of paying for me herself. What is the woman's real objective here: to prove she is my equal?

> *Sincerely,*
> *Fast-Tracker*

Questions

1. What is the main issue here?

2. Should a man always have first opportunity to pay the check?

12. Teaching Interpersonal Skills to Subordinates[1]

Purpose:
To provide students with basic skills for helping their future subordinates develop competencies in interpersonal skills.

Group Size:
Any number of groups of five to six members.

Time Required:
Semester Assignment. At least six 40- to 60-minute time periods scheduled in the second half of the course.

Preparation Required:
Lecture for early in the course on the basic parts or steps of effective skills or competency based training, e.g., (1) learner pre-assessment, (2) concept presentation, (3) concept examples for learner analysis, (4) learner practice (see also behavior modeling techniques).

➤ Introduction

You will likely, sometime in your professional career, have a management or supervisory position. Key to your success will be not only your understanding of and ability to use the interpersonal skills we examine in this course, but also your ability to impart these same valuable skills to your subordinates.

Their effective performance is also greatly dependent upon these skills, and their performance will reflect upon you as their supervisor.

This assignment is designed to help you learn how to develop effective interpersonal skills training for your future subordinates.

The five- to six-member student groups will need to meet in separate rooms, each of the groups meeting alone for 40-60 minutes once a week for six weeks. Student groups should arrange for their own meeting time and place, providing information to the instructor on how to locate them. It is helpful for the instructor to provide an open class period on six consecutive weeks to ensure that students have at least one commonly open time period per week during which to schedule a training session.

Please refer to the following notes for specific information and a checklist for preparing for and fulfilling the assignment:

Notes

On an appointed day and time of your choosing during the weeks indicated in your syllabus, you will meet with your group for 40-60 minutes and train them in some specific skill of your choice. You must clearly identify whom the members of your group represent (i.e. subordinates, line managers), and what specific skill

[1] Adapted with permission, Charles M. Vance, Loyola Marymount University, "Extending Academic Impact: Teaching Students How to Teach Interpersonal Skills to Their Future Subordinates," *Organizational Behavior Teaching Review,* 11(3), 1986-87, pp. 86-94.

objective or objectives you have for the group. The skill objective should be of a practical "how to" nature, and related in some way to this course.

Each member of your group will also conduct a training session of your group. Thus, you will act as a trainer once, and as a trainee several times. You will be graded in this project on both your training performance (30 points), and on your awareness and understanding of effective subordinate training, as reflected in the quality of your evaluation of others' training (20 points).

Please use the following for a checklist:

✔   *Set Objectives* – clearly identify the specific skill or small set of skills. (Keep it simple.)

✔   *Meet* with your assigned group as often as needed early in the course to identify a different training topic for each group member. Be sure that the topics are different enough that no two training sessions cover the same information or skills. Once you have identified your different training topics, decide upon the time and place in which each group member will conduct his or her training session. Then hand in to your instructor as early as possible a sheet of paper indicating which group member is conducting a training session on what, where, as well as the date and time.

✔   *Go to the library* and get as much resource material as you can on your topic. Now is your time to become a subject matter expert on your specific topic. After you become very familiar with the subject matter, then begin to focus on how to design and actually conduct the training. Don't try to teach your group everything you've learned on the topic. Again, keep it simple!

✔   *See your class instructor early* for help or suggestions on the design of your training session, or for assistance in obtaining the audiovisual resources you'll need.

✔   *Conduct your sessions.* Don't just lecture to the group! Reserve 10 minutes at the end for individual group member written evaluation of your performance.

   Collect the evaluations. A handwritten evaluation on a blank sheet of paper is acceptable. The quality of each of these evaluations will also be assessed. *The individual evaluations should be based on the steps for effective skill training as presented in class by your instructor.* Be sure that you are very familiar with those steps, for your instructor will look for your awareness of them when you evaluate your fellow students' training performance. Optional: To make it easier for the instructor to grade the perceptiveness of your evaluation, write the last four digits of your identification on the back of each of the individual, otherwise anonymous, evaluations you hand in to the group trainer.

✔   *Hand in* at the next class (late papers docked points) a four- to five-page two-part report containing (1) Design: Your intended training design, including learner objectives, planned delivery outline with justification for methods used, and references; and (2) Evaluation: Your personal evaluation of your actual training performance and your analysis of the group members' handwritten evaluations of your training, with thoughtful recommendations for improvement if you were to do the assignment over again. Also attach the handwritten evaluations of your group members.

Consider the following interpersonal skill topics for your training session, but don't be limited by them:

Handling angry customers	Correctional interview	Employee selection interview
Giving feedback	Disciplinary interview	Nonverbal communication
Soliciting feedback	Termination interview	Disagreeing effectively
Asserting oneself	Managing interpersonal conflict	
Active listening	Managing group conflict	

13. Dealing With Difficult People[1]

Purpose:
To learn how to handle difficult people.

Time:
10-55 minutes, depending on optional role-plays.

Exercise Schedule

		Unit Time	Total Time
1.	**Pre-class** Complete the instrument.		
2.	**Class discussion** Instructor leads a discussion on difficult people.	**10-20 min**	**10-20 min**
3.	**Role-plays (optional)** Instructor asks class for examples of when they have interacted with a "difficult" person. After writing them on the board, the instructor chooses a few and asks for volunteers to role-play them in front of the class. Students give feedback on the effectiveness of the interaction and how to deal with difficult people.	**15-25 min**	

➨ Introduction

Do you have clients or associates who drive you crazy? As the time approaches for a meeting with them, do you find yourself dreading their arrival and your heart sinking as they enter the door?

Or perhaps you have colleagues who make you so angry your blood boils: always cutting you down, never saying what they mean, or bossing you around and criticizing what you do.

At any rate, these people make your day more difficult and sometimes make you wish you worked somewhere else. The reality is that if you got another job, there would be difficult people there, too. You can't get away from them.

What's the solution? First of all, stop trying to change them and wishing they would change. Accept the fact that they will not change and will probably continue on as before. Most of our energy in dealing with difficult people is spent wanting them to be something else. To understand "your" difficult person quotient, fill out the quiz on the next page.

Difficult Person Interaction Index

For the statements below, use the following scale:

    5   strongly agree
    4   somewhat agree
    3   indifferent
    2   somewhat disagree
    1   strongly disagree

____   1. When someone shouts at or belittles me, I cringe inside and am careful not to say anything to upset that person again.

____   2. Dirty looks or sarcastic comments from another person easily make me feel guilty.

____   3. When I make a mistake, I go overboard trying to make it up to the other person.

____   4. When someone bothers me, I don't confront the person but rather backbite with others about the situation.

____   5. If I have a conflict with someone I will stew about it, sometimes for days or longer.

____   6. There are a number of people I work with or who come in the office (or I otherwise interact with) who really need to learn better interpersonal skills.

____   7. There are problems I have with people that never seem to get better.

____   8. It is hard for me to entrust important tasks to others in the office.

____   9. Sometimes my motivation in resolving a problem situation is "he/she needs to learn this lesson."

____ 10. I easily get annoyed when people do things I see as inappropriate or incorrect.

____ 11. I often criticize people with others in the office.

____ 12. I often give others dirty looks, glare, raise my eyebrows or sign at them when they do something stupid or improper.

____   Total Score

Scoring:

48-60   You have a high need for control and spend much time wishing you could change others. You need to focus more on your own behavior and why you react so negatively to others. Your self-esteem is probably low.

29-47   You alternate between letting people be who they are and wishing they were different. Try to work on building up the "acceptance of others" more. Your self-esteem fluctuates between high and low.

12-28   You are relatively easy-going and have learned to accept people as they are. You probably have high self-esteem and get along well with most people.

Suggestions?

You might...

...learn to accept others for what they are.

Actually, the problem with difficult people is not "them," but how you react to them. You get angry, upset, frustrated. Sometimes you get ulcers or cannot sleep at night. Does all of this change those difficult people? Not in the slightest. It only makes you miserable. The one thing you can change is yourself. Work on accepting them for what they are.

Remember that no one is perfect and try focusing on their positive qualities, even if you have to look hard to find them.

> *Everyone does have something good about them.*

...change your behavior.

The next thing you can do is change how you relate to the difficult person. Every relationship is like a mobile. When one person changes his or her behavior, it forces a different reaction. If the person criticizes you, stop putting up with it or responding with negative comments. You might try a response in a pleasant tone of voice, such as, "I don't agree with your opinion. That's not how I see it."

When we get upset or hop around trying to please someone, we are allowing that person to control our behavior. Eleanor Roosevelt said that no one can make you feel inferior without your permission. The same is true with other emotions:

> *No one can make you angry without your permission.*

...look at behavior patterns.

Do you have the same problem over and over again with people? Perhaps many people try to tell you how to live your life, or others criticize you frequently. If there is a pattern, then you need to do some careful, honest self-evaluation and figure out what you are doing to encourage that behavior from others. Jessie Potter, a communications expert, restates what her grandmother told her:

> *"If you continue to do what you've always done, you'll continue to get what you've always got."*

Read that over again and think about it. When people are doing the same things to you repeatedly, perhaps you are asking for it in some way. That's the time to change your behavior and re-fashion that unsatisfactory interaction pattern: i.e., try something else!

...continue to work on self-esteem.

When your self-esteem is high, it is much easier to let nasty comments or harsh looks roll off like raindrops on a slippery umbrella. Days when you are not feeling good about yourself are the times when those difficult people are going to bother you more.

Therefore, all the guidelines for building self-concept will help you work more effectively with difficult persons.

> *Like yourself and it is infinitely easier to like others, even if they are not particularly likable.*

And don't let that difficult person rule your life!

Think for a moment how much energy and attention you have spent as a result of that difficult person. What if you took all that time and energy and instead put it into improving your skills? It is very common to give power to difficult people, to let them control our thoughts and behavior. If you do that, you lose control of your own life.

Start noticing those situations where you avoid saying certain things to someone. When you speak cautiously, it means that you are trying to prevent some negative reaction from that person. You have learned from past experience that bringing up that subject or speaking in one tone of voice means you get back angry glares, shouting, screaming, pouting, sighs, or deadly silence – none of which is pleasant.

Instead you act in a way to keep these reactions at bay, which means the other person is directing your behavior. You are allowing the other person to determine how you will act. Stop letting that difficult person control you.

Chapter 5
Learning and Reinforcement

14. Learning Organizations[1]

Purpose:
To learn and apply skills needed to create learning organizations.

Group Size:
Four to six members.

Time:
35 minutes or more.

Exercise Schedule

1. **Pre-class**
   Read "Background," and fill in items and answer questions.

		Unit Time	Total Time
2.	**Small groups (optional)**	20 min	

   Groups of four to six members discuss answers to questions in various sections.

---

3.   **Class discussion**   10+ min   10+ min

Instructor leads discussion on the Five Disciplines and how managers can help create such a work environment.

4.   **Role-play**   15+ min   25+ min

Choose two members from each group to role-play a conflict situation. The other members are observers. For five minutes dyad uses advocacy approach and the next five minutes uses dialogue. Observers comment on differences in quality of conflict resolution: how advocacy is done and to what extent arguers can use the inquiry approach successfully. How did the nature of the interaction change?

5.   **Final discussion**   10+ min   35+ min

Class discusses differences in advocacy versus dialogue approaches and when each is used, as well as when each is most effective.

☐ Background on the Five Disciplines[2]

1. Personal Mastery

When individuals keep learning and improving their skills. Good teams require competent individuals. Personal mastery is an ongoing process, for no one ever "arrives."

2. Mental Models

Internal images of how things work, including generalizations or assumptions held. Examples of assumptions or generalizations would be: doctors are closed-minded, nurses are co-dependent, doctors don't understand management. Other examples might include organizational issues, such as, that people at higher levels are treated differently than those at lower ones (which may be an unconscious assumption), or "this is the way we do it."

3. Shared Vision

Senge talks about "creating a shared vision," for it is not an idea, but a force in people's hearts and provides a sense of purpose to what everyone does. Learning organizations are not possible without a shared vision, for without it the many needs of individuals pull at one another. As Robert Fritz said, "In the presence of greatness, pettiness disappears." Shared vision is not the same as strategic planning, which generally involves the top announcing its plans.

4. Team Learning

Bill Russell of the Celtics wrote about being on a team of specialists whose performance depended on one another's individual excellence and their ability to work together. In order to do this there must be alignment, where the team functions as one group, not as individuals operating at cross-purposes. For true team learning there needs to be both dialogue and discussion, but most teams cannot differentiate between the two and tend to use discussion more. The purpose of dialogue is to understand, to share, not to win. Judgments are suspended and an openness prevails. Discussion, which comes from the root word percussion (or to throw), often involves a verbal banter (or even batter) and has as its object winning.

---

[2]From Peter Senge, *The Fifth Discipline.* New York: Doubleday, 1990.

5. Systems Thinking

Senge determines this to be the most important discipline, hence the title of this book, *The Fifth Discipline*. Without systems thinking, none of the others has a great impact. Personal mastery alone, for example, would lead to internal competition. Structural and systemic issues need to be addressed and understood. Each member needs to understand how they play a part in *any* problem in the organization. There is no finger pointing or blaming. "I have found the enemy and he is us," as Pogo used to say.

Part One:
Learning Disabilities in Organizations

This is an exercise to look carefully at how your organization functions in terms of learning disabilities as well as the Five Disciplines.

Give examples of where you have seen learning disabilities working:

1.   I am my position

2.   The enemy is out there/shifting the burden

3.   The illusion of taking charge

4.   The fixation on events

5.   Parable of the boiled frog

6.   The delusion of learning from experience

7.   The myth of the management team

Part Two:
The Five Disciplines

Fill in the boxes on the table to indicate how your work environment or your school is relative to each of the five disciplines.

	What is the current situation?	What you can do to improve:	What you can help your organization do:
Personal Mastery			
Mental Models			
Team Learning			
Shared Vision			
Systems Thinking			

Part Three:
On Balancing Advocacy and Inquiry

Definitions: Advocacy – *to win an argument*

Inquiry – *to find the best argument*

When advocating...

   ✔   Make your reasons explicit; say how you arrived at them.

   ✔   Encourage others to explore your views.
          "Do you see any gaps in my reasoning?"

   ✔   Encourage others to provide other views.
          "Do you have any different data or conclusions?"

   ✔   Actively inquire into others' views that differ from yours.
          "How did you arrive at that?"
          "Are you taking into account data different from what I have?"

When you arrive at an impasse...

   ✔   Ask what data or logic might change their views.

   ✔   Ask if there is any way to design an experiment (or other inquiry) to provide new information.

When others are hesitant to express their views...

   ✔   Ask what makes it difficult to share their opinions.

   ✔   Jointly design ways to remove those barriers.

15. The Learning-Model Instrument

Purpose:
To determine what type of learners students are.

Group Size:
Any number.

Time Required:
30 minutes.

Preparation Required:
Complete and score the instrument.

Exercise Schedule

1.   **Instrument (pre-class)**
     Complete and score the instrument.

		Unit Time	*Total Time*
2.	**Small groups**	**15 min**	**15 min**

Instructor divides class into four groups: Thinking Planners, Feeling Planners, Task Implementors and Participative Implementors. Each group discusses:

   a.   What is the ideal learning environment?

   b.   Describe the best learning situation for your opposite type.

   c.   What was your worst learning experience?

3.	**Class discussion**	**15 min**	**30 min**

The instructor gets reports from each group and leads a discussion on learning styles.

The Learning-Model Instrument[1]

Instructions: For each statement choose the response that is more nearly true for you. Place an X on the blank that corresponds to that response.

1. When meeting people, I prefer
    _____ (a)   to think and speculate on what they are like.
    _____ (b)   to interact directly and to ask them questions.

2. When presented with a problem, I prefer
    _____ (a)   to jump right in and work on a solution.
    _____ (b)   to think through and evaluate possible ways to solve the problem.

3. I enjoy sports more when
    _____ (a)   I am watching a good game.
    _____ (b)   I am actively participating.

4. Before taking a vacation, I prefer
    _____ (a)   to rush at the last minute and give little thought beforehand
                to what I will do while on vacation.
    _____ (b)   to plan early and daydream about how I will spend my vacation.

5. When enrolled in courses, I prefer
    _____ (a)   to plan how to do my homework before actually attacking the assignment.
    _____ (b)   to immediately become involved in doing the assignment.

6. When I receive information that requires action, I prefer
    _____ (a)   to take action immediately.
    _____ (b)   to organize the information and determine what type of action
                would be most appropriate.

7. When presented with a number of alternatives for action, I prefer
    _____ (a)   to determine how the alternatives relate to one another
                and analyze the consequences of each.
    _____ (b)   to select the one that looks best and implement it.

8. When I awaken every morning, I prefer
    _____ (a)   to expect to accomplish some worthwhile work without considering
                what the individual tasks may entail.
    _____ (b)   to plan a schedule for the tasks I expect to do that day.

9. After a full day of work, I prefer
    _____ (a)   to reflect back on what I accomplished and think of how
                to make time the next day for unfinished tasks.
    _____ (b)   to relax with some type of recreation and not think about my job.

---

[1] © 1987 by Dr. Kenneth L. Murrell, University of West Florida. Used with permission.

The Learning-Model Instrument (cont'd)

10. After choosing the above responses, I
    _____ (a) prefer to continue and complete this instrument.
    _____ (b) am curious about how my responses will be interpreted and prefer some feedback before continuing with the instrument.

11. When I learn something, I am usually
    _____ (a) thinking about it.
    _____ (b) right in the middle of doing it.

12. I learn best when
    _____ (a) I am dealing with real-world issues.
    _____ (b) concepts are clear and well-organized.

13. In order to retain something I have learned, I must
    _____ (a) periodically review it in my mind.
    _____ (b) practice it or try to use the information.

14. In teaching others how to do something, I first
    _____ (a) demonstrate the task.
    _____ (b) explain the task.

15. My favorite way to learn to do something is
    _____ (a) reading a book or instructions or enrolling in a class.
    _____ (b) trying to do it and learning from my mistakes.

16. When I become emotionally involved with something, I usually
    _____ (a) let my feelings take the lead and then decide what to do.
    _____ (b) control my feelings and try to analyze the situation.

17. If I were meeting jointly with several experts on a subject, I would prefer
    _____ (a) to ask each of them for his or her opinion.
    _____ (b) to interact with them and share our ideas and feelings.

18. When I am asked to relate information to a group of people, I prefer
    _____ (a) not to have an outline, but to interact with them and become involved in an extemporaneous conversation.
    _____ (b) to prepare notes and know exactly what I am going to say.

19. Experience is
    _____ (a) a guide for building theories.
    _____ (b) the best teacher.

20. People learn more easily when they are
    _____ (a) doing work on the job.
    _____ (b) in a class taught by an expert.

The Learning-Model Instrument Scoring Sheet

Instructions: Transfer your responses by writing either "a" or "b" in the blank that corresponds to each item in the Learning-Model Instrument.

	Abstract/Concrete		Cognitive/Affective	
	Column 1	Column 2	Column 3	Column 4
	1. _____	2. _____	11. _____	12. _____
	3. _____	4. _____	13. _____	14. _____
	5. _____	6. _____	15. _____	16. _____
	7. _____	8. _____	17. _____	18. _____
	9. _____	10. _____	19. _____	20. _____
Total Circles	_____	_____	_____	_____
Grand Totals	_____		_____	

Now circle every "a" in Column 1 and Column 4. Then circle every "b" in Column 2 and in Column 3. Next, total the circles in each of the four columns. Then add the totals of Columns 1 and 2; plot this grand total on the vertical axis of the Learning-Model for Managers and draw a horizontal line through the point. Now add the totals of Columns 3 and 4; plot that grand total on the horizontal axis of the model and draw a vertical line through the point. The intersection of these two lines indicates the domain of your preferred learning style.

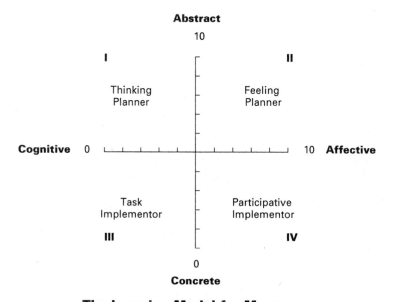

The Learning-Model for Managers

The Learning-Model Instrument Interpretation Sheet

The cognitive-affective axis or continuum represents the range of ways in which people learn. Cognitive learning includes learning that is structured around either rote storing of knowledge or intellectual abilities and skills, or both. Affective learning includes learning from experience, from feelings about the experience, and from one's own emotions.

The concrete-abstract axis or continuum represents the range of ways in which people experience life. When people experience life abstractly, they detach themselves from the immediacy of the situation and theorize about it. If they experience life concretely, they respond to the situation directly with little subsequent contemplation.

The two axes divide the model into four parts or domains. Most people experience life and learn from it in all four domains but have a preference for a particular domain. Liberal arts education has typically concentrated on abstract learning (Domains I and II), whereas vocational and on-the-job training usually takes place in the lower quadrants, particularly Domain III.

Occupations representative of the four styles include the following: Domain I, philosopher or chief executive officer; Domain II, poet or journalist; Domain III, architect or engineer; Domain IV, psychologist or personnel counselor.

Managerial jobs require an ability to learn in all four domains, and a manager's development depends on his or her ability to learn both cognitively and affectively. Thus, management education and development demand the opportunity for the participants to learn how to learn in each domain.

Scoring the Instrument: The scoring sheet indicates which answers receive a score of one point. The rest of the answers receive a score of zero. The total of the scores in the first half of the instrument is plotted on the vertical axis and a horizontal line is drawn from the point. The total of the scores in the last half is plotted on the horizontal axis and a vertical line is drawn through that point. The point of intersection of the two lines indicates the domain of the respondent.

Interpreting the Scores

The next four paragraphs give an interpretation of the four end points of the axes in the Learning-Model for Managers. Following these are explanations of the four domains in the model.

Cognitive Learning

A person who scores low on the cognitive-affective axis shows a marked preference for learning through thought or other mental activity. People who grasp intellectually very quickly what they are trying to learn or who simply prefer to use controlled thought and logic will be found on the cognitive end of this axis. Rationality appeals to these individuals, as do logic and other thinking skills that are necessary for this type of learning. Although this statement is not based on hard research, it appears that a high cognitive orientation correlates with a high task orientation rather than with a people orientation. The research about possible left-versus right-brain functioning correlates a cognitive orientation to individuals who are left-brain dominant. Therefore, the left side of the axis was deliberately assigned to the cognitive orientation to serve as an easy reminder.

Affective Learning

A person who scores high on the cognitive-affective axis shows a marked preference for learning in the affective realm. Such an individual is more comfortable with and seeks out learning from his or her emotions and feelings. These individuals desire personal interaction and seek to learn about people by experiencing them in emotional ways. This type of learner would potentially be highly people-oriented. A manager with this orientation would probably seek out social interaction rather than to focus exclusively on the task components of the job. In right-brain research, affective learners are said to be more intuitive, more spontaneous, and less linear. They seek out feelings and emotions rather than logic.

Concrete Life Experiencing

People with a preference for the concrete enjoy jumping in and getting their hands dirty. Hands-on experiences are important to them. As managers, these people want to keep busy, become directly involved, and physically approach or touch whatever they are working with. If they work with machines, they will get greasy; if they work with people, they will become involved.

Abstract Life Experiencing

Individuals preferring this style have no special desire to touch, but they want to keep active by thinking about the situation and relating it to similar situations. Their preferred interaction style is internal – inside their own heads.

The Four Learning Domains

A person is unlikely to be on the extreme end of either axis, and no one type of learning is "best." Any mixture of preferences simply represents a person's uniqueness. The model is useful in helping people differentiate themselves, and it offers a method for looking at the way different styles fit together. This section describes the four domains that are represented in the model.

The descriptions of these domains could be of special interest to managers, because they will help the manager understand the relationship between managerial action and learning style. A manager should be capable of learning and functioning well in all four domains, especially if he or she expects to face a variety of situations and challenges. The successful manager is likely to be the one who can operate in both a task and a people environment with the ability to see and become involved with the concrete and also use thought processes to understand what is needed. The normative assumption of the model is that a manager should learn how to learn in each of the four domains. In doing this, the manager may well build on his or her primary strengths, but the versatility and flexibility demanded in a managerial career make clear the importance of all four domains.

Domain I: The Thinking Planner

A combination of cognitive and abstract preferences constitutes Domain I, where the "thinking planner" is located. This domain might well be termed the place for the planner whose job is task-oriented and whose environment contains primarily things, numbers, or printouts. The bias in formal education is often toward this learning domain, and Mintzberg (1976) was critical of this bias. In this domain, things are treated abstractly and often their socio-emotional elements are denied.

The Domain-I learner should do well in school, should have a talent for planning, and is likely to be successful as a staff person or manager in a department that deals with large quantities of untouchable things. This domain represents an important area for management learning. Of the four domains, it seems to receive the heaviest emphasis in traditional university programs and in management-development seminars, particularly those in financial management.

Domain II: The Feeling Planner

A combination of affective and abstract preferences constitutes Domain II, where the "feeling planner" is located. The managerial style associated with this domain is that of the thinker who can learn and who enjoys working with people but has limited opportunity to get close to them. This domain is important for the personnel executive or a manager with too much responsibility to interact closely with other employees. Social-analysis skills are represented in this area. Managers in this domain should be able to think through and understand the social and emotional factors affecting a large organization.

Difficulties in this area sometimes arise when good first-line supervisors who have a natural style with people are promoted into positions that prevent them from having direct contact with others and are expected to determine without concrete experience the nature of and solutions to personnel problems.

Domain III: The Task Implementor

A combination of cognitive and concrete preferences constitutes Domain III, where the "task implementor" is located. This domain contains decision makers who primarily want to understand the task and who can focus on the details and specifics of the concrete in a thoughtful manner. If these people are allowed to think about a situation, they can see the concrete issues and, after close examination, can make a well-thought-out decision. A person in this domain is often a task-focused doer. If the interpersonal skill demands are low and if the emotional climate is not a problem, this person is likely to do well.

Domain IV: The Participative Implementor

A combination of affective and concrete preferences constitutes Domain IV, where the "participative implementor" is located. The manager with people skills who has the opportunity to work closely with people is found in this category. This is the place where implementors and highly skilled organization development consultants reside. This domain is for those who like to become involved and who have the ability and interest in working with the emotional needs and demands of the people in an organization. This is the domain that is emphasized by most of the practical management programs, and it can be used to complement the traditional educational programs of Domain I.

References

Blake, R.R., and J. S. Mouton. *Managerial Grid.* 3rd ed. Houston, Texas: Gulf, 1984.

Jung, C.G. *Second Impression* Trans., H. Godwin. New York: Harcourt Brace, 1924.

Kolb, D.A., I.M. Rubin and J. M. McIntyre. *Organizational Psychology: An Experiential Approach.* 2nd ed. Englewood Cliffs, NJ: Prentice-Hall, 1974.

Mintzberg, H. "Planning on the Left Side and Managing on the Right." *Harvard Business Review*, July-August, 1976, pp. 49-58.

Peters, D. *Directory of Human Resource Development Instrumentation.* San Diego, Ca.: University Associates, 1985.

Pfeiffer, J. W., R. Heslin, and J.E. Jones. *Instrumentation in Human Relations Training.* San Diego, Ca.: University Associates, 1976.

Rogers, C.R. *Freedom to Learn.* Columbus, Ohio: Charles E. Merrill, 1982.

16. Positive and Negative Reinforcement

Purpose:
To examine the effects of positive and negative reinforcement on behavior change.

Group Size:
Any number, although it is especially effective in large classes.

Time Required:
25 minutes for Part A.
10 minutes for Part B.

Related Topics:
Motivation, Interpersonal Communication

➼ Introduction

Behavior Modification (Behavior Management) and Reinforcement are based on the work of B. F. Skinner and have proven to be effective in behavior change in organizations. The following exercise will help you see what happens when positive and negative reinforcement are used.

Exercise Schedule

Part A – Positive and Negative Reinforcement Exercise[1]

	Unit Time	Total Time
Steps 1-4: Exercise overview	**5 min**	**5 min**

1. Two (or three) volunteers are selected to receive reinforcement from the class while performing a particular task. The volunteers leave the room.

2. The instructor identifies an object for the student volunteers to locate when they return to the room. (The object should be unobtrusive but clearly visible to the class. Examples that have worked well include a small triangular piece of paper that was left behind when a notice was torn off a classroom bulletin board, a smudge on the chalkboard, and a chip in the plaster of a classroom wall.)

3. The instructor specifies the reinforcement contingencies that will be in effect when the volunteers return to the room – for negative reinforcement students should hiss, boo and throw things (although you should not throw anything harmful) when the first volunteer is moving away from the object; for positive reinforcement they should cheer and applaud when the second volunteer is getting closer to the object; and, if a third volunteer is used, students should use both negative and positive reinforcement.

4. The instructor should assign a student to keep a record of the time it takes each of the volunteers to locate the object.

---

[1]By Larry Michaelson. Used with permission.

Steps 5 & 6: Volunteer #1   **5 min**   **10 min**

5. Volunteer #1 is brought back into the room and is instructed: "Your task is to locate and touch a particular object in the room, and the class has agreed to help you. You may not use words or ask questions. You may begin."

6. Volunteer #1 continues to look for the object until it is found, while the class assists by giving negative reinforcement.

Steps 7 & 8: Volunteer #2   **5 min**   **15 min**

7. Volunteer #2 is brought back into the room and is instructed: "Your task is to locate and touch a particular object in the room, and the class has agreed to help you. You may not use words or ask questions. You may begin."

8. Volunteer #2 continues to look for the object until it is found, while the class assists by giving positive reinforcement.

Steps 9 & 10: Volunteer #3   **5 min**   **20 min**

9. Volunteer #3 is brought back into the room and is instructed: "Your task is to locate and touch a particular object in the room, and the class has agreed to help you. You may not use words or ask questions. You may begin."

10. Volunteer #3 continues to look for the object until it is found, while the class assists by giving both positive and negative reinforcement.

11.   Class discussion   **5 min**   **25 min**

In a class discussion answer the following questions:

    a.   What was the difference in behavior change of the volunteer when different kinds of reinforcement (positive, negative, or both) were used?

    b.   What were the emotional reactions of the volunteers to the different kinds of reinforcement?

    c.   Which type of reinforcement is most common in organizations, positive or negative? What effect do you think this has on motivation and productivity?

Part B – Reinforcement: Its Application and Results[2]

In order to better understand the impact reinforcement can have on the behavior, attitudes, and reactions of others, this exercise requires you to experiment and analyze its application.

1.   During the next week, look for a situation where you can practice reinforcement.
Be alert for situations in which someone does something that you consider to be worthy of a compliment. When such a situation occurs, make a deliberate effort to give them a compliment in a sincere and specific way (e.g., perhaps a roommate washes a sink full of everyone's dirty dishes, or your boss provides you with some helpful information, or a fellow student gets an interview request from a good company, etc.)

---

[2]By Mary Gander. Used with permission.

2.   **After you have completed the experiment, answer the following questions.**

Analyze:

1)   What kind of reinforcement did you use? Why?

2)   What was the other person's reaction?

3)   What short-term and/or long-term outcomes, if any, were achieved or do you expect to occur?

4)   How did you feel after the incident?

Briefly describe an incident in which another person used reinforcement on you. How did you feel/respond?

3.   **Share experiences**   **10 min**   **10 min**

In class, the instructor will ask for volunteers to explain their experiences and may ask you to turn in this page or another sheet with answers to the above four questions.

Chapter 6
Work Motivation

17. Robert Princeton[1]

Purpose:
To understand job motivation.

Time Required:
10-25 minutes.

Preparation:
1. Read the "Robert Princeton" case study.
2. Report your conclusions in a memo format, directed to the instructor.

Guidelines:

In your memo, explain why Robert Princeton quit his job.

- Explain how the situation could have been avoided, or at least handled more effectively.

- Be specific about *who* should have done *what* differently at *which* point in time.

- The appropriate use of the concepts and theories is sufficient; you may assume that the instructor has a sufficient understanding of all textbook concepts and terminology.

- If necessary, you may make appropriate assumptions in cases where data is missing or unclear. However, it is very important that you label such information as assumption, and that you justify its appropriateness on the basis of case data.

In class, discuss the memos and motivation theories which support students' decisions.

---

[1] © 1994 by David M. Leuser, Ph.D., Plymouth State College of the University System of New Hampshire. Used with permission.

Case Study: _____

Robert Princeton

In May of 1987, Robert Princeton, age 24, graduated from Middlebury College with a Bachelor's degree in theater. In October of 1987, he accepted a job as the Assistant Manager of Falls Video, a rapidly growing chain of video rental outlets located in northeastern New York State.

Falls Video had been founded by "Momma and Poppa" Valenchia in 1983. The operation began as a video rental business in a corner of their Glens Falls grocery store. They experienced immediate success, and expanded the operation to include four new video rental outlets by 1985. At the same time that the video business was expanding, so was the grocery business, with three new stores established in surrounding towns. Momma Valenchia was the mastermind behind this growth; Poppa Valenchia was content to remain in the Glens Falls office and keep the books for the growing business. One of the decisions that Momma had made was to separate the grocery and video stores. As she expanded the number of grocery and video outlets, it became apparent that she needed management assistance. In June of 1985, she split the management duties of the organization. Momma continued to manage the grocery stores, but she brought in her son, Mario, to run the video business. Mario had just earned an Associate's degree in business from a nearby community college, and was eager to take charge of the rapidly growing video business. Mario was put in charge of hiring, firing, loss prevention, video buying, and the day-to-day management of all the video stores, including the supervision of personnel.

By the summer of 1987, Falls Video had eight rental outlets within a twenty-five mile radius of Glens Falls. However, problems had begun to arise. Losses due to stolen or misplaced videos were up, there were inadequate supplies of newly released films to satisfy customer demand, and turnover, absenteeism and tardiness were way up among the 35 full- and part-time employees of the chain. Momma Valenchia was particularly puzzled by the personnel problems, since she was experiencing no such difficulties with her grocery staff. When she asked Mario about it, he replied that she had only four stores to manage, and he had eight! Besides, he insisted, it was hard to attract competent workers at the low wages that they had to pay to remain profitable.

In the early fall of 1987, Momma Valenchia decided to hire Robert Princeton as the Assistant Manager of Falls Video in order to help Mario out. He was hired at an annual salary of $21,500 because Momma Valenchia believed that he had a lot of potential.

Princeton began his work with enthusiasm. He made it a point to visit each store at least two times a week, and, over time, got to know every staff member personally. He found that by taking a staff member out to lunch or dinner, he could really get them to open up about their perceptions of the organization. Princeton found this contact with the staff very gratifying. However, he quickly encountered some misunderstandings with his boss, Mario. On one occasion, he allowed a part-time employee to take the weekend off in order to attend an out-of-state funeral. When Mario found out, he was furious that the store was understaffed during the critical weekend period, and he informed Princeton that all future schedule changes would have to have his personal approval. Feeling somewhat embarrassed, Princeton sheepishly agreed. On another occasion, Princeton offered to train the staff in the basics of film appreciation, since he felt that this would help them to better assess and satisfy customer needs. Mario said that it was a foolish idea, and told Princeton not to waste any company time on it. Although Princeton still felt that his idea was a good one, he did not pursue it any further. At one point Princeton mentioned to Mario that many of the full-time employees wanted the company to institute an employee health insurance program. Mario's casual response was that they could not afford the expense, and that Princeton should be channeling his efforts into saving money rather than spending it. Even though Princeton was convinced that such a program would boost morale and reduce turnover, he let the matter drop.

> Princeton **began** his work with enthusiasm.

In spite of all these frustrations, Princeton kept up his efforts. While he was troubled by the lack of guidance that he received from Mario, he felt that he could demonstrate his value to the organization. After all, when he had approached Momma Valenchia with his concerns about his working relationship with Mario, she had said: "Mario is a good and capable boy, and so are you. Work hard and you will be successful." This discussion motivated Princeton to take a more strategic perspective in his efforts.

He immediately initiated a survey of customer preferences in movies to develop recommendations for new titles to purchase. He initiated exit interviews with employees who quit, and as a result of this, did an informal survey of staff members' perceptions of Falls Video management. Finally, he developed a proposal to track video rentals and customer creditworthiness on a microcomputer system.

In early January of 1988, Robert Princeton scheduled a meeting with Mario to discuss his accomplishments of the previous three months. Mario was silent and looked sullen as Princeton presented the results of his work. Princeton provided detailed recommendations for the purchase and resale of new titles, and suggested a variety of changes in personnel policy and management practice designed to boost morale and reduce absenteeism and turnover. He explained how the computer tracking system could reduce losses of videos and improve customer service. Princeton was taken aback by Mario's sudden response:

"Who the hell do you think you are?" (followed by a long pause...) "Strategic management is my job. Your job is to supervise the workers. I tell you what to do, and you tell them what to do! It's as simple as that. Any questions?"

"Well, yes...but...I thought..." stammered Princeton.

"You're not paid to think – you're paid to do what you're told," shouted Mario. "Poppa showed me your expense account yesterday. The poor old guy almost had a coronary when he tallied it. It's off the wall! Your travel and entertainment expenses in one week are more than mine in a whole month! We give you an office and a telephone here in Glens Falls. I expect you to use them! We're not rich like your family and that snobby private school they sent you to. We have to run this operation on a shoestring. As I've told you before, that's where I need your help. Now get to work on making a real contribution to this organization's bottom line."

> **"You're not paid to think:** you're paid to do what you're told," shouted Mario.

Princeton was flabbergasted! He was proud of his accomplishments, and thought that they proved his value to the organization. But, rather than get into a heated argument on the spot, Princeton felt that he had better sleep on it.

The next morning when Princeton arrived for work, he found a sealed envelope on his desk with his name on it, marked "Personal and Confidential." At first he assumed that it must be an apology from Mario. He was surprised to find that it was a letter of reprimand for abuse of his expense account and insubordination, signed by both Poppa and Mario Valenchia. It concluded with the statement: "If you wish to continue your employment with Falls Video, you must learn to become more cost conscious!"

Princeton spent the rest of the morning in his office with the door closed, thinking.

At 11:30, he asked Momma Valenchia to have lunch with him. After some hesitation, she agreed. During lunch, Princeton complained that he was not being allowed to have a strategic impact on the organization. Momma's response had been: "Roberto, I hired you as an assistant manager to Mario. Your job is to work for Mario. Mario's job is strategic planning. I still believe that you have a lot of potential. But you must understand the ways of the family. Poppa and Mario run the business. You must cooperate with them. Without cooperation, we cannot run a successful family business."

At 1:30 p.m., Robert Princeton submitted his resignation. He had no job prospects, and wasn't sure what his next move would be.

18. Expectancy Theory Activity[1]

Purpose:
To see how expectancy theory works in practice.

Group Size:
An even number of up to 10 groups of five to eight members.

Time Required:
50 minutes.

Preparation Required:
Read the background below and each of the case studies.

Related Topics:
Motivation, Need Theory, Organizational Research, Job Design

☐ Background

The essence of expectancy theory is that people choose actions that benefit themselves the most: they maximize the value of their actions. Seen another way, from the point of view of the organization, individuals are motivated to perform behaviors that are in their best interest. In other words, employees will work hard when they are rewarded for working hard. If they are not rewarded, they will not work hard. It is in their better interest to expend less effort. If we are talking about motivating choice of tasks rather than effort, then we can say that people will choose tasks that benefit them.

Expectancy theory is of course more complicated in its completeness than the simple description above. It specifies the components of the connection between behavior and reward, saying that for reward to motivate behavior,

(1) *rewards must be valued,*

(2) *performance must lead to rewards, and*

(3) *behavior must lead to performance.*

Each of these components is necessary; if one is missing or weak, the entire connection is weak and behavior is poorly motivated. These three components are called (1) valence, (2) instrumentality, and (3) expectancy, and are described more fully below. The theory also specifies how these components are combined to calculate motivational force. This is also described below.

Valence

This refers to the value of the rewards of performance for the individual. Some people value money, for example, more than other things or more than other people do. Some people may value the personal satisfaction they get from doing their job well most of all. Some people may value their relationships with co-workers.

Different people will value different job or task rewards differently. These rewards have differing *valence*, therefore, and have differing potential to motivate behavior.

Expectancy theory does not specify all the rewards that must be considered. We do know, though, that pay, co-worker relationships, personal satisfaction, promotions, and the characteristics of the job are common job rewards. To measure valence we must determine how valuable or important to a person the rewards offered by the job are.

> Valence is best measured on a scale from 0 to 1. The valence of a particular reward is high, or close to 1, when that reward is highly valued. When a reward is not valued it has 0 valence. To make calculations simpler to the exercise that follows, rather than estimating expectancy between 0 and 1 you will use a scale from 0 to 100.

Because jobs have multiple rewards and individuals value more than just one reward, all relevant job outcomes should be taken into account to best predict or enhance motivation. In the exercise that follows, though, you will be considering only the two most important rewards.

Instrumentality

This refers to the perceived relationship between performance and rewards, or how well performance on a job leads to job rewards. Often this component is called Performance-Reward Expectancy, sometimes referred to as E_2. Here we will call it instrumentality. This comes from the idea that performance is instrumental for rewards – it is the means to achieve rewards.

Because jobs have multiple rewards they also have more than one instrumentality. For each reward, instrumentality is the degree to which performance on the job is perceived to cause the reward to be received. If high performance and only high performance leads to high amounts of the reward and low performance and only low performance leads to low reward, then instrumentality is high – performance causes the reward to follow. If a reward is achieved whether performance is high or not, then performance is not instrumental for the reward and instrumentality is low. In some jobs people get paid the same whether their performance is high or low.

> Instrumentality for each reward is best measured on a scale from -1 to +1. When high performance and only high performance leads to high pay, for example, and low performance and only low performance leads to low rewards, then performance is highly instrumental for pay and instrumentality for that reward is high and positive, or close to +1. If there is no relationship between performance and promotions, for example, the instrumentality is absent or close to 0. It is even possible that performance on some jobs leads to lower rewards, such as when doing well in a job lessens the chance of a transfer. In this case instrumentality is negative, or between 0 and -1. In the exercise, though, you will estimate instrumentality on a scale from -100 to +100.

Instrumentality is measured between performance and each reward. For example, if two rewards, pay and promotion, are present, there is an instrumentality of performance of pay (we'll call this first instrumentality I_1 in the exercise) and an instrumentality of performance for promotion (which we will call I_2 in the exercise). These multiple instrumentalities are combined with the multiple valences in the way described later, "Combining Valence, Instrumentality, and Expectancy." In the exercise you will estimate instrumentality for the two most important rewards.

Expectancy

This refers to the perceived relationship between effort and performance. Often this component is called effort-performance expectancy, sometimes referred to as E_1. Here we'll call it expectancy.

Expectancy is the degree to which effort is perceived to cause performance. If effort leads to performance and lack of effort leads to lack of performance, then expectancy is high. If no matter how much effort a person expends, performance does not change (that is, it remains low or high), then expectancy is low. Expectancy is high when changes in behavior cause corresponding changes in performance. So expectancy is low when jobs are too easy or too difficult, when a person's behavior is not what is required to cause performance.

Another way of thinking about expectancy is the amount of control a person perceives they have over their performance. If they can believe that they control performance with their behavior, then expectancy is high.

> Expectancy is best measured on a scale from -1 to +1. When high effort and only high effort leads to high performance and low effort and only low effort leads to low performance, then expectancy is high and positive, or close to 1. When there is no relationship, then expectancy is absent or close to 0. Because it is possible for more effort to lead to lower performance (such as when working harder interferes with productivity) expectancy can be negative. The stronger this negative relationship, the closer expectancy is to -1. You will estimate expectancy on a scale from -100 to +100 in the exercise.

Combining Valence, Instrumentality and Expectancy

> In order for rewards to motivate behavior, the rewards must be valued, performance must lead to rewards, and effort must lead to performance. From the employee's perspective, the "line of sight" from effort to rewards must be clear. Each link in the chain is necessary; effort causing performance, performance causing rewards, and rewards being valued.

> In expectancy theory, motivational force, which is a person's tendency to choose to expend effort, is equal to the product of expectancy, instrumentality, and valence. It is each of these multiplied by each other. In this way, if any one is absent, or equal to 0, then the whole equation is equal to 0: no force is present.

> *Specifically the formula is written as follows:* $MF = E \times (I \times V)$

> The formula can be read as "motivational force is equal to the product of expectancy times the sum of the product of each instrumentality times each valence." To illustrate, once all components are measured, (1) each reward valence (V_1, V_2, ...) is multiplied by each instrumentality for the corresponding rewards (I_1, I_2, ...), (2) these products (VI_1, VI_2, ...) are summed or added together, and (3) this total (VI) is multiplied by expectancy, the resulting figures is what we would predict the force to expend effort to be. For example, if V_1 and V_2 are equal to .8 and .6, I_1 and I_2 are equal to .8 and .9, and E is equal to .7, then MF = $.7 \times [(.8 \times .8) + (.6 \times .9)] = .83$.

In the following exercise you will be estimating or measuring the valence, instrumentality, and expectancy that is present for the individuals described in the following case studies. You will also calculate motivational force. To test the validity of expectancy theory, you will also be predicting how hard the individuals described are likely to work. Your motivation calculations will be compared to the effort predictions made by other groups, and vice versa. If expectancy theory works, then we would expect predictions of level of effort to match calculated motivational force.

*Case Studies:*_____

A is for Arthur. Arthur has been working for the same insurance firm for 20 years. He was recently transferred to a position where he supervises a group of young managers-in-training. As a senior employee he is well paid. Money, though, doesn't mean much to Arthur. His investments have done well and he has no family to support. Arthur's principal interest has always been the work itself. If he is diligent, Arthur is able to do a good job. But the transfer has taken him away from his previous work and he finds supervision uninteresting. In recognition of this, Arthur has been given a raise and promised more of the same work.

B is for Barbara. Barbara is an entry-level accountant for a small bookkeeping firm. One of the things that attracted her to this firm is their way of paying people – Barbara receives a share of the firm's monthly profit based on her monthly performance. As a young person, Barbara wants to be successful, and for her that means earning money and moving upward in the firm. When Barbara works hard she feels that she accomplishes a lot; more, she thinks, than her co-workers. But when her bosses appraise her performance she feels unfairly treated. On months that she has done well she doesn't get any more profit than other months. What really angered her was when she was overlooked for a promotion after her best month yet.

C is for Charles. The assembly line at the Mayfair Appliance Plant runs at a steady one foot per second. Charles' job is attaching refrigerator door hinges, for which he's not paid very much. Whether he works harder or takes it easy makes no difference – the line moves on. Mayfair's slogan is "Quality Comes First." But though Charles pays special attention to quality, no one notices. Although he'd like to socialize, his co-workers ignore him – Charles is the only American Indian in this plant.

D is for Diane. Diane works as a software designer for an innovative microcomputer manufacturer. She enjoys her work because it provides her with challenging and interesting work and it pays well. In her firm, bonuses are awarded every quarter on the basis of individual employee accomplishments. People who perform well are also given first choice of new projects. As a well-trained and competent worker Diane, is able to do her job very well so long as she works hard.

E is for Earl. Earl only wants two things out of his job – the friendship of his buddies in the machine shop and his paycheck. Earl is paid on a piece rate basis – the harder he works and the more parts he finishes, the more money he makes. Earl is a good machinist and can be very productive if he tries. Unfortunately, when Earl outperforms the rest of his work group, they scorn him as a "rate-buster." The more he produces the worse the scorn. It seems that in the past, the shop's owners have used high performance to lower the amount workers receive for each piece produced.

F is for Fay. Fay recently returned to the workforce after a long absence. During that time much of the way her job is done has changed. It used to be that hard work and creativity were necessary to do a good job, which earned her praise and a good salary. She is still recognized for high performance, but she doesn't feel personally responsible. Now a computer program does most of her work for her – her effort or creativity isn't required. Fay's work is always good.

Exercise Schedule

		Unit Time	Total Time
1.	**Introduction**	**10 min**	**10 min**

The instructor will discuss the expectancy model of motivation and will divide the class into an even number of groups, each with about five members.

		Unit Time	Total Time
2.	**Group calculations**	**25 min**	**35 min**

Each group will first use the expectancy model to calculate the motivational force present in half of the case studies by judging their valence, instrumentality and expectancy. For the remaining cases each group will predict how hard the individual described is likely to work. Groups with odd numbers will calculate motivation for cases in Set I (A, B and C). Even-numbered groups will calculate motivation for cases in Set II (D, E, F) and predict motivation for cases in Set I (A, B, C).

a. First, read one case study at a time in the appropriate set and come to a group consensus on the two most salient rewards present for the individual. For each of these rewards, assign a number between 0 and 100 representing the importance or value of performance and each reward, or instrumentality, that is present. Use the description of instrumentality in the background and assign numbers between -100 and +100. Record the instrumentality of performance for the first reward in Column 2 and that of the second reward in Column 5.

b. Second, achieve consensus on the degree of expectancy, or the strength of relationship between effort and performance, that is present. Again, refer to the background and assign a number between -100 and +100. Record this in Column 8.

c. Third, perform the appropriate calculations:

   — multiply Column 1 and Column 2 and divide by 100, and then place the result (which should be between 0 and + 100) in Column 3;

   — do the same for Columns 4 and 5, placing the result in Column 6;

   — add Columns 3 and 6 and place the result in Column 7;

   — multiply Columns 7 and 9 and divide by 100, and place this result in Column 9. This represents the degree to which effort is rewarded in the case. The maximum is 200. Transfer Column 9 to the Class Tally Sheet in the appropriate column of the Calculated section.

3.   Case calculations   **5 min**   **40 min**
For each of the case studies in the other set (Set I for even-numbered groups, Set II for odd-numbered groups), as a group, predict how the individual described in the case is likely to be motivated to expend high effort. Don't do the calculations in the way you just did, rather think about how hard you would work if you were the individual described. Assign a number between 0 and 100 to how hard you would work, and place this number in the appropriate column of the Predicted section of the Class Tally Sheet.

4.   Reports   **10 min**   **50 min**
Each group reports to the class on their calculated and predicted motivational force for Cases A through F to complete the Class Tally Sheet. Together the class will compute the average calculated and predicted scores for each force and discuss the match between them. Instructor leads a discussion of the questions below.

Discussion Questions

1. Did the average calculated motivational force for the cases match the predicted effort? How would you explain instances where the match is poor?

2. In your small group discussion, did you notice differences in how people rated valence, instrumentality, or expectancy? What are the implications of these differences for motivating people?

3. In those cases where predicted motivation or calculated force was low, what would you do to redesign the job so that it *was* motivating?

Group Tally Sheet

Calculated Force

Group #:_____

	(1) V^1	(2) I^1	(3) VI^1	(4) V^2	(5) I^2	(6) VI^2	(7) VI	(8) E	(9) $E\ VI$

Case A
Case B } OR { D
E
Case C F

_____

_____

_____

$$\frac{(1)\times(2)}{100} = (3) \qquad \frac{(4)\times(5)}{100} = (6) \qquad (3)+(6) = (7) \qquad \frac{(7)\times(8)}{100} = (9)$$

Predicted Effort
(10)

Case A
Case B } OR { D
E
Case C F

_____

_____

_____

_____

Class Tally Sheet

	Calculated Force (9)*						**Predicted Effort (10)****					
Group	1	3	5	7	9	$\overline{X}$	2	4	6	8	10	$\overline{X}$
Case A												
B												
C												
Group	2	4	6	8	10	$\overline{X}$	1	3	5	7	9	$\overline{X}$
Case D												
E												
F												

19. Work vs. Play[1]

> **Purpose:**
> To introduce the concept of motivation.
>
> **Group Size:**
> Any number of groups of four to five members.
>
> **Time Required:**
> 40-55 minutes.

Exercise Schedule

		Unit Time	*Total Time*
1.	**Group discussion**	**20-30 min**	**20-30 min**

Groups discuss the following:

What drives you to expend energy on play activities? That is, assuming you have some amount of leisure, non-work-oriented time, why do you choose those play activities? Keep the focus on why, not which particular activities. Choose a reader to present ideas to the class.

2.	**Group presentation**	**10-15 min**	**30-45 min**

Each group presents its main discussion points to the class. The instructor will draw on the board a table similar to the one below, based on the information from group discussion.

Activities	Outcome #1	Outcome #2	Outcome #3	Outcome #4	Outcome #5	Outcome #6
Example: #1. Soccer	high-energy	team bonding	fitness			
#2.						
#3.						
#4.						

3.	**Class discussion**	**10 min**	**40-55 min**

Class discussion on the following questions:

a. How can you build some of these motives for play into a work environment?

b. What prevents you from making work more intrinsically motivating, like play is?

c. If you have already covered motivation theorists, which are relevant here?

---

[1] Adapted from Phil Anderson, College of St. Thomas. Used with permission.

20. Manifest Needs[1]

Purpose:
To examine levels of motivation according to Murray, McClelland, and others.

Group Size:
Any number of groups of four to six members.

Time Required:
35 minutes.

Preparation Required:
Complete the "Motivation Needs" instrument and answer the questions after the case studies.

Exercise Schedule

		Unit Time	Total Time
1.	**Complete instrument (pre-class)**		
2.	**Group discussion**	**20 min**	**20 min**

Groups share their responses to the questionnaire and try to achieve consensus on the problems at the end of the case studies and problems.

3.	**Class discussion**	**15 min**	**35 min**

Instructor leads a discussion on McClelland's motivation theory, as well as the other dimension of autonomy (from Murray's work).

Motivation Needs Instrument

1. At work or in class, I would rather work
   a. alone.
   b. in a group.

2. When working on a project, I usually
   a. spend a great deal of time so it is really good.
   b. try to make it just acceptable.

3. In a group,
   a. I really try to be a leader.
   b. I let others take the lead.

4. With a project, I prefer
   a. to do it my way.
   b. to see how others have done it or want it done.

5. My goals at work or school are usually to
   a. be good enough, to get by.
   b. to outperform others.

6. When there is a disagreement, I usually
   a. refrain from saying much if people I like are arguing against my opinion.
   b. speak my mind.

7. In a group,
   a. I let the ideas or recommendations develop naturally.
   b. I try to influence those in the group to my opinion.

8. At work, I pretty much
   a. keep to myself and get the work done.
   b. enjoy chatting with other people.

9. At work or school, I usually
   a. avoid risks.
   b. stick my neck out and take moderate risks to get ahead.

10. Regarding rules and regulations, I generally
    a. follow them unless there is a compelling reason not to.
    b. disregard them if they get in the way of my freedom.

Motivation Needs Instrument (cont'd)

11. When involved in sports or other games, I usually play
    a. to have a good time.
    b. to win or at least do better than I have previously.

12. When working on a project, I like to
    a. have a lot of say in the outcome.
    b. be an accepted "team player."

13. In my worklife, I often
    a. make certain I give adequate time to my personal life (family, friends, etc.).
    b. get so over-scheduled I have less time for my personal life.

14. When I am working with other people, I usually want to
    a. do better than they do.
    b. organize and direct the activities of the others.

Scoring

Score one point in the following categories if you marked the appropriate letter.

N Aut	N Power	N Ach	N Aff
1a	3a	2a	1b
4a	5b	9b	6a
6b	7b	11b	8b
8a	12a	13b	12b
10b	14b	14a	13a

Totals   _____   _____   _____   _____

❑ **Background**

Henry Murray (1938) developed a theory of personality and motivation needs in the 1930s, which was later developed further by David McClelland (1953). Four needs were identified: need for autonomy (N Aut), need for power (N Pow), need for achievement (N Ach), and need for affiliation (N Aff). Murray called these manifest needs.

These four needs co-exist in each person, but at varying levels. N Aut determines a person's requirement to do things alone, with a minimum amount of supervision or outside structure. N Pow relates to the desire to be in charge, in control, where the person is influencing and directing others. N Ach describes the desire to excel, to do better than others, to accomplish goals. Finally, N Aff has to do with someone's need to be part of a group, to be accepted and liked, to be included.

What Your Score Means

This test measures your needs in each of the four areas. Results only show a general tendency towards the four needs and are not meant to be a definitive calibration. Use the results only in a general sense, to get a basic idea of where your need levels are.

Each of the four areas has a possible total of five points. Whichever area you have the highest number of points in is probably the area where your need level is greatest. There are no "good" or "bad" scores. Any combination of need levels can work for you, depending on what you want to do with your life. Someone with a low need for power, for example, is less likely to be drawn to management positions, while a person with a high need for affiliation would, most likely, do well in work that requires people skills and would not tend to desire work that requires a great deal of rejection or conflict (commodities traders, for example).

Case Studies and Problems

1 – Case Studies[2]

Read the following cases and determine which of the four dimensions would be most important and which would be second most important when that person is making a decision about which action to take.

A. Martha Merriweather

Martha has been with Performance Horizons for seven years, steadily moving up the corporate ladder. She was noticed early on by the CEO when she developed a new marketing plan which increased sales by 14%. Her current position involves developing strategic plans, and she has managed to enthuse many in the organization to the new mission of the company which she helped develop. Her long-range goals include working overseas for several years and helping to build up those operations. She would like to eventually be at or near the top.

Which of the four motivates Martha? List the first and second most important ones.

B. Steven Soldenberg

Steven has been one of the stable employees of Performance Horizons for nearly 20 years. In fact, few can remember the company without him around. In addition to being a decent salesperson, he's the first one to remember birthdays and to spearhead plans for holiday parties. Whenever anyone has a problem, Steven is often the first one they go to for help. Several years ago, Steven was offered a promotion at a different site. He turned it down, though, citing family reasons. Many suspected, though, that he just felt too comfortable with the crew at his location.

Which two of the four motivate Steven?

---

[2]Idea for case studies came from Patrick Doyle, Management for Tomorrow in Impact Ground Zero. Used with permission.

C. Joanne Jamison

Joanne started with Performance Horizons five years ago, after receiving her MBA from the Wharton Business School. She has told people the reason she went to Wharton was to have the best opportunities at jobs that would offer quick advancement. Joanne has a keen sense of what makes organizations tick and who to go to when things need to get done. She doesn't "waste" her time with chit-chat, as she calls it. Her time is all spent on getting the job done and making sure she makes the right connections.

Which two motivate Joanne?

D. Mark Mendelson

Mark has worked for 10 years in several departments (all in creative units) at Performance Horizons. He likes to move around, he says, to keep from being bored. His co-workers say he does it so that he won't get entrenched in one spot or stuck with one way of doing things. He takes pride in his work, which is always top-class. And he frequently comes up with unusual ways of doing things. Mark is seldom in his office. He might be in the lab, the art room, or meeting with people in their offices. No one is quite sure how he does it, but his productivity is quite high. Mark rarely shows up at company events. He does like to send people electronic mail, though, on his new ideas.

Which two needs motivate Mark?

2 – Presidential Choices

Consider the last several presidents: Nixon, Ford, Carter, Reagan, Bush, and Clinton. Examine how they campaigned, what they sought as presidents, and – for the past presidents – what they occupied themselves with after they were out of office.

    a. What need levels seem dominant in each of the six presidents?

    b. What would be your ideal mix of needs for a president of the United States?

3 – Bosses

Think about the best boss and the worst boss you have had.

    a. What need levels did those two have?

    b. Is there an ideal need mix for a manager?

    c. Should managers at different levels or in different organizations have different levels of needs to be effective? Explain.

4 – Higher Education

As an undergraduate or graduate student, what types of activities or requirements fill the four needs?
List them below.

N Aut   N Pow

N Ach   N Aff

References

McClelland, David. *The Achievement Motive.* New York: Appleton-Century-Crofts, 1953.

_____. *The Achieving Society.* Princeton, NJ: Van Nostrand, 1961.

Murray, Henry A.; William J. Barrett and Erik Homberger. *Explorations in Personality.* London: Oxford University Press, 1938.

_____. *Thematic Apperception Test Manual.* Cambridge, Mass: Harvard University Press, 1943.

Steers, Richard M. and Daniel N. Braunstein. "A behaviorally-based measure of manifest needs in work settings," *Journal of Vocational Behavior*, Vol. 9, pp. 251-266, 1976.

21. Job Involvement[1]

Purpose:
To examine job involvement.

Time Required:
5-10 minutes to complete inventory.

Job Involvement Inventory

The comments below were made by people about their work. Consider how much you agree with each item regarding your current or previous job (or your "job" as a student). Use a five-point scale, as shown:

Strongly agree	Agree	Indifferent	Disagree	Strongly disagree
5	4	3	2	1

_____ 1. I'll stay overtime to finish a job, even if I'm not paid for it.

_____ 2. You can measure a person pretty well by how good a job he or she does.

_____ 3. The major satisfaction in my life comes from my job.

_____ 4. For me, mornings at work really fly by.

_____ 5. I usually show up for work a little early to get things ready.

_____ 6. The most important things that happen to me involve my work.

_____ 7. Sometimes I lie awake at night thinking ahead to the next day's work.

_____ 8. I'm really a perfectionist about my work.

_____ 9. I feel depressed when I fail at something connected with my job.

_____ 10. I have other activities more important than my work.

_____ 11. I live, eat, and breathe my job.

_____ 12. I would probably keep working even if I didn't need the money.

_____ 13. Quite often I feel like staying home from work instead of coming in.

_____ 14. To me, my work is only a small part of who I am.

_____ 15. I am very much involved personally in my work.

_____ 16. I avoid taking on extra duties and responsibilitites in my work.

_____ 17. I used to be more ambitious about my work than I am now.

_____ 18. Most things in life are more important than work.

_____ 19. I used to care more about my work, but now other things are more important to me.

_____ 20. Sometimes I'd like to kick myself for the mistakes I make in my work.

[1]Source: Thomas M. Lodahl and Mathilde Kejner, "The Definition and Measurement of Job Involvement," *Journal of Applied Psychology*, February 1965, Vol. 49, No. 1, p. 29. © 1965 by the American Psychological Association. Reprinted with permission.

Job Involvement

In recent decades, the concept of job involvement has been added to the ideas of organizational behavior and management. Some writers and researchers believe strong ego commitment is a necessary part of job involvement; others disagree. However, a good way to think of job involvement is the extent to which a person is psychologically committed to his or her work, and the extent to which "blunders" will not be tolerated and would decrease self-esteem. In other words, if you have high job involvement, you care about your work and the quality of your output. People with high job involvement usually have lower rates of absenteeism and turnover.

Job involvement can, however, go too far. Recent research on work addiction indicates social costs for overdoing it: these include health problems and estrangement from family and friends. Howard Schwartz (1982) wrote that job involvement can be seen as obsessive/compulsive behavior.

What do you think?

Chapter 7

Motivating Performance, Goal-Setting and Reward Systems

22. Job Design

Purpose:
To redesign a job using job characteristics theory (Hackman and Oldham, 1976).

Group Size:
Any number of groups of four to six members.

Time Required:
50 minutes.

Preparation Required:
Read overview of job characteristics theory.

Job Characteristics Theory: An Overview[1]

Generally speaking, job design is concerned with the specific tasks that are performed on a job, how those tasks are performed, and the types of reactions employees experience as a result of performing the job. The most

---

[1]Based on a case by Loren W. Kuzuhara and Randall B. Dunham, in the *Instructor's Resource Manual for Management* by Randy Dunham and J.L. Pierce, Glenview, IL.: Scott Foresman, 1989. Used with permission.

comprehensive model of job design that exists today is called job characteristics theory (Hackman and Oldham, 1976). Specifically, this theory is concerned with how various job characteristics influence worker reactions (see Figure 1).

Core Job Characteristics

According to Hackman and Oldham (1976), there are five critical characteristics of a job:

1. Skill variety   The extent to which a job involves a variety of different activities that require different skills and abilities.

2. Task identity   The extent to which a job involves the completion of a whole, identifiable task from beginning to end.

3. Task significance   The extent to which the worker perceives that the job is important and has a significant impact on other people.

4. Autonomy   The extent to which the job allows the worker to determine how his or her work will be completed.

5. Feedback   The extent to which performing the job results in the worker receiving clear information regarding his or her level of performance.

Critical Psychological States

The five core job characteristics combine to determine the degree to which a worker experiences three critical psychological states. As shown in Figure 1, skill variety, task identity, and task significance are said to determine the extent to which the worker will perceive the job as being a meaningful work experience. Autonomy determines the level of responsibility for work outcomes that a worker experiences. Finally, feedback provides the worker with knowledge about the results of his or her work activities.

Personal and Work Outcomes

The three critical psychological states combine to determine the following personal and work outcomes: work motivation, work performance, work satisfaction, and absenteeism and turnover behavior.

Growth-Need Strength (GNS)

Growth-need strength (GNS) may be defined as the degree to which an individual values complex, challenging work. Its role in the job characteristics model may be described as follows: 1) High GNS individuals will experience high levels of the critical psychological states, if the core job dimensions are high, and lower levels of the critical psychological states if the core job dimensions are low; 2) High GNS individuals will react favorably to high levels of critical psychological states by exhibiting high internal motivation, high work performance, high work satisfaction, and low absenteeism and turnover; 3) Low GNS individuals will still respond favorably to core job characteristics, but not as strongly as will high GNS people.

Exercise Schedule

		Unit Time	*Total Time*

1. **Preparation (pre-class)**
   Read the overview of job characteristics.

2.	**Groups analyze characteristics**	10 min	10 min

   In groups of five to seven members, analyze the levels of the core job characteristics in the case relative to the national norm scores.

3. **Develop job design**   15 min   25 min
   Based on the analysis conducted in Step Two, formulate a new job design that will increase the levels of the core job characteristics.

4. **Group presentations**   15 min   40 min
   Have each group present a brief description of its job redesign plan.

5. **Class discussion**   10 min   50 min
   The instructor leads a discussion on job design.

Topics for Discussion

1. Explain why you chose to redesign the clerical worker jobs at Wyatt-Boyer Insurance in the way you did.

2. Describe the expected effects of the job redesign on core job characteristics.

3. Describe the expected worker reactions to the changes in core job characteristics.

4. How do you think the workers would respond to the changes in core job characteristics if they had low growth-need strength?

5. Compare and contrast your job redesign plan with the actual job redesign plan that was used at Wyatt-Boyer Insurance. Which job redesign plan do you prefer? Why?

6. Discuss the changes in core job characteristics and personal and work outcomes that resulted from the actual job redesign plan used at Wyatt-Boyer Insurance. Why do you think they changed in the direction expected or not expected? (Note: Refer to Figure 5 to answer this question.)

Self-Generated Personal Experiences (Optional)

a) Think of a job you have held that you did or did not like.

b) Describe the specific tasks that the job involved.

c) Assess the levels of core job characteristics with respect to your job.

d) If you could, how would you redesign your job? What impact would you expect the job redesign to have on levels of core job characteristics?

Summary

The basic aim of job characteristics theory (Hackman and Oldham, 1976) is to explain how various aspects of a job can influence worker reactions. The fundamental argument of this theory is that for individuals with high growth-need strength, high levels of core job characteristics will lead to high levels of critical psychological states, which will result in favorable personal and work outcomes (see Figure 1 for a summary of how job characteristics theory works).

Background on The Wyatt-Boyer Insurance Company

Wyatt-Boyer Insurance is a multi-line insurance firm located in a major city of a Midwestern state. The company's primary functions are to accept policy applications from agents, rate (price) the policies, and prepare and issue the policies.

Figure 2 illustrates the initial work flow layout (i.e., job design) at Wyatt-Boyer Insurance. Policy applications received (new work) were first routed to a general sorting room, where policies were separated by type (A, B, or C). The sorted policies were then sent to the appropriate policy type sort rooms (sort room A, B, or C) where they were prepared for distribution to policy type supervisors. These supervisors assigned the work to entry clerks, who entered policy information into a computer and sent the work on to underwriters. The underwriters authorized the policies and sent them to rating clerks, who were responsible for pricing (rating) the policies. The rated policies were then printed out and sent to a policy type sorting room, where the work was processed and assigned to distribution clerks. Three copies of each policy were made by distribution clerks and then sent on to the mailroom. The mailroom sent one copy of the policy to Wyatt-Boyer files, one copy to the policy holder, and one copy to the appropriate insurance agent.

Recently, management at Wyatt-Boyer administered a survey to clerical workers in order to assess core job characteristics and worker responses. Results of this survey are displayed in Figure 3. The dotted line running across each of the bar graphs represents the national norm (i.e., average value) for a large, representative sample of clerical workers in the United States. The top graph shows clerical worker perceptions of core job characteristics. The bottom graph represents workers' satisfaction with various aspects of their jobs, along with attendance levels and an index of productivity. Finally, it should be noted that the clerical workers at Wyatt-Boyer Insurance were generally very competent individuals who had a strong desire to engage in challenging work (i.e., they had high growth-need strength).

Figure 1. Job Characteristics Theory

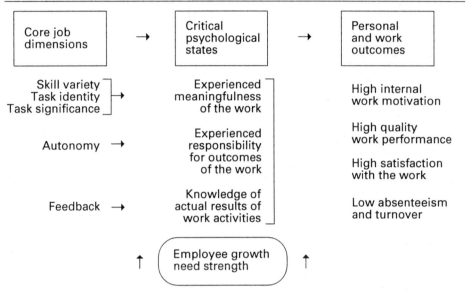

Source: J.R. Hackman and G.R. Oldham (1976). Motivation through the design of work: Test of a theory. *Organizational Behavior and Human Performance*, 16, 250-279.

Figure 2. Initial Work Flow (Job Design) at Wyatt-Boyer Insurance

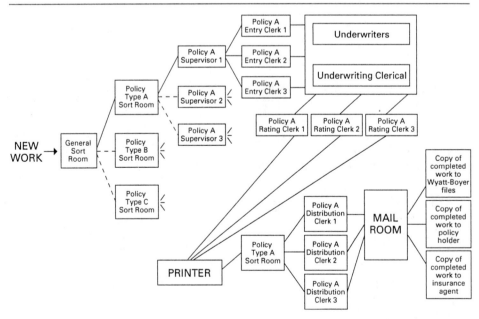

Figure 3. Core Job Characteristics and Worker Reactions for the Initial Work Flow (Job Design) at Wyatt-Boyer Insurance

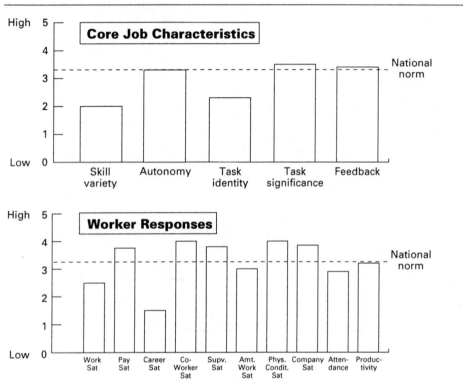

Figure 4. Work Flow at Wyatt-Boyer Insurance after the Job Redesign

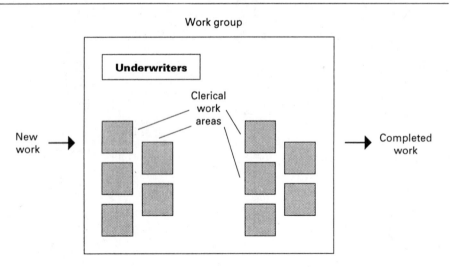

Figure 5. Core Job Characteristics and Worker Reactions to the Job Redesign at Wyatt-Boyer Insurance

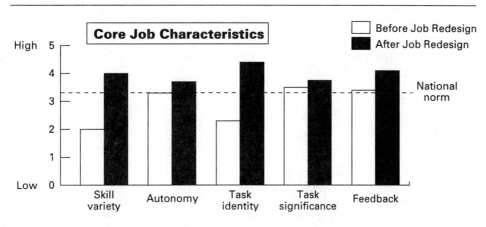

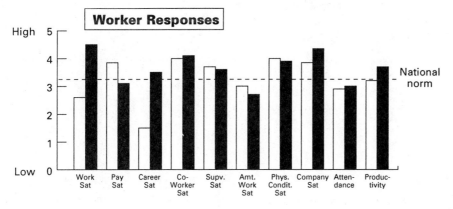

23. Team Ring-Toss – An Experiential Exercise[1]

Purpose:
Understanding the effects of motivation on individual and group behavior.

Group Size:
Four to six members.

Time Required:
26-36 minutes or more.

Materials and Preparation Needed:
1. You will need a small plastic ring-toss peg and four plastic rings. These can be purchased at any toy store or toy department for under five dollars. You will also need some masking tape and a ruler to prepare the tossing range.
2. Place a 5- or 6-inch piece of tape at 1-foot intervals up to 14 feet from the peg. Tape down the peg to make sure it does not tip over. Mark each piece of tape according to how far it is from the peg (i.e., 1', 2', . . . 14').

Exercise Schedule

Object:
To win as many points as possible.

	Unit Time	*Total Time*
1. Teams select one member to toss the ring	5 min	5 min

Each team will have eight practice tosses. Before, during, and after the practice session, the designated player may consult with the team. The rings may be tossed from any distance.

2. Each team plays one round	3 min	8 min

The designated player takes four tosses, which constitute one round. Once the player selects a distance and throws the first ring, all other rings must be tossed from that distance. The player achieves the points according to the payoff schedule below if two rings fall on the post and remain there. (The same player must toss for all three rounds.)

3. Caucus	2 min	10 min

After all teams have completed one round, a brief team meeting may be held to reorganize strategy.

4. Groups complete Rounds Two and Three	6 min	16 min
5. Small group discussion (optional)	10-20 min	
6. Group discussion	10-20 min	26-36 min

Groups discuss winning strategies and Achievement Motivation issues (see background below).

---

[1]Used by permission of the authors, William P. Ferris and Russell Fanelli, School of Business, Western New England College.

Explanation of Scoring

If a player tosses from one, two, or three feet and succeeds in landing two rings on the post, the team is awarded one point. If a player tosses from four feet and is successful, the team receives two points, etc. The maximum score possible for one round is 100 points.

Payoff Schedule With Successful Ring Toss

Feet	Return
1	1
2	1
3	1
4	2
5	4
6	6
7	8
8	12
9	16
10	24
11	32
12	42
13	60
14	100

Background on Achievement Motivation

I. *Risk-Taking*

   A. What were you thinking and feeling as you began the game?

   Did you have a goal in mind? What were you trying to do?

   How did you decide where to stand?

   Did you consciously estimate or think about your chances as you played?

   Did you expect to succeed or fail? How did these feelings affect your performance?

   B. What conclusions can be drawn from the performance data?
   What seem to be the winning strategies?

   How would you describe the goals set by those who were most successful?

   How is a moderate risk determined? Is it the same for everyone?

   Could you define risk-taking in terms of probabilities?

   What kinds of odds are involved in moderate risk-taking?

   C. Would you consider your behavior in this game typical of you in competitive situations?
   Can you draw analogies from other areas of your life?
   What kinds of risks do you usually take?

   What kinds of goal-setting and risk-taking are involved in your work or hobbies?
   Competition?

   What does your behavior in the game suggest about your attitude toward yourself?

II. *Use of Immediate Concrete Feedback to Modify Goals*

   How did you feel about your performance from round to round?
   What effect did those feelings have?

   How well did you use your feedback from the score you made in setting succeeding goals
   in the game? Did you pay any attention to it?

   Did others provide any helpful feedback?

   What occupations or situations do actually offer immediate concrete feedback
   as a measure of progress toward an achievement goal?

   Is concrete and immediate feedback available to you in your work?

III. *Personal Responsibility*

   What is your usual attitude toward games of chance and games of skill?
   Would you ever call yourself a gambler?

   How important is it for you to have control over a situation?

   How can personal responsibility be facilitated at work?

IV. *Researching the Environment*

   How actively aware of your environment are you?

   Do you test limits? Do you test your own limits?

   Is environment probing encouraged at work?

Characteristics of Achievement Motivation

I. *Moderate Risk-Taking*

Examples?

Differences among high, moderate, low risks?

How are these communicated where you work?

II. *Goal-Setting*

Examples?

What kinds of goals are currently in force at work?

What new ones could be?

III. *Use of Immediate Concrete Feedback (to modify goals and behavior)*

Examples?

How can you make IFC available where you work?

IV. *Desire for Personal Responsibility*

Examples?

How could you facilitate Personal Responsibility at work?

V. *Need to Research Environment*

Examples?

How actively aware of your environment are you?

. Is environment probing encouraged at work?

Notes: An N-Ach Vocabulary

AIM: thoughts about successfully reaching a goal that requires excellence

NEED: deep desire to reach that goal

HOS: hope of success; imagining reaching that goal

FOF: fear of failure

ACT: action; plans and action that help one reach that goal

PO: personal obstacles; blocks within the person himself or herself

WO: world obstacles; blocks outside the person

HELP: expert help or advice to overcome obstacles

FaF: failure feelings

SuF: success feelings

24. The Merit Bonus Activity[1]

Purpose:
1. To familiarize the individual with various criteria that can be used to make decisions regarding organizational rewards.
2. To introduce issues of money as a motivator, the use of bonus systems, and the concept that people tend to behave in ways for which they are rewarded.

Group Size:
Any number of groups of four to six members.

Time Required:
50 minutes, or 20 minutes if done only as a class discussion.

Preparation Required:
Read the "Merit Bonus Case Study" and assign a merit bonus to each person on the list.

Exercise Schedule

1. **Preparation (pre-class)**
   Read the Merit Bonus Case Study and assign a merit bonus to each person on the list.

		Unit Time	*Total Time*
2.	**Group consensus**	**20 min**	**20 min**

   a. In groups of four to six members, reach a consensus on merit bonus assignments. The exercise may be done individually, followed by a class discussion.

   b. Identify and write below the criteria which should be used when giving rewards.

   c. Write down the criteria you would use as a manager.

3.	**Reports**	**10 min**	**30 min**

   Groups report their decisions and record them on the blackboard. Where discrepancies exist between groups, they must then defend their decisions.

4.	**List generation**	**5 min**	**35 min**

   The instructor will generate a list of the responses for #2c (criteria) on the blackboard.

---

[1] Adapted from E. Gil Boyer (St. Joseph's University), Steven I. Meisel (La Salle University), Joseph Seltzer (La Salle University), and Joan Weiner (Drexel University). Used with permission.

5.   **Scoring key**   **5 min**   **40 min**

The instructor will give the scoring key to you so that you can obtain total scores for each criteria. Individuals should total scores and each group's decision should be totaled as well.

6.   **Class discussion**   **10 min**   **50 min**

The instructor will lead a discussion on how rewards affect behavior.

Case Study: _____

The Merit Bonus Case

You are a manager of a department that was formed just under a year ago. At that time, 10 recent technical graduates were hired to perform a variety of maintenance tasks. You have finished the annual performance reviews except for one new form that the Personnel Department introduced this year. Under an innovative agreement with the union, it requires you to make a recommendation for a percentage increase that will be given as a merit bonus. Then the division General Manager will review your recommendations and make the final decision. You are not happy about having to do the task because it's hard to tell how well each person is doing and also the G.M. said at a meeting that "all employees aren't the same. I want to see the managers give their employees different bonuses. I wouldn't want more than a third of your department to get the same amount. I also don't think anyone deserves more than 15%." The company has a cost of living pay raise, so you just have to make recommendations about the merit bonus. All 10 should add up to 100%.

_____   **Alice Adams** – Alice puts a lot of effort into her work and, because of her superior ability and the respect she has earned from others, seems to have a good performance record.

_____   **Bob Burns** – Bob is a real nice fellow. He is very friendly and tries hard to do a good job. You think he has the skills, but he makes a lot of mistakes.

_____   **Charlene Carlson** – Charlene is a hard worker, but tends to be a loner. She is quite skilled and has good performance.

_____   **Dan Dunn** – Dan is lazy and doesn't get much done. The only reason he got the job in the first place is that his uncle is the assistant general manager.

_____   **Ed Enders** – Ed is very skilled at his job and therefore doesn't have to work too hard to have good performance. He is quite friendly with the others.

_____   **Fran Fox** – Fran has been an important member of the work group. She understands the technical details and often tries to help others. She might be called the informal group leader, but she seems bored with her present job and doesn't work very hard. As a result, her performance seems to have been below average.

_____   **Gus Groom** – Gus has excellent technical skill and seems to have good performance even though he often gets into arguments with the other employees and rarely puts much effort into his job.

_____   **Harry Hall** – Harry is not very good at his job but puts in more time than anyone else, and often works through breaks and lunch. He gets along well with others both on and off the job.

_____   **Irene Illman** – Irene didn't do well in technical school, but she puts a lot of effort into her job. She has good performance except when she has to work with others and her temper gets in the way.

_____   **John Janis** – John has a lot of influence with the other members of the group and is well-liked. You think his performance is good because he works hard at whatever tasks he is assigned to do and makes the most of his limited skills.

<u>100%</u>   **TOTAL**

Chapter 8
Work Stress

25. Stress Management

Purpose:
To assess the stress level in your life.

Group Size:
Any number of groups of three to four members.

Time Required:
20 minutes or more.

Preparation Required:
Complete Stress Assessment before class.

Exercise Schedule

1. **Preparation (pre-class)**
   Fill out and score Stress Assessment.

	Unit Time	Total Time
2. **Group discussion (optional)**	15 min	

   In groups of three to four members, discuss responses and total scores of the inventories.

3. **Class discussion**	20 min	20 min

   The instructor leads a discussion on stress and stress management.

Personal Stress Assessment Inventory[1]

1. Predisposition[2]

Our typical behavior lies somewhere along the line described at the right and left of each 10-point scale below. Please circle the number for each item below to most closely describe your customary behavior.

a. I often feel impatient behind slow-poke drivers.   1 2 3 4 5 6 7 8 9 10   I seldom feel impatient behind slow-poke drivers.

b. I seldom speak in a loud voice or use expressive gestures.   1 2 3 4 5 6 7 8 9 10   I often speak in a loud voice or use gestures.

c. I am seldom more precise about details than others are.   1 2 3 4 5 6 7 8 9 10   I am often more precise about details than others are.

d. I seldom arrive early for appointments.   1 2 3 4 5 6 7 8 9 10   I often arrive early for appointments.

e. I often get annoyed when I must wait in line.   1 2 3 4 5 6 7 8 9 10   I seldom get annoyed when I must wait in line.

f. I seldom do several things simultaneously.   1 2 3 4 5 6 7 8 9 10   I often do several things simultaneously.

g. While involved in one task, I often think ahead to the next task.   1 2 3 4 5 6 7 8 9 10   While involved in one task, I seldom think ahead to the next task.

h. I seldom experience annoying or irritating situations.   1 2 3 4 5 6 7 8 9 10   I often experience annoying or irritating situations.

i. I often have enough time for personal errands.   1 2 3 4 5 6 7 8 9 10   I seldom have enough time for personal errands.

j. I hear others out fully without finishing a thought for them.   1 2 3 4 5 6 7 8 9 10   I anticipate what others will say and finish a thought for them.

---

[1] Adapted from Herbert S. Kindler, Ph.D., Center for Management Effectiveness, P.O. Box 1202, Pacific Palisades, CA 90272. Used with permission.
[2] Adapted from *Type A Behavior and Your Heart* by Meyer Friedman and Ray Rosenman, Fawcett Crest, 1974. Used with permission.

k.   I often hurry, even when   1 2 3 4 5 6 7 8 9 10   I seldom hurry when I
     I have plenty of time.   have plenty of time.

l.   I seldom eat rapidly.   1 2 3 4 5 6 7 8 9 10   I often eat rapidly.

m.   I often push myself,   1 2 3 4 5 6 7 8 9 10   I seldom push myself
     even when tired.   when I feel tired.

n.   I seldom feel hard-   1 2 3 4 5 6 7 8 9 10   I often feel hard-driving
     driving and competitive.   and competitive.

o.   I often compare my   1 2 3 4 5 6 7 8 9 10   I seldom compare my
     performance with others.   performance with others.

p.   I often feel I haven't   1 2 3 4 5 6 7 8 9 10   I seldom feel I haven't
     met all my goals in a day.   met all my goals in a day.

q.   I prefer respect for   1 2 3 4 5 6 7 8 9 10   I prefer respect for
     what I have achieved.   who I am.

r.   I seldom compare my   1 2 3 4 5 6 7 8 9 10   I often compare my
     performance to some standard.   performance to a standard.

s.   I often keep my feelings   1 2 3 4 5 6 7 8 9 10   I seldom keep my
     to myself.   feelings to myself.

t.   I play to win or excel.   1 2 3 4 5 6 7 8 9 10   I play to relax or have fun.

2. Intermittent Sources of Stress[3]

For each of the events that occurred during the past 12 months or so, indicate your emotional impact score (i.e., write in a number from "1," low impact, to "10," major impact). Impact may be positive or negative; scoring only reflects magnitude. "Emotional Impact" is the force that tends to disturb your emotional balance or equilibrium, or the energy you require to get back to "feeling normal." Only score events that occurred – skip items that did not occur during the past 12 months, or that don't apply.

Emotional Impact Score

a. _____ I lost my job, retired, or expect to lose my job, or I failed a class.

b. _____ I was criticized by my boss or passed over for a promotion.

c. _____ I changed my place of residence.

d. _____ A person close to me ended or changed the nature of our relationship.

e. _____ I got married, reconciled, separated, or divorced.

f. _____ I received evaluations at work or school that were unexpected.

g. _____ I wasn't adequately prepared for a deadline or assignment.

h. _____ I received some special recognition or scholastic honor.

i. _____ I was reprimanded or put on probation.

j. _____ I dropped a course after investing time to master it.

k. _____ I changed smoking, drinking, or eating habits.

l. _____ A close friend was transferred or graduated and left.

m. _____ An important source of income was interrupted, reduced, or ended.

n. _____ I was assigned a new boss.

o. _____ A new family member was added (birth, adoption, moving in).

p. _____ Work or school assignments interfered with my personal life.

---

[3] Suggested by "The Social Readjustment Rating Scale" by T.H. Holmes. *Journal of Psychosomatic Research,* 1967, pp. 213-218. Used with permission.

Personal Stress Assessment Inventory (cont'd)

q. _____ I terminated a subordinate.

r. _____ Major policy or procedural changes at work or school suddenly occurred.

s. _____ I had trouble with co-workers or group members.

t. _____ I was criticized by my boss, or I was the one criticizing others openly.

If not covered above, add two emotionally unsettling events or experiences that occurred during the past year or so, and were intermittent in nature. These may be positive or negative such as: a blind date, visit from your parents, seeing someone cheat on an exam, pregnancy, litigation, car breaking down, etc.

Emotional Impact Score

u. _____ _____

v. _____ _____

_____ Total for emotional impact score (a. - v.).

3. Ongoing Sources of Stress

For each of the events that occurred during the past month or so, indicate your emotional impact score ("1," low impact, to "10," major impact). After you have assessed the emotional impact (for example, assume you judged a "6" impact), then place the 6 in either column A or B, whichever is applicable. Alternatively, you may divide your score between Columns A and B (for example, scoring "4" in Column A, and "2" in Column B). Only score events that occurred – skip items that didn't occur or aren't applicable.

Emotional Impact Score

Events Beyond My Power to Change	Events Within My Power to Change		
Column A	Column B		
_____	_____	a.	I have continuing problems or lack of closeness with my parents or relatives.
_____	_____	b.	I don't feel as healthy as I'd like.
_____	_____	c.	Job security is a problem.
_____	_____	d.	I am not satisfied with my career or school progression.
_____	_____	e.	I must attend meetings that waste time.
_____	_____	f.	The activities or work schedule of my spouse or close friends create continuing problems.
_____	_____	g.	I feel under-appreciated at home or in my personal life.
_____	_____	h.	Family members have chronic or addictive problems.
_____	_____	i.	My lifestyle lacks adventure or doesn't serve my deepest needs.
_____	_____	j.	I feel my performance is not evaluated appropriately.
_____	_____	k.	I am involved with too much, or not enough, travel.
_____	_____	l.	My subordinates (or group members) are not as motivated as I would like them to be.
_____	_____	m.	I am not satisfied with my compensation or benefits or grades.
_____	_____	n.	I don't have enough intimacy or satisfaction in my primary relationship – or I want one and don't have it.
_____	_____	o.	Traffic congestion, commuting, or related problems are excessive.
_____	_____	p.	Expressing my feelings is a problem for me.
_____	_____	q.	I experience continuing relationship conflicts.
_____	_____	r.	Work or school situations create personal or ethical concerns.

_____ | _____ | s. I have inadequate social interactions or friendships at work or school.

If not covered above, add on two emotional events that occurred during the past month or so (positive or negative).

_____ | _____ | t. _____

_____ | _____ | u. _____

Total for Emotional Impact Score:

Column A   Column B

_____   _____

Interpreting Your Inventory Scores

Your scores highlight areas of your life that may be contributing to excessive stress. Should you decide to make changes in your lifestyle, work style, diet, or exercise patterns, start with a medical checkup.

a.   Predisposition: Scoring Key

Insert your answers in Columns 1 and 2. Subtract Column 2 number from 11 and write in your answer in Column 3. Total Columns 1 and 3.

Column 1   Column 2   Column 3

b. _____   11-_____ = _____
                                                             a.

c. _____   11-_____ = _____
                                                             e.

d. _____   11-_____ = _____
                                                             g.

f. _____   11-_____ = _____
                                                             k.

h. _____   11-_____ = _____
                                                             m.

i. _____   11-_____ = _____
                                                             o.

j. _____   11-_____ = _____
                                                             p.

l. _____   11-_____ = _____
                                                             q.

n. _____   11-_____ = _____
                                                             s.

r. _____   11-_____ = _____
                                                             t.

Total Column 1 _____   Total Column 3 _____

Grand Total _____ divided by 20 = ➡_____
     (Column 1 + Column 3)   Your Predisposition Score

Scores above 7.0 reflect "Type A" behavior, exhibited by those compulsive about time, who strive with single-minded dedication to achieve specific quantitative goals, seek approval from others, and see life as a serious competitive game to be "winners." While this behavior may have short-term benefits, in the long run it tends to undermine one's health. In fact, research has shown "Type A's" have a much greater risk of dying from a heart attack than "Type B's." Scores may be reduced by consciously giving up control and risking spontaneity; learning to relax without guilt into more creative hobbies and pure leisure; and focusing more on the quality of one's relationships.

b.   Sources of Stress/Stressors

Intermittent Sources of Stress include those life changes that demand and drain energy as one attempts to adjust and restore balance. Scores higher than 50 for stressors suggest attention to finding ways of better pacing with more spacing of future changes.

Ongoing Sources of Stress manifest as the daily "wear and tear" one experiences. Total scores of over 50 suggest the need for more active confrontation and dealing with these ongoing irritants. Where Column A scores "Beyond My Power to Change" are appreciably higher than Column B scores "Within My Power to Change," one may want to take more responsibility for events in one's life in order to feel less helpless and "victimized." Scores below 10 indicate opportunities for growth by being more adventurous.

c.   Calculating Your Overall Stress Factor

Predisposition Score   _____[1]

Emotional Impact Score –   _____
Intermittent Sources of Stress

Emotional Impact Score –
Ongoing Sources of Stress

     Column A (from page 105)   _____

     Column B (from page 105)   _____

     Total Sources of Stress
     (Add the preceding three numbers)   _____[2]

Overall Stress Factor = [1] X [2]

[1] _____ **X [2]** _____ **= ➥** _____
                            Your Overall Stress Factor

If this number exceeds 700 or so, you should review the high component scores to consider where stress level reductions seem appropriate and feasible.

Managing Stress Effectively:
You and Your Stress Source

Intermittent Sources of Stress

When a change occurs in your life, whether self-initiated or not, your equilibrium is disturbed. The energy you require to restore your balance, or homeostasis, reflects the stress level induced by change. Energy absorbed in the process of regaining harmony is not available for other purposes, such as protecting you from illness and accident.

If you are experiencing excessive stress from too many concurrent changes in your work or personal life, be especially kind to yourself, slow your pace, and avoid strenuous effort. Where feasible, defer new commitments or try to space them out over time.

Ongoing Sources of Stress

If you are experiencing excess stress from enduring a number of abrasive or hostile life events, three overlapping strategies are available to you:

(1)   You can leave the situation (e.g., change jobs to get away from smog that has become a health hazard for you).

(2)   You can attempt to change the situation (e.g., speak to your teacher when you feel he or she has treated you unfairly; speak with another group member whose performance is concerning you).

(3)   Change your own behavior (e.g., procrastinate less; say "no" more).

While multiple changes divert energy, adapting to day-in-and-day-out irritation drains it. The cost of excessive adaptation sustained over time is higher risk of illness, lower satisfaction, and impaired effectiveness. In addition to considering the three strategies outlined, also consider asking friends for help and emotional support.

26. Odyssey into Organizational Hope[1]

Purpose:
To relate and learn from our narratives of organizational hope.

Group Size:
Any number of groups of three people.

Time Required:
90 minutes.

Preparation Required:
Read the background and prepare to share your narrative or story of organizational hope.

Exercise Schedule

1. **Preparation (pre-class)**
   Students read the background and make notes to themselves about their experience in the hope of organizations.

		Unit Time	Total Time
2.	**Introduction to the topic**	10 min	10 min

   Instructor provides a context for inquiry into organizational hope.

3.	**Group storytelling and interpretation**	55 min	65 min

   In trios, each student takes his or her turn sharing a narrative of organizational hope followed by group interpretations.

4.	**Class discussion**	25 min	90 min

   The instructor leads a discussion that conceptualizes organizational hope and draws out its implications for human systems.

---

[1]Timothy B. Wilmot and James D. Ludema, Case Western Reserve University. Used with permission.

Background on Organizational Hope

Throughout Western history, hope has been heralded as a primary catalyst for human creativity, community, and transformation. Fields of study as variant as philosophy, psychology, medicine, and the fine arts converge around the notion that the act of human hoping – the collective search for unexplored possibilities of value – provides the impetus for virtually all meaningful activity. Among other things, it has been found that hope can give life meaning in the face of existential nothingness, provide the path out of the torturous psychic imprisonment of mental illness, furnish the human body with powerful emotional, spiritual, and physiological resources to conquer disease, and excite the creative imagination of the artist (for a review of the qualities and effects of hope, see, for example, Kast, 1991; Seligman, 1990; and Taylor, 1989). Philosopher Gabriel Marcel captured hope's essentiality well when he said: "Hope is for the soul what breathing is for the living organism."

> "Hope is for **the soul** what breathing is for the living organism."

The interdisciplinary literature further reveals that hoping is not just an emotional or cognitive experience residing in the heart, mind, or soul of the individual, but that it is a distinctly intersubjective phenomenon born in relationship with and sustained through dedication to concerns beyond one's own ego (Marcel, 1965). What is more, people who hope take the stance that any reality – whether events from the past, a difficult situation in the present, or an uncertain future – is always completely open to fresh interpretations and the discovery of possibilities (Moltmann, 1991; Lynch, 1965). Consequently, when we hope we inquire with others into what we fundamentally value, or what Paul Tillich (1957) would call our "ultimate concerns" (e.g., fairness, equality, cooperation, peace, goodness, beauty), and are then able to construct commonly valued futures. Once articulated, these transcendent ideals become the shared visions that, when made public, guide collective action and imbue relationships with joy, inspiration, and solidarity (Kast, 1991; Bloch, 1986).

As places where people come together every day to plan out shared futures, organizations serve as primary forums for human hoping. Common practices such as goal-setting, visioning, management by objectives, expectation sharing, and strategic planning reveal the fundamental and pervasive extent to which we are continually searching for shared constructions of the future in organizations. Herbert Simon (1947), a theorist on administrative behavior, was the first to recognize anticipation as an essential aspect of individual decision-making, for it allows human beings to experience and "satisfice" among alternative futures. Since then, writers like Cooperrider (1991) have demonstrated the towering extent to which collective anticipatory images guide organizational behavior. Yet much is still to be learned about why human hopes are so generative, how the dynamics of hope play out in organizational life, or what the generative consequences of hoping are. In the following exercise we will explore these questions by embarking on an odyssey into our own stories of organizational hope.

Part I:

Narrative Preparation (pre-class)

1. Imagine the following:

    It's 20 years from now, and we've gathered at our alumni reunion. Each of us has led a very full life of working and living in organizations. As we reflect back over our rich involvements, we begin to share stories about the events, activities, people, and understandings that best illustrate the role of hope in human organizing. What is your story of organizational hope?

    Note: Given this scenario, your story might be either an actual experience from your own past, a current involvement, or an imagined event in your likely future; whichever type you choose, what remains constant is that you are intimately involved.

2. Jot down notes about the situation:

    a. What led up to the situation?

    b. Who was involved?

    c. What happened?

    d. What was your involvement?

    e. What were others doing?

    f. What were the consequences?

Part II:

Questions for Narrative Interpretation (in class)

1. After relating your story of organizational hope in your trio, share your interpretations of the narrative by responding to the following questions:

    a.   What was it about you that contributed to hope?

    b.   What was it about others that fostered hope?

    c.   What was it about the organization (e.g., the culture, the people, leadership, history, unique practices) that was creative of hope?

    d.   What does this story say about organizational hope?

2. Next allow the two people who listened to your tale to interpret your narrative by answering the above questions.

References

Bloch, E. *The Principles of Hope* (translated by N. Plaice, S. Plaice and P. Knight from the German *Das Prinzip Hoffnung*). Cambridge, MA: MIT Press, 1986.

Cooperrider, D. "Positive Image, Positive Action: The Affirmative Basis of Organizing." In Srivastva, S., Cooperrider, D., & Associates, *Appreciative Management and Leadership*. San Francisco: Jossey-Bass, 1990.

Kast, V. *Joy, Inspiration and Hope* (translated by D. Whitcher). College Station, TX: Texas A&M University Press, 1991.

Lynch, W.F. *Images of Hope*. Notre Dame: Notre Dame Press, 1965.

Marcel, G. *Homo viator* (translated by Emma Craufurd). Chicago: Henry Regnery, 1951.

Moltmann, J. *Theology of Hope* (translated by J.W. Leitch from the German *Theologie der Hoffnung*). New York: Harper Collins, 1991.

Seligman, M. *Learned Optimism*. New York: Pocket Books, 1990.

Simon, H.A. *Administrative Theory*. New York: MacMillan, 1947.

Taylor, S. *Positive Illusions*. New York: Basic Books, 1989.

Tillich, P. *Dynamics of Faith*. New York: Harper and Row, 1957.

Chapter 9
Dynamics Within Groups

27. Using New Product Development to Study Group Decision-Making[1]

Purpose:
To study group decision-making in an organizational context.

Group Size:
Four to six members.

Time Required:
The exercise can be run in 50 minutes if necessary, but an optimal session, including a debriefing session, requires an hour and 20 minutes.

Preparation:
Each group should have scissors, a ruler, a stapler, and a small stack of colored paper.

---

[1]Developed by P.S. Heath, H. Hopper, and D. Daniels. Used with permission.

➡ Introduction

The new product design scenario provides a fun and useful exercise in which participants design and evaluate new products. It has three primary learning objectives:

1. It aims to teach about various processes that groups use to make decisions in an organizational context and to understand a group member's role within those processes.

2. It demonstrates problems that can occur during group decision-making and attempts to restructure those processes for more effective group experiences.

3. It allows us to investigate more general concepts of group dynamics and how those are influenced by the nature of the task and the organizational context.

Exercise Schedule

		Unit Time	*Total Time*
1.	**Groups receive instructions**	**5 min**	**5 min**

The instructor, acting as the Vice-President of Marketing, goes over the instructions for each group, which are at the end of this section.

2.	**Developing a product**	**20-30 min**	**25-35 min**

The groups work to design a container according to the criteria suggested by the instructor.

3.	**Product evaluation**	**10-15 min**	**35-50 min**

When the design phase is completed, the groups each select one member to be part of the product evaluating team, which assesses the products to determine the final recommendation. The evaluating team develops its own decision-making process without input from the instructor.

4.	**Debriefing/discussion**	**15-30 min**	**50-80 min**

When the evaluation team has chosen a product to recommend to the Vice-President of Marketing (i.e., the instructor/facilitator), discussion as a large group begins. Discussion questions following the instructions provide a starting point for debriefing. Participants are encouraged to describe their individual experiences in the groups, including information about emerging decision processes and individual role formation. Discussion will initially center on differences between the processes in the individual product development teams and the evaluating team. Also addressed are group dynamics and the influence of organizational context on the nature of the decision processes and their outcomes. To close the debriefing, we discuss some improvements to the process that might increase decision-making effectiveness.

Instructions

I am the Vice-President of Marketing, and your group is one of six new product venture teams for AmeriContainer Corp. Our company is in the business of containers – all shapes and sizes. Each of the product venture teams is expected to develop a container design and present a prototype at our next meeting, scheduled in 30 minutes. The individuals of the team that produce the best design will receive (*some form of academic reward*).

I am looking for something innovative and marketable, subject to the following constraints:

> 1. The end product should be as cost-effective as possible. The container will be evaluated for the quality of materials it requires, and the difficulty in putting it together. We need something that could be mass-produced with ease.

> 2. The container must be sturdy and functional – i.e., it should be able to hold whatever the group designates the container for.

After 30 minutes, you will select one member from your group to be a part of the product evaluation team. This team will evaluate each group's design, and will then make a recommendation to me for the container that they think should be produced by AmeriContainer.

Discussion Questions

Individual Group Process

1. What process did the group use to complete the project?

2. Did everyone participate in the project? If not, why not? How did you decide what your role was in the group?

3. To what extent was members' input to the project determined by interactions on projects in the past?

4. How did you deal with conflicting criteria? What did the group do to resolve ambiguity?

5. If you had known about this project beforehand, would you have done it differently? That is, if this project team was permanent and your job consisted of creating new products, what would your work session look like? What roles or norms would you have?

Evaluating Group Process

1. What process did the evaluating team use to make their decision?

2. How was the process different from the individual group's process? Why do you think it was different?

3. What was the ambiguity of the situation? How was it resolved? Was there a power issue?

4. What was the goal of the evaluating team? Was there an issue of goal congruence for the evaluating members? How did each of you deal with that conflict? What did the evaluation process you developed do for that conflict?

5. What are the advantages and disadvantages of a separate review process like this instead of the vice-president doing his/her own reviewing?

6. If the evaluation team concept were used extensively in your company, what changes would you make to the process to ensure the goal achievement?

28. Tower Building Exercise: A Group Dynamics Activity[1]

Purpose:
1. To study dynamics of a group in a task-oriented situation.
2. To examine the dynamics of leadership and power in a group.

Group Size:
Any number of groups of six to eight members.

Time Required:
50 minutes.

Materials:
Each group brings materials for building a tower; these must fit in a box no greater than eight cubic feet.
Room Arrangement Requirements:
Space for each group to build a tower.

Related Topics:
Power and Influence, Interpersonal Relationships, Leadership, Interpersonal Communication, Creativity

Exercise Schedule

		Unit Time	Total Time
1.	**Preparation**	**5 min**	**5 min**

Each group is assigned a meeting place and a work place. One or two observers should be assigned in each group. Instructor may assign a manager to each group.

		Unit Time	Total Time
2.	**Planning phase**	**10 min**	**15 min**

Each group plans for the building of the paper tower (no physical construction is allowed during this planning period). Towers will be judged on the basis of height, stability, beauty, and meaning. (Another option is to have the groups do the planning outside of class and come prepared to build the tower.)

		Unit Time	Total Time
3.	**Building phase**	**15 min**	**30 min**

Each group constructs its tower.

		Unit Time	Total Time
4.	**Judging phase**	**5 min**	**35 min**

Groups inspect other towers, and all individuals rate towers other than their own. See evaluation sheet below. Each group turns in its point totals (i.e., someone in the group adds up each person's total for all groups rated) to the instructor, and the instructor announces the winner.

---

[1]Idea from Philip Hunsaker, in *Exchange*, 4(4), 1979, p. 49. Additional parts adapted from Mary Gander. Used with permission.

5.   **Group dynamics analysis**   **10 min**   **45 min**

Observers report observations to their own groups, and each group analyzes the group dynamics that occurred during the planning and building of the tower.

6.   **Group reports**   **5 min**   **50 min**

Groups will report on major issues in group dynamics that arose during the tower planning and building. *Homework:* Complete the following Tower Building Aftermath, to be turned in to your instructor.

Tower Evaluation Sheet

Criteria	Groups							
	1	2	3	4	5	6	7	8
Height								
Stability/Strength								
Beauty								
Meaning/ Significance								

TOTALS ____   ____   ____   ____   ____   ____   ____   ____

Rate each criteria on a scale of 1-10, with 1 being lowest or poorest, and 10 being highest or best.

Tower Building Project Aftermath Analysis

by Mary Gander

Your
Name_____Group_____

1. Were you a manager? yes_____ no_____

    Who was informal leader? _____

    Did you have a deviant or isolate? yes_____ no_____

2. Did you feel like you "fit" the group or its norm? yes_____ no_____

    Explain briefly:

3. Was there any conflict? Briefly explain. Was it resolved?

4. Did any problems arise? How were they handled?

5. How cohesive were you as a group by the end of the project?

    very_____   moderately_____   not very_____   not at all_____

6. How do you feel about your personal performance/contribution to the work group?

    excellent_____   good_____   fair_____   poor_____

    Explain:

7. How do you feel about the functioning of your group as a whole?

8.   Do you feel your group produced a good product?

very much_____   it's okay_____   no_____

9.   Please express your opinion of the usefulness of this project involving work group dynamics and supervising peers:

a.   great, we learned a lot_____

b.   not bad, learned some things_____

c.   a waste of time, don't do it next semester_____

d.   it was fun: I didn't learn much, but it was good to apply things from class_____

Additional comments:

10.   How much planning did your group do?

a lot_____   some_____   we were pretty spontaneous_____

11.   How many times did you meet (if applicable)?

once_____   twice_____   three times_____   more than three times_____

12.   A.   Group members: Evaluate your manager's performance (if applicable).

effective_____   somewhat effective_____   ineffective_____

Explain:

B.   Managers: Evaluate each of your subordinates (if applicable).

1.

2.

3.

4.

5.

6.

29. Group Socialization: The United Chemical Company

Purpose:
To explore issues of socialization in groups.

Group Size:
Any number of groups of six to nine members.

Time Required:
45 minutes.

Preparation Required:
Read the case study below and answer the questions at the end.

Related Topics:
Organization Culture and Socialization, Interpersonal Communication

Exercise Schedule

1. **Preparation (pre-class)**
   Read the case and answer the questions.

		Unit Time	Total Time
2.	**Groups discuss case**	10 min	10 min

In groups of six to nine members, discuss the answers to the six questions at the end of the case.

| 3. | **Volunteers** | 5 min | 15 min |

Discussion is stopped and the instructor asks for two volunteers from each group, one to be an observer and one a "risk-taker." These members go out into the hall with the instructor.

| 4. | **Groups discuss more** | 10 min | 25 min |

Members return to class and groups continue discussion.

| 5. | **Evaluate group process** | 10 min | 35 min |

Class discusses group process.

| 6. | **Class discusses case** | 10 min | 45 min |

Continue class discussion on the United Chemical Company, relating it to the experienced group process.

Case Study: _____

The United Chemical Company[1]

The United Chemical Company is a large producer and distributor of commodity chemicals with five chemical production plants in the United States. The operations at the main plant in Baytown, Texas, include not only production equipment: it is also the site of the company's research and engineering center.

The process design group consisted of eight male engineers and the supervisor, Max Kane. The group had worked together steadily for a number of years, and good relationships had developed among all members. When the workload began to increase, Max hired a new design engineer, Sue Davis, a recent Master's degree graduate from one of the foremost engineering schools in the country. Sue was assigned to a project whose goal was expansion of one of the existing plant facility's capacity. Three other design engineers were assigned to the project along with Sue: Jack Keller (age 38, fifteen years with the company); Sam Sims (age 40, ten years with the company); and Lance Madison (age 32, eight years with the company).

As a new employee, Sue was very enthusiastic about the opportunity to work at United. She liked her work very much because it was challenging and it offered her a chance to apply much of the knowledge she had gained in her university studies. On the job, Sue kept fairly much to herself and her design work. Her relations with her fellow project members were friendly, but she did not go out of her way to have informal conversations during or after working hours.

Sue was a diligent employee who took her work quite seriously. On occasions when a difficult problem arose, she would stay after hours in order to come up with a solution. Because of her persistence, coupled with her more current education, Sue completed her portion of the various project stages usually a number of days before her colleagues. This was somewhat irritating to her, because on these occasions she went to Max to ask for additional work to keep her busy until her fellow workers caught up to her. Initially, she had offered to help Jack, Sam, and Lance with their portion of the project, but each time she was turned down very tersely.

About five months after Sue had joined the design group, Jack asked to see Max about a problem the group was having. The conversation between Max and Jack was as follows:

Max: Jack, I understand you wanted to discuss a problem with me.

Jack: Yes, Max, I didn't want to waste your time, but some of the other design engineers wanted me to discuss Sue with you. She is irritating everyone with her know-it-all, pompous attitude. She just is not the kind of person that we want to work with.

Max: I can't understand that, Jack. She's an excellent worker whose design work is always well done and usually flawless. She's doing everything the company wants her to do.

Jack: The company never asked her to disturb the morale of the group or to tell us how to do our work. The animosity of the group can eventually result in lower quality work for the whole unit.

Max: I'll tell you what I'll do. Sue has a meeting with me next week to discuss her six-month performance. I'll keep your thoughts in mind, but I can't promise an improvement in what you and the others believe is a pompous attitude.

> "She just is not **the kind of person** that we want to work with."

Jack: Immediate improvement in her behavior is not the problem, it's her coaching others when she has no right to engage in publicly showing others what to do. You'd think she was lecturing an advanced class in design with all her high-powered, useless equations and formulas. She'd better back off soon, or some of us will quit or transfer.

[1]From *Organizational Behavior and Performance*, 4/e, by Andrew D. Szilagi, Jr. and Marc J. Wallace, Jr. © 1987, 1983, 1980, 1977 by Scott, Foresman and Co. Reprinted by permission of HarperCollins Publishers, Inc.

During the next week, Max thought carefully about his meeting with Jack. He knew that Jack was the informal leader of the design engineers and generally spoke for the other group members. On Thursday of the following week, Max called Sue into his office for her mid-year review. Certain excerpts of the conversation were as follows:

Max: There is one other aspect I'd like to discuss with you about your performance. As I just related to you, your technical performance has been excellent; however, there are some questions about your relationships with the other workers.

Sue: I don't understand; what questions are you talking about?

Max: Well, to be specific, certain members of the design group have complained about your apparent "know-it-all attitude" and the manner in which you try to tell them how to do their job. You're going to have to be patient with them and not publicly call them out about their performance. This is a good group of engineers, and their work over the years has been more than acceptable. I don't want any problems that will cause the group to produce less effectively.

Sue: Let me make a few comments. First of all, I have never publicly criticized their performance to them or to you. Initially, when I was finished ahead of them, I offered to help them with their work, but was bluntly told to mind my own business. I took the hint and concentrated only on my part of the work.

Max: Okay, I understand that.

> "I don't want any problems that will cause the group to **produce less effectively**."

Sue: What you don't understand is that after five months of working in this group, I have come to the conclusion that what is going on is a "rip-off" of the company. The other engineers are "goldbricking" and setting a work pace much less than they're capable of. They're more interested in the music from Sam's radio, the local football team, and the bar they're going to for TGIF. I'm sorry, but this is just not the way I was raised or trained. And finally, they've never looked on me as a qualified engineer, but as a woman who has broken their professional barrier.

Max: The assessment and motivation of the engineers is a managerial job. Your job is to do your work as well as you can without interfering with the work of others. As for the male-female comment, this company hired you because of your qualifications, not your sex. Your future at United is quite promising if you do the engineering and leave the management to me.

Sue left the meeting very depressed. She knew that she was performing well and that the other design engineers were not working up to their capacity. This knowledge frustrated her more and more as the weeks passed.

Case Questions

1. Does Sue value her membership in the group? Explain.

2. What is Sue seeking from membership in the design group?
   What are the other members seeking from membership in the group?

3. How do you rate the way Max handled his meeting with Sue?

4. Discuss this situation in terms of the stages of group development.

5. Discuss this situation in terms of structural dimensions of the group.

6. What should Sue do next? What should Max do next?

30. Sunset Community Hospital: Using Nominal Group Technique[1]

Purpose:
To practice using the Nominal Group Technique.

Group Size:
Any number of groups of seven members, where one person is designated as "leader."

Time Required:
50 minutes.

Preparation Required:
Read the case study on Sunset Community Hospital.

Materials Required:
1. Flip chart/markers or chalkboard for each group.
2. 3" x 5" index cards (about seven per class member).

Related Topics:
Interpersonal Communication

➤➤ Introduction

To resolve the problem in the case below, your group will use the Nominal Group Technique (NGT), which has proven to be an effective means of idea generation for a group examining new issues.

Exercise Schedule

1. **Preparation (pre-class)**
   Read the case study.

		Unit Time	Total Time
		5 min	**5 min**

2. **Idea generation**
   Silent generation of ideas in writing. In groups of seven, the question is read aloud by the leader, after which each member individually writes ideas in brief phrases or statements. It is important for each member to work silently and independently.

		10 min	**15 min**

3. **Record ideas**
   Round-robin recording of ideas on a flip pad or blackboard. Each person presents ideas in a few words or phrases, going one at a time. Any member may "pass" if his/her ideas are duplicated and may "re-enter" later. It is important not to start any discussions on ideas until the listing is complete.

---

[1]By Andre Delbecq. Used with permission.

4.   **Discussion**   10 min   25 min

Serial discussion for clarification. Each member takes a turn discussing the various ideas in order to clarify the meaning of the items and explain reasons for agreement or disagreement.

5.   **Voting**   5 min   30 min

Preliminary vote on item importance. Group chooses five to nine items as "priority items." Each priority item is written down on a 3" x 5" index card. Members then individually and silently rank order the items. A member writes a "1" in the upper right hand corner for the most important item, "2" for the next most important, and so on. Cards are collected by the leader and shuffled so that anonymity is retained. Votes are then tallied and posted on the flip chart or board in front of the group.

6.   **Discussion on vote**   10 min   40 min

Discussion of the preliminary vote. Each person has a chance to *briefly* clarify issues.

7.   **Final vote**   5 min   45 min

Repeat "Preliminary Vote," Step 5.

8.   **Class discussion**   5+ min   50 min

The instructor will lead a discussion on the benefits of the Nominal Group Technique.

Case Study: _____

A Student Service HMO: Sunset Community Hospital

Fred Feister was meeting with Joseph Collins, Academic Vice-President of a neighboring Ivy League University. Sunset Community Hospital itself is located in a New England community and has traditionally found a substantial portion of its patient population drawn from area colleges and universities.

However, universities as well as local industries were expressing increased concern about the cost of medical care. At a recent meeting of faculty and students at Mr. Collins' university, both the faculty and student senate voted on a motion requesting their school to explore the possibility of an HMO in collaboration with an area hospital. The university has also asked that the HMO include a relationship with a physician group practice so that outpatient services as well as hospital care would be included.

Mr. Feister would like his hospital and a physician group practice which utilizes his hospital to be selected as joint providers for the university HMO plan. In order to respond in a way that is both sensitive and competitively astute, he is proposing to Mr. Collins that his staff be allowed to meet with a "focus group" composed of faculty members and a focus group composed of students to examine their special preferences with respect to medical care. He has suggested that a focus group of 24 students (divided into four subgroups representing each class) be arranged. A similar faculty group of the same size, drawn from across faculty ranks, has also been suggested. The central questions for the focus groups would be as follows:

Student Question:

What are the *attributes of medical care* that are important to you as a student while living in dormitory residences away from home?

Faculty Question:

What are the *attributes of medical care* that are important to you and your family at this stage of your professional career?

Mr. Collins: "Fred, if you did meet with groups of students and faculty, I wonder if this question could be answered in one meeting? We know that everyone is concerned with quality and reasonable cost. But beyond this, what exactly do you expect the students and faculty will say that you don't already know? I'm going to have some problems selling this idea. We're close to the end of the quarter and both faculty and students are busy trying to wind up their spring! They have limited time."

Fred Feister: "The purpose for using this broad question, Mr. Collins, is exactly for me not to prescribe what the students or faculty may say. Students living in dormitory residences away from their families are going to think about medical care in a different manner than they have in the past. It's no longer seeing their family doctor but perhaps a stranger. What are the circumstances that will make this experience comfortable for them? What hours of the day are going to be critical in the provision of services, etc.
The same is going to be true for faculty. They are particularly insightful health care consumers and will have special concerns that we might be able to respond to. Indeed, your faculty and students may help us develop an HMO that is not simply effective and efficient in terms of medical quality and cost, but is also particularly responsive to the special problems of your academic community. Believe me, I know that students participating in such a group will present ideas to us that we as providers will be able to respond to in order to serve them better."

Mr. Collins: "Well, Fred, I'm willing to try this once and see whether or not it's worth going through the trouble of recruiting a larger group of students and faculty. Suppose I arrange for you to meet the officers of the Student Senate and have them participate in this focus group you are talking about. Let's see what happens and determine whether or not the ideas produced are worth the energy I would have to invest to get a broader campus sample."

> "Well, Fred, I'm willing to try this once..."

Assignment:

Imagine that you are Fred Feister, negotiating with the university in competition with several different medical clinics and hospitals to provide prepaid care. You must conduct the focus group for the purpose of idea generation, and you have decided to utilize the Nominal Group Technique (NGT) for structuring the meeting.

The NGT question for the meeting with students is:

"What are the *attributes of medical care* that are important to you as a student while living in dormitory residences away from home?"

Reference
Delbecq, Andre L., Andrew H. VandeVen and David H. Gustafson. *Group Techniques for Program Planning.* Middleton, Wis: Greenbriar Press, 1986, pp. 15-82.

31. Wilderness Survival[1]

Purpose:
To understand group dynamics and group decision-making processes.

Group Size:
Any number of groups of six to nine members.

Time Required:
50 minutes (more time for larger groups or if longer discussions are desired).

Related Topics:
Leadership, Communications

☐ Background

Sometimes group decision-making is more effective than individual decision-making. Research shows that if the decision is simple, it is better to have one person responsible; however, if the problem is more complex, group decision-making is more effective. In this exercise, you'll get a chance to compare the results of individual and group decision-making.

The Situation

You have gone on a Boundary Waters canoe trip with five friends to upper Minnesota and southern Ontario in the Quetico Provincial Park. Your group has been traveling Saganagons Lake to Kawnipi Lake, following through Canyon Falls and Kennebas Falls and Kenny Lake.

Fifteen to 18 miles away is the closest road, which is arrived at by paddling through lakes and rivers and usually portaging (taking the land path) around numerous falls. Saganagons Lake is impossible to cross in bad weather, generally because of heavy rain. The nearest town is Grand Marais, Minnesota, 60 miles away. That town has plenty of camping outfitters, but limited medical help, so residents rely on hospitals further to the south.

The terrain is about 70 percent land and 30 percent water, with small patches of land here and there in between the lakes and rivers. Bears are not uncommon in this region. It is now mid-May, when the temperature (daytime) ranges from about 25° to 70°, often in the same day. Nighttime temperatures can be in the 20s.

Rain is frequent during the day (nights, too) and can be life-threatening if the temperature is cold. It is unusual for the weather to stay the same for more than a day or two. Generally, it will rain one day and be warm and clear the next, with a third day windy – and it is not easy to predict what type of weather will come next. In fact, it may be clear and warm, rainy and windy, all in the same day.

---

[1] © 1992 by Dorothy Marcic. Expert advisers Jeff Stemmerman and Ken Gieske. All rights reserved.

Your group of six was in two canoes going down the river and came to some rapids. Rather than taking the portage route on land, the group foolishly decided to shoot the rapids by canoe. Unfortunately, everyone fell out of the canoes and some were banged against the rocks. Luckily no one was killed, but one person suffered a broken leg and several others had cuts and bruises.

Both canoes were damaged severely. Both were bent clear in half, one with an open tear of 18", while the other had two tears 12" and 15" long. Both had broken gunwales (upper edges on both sides). You lost the packs that held the tent, most clothing, nearly all the food, cooking equipment, fuel, first aid kit, and flashlight. Your combined possessions include one jack-knife, four canoe paddles, a pocketful of hard candies, five dollar bills and 65 cents in change.

Luckily **no one was killed**, but the nearest town is 60 miles away...

You had permits to take this trip, but no one knows for sure where you are and the closest phone is in Grand Marais. You were scheduled back four days from now, so it is likely a search party would be sent out in about five days (since you may have been delayed a day or so in getting back). Just now it has started to drizzle and it looks like rain will follow.

Your task now is to figure out how to survive in these unpredictable and possibly harsh conditions until you can get help.

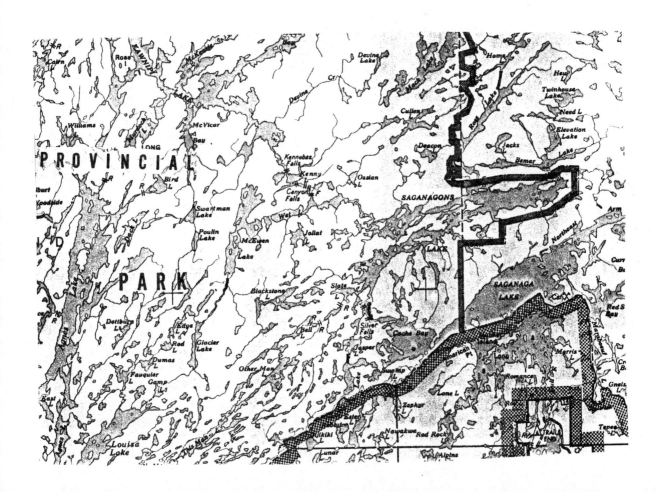

Exercise Schedule

		Unit Time	*Total Time*

1. Introduction and individual ranking   5 min   5 min

Instructor gives brief background on case and asks students to rank order the 14 items on the list in terms of survival value. The item considered most valuable should be ranked "1" while the least valuable should be ranked "14." Individuals should place their rankings on Table 1, Column B.

2. Group discussion   20 min   25 min

In groups of six to nine members (with one or two optional observers who are asked to refer to "What to Observe in a Group" in the Appendix of this book – observers take notes and later give feedback) come to a consensus on the ranking of the items. Use Table 1, Column C for this. Members should not vote or "horse trade," but rather should try to have everyone more or less agree on the ranking. When someone disagrees, members should try to listen carefully. And when someone feels strongly, that person should attempt to use persuasive techniques.

3. Correct answers given   5 min   30 min

Instructor posts the correct answers and gives the reasons for these rankings, according to the experts. Students put correct rankings in Column D of Table 1.

4. Computation of Table 1   5 min   35 min

a. Compare your answer, listed under Column B, with the correct answer, listed under Column D. Subtract D from B in each row, taking the absolute value (do not count minus signs). That will be the individual error which is then listed under Column A. For example:

if you answered...	if correct answer was...	difference is:
2	11	9
10	5	5
12	1	11

b. Total up the numbers in Column A (none of which should be negative numbers). This gives you your Individual Score.

c. Subtract Column D from Column C in each row, again using absolute values, to get the group error, which should be listed under Column E.

d. Total up the numbers in Column E (none of which should be negative numbers). This gives you your Group Score.

e. Subtract the numbers in Column C from Column B and put the results (absolute value) in Column F. This is your persuasion score, which measures how much you are able to influence other group members to your thinking. Spend a few minutes during your group discussion talking about the persuasion score. Who had the lowest (this person was the most persuasive) and who had the highest (this person was the least persuasive) scores? Table 1 should now be complete.

5. Computation of Table 2   5 min   40 min

a. Average Member Score
Add up the Individual Score (Step B; Column A) of all group members and divide by the number of members in the group. Put this number in the indicated column.

b. Group Score (Step D, Column E)
Put this number in the indicated column.

c. Synergy

If your Group Score is lower than your average member score, then put "yes" in the column for Synergy. If your Group Score is higher than your average member score, then put "no" in the column for Synergy.

d. Best Member Score

This is the number of the member who has the lowest Individual Score. Put this score in the indicated column.

Table 1

Rank order the following in terms of survival assistance, putting the most valuable as "1."

Items	A (B-D) Individual Error	B Your Ranking	C Group Ranking	D Expert Ranking	E (C-D) Group Error	F (B-C) Persuasion
Fanny pack of food – cheese, salami, gorp						
Plastic-covered map of Boundary Waters						
Six PFD's – Personal Flotation Devices						
Two fishing poles, broken						
Set of clothes for three (wet)						
One yellow Frisbee						
Water purification tablets						
Duct tape, one 30' roll						
Whiskey, one pint, 180 proof						
Insect repellent, one bottle						
Matches, 30, dry						
Parachute cord, 35'						
Compass						
Six sleeping bags, synthetic, medium weight						

Individual Score (Total of A)   _____

Group Score (Total of E)   _____

Persuasion Score (Total of F)   _____

6. **Group feedback (optional)**   **10+ min**
    Observers give feedback to group and group talks about how it did in terms of decision-making, who was most persuasive, and so on.

7. **Class discussion**   **10+ min**   **50 min**
    Instructor leads discussion on group decision-making and how each group did in this exercise, answering the following questions.

8. **Group discussion**
    As a class, discuss the following questions:

    1. To what extent did group discussion change the accuracy of the answers?

    2. Which behaviors helped/hindered the decision-making process?

    3. What happened if a person had a very accurate Individual Score, but was not very persuasive in the group; and, conversely, what if a person had a poor Individual Score and was very persuasive in the group?

Table 2

Groups

	1	2	3	4	5	6
Average Member Score						
Group Score						
Synergy						
Best Member Score						

Chapter 10
Dynamics Between Groups

32. Prisoner's Dilemma: An Intergroup Competition

Purpose:
1. To explore trust and its betrayal between group members.
2. To demonstrate effects of interpersonal competition.

Group Size:
Groups of no more than eight members each.

Time Required:
50 minutes.

Room Arrangement Requirements:
Enough space for the opposing teams to meet separately without overhearing each other.

Exercise Schedule

		Unit Time	*Total Time*
	Introduction (Steps 1 & 2)	**5 min**	**5 min**

1.   The instructor explains what will take place in this exercise and assigns people to groups.
Two types of teams are formed and named Red and Blue (with no more than eight members per group). Each team must not communicate with the other team in any way, verbally or nonverbally, except when told to do so by the instructor.

2.   Groups are given time to study the Prisoner's Dilemma Tally Sheets.

3.	**Round 1**	**3 min**	**8 min**

Each team has three minutes to make a team decision. Write down your decisions when the instructor says time is up.

4.	**Choices announced**	**2 min**	**10 min**

The choices of the teams are announced for Round 1. The scores are entered on the Tally Sheet.

5.	**Round 2**	**5 min**	**15 min**

Round 2 is conducted in the same manner as Round 1 (Steps 3 & 4).

6.	**Round 3**	**6 min**	**21 min**

Round 3 is announced as a special round for which the payoff points are doubled. Each team is instructed to send one representative to chairs in the center of the room. After representatives have conferred for three minutes, they return to their teams. Teams then have three minutes, as before, in which to make their decisions. When recording their scores, they should be reminded that points indicated by the payoff schedule are doubled for this round only.

7.	**Rounds 4 & 5**	**9 min**	**30 min**

Rounds 4-5 are conducted in the same manner as the first two rounds.

8.	**Round 6**	**6 min**	**36 min**

Round 6 is announced as a special round, in which the payoff points are "squared" (multiplied by themselves: e.g., a score of 4 would be $4^2 = 16$.) A minus sign should be retained: e.g., $(-3)^2 = -9$. Team representatives meet for three minutes, after which the teams meet for three minutes. At the instructor's signal, the teams write down their choices; then the two choices are announced.

9.	**Round 7**	**6 min**	**42 min**

Round 7 is handled exactly as Round 6 was. Payoff points are squared.

10.	**Closing**	**8+ min**	**50 min**

The point total for each team is announced, and the sum of the two team totals is calculated and compared to the maximum positive or negative outcomes (+108 or -108 points). A discussion on win-lose situations, competition, etc., will be conducted.

Prisoner's Dilemma Tally Sheet

Instructions: For seven successive rounds, the Red team will choose either an A or a B and the Blue Team will choose either an X or a Y. The score each team receives in a round is determined by the pattern made by the choices of both teams, according to the schedule below.

Payoff Schedule

AX – Both teams win 3 points.

AY – Red Team loses 6 points; Blue Team wins 6 points.

BX – Red Team wins 6 points; Blue Team loses 6 points.

BY – Both teams lose 3 points.

Scorecard

Round	Minutes	Choice		Total Points	
		Red Team	**Blue Team**	**Red Team**	**Blue Team**
1	3				
2	3				
3*	3 (reps) 3 (teams)				
4	3				
5	3				
6**	3 (reps) 5 (teams)				
7**	3 (reps) 5 (teams)				

*   Payoff points are doubled for this round.

** Payoff points are squared for this round (retain the minus sign).

33. WINDSOCK, INC.[1]

Purpose:
To explore intergroup relationships.

Time Required:
50 minutes or more.

Materials:
Plastic milk straws (500) and a box (750) of straight pins.

Related Topics:
Leadership, Interpersonal Communications

Exercise Schedule

		Unit Time	Total Time
1.	**Introduction**	**5 min**	**5 min**

Class is divided into four groups: Central Office, Product Design, Marketing/Sales, and Production. Central Office is a slightly smaller group. If groups are large enough, assign observers to each one.

Central Office is given 500 straws and 750 pins. Each person reads *only* the role description relevant to that group.

		Unit Time	Total Time
2.	**Perform task**	**30+ min**	**35 min**

Depending on length of class, Step 2 may be longer, up to 60 min. Groups perform functions and prepare a two-minute report for "stockholders."

		Unit Time	Total Time
3.	**Group reports**	**10 min**	**45 min**

Each group gives a two-minute presentation to "stockholders."

		Unit Time	Total Time
4.	**Observers' reports (optional)**	**15 min**	

Observers share insights with subgroups.

		Unit Time	Total Time
5.	**Class discussion**	**5+ min**	**50 min**

Instructor leads class discussion in areas of intergroup cooperation and coordination, open vs. closed communication, leadership.

---

[1] Adapted from Christopher Taylor and Saundra Taylor in "Teaching Organizational Team-Building Through Simulations," *Organizational Behavior Teaching Review,* Vol. XI(3), pp. 86-87. Used with permission.

Roles

Central Office

Your team is the central management and administration of WINDSOCK, INC.

> *You are the heart and pulse of the organization, because without your coordination and resource allocation, the organization would go under.*

Your task is to manage the operations of the organization, not an easy responsibility because you have to coordinate the activities of three distinct groups of personnel: the Marketing/Sales group, the Production group, and the Product Design group. In addition, you have to manage resources, including materials (pins and straws), time deadlines, communications, and product requirements.

In this exercise, you are to do whatever is necessary in order to accomplish the mission and to keep the organization operating in a harmonious and efficient manner.

WINDSOCK, INC. has a total of 30 minutes (more if instructor assigns) to design an advertising campaign and ad copy, design the windmill, and to produce the first windmill prototypes for delivery. Good luck to you all.

◆

Product Design

Your team is the research and product design group of WINDSOCK, INC.

> *You are the brain and creative aspect of the operation, because without an innovative and successfully designed product, the organization would go under.*

Your duties are to design products which will compete favorably in the marketplace, keeping in mind function, aesthetics, cost, ease of production, and available materials.

In this exercise, you are to come up with a workable plan for a product which will be built by your production team. Your windmill must be light, portable, easy to assemble, and aesthetically pleasing. Central Office controls the budget and allocates material for your division.

WINDSOCK, INC. has a total of 30 minutes (more if instructor assigns) to design an advertising campaign, design the windmill (your group's task), and to produce the first windmill prototypes for delivery. Good luck to you all.

◆

Marketing/Sales

Your team is the marketing/sales group of WINDSOCK, INC.

> *You are the backbone of the operation, because without customers and sales, the organization would go under.*

Your task is to determine the market, develop an advertising campaign to promote your company's unique product, produce ad copy, and develop a sales force and sales procedures for both potential customers and the public at large.

For the purpose of this exercise, you may assume that a market analysis has been completed. Your team is now in a position to produce an advertising campaign and ad copy for the product. To be effective, you have to become very familiar with the characteristics of the product and how it is different from those products already on the market. The Central Office controls your budget and allocates materials for use by your division.

WINDSOCK, INC. has a total of 30 minutes (more if instructor assigns) to design an advertising campaign and ad (your group's task), to design the windmill, and to produce the first windmill prototypes for delivery. Good luck to you all.

◆

Production

Your team is the production group of WINDSOCK, INC.

> *You are the heart of the operation, because without a group to produce the product, the organization would go under.*

You have the responsibility to coordinate and produce the product for delivery. The product involves an innovative "windmill" design which is cheaper, lighter, more portable, more flexible, and more aesthetically pleasing than other designs currently available on the market. Your task is to build windmills within cost guidelines, according to specifications, within a prescribed time period, using predetermined materials.

For the purpose of this exercise, you are to organize your team, set production schedules, and build the windmills. Central Office has control over your budget and materials, as well as the specifications.

WINDSOCK, INC. has a total of 30 minutes (more if instructor assigns) to design an advertising campaign, design the windmill, and to produce the first windmill prototypes (your group's task) for delivery. Good luck to you all.

Chapter 11
Leadership

34. In Search of Great Leaders

Purpose:
To identify characteristics that make a great leader.

Group Size:
Teams of three to six members.

Time Required:
40 minutes, or more.

Exercise Schedule

		Unit Time	*Total Time*
1.	**Groups list leaders**	**10 min**	**10 min**

Divide into groups of three to six people. Your task is to identify two great leaders and two poor leaders from any of the categories below. These leaders can be historical figures, or people alive now.

Social Activists	Science/Medicine
Dissidents	Sports
Business	Entertainment Industry
Religion	

2.   **Groups answer questions**   **15-30 min**   **25-40 min**
     Now discuss and answer the following questions:

a.   What did these leaders accomplish?

	Great Leaders	Poor Leaders
Names of leaders		
What they accomplished		

b.   What similarities do you see in the leaders above? Were they transformational leaders?

c.   What is the difference between a great leader and a poor leader?

d.   Are some leaders able to achieve only under certain historical, economic, or cultural conditions? Explain.

3.   **Class discussion**   **15-25 min**   **40-65 min**
     Instructor leads discussion on "great" leaders.

35. Leadership Style Inventory[1]

Purpose:
To assess your leadership style along the Leader-Centered/Subordinate-Centered continuum.

Time Required:
10-20 minutes.

Preparation Required:
1. Read the Introduction below.
2. Complete and score "Leadership Style Inventory."

Exercise Schedule

1. **Pre-class**

   Complete and score the Leadership Style Inventory, paying attention to your present leadership repertoire, your leadership inclinations, interpretive guide, and personal analysis.

	Unit Time	*Total Time*
2. **General group discussion**	**10-20 min**	**10-20 min**

   Instructor leads class discussion on leadership style and its implications for management.

➤➤ Introduction

Over the last decade the contingency approach to management has gained wide acceptance – an approach which traces some of its intellectual origins to the pioneering work of Robert Tannenbaum and Warren H. Schmidt ("How to Choose a Leadership Pattern," *Harvard Business Review*, March-April 1958, pp. 95-101). While Tannenbaum and Schmidt did not call their work a contingency approach, their concepts represent some of the earliest efforts in this area.

In essence, the contingency approach suggests that there is no right or wrong answer when it comes to managing subordinates. Hence, choosing a leadership behavior becomes analogous to a golfer's dilemma in choosing a golf club. This inventory, while not designed to tell you which behavior to select and when to select it, is designed to help you assess the ways of leading you tend to favor. The inventory owes an intellectual debt to Robert Tannenbaum and Warren H. Schmidt, whose work is still recognized today as a major contribution to our understanding of leadership. The inventory is based on research data gathered over an eight-year period from practicing managers and administrators in both the private and public sectors, representing the broadest spectrum of specializations and levels in several hundred different organizations.

The Leadership Behavior Inventory is essentially a personal assessment tool. It is intended to be used as a mirroring device to aid individuals who wish to explore how they behave when they attempt to influence others. As with any self-assessment tool, the results are only as valid as the respondent wishes them to be. While

---

[1]By John F. Veiga, Leadership Development Group, Storrs, CT 06268. Reprinted with permission.

it is possible to "fake" your answers in order to look good, it is strongly recommended that you try to answer honestly in order to gain some valuable insights about yourself. In responding, you must continually ask yourself, "Is this the way I am, or is this the way I'd like to be?" Having someone else who knows you well fill out the inventory on you can provide an even stronger basis for purposeful self-reflection.

Leadership Style Inventory

This inventory is designed to provide you with personal data about the frequency with which you tend to select particular leadership behaviors. As you fill out the inventory, give a high rank to those words which best describe the way you most often behave as a leader and a low rank to the words which describe the way you least often behave as a leader.

You may find it hard to choose the words that best describe your leadership behavior, because there are no right or wrong answers. Different behaviors described in the inventory are equally good.

There are nine sets of four words listed below. Rank order the four words in each set across the page, assigning a 4 to the word which best describes your leadership behavior, a 3 to the next best, a 2 to the next best, and a 1 to the word which is least descriptive of your behavior as a leader. Be sure to assign a different rank number to each of the four words in each set. Do not make ties.

	A	B	C	D
1.	____ Forceful	____ Negotiating	____ Testing	____ Sharing
2.	____ Decisive	____ Teaching	____ Probing	____ Unifying
3.	____ Expert	____ Convincing	____ Inquiring	____ Cooperative
4.	____ Resolute	____ Inspirational	____ Questioning	____ Giving
5.	____ Authoritative	____ Compelling	____ Participative	____ Approving
6.	____ Commanding	____ Influential	____ Searching	____ Collaborating
7.	____ Direct	____ Persuasive	____ Verifying	____ Impartial
8.	____ Showing	____ Maneuvering	____ Analytical	____ Supportive
9.	____ Prescriptive	____ Strategical	____ Exploring	____ Compromising

Scoring

Each column corresponds to a different leadership behavior: Column A – Tell; Column B – Sell; Column C – Consult; Column D – Join. To determine how frequently you use each of these behaviors, insert into the boxes directly below each column how you ranked the designated words. For example, in Column A (the "Tell" column), words numbered 2, 3, 4, 5, 7, and 8 are designated. Now do the same for the other three columns. After you have completed this, add up the numbers in each box to get column scores.

Words Numbered:	Words Numbered:	Words Numbered:	Words Numbered:
– – – – – – = ___	– – – – – – = ___	– – – – – – = ___	– – – – – – = ___
2 3 4 5 7 8	1 3 6 7 8 9	2 3 4 5 8 9	1 3 6 7 8 9
Column A (Tell Score)	Column B (Sell Score)	Column C (Consult Score)	Column D (Join Score)

Your Present Leadership Repertoire

The chart below can be developed into a graphic profile of your present repertoire of leadership behavior. Shade in the area which corresponds to each of your scores from the Leadership Style Inventory. For example, if you scored 15 on Tell behavior, then shade the area up to the 15 on the chart under Tell. The ruled-in percentile provides you with a way of comparing yourself to other managers who have taken the inventory. The percentiles are keyed to indicate the number of managers who scored below a particular score. For example, a score of 17 on Tell means over 80 percent of the managers tested use a Tell behavior less frequently than you do.

	Tell	Sell	Consult	Join	
100%					100%
	20	21	21	21	
	17	19	19	19	
80%					80%
				18	
		18	18	17	
	15				
			16		
60%					60%
		17		16	
	14	16	15	15	
	13				
40%					40%
		15		14	
	12	14	14	13	
	11		13		
20%					20%
	10			11	
		12	10		
	8			9	

Your Leadership Inclinations

Two additional scores may be obtained from the inventory: Manipulativeness and Emphasis on Human Resources. To obtain these, complete the following calculations by first inserting your Tell, Sell, Consult and Join scores into the blanks below.

Manipulativeness:

$$\underline{\quad\quad} + \underline{\quad\quad} - \underline{\quad\quad} - \underline{\quad\quad} = \underline{\quad\quad} \text{ (preserve minus sign, if any)}$$
$$\text{Sell} \qquad \text{Consult} \qquad \text{Tell} \qquad \text{Join}$$

Human Resources:

$$\underline{\quad\quad} + \underline{\quad\quad} - \underline{\quad\quad} - \underline{\quad\quad} = \underline{\quad\quad} \text{ (preserve minus sign, if any)}$$
$$\text{Join} \qquad \text{Consult} \qquad \text{Tell} \qquad \text{Sell}$$

These scores may now be charted below. (Note that it is possible to chart a negative score.)

	Manipulative-ness	**Emphasis on Human Resources**	
100%	____15____	____16____	100%
	____10____	____9____	
80%	____9____		80%
	____6____	____7____	
		____4____	
60%	____4____		60%
		____1____	
		____0____	
40%	0		40%
	____(-2)____	____(-2)____	
		____(-5)____	
20%			20%
	____(-4)____	____(-7)____	
	____(-9)____		
		____(-17)____	

Interpretive Guide

Figure 1 below depicts four primary ways a leader may choose to behave in a given situation. The rectangle represents the amount of authority a leader has in a particular situation, so that "Tell" represents a point on the continuum where maximal use of authority is made by the leader and minimal freedom is given to subordinates in the decision-making process. Each of these primary leadership behaviors is more fully explained in Table 1.

Figure 1 Continuum of Leader Behavior

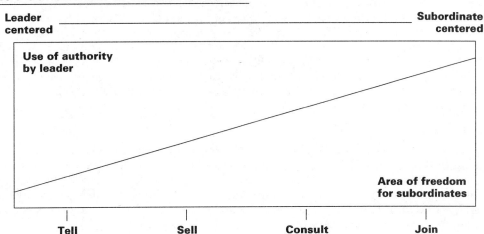

Based largely on R. Tannenbaum and W.H. Schmidt, How to choose a leadership pattern, *Harvard Business Review* (March-April 1958): 95-101.
In the original article, Tell was represented by position 1; Sell by position 2; Consult by positions 3, 4 and 5; and Join by positions 6 and 7

What the Tell, Sell, Consult, and Join Scores Mean

Your Tell, Sell, Consult, and Join scores indicate the frequency with which you use each of the primary leadership behaviors. In part, your use of these behaviors reflects how you see yourself, your subordinates, and your current work situation. For example, if you work in an environment where subordinates are perceived as mature and experienced, then chances are you are going to use more frequently Consult and Join behaviors. On the other hand, if you have little tolerance for ambiguity, then you may tend to frequently use Tell and Sell behaviors. Your scores are also a reflection, in part, of your leadership inclinations. Generally, people tend to emphasize leadership behaviors which fit their personality, which they have learned work for them, or with which they feel comfortable. Some managers, by their very nature, find it very hard to be assertive and use a Tell approach, while others are very comfortable behaving that way. The point to remember is that your present repertoire of leadership behavior is not an unchangeable part of your personality, but rather represents how you presently choose to behave on the job. Hence, it is more important to begin to explore why you emphasize the behaviors you do and whether or not such behaviors are the most effective than to conclude, "That's just the way I am." In addition, you will want to explore why you tend to use some of the leadership behaviors less frequently. In the personal analysis section, there is a place set aside for you to consider which forces tend to shape your leadership inclinations.

What the Manipulativeness and Human Resources Scores Mean

The manipulativeness score measures the degree to which the leader attempts to gain subordinates' acceptance of his or her decisions. Manipulation, as defined by the dictionary, is "artful management or control." It is in this context that manipulativeness is used here and not in the context of unfair or dishonest actions. If we examine the beliefs underlying the Tell and Sell behavior in Table 1, we find the primary difference between Tell and Sell is that in Sell the leader also "seeks to reduce any resistance through persuasion" – hence, a manipulative act is added to Sell. Similarly, the difference between Consult and Join is the leader's belief that consulting subordinates is useful in order "to increase subordinates' ownership and commitment" – hence, Consult also involves a manipulative act. If you score high on manipulativeness, it may be because you have experienced a strong need to insure subordinate acceptance of your decisions or because you perceive that your subordinates or work setting would necessitate such behavior. While some managers tend to employ manipulative behavior even when such behavior is really unnecessary, whether or not you tend to do so depends upon a careful diagnosis of the forces in your work setting. Do you tend to frequently Sell or Consult, even when Telling is all that is necessary; do you tend to avoid Join situations because you don't want to give up control even though Joining is called for? Do you use manipulative behaviors because you are comfortable doing so or because your situation or subordinates necessitate such action?

The human resources score measures the tendency of the leader to use behaviors which reflect confidence in his or her subordinates' ability to make decisions. As one moves to the right on the leadership continuum, in Figure 1, there is an increasing emphasis placed on the use of subordinates as resources. Hence, the leader who relies more on Consult and Join rather than Tell and Sell tends to utilize subordinates more often in joint decision-making situations. Again, to what extent you rely on these behaviors because of your own tendencies or out of real necessity should be carefully evaluated by you.

Table I

A Description of Leadership Behaviors

Leadership Behavior	Action Taken	Underlying Beliefs
Tell	Leader identifies the problem, considers alternative solutions and announces the final decision to subordinates for implementation.	Leader feels subordinate participation in the decision is unnecessary, unwarranted or not feasible. Hence, no opportunity to participate is provided.
Sell	Leader takes responsibility for identifying the problem and determining the final decision. But rather than simply announcing the decision, the leader takes the added step of trying to persuade subordinates to accept the decision.	Leader recognizes the potential for subordinate resistance from merely announcing the final decision and therefore seeks to reduce any resistance through persuasion.
Consult	Leader identifies the problem, consults subordinates for possible solutions, and then announces the final decision.	Leader recognizes the potential value of effectively culling ideas from subordinates and believes such action will increase subordinates' ownership and commitment to the final solution.
Join	Leader defines the problem and then joins subordinates in making the final decision. The leader fully shares decision-making authority with subordinates.	Leader believes subordinates are capable of making high-quality decisions and that subordinates want to do the right thing. The leader believes human resources are best utilized when decision-making authority is fully shared.

Which Behaviors Are Best?

By now it should be clear that one leadership behavior is no better than any other – to be effective, the leader must be able to choose correctly the behavior that a particular work situation calls for and be effective in the use of that behavior. While this instrument cannot help you decide how to behave, it can help you examine more carefully your present leadership inclinations and help you begin to explore whether or not it might be useful to begin developing other behaviors. For example, if you frequently use Tell and Sell behaviors, you might want to think about why you tend to favor these over Consult and Join. Are you uncomfortable with less directive behaviors? Do your subordinates have difficulty working independently? Or does the nature of the job require acting this way? In general, the more you understand why you choose the leadership behaviors you do, the more potentially effective you can be as a leader. And, much like the golfer, the more you are comfortable and skilled using the various clubs available to you, the greater your potential versatility in selecting a behavior that is likely to be effective. Below, space is provided for some personal reflection and analysis of your present work situation.

Personal Analysis

A. I tend to frequently use (_____ Tell; _____ Sell; _____ Consult; _____ Join) behaviors because of:

1st, the way I see myself

2nd, the way I see my present or past boss

3rd, the way I see my work/school situation

B. I tend to less frequently use (_____ Tell; _____ Sell; _____ Consult; _____ Join) behaviors because of:

1st, the way I see myself

2nd, the way I see my present or past boss

3rd, the way I see my work/school situation

36. What's the Best Leadership Style? Vroom and Yetton's Model[1]

Purpose:
To show how situational leadership can work in practice.

Group Size:
Any number of groups of five to eight members.

Time Required:
30 minutes.

Preparation Required:
Read the "Background" below and decide which leadership style is best for each of the three case studies.

Related Topics:
Decision-Making

Exercise Schedule

		Unit Time	*Total Time*
1.	**Introduction**	**5+ min**	**5 min**

The instructor will discuss Vroom & Yetton's Managerial Decision Tree and divide the class into groups of five to eight members.

2.	**Group consensus**	**15+ min**	**20 min**

Groups try to achieve consensus, using Vroom & Yetton's model, on which leadership style is most appropriate for each of the three cases.

3.	**Group reports**	**10+ min**	**30 min**

Each group reports on which leadership style it chose for Case I. After this the instructor reads Victor Vroom's choice of leadership style for this case. This is repeated for the other two cases.

❏ Background

Decision-making is a vital part of being a manager. In recent years much has been written about contingency or situational leadership styles. The research indicates there is no *one* best way to lead, but rather variables in the situation indicate which style is most appropriate.

---

[1]Adapted and reprinted, by permission of the publishers, from "A New Look at Managerial Decision-Making" by Victor H. Vroom, pp. 67-70, *Organizational Dynamics*, Spring 1973. © 1973 American Management Association, New York. All rights reserved.

Vroom and Yetton have developed a normative model to show how to work this. It uses a decision tree, answering a series of questions along the way. Similar models are used in medicine and are called protocols or algorithms.

Table 1 shows a set of alternative decision processes that we have employed in our research. Each process is represented by a symbol (e.g., AI, CI, GII) that will be used as a convenient method of referring to each process. The first letter in this symbol signifies the basic properties of the process (A stands for autocratic; C for consultative; and G for group). The Roman numerals that follow the first letter constitute variants on that process. Thus, AI represents the first variant on an autocratic process, and AII the second variant.

Table I

Types of Management Decision Styles

A I   You solve the problem or make the decision yourself, using information available to you at that time.

A II   You obtain the necessary information from your subordinate(s), then decide on the solution to the problem yourself. You may or may not tell your subordinates what the problem is in getting the information from them. The role played by your subordinates in making the decision is clearly one of providing the necessary information to you, rather than generating or evaluating alternative solutions.

C I   You share the problem with relevant subordinates individually, getting their ideas and suggestions without bringing them together as a group. Then you make the decision which may or may not reflect your subordinates' influence.

C II   You share the problem with your subordinates as a group, collectively obtaining their ideas and suggestions. Then you make the decision which may or may not reflect your subordinates' influence.

G II   You share the problem with your subordinates as a group. Together you generate and evaluate alternatives and attempt to reach agreement (consensus) on a solution. Your role is much like that of chairman. You do not try to influence the group to adopt to "your" solution and you are willing to accept and implement any solution that has the support of the entire group.

To aid in understanding the conceptual basis of the model, it is important to distinguish among three classes of outcomes that bear on the ultimate effectiveness of decisions. These are:

1) The quality or rationality of the decision
2) The acceptance or commitment on the part of the subordinates to execute the decision effectively
3) The amount of time required to make the decision

We have found that managers can diagnose a situation quickly and accurately by answering this set of seven questions concerning it. But how can such responses generate a prescription concerning the most effective leadership style or decision process? What kind of normative model of participation in decision-making can be built from this set of problem attributes? Figure 1 shows one such model expressed in the form of a decision tree.

Figure 1. Decision Model

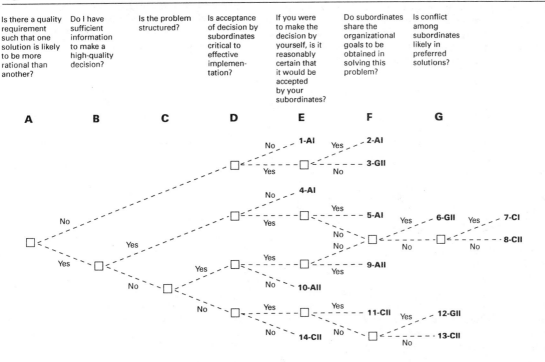

A. Is there a quality requirement such that one solution is likely to be more rational than another?

B. Do I have sufficient information to make a high-quality decision?

C. Is the problem structured?

D. Is acceptance of decision by subordinates critical to effective implementation?

E. If you were to make the decision by yourself, is it reasonably certain that it would be accepted by your subordinates?

F. Do subordinates share the organizational goals to be obtained in solving this problem?

G. Is conflict among subordinates likely in preferred solutions?

Case Studies: _____

Case Study I

You are the senior manager for a group of 10 highly educated engineers. Plans are now being finalized to build a newer and more suitable building, which you will move into within a few months.

All the group members get along reasonably well, with only minor conflicts, most of which are solved in time. Everyone has been looking forward to the new building and talking about who will get which office, types of desks, etc. The best part, it seemed, was that the parking lot for the new building would make access much easier than it is now.

However, today you received the following memo from your boss:

Due to unsolvable disagreements with the contractor and some recent disputes with the adjoining landowner over property lines, we will now have two parking lots. Lot Number One will be in the previously planned place, right next to the building. Lot Number Two will be some distance away, approximately the length of two city blocks. Your department has been assigned seven spaces in Lot One and five spaces in Lot Two, since there are 12, total, including yourself. I trust you will make the fairest decision when allocating the parking spaces.

Which decision style do you use?

Case Study II

You are the public relations manager for a software company which has just developed a new and revolutionary product. In fact, all indications are that this product will completely change the way people use computers.

The problem is how to market it, since the product is so vastly different it is not clear whether previous methods would work or not. There is considerable disagreement among your subordinates on what approach to use. Each of your five subordinates has been talking to different advertising agencies, and each one has what he or she thinks is the absolute best advertising/marketing program.

Which decision style do you use?

Case Study III

You are the manager in a large printing company. In the past few days several machines have been breaking down and causing decreased productivity. It has caused the workers to get more edgy and they have started yelling at one another, blaming each other for the problems. They are tired of the problems and want the machines to work at maximum like they used to.

Just now you have been handed the reports from the senior technician outlining the cause of the problems. This technician is quite competent and has always turned in thorough reports previously. You must decide how to fix the machines.

Which style do you use?

37. What to Do With Bob and Nancy?[1]

Purpose:
To determine styles of leadership which would be effective in a given situation.

Group Size:
Any number of groups of four to eight members.

Time Required:
40 minutes.

Preparation Required:
Read the case study below.

Related Topics:
Management of Diversity, Interpersonal Communication

Exercise Schedule

		Unit Time	Total Time
1.	**Group case analysis**	**20+ min**	**20 min**
	In groups of four to eight members, discuss what actions Dave should take.		
2.	**Group reports**	**20+ min**	**40 min**
	Groups report their proposed strategies to the whole class.		

Case Study: _____

What to Do With Bob and Nancy?

Dave Simpson was sitting at his desk wondering how the devil to handle this situation. In engineering school they don't tell you what to do when you think two of your key subordinates are having an affair! Dave knew a lot about the relative conducting properties of metals – but what about the properties of people?

Dave was Engineering Manager of a division in a large corporation situated on the East Coast. The division comprised three engineering supervisors, five lead engineers and approximately 55 engineers (see Exhibit 1). The past two years had seen several reductions in manpower due to a temporary decline in the business base. The remaining men and women in the organization were the "cream of the crop," all hard workers with a professional attitude about their jobs; any deadwood was long gone. The division had just won a large contract which would provide for long-term growth, but would also require a heavy workload until new people could be hired and trained. The work of the organization was highly technical, and required considerable sharing of ideas within and between the individual groups. This need for internal cooperation and support had been amplified because the organization was still understaffed.

---

[1]By David L. Bradford. Reprinted with permission of Stanford University Graduate School of Business, © 1985 by the Board of Trustees of the Leland Stanford Junior University.

Dave's previous secretary had transferred to an outplant location just before the new contract award, and it had taken a long time to find a suitable replacement. Because of a general shortage within the company, Dave had been forced to hire temporary help from a secretarial service. After several months he found Nancy, and felt very fortunate to have located an experienced secretary from within the company. She was in her mid-30s, attractive and very competent.

In the electronic design group was an enthusiastic, highly respected lead engineer named Bob. Bob and Dave had been close friends for several years, having started with the company at the same time. They shared several common interests that had led to spending a fair amount of time together away from work. Bob was struggling to get into management, and Dave's more rapid advancement had put a strain on the friendship. Dave had moved up from co-worker to being his boss and finally, his boss's boss. Dave felt they could still be good friends at work, but he could not show Bob any favoritism. Bob understood the situation.

From Nancy's first day on the job, Bob began to hang around her desk. He would go out of his way to start conversations and draw her attention. This was not a surprise since Nancy was attractive and Bob had gained a reputation over the years as being a bit of a "wolf." He was always the first on the scene when an attractive new female joined the program.

Before long Bob and Nancy began eating lunch together. As time passed, the lunch date became a regular routine, as did their trips together to the coffee machine. Their conversations during the work day also became more frequent. Dave felt slightly concerned about the wasted time, but since the quality and quantity of their work was not suffering in any measurable way, he did not say anything to either person. Furthermore, it was not unreasonable for Bob to be having numerous conversations with her since she had been instructed to provide typing and clerical support to the engineers whenever she had idle time. (Bob's section was temporarily looking for a secretary and the engineers were developing several new documents.)

After a few months Bob and Nancy introduced their spouses to each other and the two couples began to get together for an increasing number of social gatherings. Bob and Nancy continued their frequent lunch dates, now leaving the plant for lunch and occasionally returning late. This was not considered a major rule infraction, if the lateness was infrequent and if the time was made up in the long run. This tolerance policy was generally respected by all, including Bob and Nancy. On balance, the company seemed to be receiving at least a full week's work from both of them, since they often worked late.

> Dave felt **slightly concerned** about the wasted time, but...

What was also going on (but Dave didn't learn about until later) was that Bob and Nancy were calling each other on the phone during the work day, even though they worked in the same general area, just desks apart. They would wait until Dave had left the office, and then chat on the phone. However, Nancy's work performance was not visibly affected.

Of course, the internal grapevine was at work, and occasionally Dave would be asked about the situation between Bob and Nancy. "Do you know they've been seen having cocktails in the evenings?" "Did you know Nancy had marital problems?" "Does Bob's wife know what's going on?"

It was apparent that Bob and Nancy were starting to have an affair, but how serious it was, and how long it would last, wasn't known. They were being very careful around Dave, and almost all of what Dave knew was based upon second- and third-hand information and rumors. At this point, about four months after Nancy had started work, Dave did speak to Ron, Bob's supervisor, about it, but Ron was anxious to downplay the whole thing. He was willing to talk to Bob about the late lunches, but unwilling to discuss anything else. This seemed appropriate since, from the company's standpoint, employees' private lives were their own business. Ron was new to the organization and this factor contributed to his reluctance to discuss a delicate issue.

Dave decided not to confront Bob directly. If their relationship were as close as it had been in years past, he might have spoken to Bob about the rumors going around, but during this period the friendship had further deteriorated. They were talking on a less personal level, and Bob was spending less off-hours time with old friends. Furthermore, Dave knew from previous discussions that Bob was particularly sensitive about private matters. "He probably wouldn't welcome my advice," thought Dave.

Dave did speak to Nancy about the need to be back in the office at the end of the lunch hour, but he had not made an issue out of it. Even though it was a definite annoyance when she was not there to answer the phone or type a memo, her performance had not declined. Dave certainly did not want to bring up the issue of an affair with Nancy. He imagined what might arise: tears, defensive denial (much of what Dave thought was going on would be difficult to substantiate if Nancy was to challenge his assessment), and even potential legal ramifications if the situation was handled improperly. Bob and Nancy could claim that their reputations or careers had been damaged. (Dave also didn't want to raise this issue with Personnel; it might permanently tarnish both of their records.)

During this same time frame there was a dramatic change in Bob's personal appearance. Instead of his usual coat-and-tie attire, he started wearing open-front shirts and a beaded necklace in an attempt to acquire the current "macho" look. Although perhaps acceptable in a Southern California business office, it certainly was out of place in the Northeast with the more conservative environment of the company. As a lead engineer, Bob directed, and often presented to management, the work of 12 other engineers. The custom was for all engineers and managers to wear a coat and tie, especially since they might be called upon, with little notice, to meet with a customer or higher management. Even though Bob's attire was considered unprofessional, there was nothing in the company's written dress code requirement to forbid it.

Up to this point there had been no serious violation of company rules by either Bob or Nancy, although rules were being bent and tolerance policies abused. Then the situation took a turn for the worse while Dave was on a two-week company trip with Ron. Bob and Nancy used the opportunity to go out for a very long lunch. When they returned just before quitting time, George, one of the other supervisors, called Bob into his office and suggested that he "clean up his act." George told Bob that he was being foolish in chasing Nancy and that, among other things, he was jeopardizing his career opportunities with the company. Bob denied being anything more than friends with Nancy, and politely told George to stay out of his private affairs.

> # Rules were being **bent** and tolerance policies **abused**.

When Dave returned from his trip and heard of the incident, he told Ron to reprimand Bob and make it clear to him that "his actions are unacceptable, and that further long lunch periods will not be tolerated." Bob apologized, said he would make up the time, and that it wouldn't happen again.

Dave spoke to Nancy, and she also promised that there would be no more long lunches. But this was not the end of their noontime, out-of-plant lunch dates and before long, Nancy's husband, Ted, got involved. Ted was a salesman for the company and worked in the same building. He began to drop by at lunchtime to question the engineers about Nancy's whereabouts. In addition, he started calling Dave after work, wanting to know when Nancy had left and expressing concern that she had not yet arrived home. This questioning was an unpleasant experience for everybody.

By now the entire organization was well aware of the irregular relationship, and was growing disrespectful of both Bob and Nancy. This was a difficult situation for the engineers. The attitudes of the organization had always been very professional, and the success of each group depended upon teamwork and strong leadership from its lead engineer. Bob had been highly respected for his technical competence and ability to direct. In addition, the members of his group knew Bob's family, and had always considered him to be a good family man. Now this image had been destroyed. From a technical standpoint, Bob was still an excellent engineer and a vital resource on the new contract. But with the group's declining respect, Bob was becoming less effective as a leader. Bob's own engineers felt very uncomfortable about the situation. They believed that Bob's real interests at work were more with Nancy than with them.

The situation had now deteriorated to the point where total organization effectiveness was being measurably affected. Something had to be done to remedy this situation. But what to do?

Exhibit 1. What to Do with Bob and Nancy?

Table of Organization

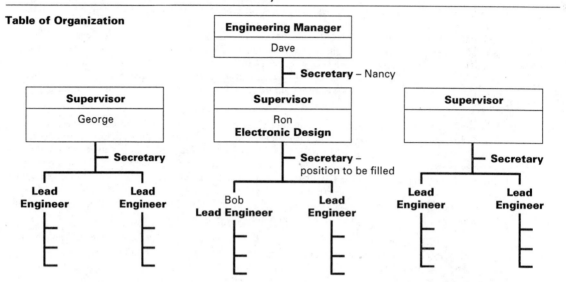

38. The President's Decision: A Role-Play[1]

Purpose:
To explore the effects of different types of leadership styles on group members.

Group Size:
Any number of persons.

Time Required:
50 minutes or more.

Room Arrangement Requirements:
Four chairs placed in a semi-circle in the front of the room.

Related Topics:
Dynamics Within Groups, Interpersonal Communications

Exercise Schedule

		Unit Time	Total Time
1.	**Assign roles**	**5+ min**	**5 min**

a. Five persons are needed to play the roles. (When possible, role assignments for this case should be given before the meeting of the class in order to permit the participants to study the roles carefully.) Two participants play the role of John/Joan Ward, president of the company, and the other three are the vice-presidents: William/Wanda Carson, in charge of manufacturing and product development, James/Jane Jackson, in charge of sales: and Russell/Rita Haney, in charge of personnel and industrial relations. Role descriptions are in the Appendix.

b. The remaining persons in the class serve as observers.

c. All group members read the background information. The instructor writes on newsprint or blackboard the name, position, age, and years with the company of all four participants.

d. The participants study their roles so they can role play without referring to the written material. They do not read any role except their own.

e. Observers read the "Instruction for Observers."

		Unit Time	Total Time
2.	**Role-play**	**30+ min**	**35 min**

a. When all participants are ready, Ward I enters the office and sits at the desk. After a few moments, the vice-presidents enter, one at a time, and seat themselves so that Carson will be at Ward's left, with Jackson next to Carson, and Haney at the end, on Ward's right. Ward II remains in the hall.

b. Ward I greets each person while entering and shows him/her the correct seat.

c. When everyone is seated, Ward I begins the discussion.

---

[1] Adapted from *The Role-Play Technique* by Norman R.F. Maier, Allen R. Solem and Ayesha Maier. Used with permission.

d. Fifteen to thirty minutes is usually needed for role playing.

e. The leader is permitted to finish or ask for help whenever he wishes. If conflict develops and persists so that no progress is made after ten minutes, the role-play is interrupted by the instructor and the problem is thrown open for general discussion. Role-playing is resumed after the president feels he/she has gained enough hints to proceed.

f. The scene is repeated with Ward II.

3. **Class discussion**   **15+ min**   **50 min**

The instructor will lead a discussion on areas shown in the next sections.

a. *Evaluation of the solution*

1. Discuss the merits of the solution from the point of view of the future of the company and determine the extent of agreement among the observers. Compare the opinions of observers, vice-presidents, and Ward. In case these opinions differ, each role-player introduces any relevant information that was given in that role to see if the new facts will alter the opinions of the observers.

2. Discuss the merits of the solution from the president's point of view.

3. What are Ward's prospects of being retained by the board of directors if the solution does not result in marked improvement?

4. Discuss the part the vice-presidents played in making the decision. Will they give Ward the support to retain his/her job?

b. *Analysis of the conference*

1. Did Ward give the vice-presidents an opportunity to help solve the real problem faced, or were they given a somewhat different problem? Ward can describe why this situation caused him/her to act so.

2. Would Ward have given his/her side of the problem or confined the discussion to company matters as much as possible? Compare views of participants and observers.

3. Which participants persisted in discussing matters from their points of view? What could have been done to get everyone working together?

4. How did the specialized information that different conferees possessed become integrated into the discussion? Was there an interest in getting facts or did Ward attempt to suppress facts?

5. Stubbornness, aggression, and childish behavior indicate frustration. Enumerate the examples of these behaviors that were evidenced in the discussion and evaluate how they were handled.

c. *Discussion of Ward's situation*

1. How many observers would have taken the advice given by the vice-presidents (in this situation) had they played the part of Ward? How many would have declined the advice? List the arguments in favor of each position.

2. What would happen if a president's decision was always the joint decision of the vice-presidents? Discuss the favorable and unfavorable aspects of such a philosophy of leadership.

Background on the ABCO Electrical Manufacturing Company

The ABCO Electrical Manufacturing Company produces various part and subassemblies for radio, television, and other electronic industries. The factory is located in Philadelphia; there are sales offices in several of the eastern cities, in or near their major market area. During the Vietnam War, the company also operated a government-built plant in Kansas City which supplied equipment for military aircraft. However, this operation was abandoned when numerous military orders were canceled; the plant was bought shortly thereafter by one of the large electronics manufacturing companies.

Two years ago, the company went through a major management reorganization, brought about by increasing losses in its operations and a steadily diminishing share of the market. The previous top management personnel were extremely conservative in their outlook and methods, and for many years had operated on a small share of the market as suppliers to the radio and broadcasting industries. During the Vietnam War, they made a good showing as a result of increased business and profits from military orders. For several years, there has been considerable growth in the electronics industry. At the same time, new problems have been created for the smaller producers, such as ABCO, by the unusually rapid technological developments and strong competition from the larger companies in the field.

The company's inability to compete for large-volume business has made it necessary to depend more and more on specialty orders. Although the unit profit margin on such orders is somewhat larger, the shifting demands of this type of market call for unusual flexibility in manufacturing processes and procedures and a highly alert, aggressive sales force in order to maintain demand for regular lines and push the sales of new products. Similarly, product development and engineering ingenuity are at a premium in order to meet competition, provide for economical changeover from one product to another, and achieve the quick solution of a variety of complex production problems. It is also necessary for production employees and foremen to adapt to frequent changes in jobs and methods without undue training or confusion.

Previous management had been **unable to adapt** to changing conditions.

It was the inability of the previous management to adapt to these changing conditions that led to the reorganization of the company and the installation of a new top management group. Following are the names of the present group of senior officers of the company, together with a summary of their previous background and experience:

John/Joan Ward, president of the company. Ward is 49 years old and has been with the company twelve years - first as an accountant, then as controller for six years - before being promoted to the present position two years ago. Ward has a college degree in accounting and is a CPA.

William/Wanda Carson, vice-president in charge of manufacturing and product development. Carson has an electrical engineering background and was hired fifteen years ago as a potential management person. Having progressed to general foreman of the night shift at the time, Carson was sent to Kansas City as superintendent. When the Kansas City plant was closed, Carson returned to Philadelphia as plant superintendent, and was promoted to the present position two years ago when Ward took over as president. Carson is 45 years old.

James/Jane Jackson, vice-president in charge of sales. Jackson came to the company five years ago from the position of assistant sales manager for one of the divisions of a larger company. Jackson is the only holdover as vice-president from the previous management, having been brought in to set up a sales organization to attempt to recapture lost accounts and widen the market for company products. Jackson started in sales work from business administration school and is 46 years old.

Russell/Rita Haney, vice-president, personnel and industrial relations, is 39 years old. Haney was hired as personnel director for the Kansas City plant and then came to Philadelphia in a similar capacity. Previously, personnel functions had been the responsibility of the office manager. Haney remained as personnel director until a promotion to the vice-presidency one and one-half years ago.

Instructions for Observers

On the basis of what you already know about the ABCO Company and the four top executives, Ward, Carson, Jackson, and Haney, you probably have formed certain impressions about the situation. Most of the things you have learned so far are facts. However, you also know that these facts may be relatively unimportant except as background, and that the attitudes, feelings, and personalities of these people, as well as their relationships with each other, may be more important. It is important to observe the feelings that are indicated and not be misled by the actual words spoken if you are to sense the developments as they occur in the role-play. The following questions give you clues as to what to watch and listen for.

Discussion Questions

1. Observe how Ward opens the discussion. Does Ward seem at ease? Did he/she state a problem with all relevant facts for open discussion? Is Ward being open-minded about things?

2. What are Ward's reasons for calling this meeting? How do the other members react to Ward's views? To what extent does Ward accept their views? What evidence is there, if any, that Ward is defensive?

3. To what extent is this a problem-solving discussion? If not, why not? What do you think is the real problem here? What did Ward do to help or hinder the group?

4. Did any of the participants become stubborn? Why?

5. Note behaviors that indicate a member was holding back relevant information.

6. How acceptable is the decision to each of the members? Note behaviors that support your evaluation.

7. What evidence is there to indicate that fear or threat influenced the relationships of the various persons in the discussion?

8. What were the differences between Ward I and Ward II?

39. Path-Goal Leadership[1]

Purpose:
To determine what leadership styles are most effective with different subordinates.

Group Size:
Eight people.

Time Required:
45 minutes per round (second round optional), plus 15 minutes class discussion.

Exercise Schedule

Round 1

	Unit Time	Total Time
1. Assigning roles	**10 min**	**10 min**

Four students adopt the role of Pat Howard (the supervisor), and the remaining four students adopt the role of one of the four subordinates (Jan Perez, Chris McBride, Jamie Johnson, or Fran Fulton). Each person reads the background information only for his or her role. The Meeting Schedule lists the names of the three subordinates with whom each supervisor will meet. Each supervisor should use the Pre-Meeting Planning Sheet to write some notes about what he or she plans to do when meeting with each subordinate.

2. Supervisor-Subordinate meetings	**20 min**	**30 min**

Form pairs within each group such that each supervisor meets with the first subordinate designated on his or her schedule (see the Meeting Schedule). For example, the schedule for Round 1 indicates that Person #1 will play the role of Pat Howard, first meeting with Jan, then Fran, and finally Jamie. Person #2 will also play the role of Pat Howard, first meeting with Fran, then Jamie, and finally Chris. Person #5 will play the role of Chris, and Person #6 will play the role of Jan, etc. The supervisor-subordinate pair is given five minutes for their one-on-one meeting. After five minutes, the instructor says "Stop" and asks the people to individually fill out their respective Role-Play Evaluation Forms. After one minute, the supervisor begins meeting with the next designated subordinate on his or her schedule. Repeat this process until all supervisors have met with the three subordinates designated on their schedules.

3. Subordinate-to-Supervisor feedback	**15 min**	**45 min**

Each designated subordinate-supervisor pair then meets again (in the same order that they met in Step 2) for three minutes to allow the subordinate to provide feedback to the supervisor concerning the effectiveness of the supervisor's behavior. Subordinates should review the Guidelines for Subordinate-to-Supervisor Feedback before providing feedback to supervisors. We recommend that the subordinate give his or her copy of the Role-Play Evaluation Form to the supervisor after providing oral feedback, so the supervisor can compare his/her self-ratings with the ratings provided by subordinates.

---

[1]Joseph Seltzer, "Path-Goal Theory in the English Language Throughout the World," *Journal of Management Education,* in press. Reprinted by permission of Sage Publications, Inc.

4.   **Round 2 (optional)**   **45 min**

In Round 2, students who played the supervisor in Round 1 will play a subordinate, and students who played a subordinate will play the supervisor. (See the Meeting Schedule for details.) For example, the schedule for Round 2 indicates that Person #5 will play the role of Pat Howard, first meeting with Jan, then Fran, and finally Jamie. Person #6 will also play the role of Pat Howard, first meeting with Fran, then Jamie, and finally Chris. Person #1 will play the role of Chris, and Person #2 will play the role of Jan, etc. Repeat Steps 1 through 3 using the Round 2 role descriptions.

5.   **General discussion**   **15 min**   **60 min**

Focus on the following questions:

a. for subordinates:

Were each of the supervisors who met with you equally effective?

What made some supervisors more or less effective than others?

What differences did you observe in the behavior of the different supervisors?

What was effective? What was ineffective?

b. for supervisors:

Did you vary your behavior with different subordinates?

Did some behaviors appear to be more effective with one person than with another?

c. for the class:

What leadership style(s) should be most effective for each of the subordinates? Why?

Pat Howard Role-Play

Meeting Schedule

Group Member	Assignments for Round 1	Assignments for Round 2
	Supervisor (Pat)	**Subordinate**
#1	Jan, Fran, Jamie	Chris
#2	Fran, Jamie, Chris	Jan
#3	Jamie, Chris, Jan	Fran
#4	Chris, Jan, Fran	Jamie
	Subordinate	**Supervisor (Pat)**
#5	Chris	Jan, Fran, Jamie
#6	Jan	Fran, Jamie, Chris
#7	Fran	Jamie, Chris, Jan
#8	Jamie	Chris, Jan, Fran

Pat Howard Role-Play

Role for Pat Howard, Round 1

It is Monday morning and your first day on the new job. You were delighted to take a lateral transfer in your company because it meant that you and your family could return to Philadelphia, and be closer to your elderly parents. You are the sales manager of a specialized systems development group for a large, diversified multinational corporation. The representatives in your group do sales, interact with the engineering and design group, and do some customer support for a number of custom-designed control systems. An individual sale is usually in the $20,000-$60,000 range. Previously you held a similar position in the Orlando branch of the company. Leslie Little, the previous sales manager, took early retirement. You have heard through the grapevine that Leslie wasn't meeting the sales projections, especially with regard to the new HX11 control system. The HX11 was the brainchild of the Division VP. In Orlando, you hadn't gotten much pressure to push the HX11 because few of the industries where it would be used were in your region. You are familiar with the product because one of your salespeople had been able to make two sales. It is an ingenious device that uses a radically different approach. You think the VP might be right in thinking that "the HX11 is the future of the division."

> It's your
> **first day**
> on the new job.

Last week, you had a chance to have dinner with Leslie Little, who explained that there had been a lot of turnover in the department recently, but didn't seem to know the reason. As a result, only four of the six positions were currently filled. Leslie gave you a perspective on each individual. Jan Perez had been the top (i.e., most productive) salesperson in the group for the past two years. Leslie said that Jan is confident about his/her abilities, and is the kind of person who believes that he/she can achieve difficult goals (and the rewards that come with them) by working hard. Fran Fulton has been in the group for a couple of years and has been an average performer. Fran seems uncomfortable with the inevitable conflicts that sometimes arise in a sales organization. Chris McBride, a new hire, is bright and personable, but this is Chris' first direct sales position. Jamie Johnson often appears uncomfortable with the "high-tech" aspects of the products and has trouble keeping up with the frequent changes in the product line. Jamie seems to feel that success as a sales rep depends more on product design, pricing, and marketing plans than on his/her own efforts. With only a few years to retirement, Jamie seems worried and a bit lost.

You know that all the people in your group will be in the office this morning for the district sales meeting. You had a chance to meet and speak informally (i.e., socially) with each of the sales representatives last evening at a company social event. At that time you told them you would be in the office early this morning and would like to speak with each sales representative individually for five minutes before the district sales meeting to begin to talk about work issues and concerns. You will have time to meet individually with three of your sales reps before the meeting. You want to motivate them toward better performance and, if necessary, influence them to push sales of the HX11. You have a few minutes to plan how you will interact with each one.

Pat Howard Role-Play

Role for Jan Perez, Round 1

You are a sales representative of a specialized systems development group for a large, diversified multinational corporation. You do sales, interact with the engineering and design group, and provide some customer support for a number of custom-designed control systems. An individual sale is usually in the $20,000-$60,000 range. It is Monday morning and the first day for Pat Howard, your new boss. Pat just took a lateral transfer from the Orlando branch of the company. You heard it was because Pat wanted to be close to elderly parents. Also, your previous manager, Leslie Little, took early retirement. You have heard through the grapevine that Leslie wasn't meeting the sales projections, especially with regard to the new HX11 control system. The HX11 was the brainchild of the Division VP. You went to a training program on the HX11 a few months ago. It is an ingenious device that uses a radically different approach. You were enthusiastic about it and made two quick sales, but have found that it requires substantially more time for support. One of your customers had a number of substantial problems with the system. You are not sure if the customized design was inappropriate or if the HX11 just didn't do everything it was promised to do, but you haven't tried very hard to sell one since. By concentrating on the other products you handle, you have been able to maintain your position as the top salesperson in your group. Several other salespeople have recently left the company. In part, it was because of Leslie Little. You are glad you have a new boss. You feel like you know how to do your job well, so you hope Pat will leave you alone and allow you to have a lot of input in establishing your work plans and goals. You have always believed that you can achieve your goals and the rewards you want by working hard, and you enjoy the sense of satisfaction that comes from a successful sale.

> You feel like you know how to **do your job well.**

You are in the office this morning for the district sales meeting. You and the other sales representatives had a chance to meet and speak informally (i.e., socially) with Pat last evening at a company social event. Pat will be in the office early this morning and would like to speak with you individually for five minutes before the district sales meeting to begin to talk about work issues and concerns.

Role for Chris McBride, Round 1

You are a sales representative of a specialized systems development group for a large, diversified multinational corporation. You were recently hired to do sales, interact with the engineering and design group, and provide customer support for a number of custom-designed control systems. An individual sale is usually in the $20,000-$60,000 range. Your previous job was in a marketing organization in a related field, but this is your first job in direct sales. It is Monday morning and the first day for Pat Howard, your new boss. Pat just took a lateral transfer from the Orlando branch of your company. You heard it was because Pat wanted to be closer to elderly parents. Also, the previous manager, Leslie Little, took early retirement right after you were hired. You have just been introduced to the new HX11 control system. The HX11 was the brainchild of the Division VP. It is an ingenious device that uses a radically different approach. The product line, especially the HX11, seems very complex, and you are concerned about your ability to successfully sell these systems. Also, a couple of experienced sales representatives have expressed some skepticism about the HX11. You wonder, if they have concerns about the system, how can you possibly be expected to sell it? You hope this new job works out well for you. You are enthusiastic, but concerned. Because you want to make a good first impression with Pat, you are not sure if it is okay to admit to your self-doubt and concerns.

> You are enthusiastic, but **concerned**.

You are in the office this morning for the district sales meeting. You and the other sales representatives had a chance to meet and speak informally (i.e., socially) with Pat last evening at a company social event. Pat will be in the office early this morning and would like to speak with you individually for five minutes before the district sales meeting to begin to talk about work issues and concerns.

Role for Fran Fulton, Round 1

You are a sales representative of a specialized systems development group for a large, diversified multinational corporation. You do sales, interact with the engineering and design group, and provide some customer support for a number of custom-designed control systems. An individual sale is usually in the $20,000-$60,000 range. It is Monday morning and the first day for Pat Howard, your new boss. Pat just took a lateral transfer from the Orlando branch of your company. You heard it was because Pat wanted to be closer to elderly parents. Also, your previous manager, Leslie Little, took early retirement. You have heard through the grapevine that Leslie wasn't meeting the sales projections, especially with regard to the new HX11 control system. The HX11 was the brainchild of the Division VP. You went to a training program on the HX11 a few months ago. It is an ingenious device that uses a radically different approach. It seemed pretty good and you were able to make a quick sale, but then providing follow-up support to the customer sometimes put you in conflict with the people in the engineering and design group. This especially troubles you because you are very uncomfortable with conflict. In fact, you left your previous job because there was so much tension and conflict among co-workers. Leslie Little also wasn't very good at creating a supportive or cooperative climate among the sales representatives, and you found yourself becoming uncomfortable at meetings with other sales representatives because of the tension and conflict sometimes created by competition among the sales reps. You are hoping that Pat will create a better climate in which to work. Your performance has been about average compared to the other sales reps.

> You are very **uncomfortable** with conflict.

You are in the office this morning for the district sales meeting. You and the other sales representatives had a chance to meet and speak informally (i.e., socially) with Pat last evening at a company social event. Pat will be in the office early this morning and would like to speak with you individually for five minutes before the district sales meeting to begin to talk about work issues and concerns.

Role for Jamie Johnson, Round 1

You are a sales representative of a specialized systems development group for a large, diversified multinational corporation. You job is to do sales, interact with the engineering and design group, and provide some customer support for a number of custom-designed control systems. An individual sale is usually in the $20,000-$60,000 range. It is Monday morning and the first day for Pat Howard, your new boss. Pat just took a lateral transfer from the Orlando branch of your company. You heard it was because Pat wanted to be closer to elderly parents. Also, your previous manager, Leslie Little, took early retirement.

The product line you sell is very complicated and "high-tech." You have been trying really hard to keep up with the frequent changes in technology of the product line. Despite all your effort, you find that you are still struggling. You think that the younger sales representatives have an advantage because their college education and training is more recent and helped make them knowledgeable and comfortable with all the recent computer hardware and software. You hope that Pat Howard will offer more help and guidance than you received from Leslie Little. You've always been willing to accept authority and you're looking forward to someone who can provide a sense of direction to the sales group. You often have felt that your success as a sales representative is more dependent on product design, pricing, and marketing plans (and economic conditions in general) than your own efforts. The new HX11 is a case in point. The HX11 was the brainchild of the Division VP and it seems especially complex. You want to do a good job, but at this point you'd be happy to just "hang on" for a few more years until you can retire.

> You've always been willing to **accept authority.**

You are in the office this morning for the district sales meeting. You and the other sales representatives had a chance to meet and speak informally (i.e., socially) with Pat last evening at a company social event. Pat will be in the office early this morning and would like to speak with you individually for five minutes before the district sales meeting to begin to talk about work issues and concerns.

Supervisor's Pre-Meeting Planning Sheet

Before you begin your meetings, complete the following concerning each of the three subordinates with whom you will meet.

What do you plan to do when you meet with Jan Perez?

What do you plan to do when you meet with Fran Fulton?

What do you plan to do when you meet with Chris McBride?

What do you plan to do when you meet with Jamie Johnson?

Supervisor's Role-Play Evaluation Form

Complete this form after you meet with each of the three subordinates.

> **Path-Goal Theory defines four types of leader behaviors:**
>
> *Supportive* – providing consideration for the needs of subordinates, showing concern for their welfare, and creating a friendly feeling in the work group.
>
> *Directive* – informing subordinates about job tasks and processes, scheduling and coordinating work, giving specific guidance, specifying rules and procedures.
>
> *Participative* – listening to suggestions, consulting with subordinates, and inviting their participation in decisions that directly affect them.
>
> *Achievement-Oriented* – setting challenging goals, showing confidence that subordinates will attain high standards, emphasizing excellence in performance, providing feedback on performance.

In the role-play with Jan Perez, what leader behaviors did you use?

	Low						High
Supportive	1	2	3	4	5	6	7
Directive	1	2	3	4	5	6	7
Participative	1	2	3	4	5	6	7
Achievement-Oriented	1	2	3	4	5	6	7

How successful were you in meeting Jan's needs and addressing his/her concerns?

	Low						High
Success	1	2	3	4	5	6	7

To what extent did you influence or motivate Jan toward high or better performance?

	Low						High
Influence	1	2	3	4	5	6	7

In the role-play with Fran Fulton, what leader behaviors did you use?

	Low						High
Supportive	1	2	3	4	5	6	7
Directive	1	2	3	4	5	6	7
Participative	1	2	3	4	5	6	7
Achievement-Oriented	1	2	3	4	5	6	7

How successful were you in meeting Fran's needs and addressing his/her concerns?

	Low						High
Success	1	2	3	4	5	6	7

To what extent did you influence or motivate Fran toward high or better performance?

	Low						High
Influence	1	2	3	4	5	6	7

In the role-play with Chris McBride, what leader behaviors did you use?

	Low						High
Supportive	1	2	3	4	5	6	7
Directive	1	2	3	4	5	6	7
Participative	1	2	3	4	5	6	7
Achievement-Oriented	1	2	3	4	5	6	7

How successful were you in meeting Chris' needs and addressing his/her concerns?

	Low						High
Success	1	2	3	4	5	6	7

To what extent did you influence or motivate Chris toward high or better performance?

	Low						High
Influence	1	2	3	4	5	6	7

In the role-play with Jamie Johnson, what leader behaviors did you use?

	Low						High
Supportive	1	2	3	4	5	6	7
Directive	1	2	3	4	5	6	7
Participative	1	2	3	4	5	6	7
Achievement-Oriented	1	2	3	4	5	6	7

How successful were you in meeting Jamie's needs and addressing his/her concerns?

	Low						High
Success	1	2	3	4	5	6	7

To what extent did you influence or motivate Jamie toward high or better performance?

	Low						High
Influence	1	2	3	4	5	6	7

Subordinate's Role-Play Evaluation Form

First Role-Play

Path-Goal Theory defines four types of leader behaviors:

Supportive – providing consideration for the needs of subordinates, showing concern for their welfare, and creating a friendly feeling in the work group.

Directive – informing subordinates about job tasks and processes, scheduling and coordinating work, giving specific guidance, specifying rules and procedures.

Participative – listening to suggestions, consulting with subordinates, and inviting their participation in decisions that directly affect them.

Achievement-Oriented – setting challenging goals, showing confidence that subordinates will attain high standards, emphasizing excellence in performance, providing feedback on performance.

In the first role-play, to what extent did Pat Howard use each of the following leader behaviors?

	Low						High
Supportive	1	2	3	4	5	6	7
Directive	1	2	3	4	5	6	7
Participative	1	2	3	4	5	6	7
Achievement-Oriented	1	2	3	4	5	6	7

To what extent did Pat seem concerned about (a) your job performance, and (b) your job satisfaction?

	Low						High
Job Performance	1	2	3	4	5	6	7
Satisfaction	1	2	3	4	5	6	7

How successful was Pat in meeting your needs and addressing your concerns?

	Low						High
Success	1	2	3	4	5	6	7

To what extent did Pat influence or motivate you toward high or better performance?

	Low						High
Influence	1	2	3	4	5	6	7

Describe leader behaviors that were effective and behaviors that were less effective.

Subordinate's Role-Play Evaluation Form

Second Role-Play

Path-Goal Theory defines four types of leader behaviors:

Supportive – providing consideration for the needs of subordinates, showing concern for their welfare, and creating a friendly feeling in the work group.

Directive – informing subordinates about job tasks and processes, scheduling and coordinating work, giving specific guidance, specifying rules and procedures.

Participative – listening to suggestions, consulting with subordinates, and inviting their participation in decisions that directly affect them.

Achievement-Oriented – setting challenging goals, showing confidence that subordinates will attain high standards, emphasizing excellence in performance, providing feedback on performance.

In the second role-play, to what extent did Pat Howard use each of the following leader behaviors?

	Low						High
Supportive	1	2	3	4	5	6	7
Directive	1	2	3	4	5	6	7
Participative	1	2	3	4	5	6	7
Achievement-Oriented	1	2	3	4	5	6	7

To what extent did Pat seem concerned about (a) your job performance, and (b) your job satisfaction?

	Low						High
Job Performance	1	2	3	4	5	6	7
Satisfaction	1	2	3	4	5	6	7

How successful was Pat in meeting your needs and addressing your concerns?

	Low						High
Success	1	2	3	4	5	6	7

To what extent did Pat influence or motivate you toward high or better performance?

	Low						High
Influence	1	2	3	4	5	6	7

Describe leader behaviors that were effective and behaviors that were less effective.

Subordinate's Role-Play Evaluation Form

Third Role-Play

Path-Goal Theory defines four types of leader behaviors:

Supportive – providing consideration for the needs of subordinates, showing concern for their welfare, and creating a friendly feeling in the work group.

Directive – informing subordinates about job tasks and processes, scheduling and coordinating work, giving specific guidance, specifying rules and procedures.

Participative – listening to suggestions, consulting with subordinates, and inviting their participation in decisions that directly affect them.

Achievement-Oriented – setting challenging goals, showing confidence that subordinates will attain high standards, emphasizing excellence in performance, providing feedback on performance.

In the third role-play, to what extent did Pat Howard use each of the following leader behaviors?

	Low						High
Supportive	1	2	3	4	5	6	7
Directive	1	2	3	4	5	6	7
Participative	1	2	3	4	5	6	7
Achievement-Oriented	1	2	3	4	5	6	7

To what extent did Pat seem concerned about (a) your job performance, and (b) your job satisfaction?

	Low						High
Job Performance	1	2	3	4	5	6	7
Satisfaction	1	2	3	4	5	6	7

How successful was Pat in meeting your needs and addressing your concerns?

	Low						High
Success	1	2	3	4	5	6	7

To what extent did Pat influence or motivate you toward high or better performance?

	Low						High
Influence	1	2	3	4	5	6	7

Describe leader behaviors that were effective and behaviors that were less effective.

Guidelines for Subordinate-to-Supervisor Feedback

Avoid vague or very general comments. Instead, describe Pat's specific behaviors, focusing especially on those behaviors that your character found to be effective or ineffective. Your comments should focus on Pat's behavior, not on Pat "as a person." Following are some suggested questions that you might address when you provide feedback for Pat.

Briefly describe Pat Howard's behavior during your meeting.

What did Pat do that your character found to be effective?

Contrast the behavior of this "Pat" with the other "Pats" with whom you met.

How do you think your character would have felt during your meeting with Pat?
(Say, "When you said such and such, I felt..."; don't say, "You made me feel...")

Did Pat focus primarily on your job performance or your job satisfaction?

What concerns of yours were *not* addressed during your meeting with Pat?

Provide Pat with at least two developmental suggestions (e.g., ways in which Pat might have been more effective with your character).

Pat Howard Role-Play

Role for Pat Howard

You have just finished your first three months as sales manager with the Philadelphia office of a specialized systems development group for a large, diversified multinational corporation. The representatives in your group do sales, interact with the engineering and design group, and provide some customer support for a number of custom-designed control systems. An individual sale is usually in the $20,000-$60,000 range. Previously, you held a similar position in the Orlando branch of the company. Your first quarter in the Philadelphia office was reasonably successful. Sales were substantially better than under your predecessor (Leslie Little) and you met your goals on all products except the HX11. The Division VP has been pushing hard for sales of "his brainchild," the HX11, and you have a ways to go if you are going to meet your annual sales goal. You have finally been able to fill the openings created by the turnover problem that the previous manager had. Two weeks ago, you hired K.C. James, who is currently at the corporate offices for technical training. Your most recent hire, Xeno Batvariana, will start next week. All of your current salespeople look as if they will stay.

> Your first quarter in the Philadelphia office was **reasonably successful.**

You have been thinking about the quarterly district sales meeting scheduled for later this morning. Although you have a few things you want to say to the group, you also want to spend about five minutes with your people individually and informally discuss current work issues and concerns, including sales of the HX11.

Over the past three months, Jan Perez has continued to be the top sales representative in the office. So far, you've given Jan a lot of latitude in setting goals. Jan has obviously been successful, but hasn't put effort into selling the HX11. Jan appears willing to work hard to reach sales goals (and obtain the rewards that come with them) and really seems to enjoy the sense of satisfaction that comes with a successful sale. Fran Fulton continues to be an average performer, although this might improve if Fran wasn't always backing away from any situation in which there was conflict. Jamie Johnson, who only has a few years to retirement, seems nice but often appears a bit overwhelmed by the complexity of the product line. You've been providing Jamie with some help and direction, but Jamie still seems to struggle. Jamie seems to feel that success as a sales rep depends more on product design, pricing, and marketing plans (and economic conditions in general) than his/her own efforts. You have also been providing a great deal of direction and guidance to Chris McBride, a recent hire, and Chris has made significant progress. Chris has learned a lot about the product line, is feeling more confident, and has made a few nice sales in the last three months.

Pat Howard Role-Play

Role Play for Jan Perez, Round 2

You are a sales representative of a specialized systems development group for a large, diversified multinational corporation. You do sales, interact with the engineering and design group, and provide some customer support for a number of custom-designed control systems. An individual sale is usually in the $20,000-$60,000 range. Three months ago, Pat Howard took over the Philadelphia office. Pat has been effective as manager. The office is way ahead of last year and seems on track for the yearly sales projections, except for the new HX11 control system. Pat has been able to address the turnover problem that the previous manager had. Two vacant positions have been filled and there is no more talk about people leaving.

You have been happy to have Pat as your manager. It has certainly been an improvement over the previous person, Leslie Little. You continue to be the top sales representative in the office. So far, Pat has pretty much let you set your own goals. You feel like you know how to do your job well, so you hope Pat will continue to leave you alone and allow you to have a lot of input in establishing your work plans and goals. Although you know Pat is pushing the HX11, there have been some customer complaints about it and it requires a great deal of follow-up support, so you have not tried particularly hard to sell it.

> So far, Pat has let you **set your own goals.**

You have always believed that you can achieve your goals and the rewards you want by working hard, and you enjoy the sense of satisfaction that comes from a successful sale.

You are in the office this morning for the quarterly district sales meeting. You are expecting to have a few minutes to talk individually with Pat before the meeting.

Role for Chris McBride, Round 2

You were hired about four months ago as a sales representative of a specialized systems development group for a large, diversified multinational corporation. You do sales, interact with the engineering and design group, and provide some customer support for a number of custom-designed control systems. An individual sale is usually in the $20,000-$60,000 range. Pat Howard took over the Philadelphia office some three months ago and has been reasonably effective as manager. The office is way ahead of last year and seems on track for the yearly sales projections, except for the new HX11 control system. Pat has been able to address the turnover problem that the previous manager had. Two vacant positions have been filled and there is no more talk about people leaving.

You have been happy to have Pat as your manager. It has certainly been an improvement over the previous person, Leslie Little. You were very anxious when you started the job several months ago (due to your lack of experience in direct sales), and Pat provided a lot of direction, as well as information and guidance about all of the product lines. You have made several nice sales and now you're feeling more knowledgeable and confident. The one item that you haven't been very successful with is the HX11 control system. Since it uses a radically different approach, it is very complex to understand.

> You're feeling **more knowledgeable and confident.**

You are in the office this morning for the quarterly district sales meeting. You are expecting to have a few minutes to talk individually with Pat before the meeting.

Role for Fran Fulton, Round 2

You are a sales representative of a specialized systems development group for a large, diversified multinational corporation. You do sales, interact with the engineering and design group, and provide some customer support for a number of custom-designed control systems. An individual sale is usually in the $20,000-$60,000 range. Three months ago, Pat Howard took over the Philadelphia office, and has been reasonably effective as manager. The office is way ahead of last year and seems on track for the yearly sales projections, except for the new HX11 control system. Pat has been able to address the turnover problem that the previous manager had. Two vacant positions have been filled and there is no more talk about people leaving.

You have been happy to have Pat as your manager. It has certainly been an improvement over the previous person, Leslie Little. Pat has helped calm things down when there has been conflict between the sales representatives and the people in the engineering and design group over the HX11 designs. Your performance continues to be average. Still, you find that the competition among the sales reps, coupled with the pressure to meet high sales goals, sometimes creates conflict and tension in the group. And you really dislike having to work in a situation where there is dissention.

> Your performance continues to be **average**.

You are in the office this morning for the quarterly district sales meeting. You are expecting to have a few minutes to talk individually with Pat before the meeting.

Role for Jamie Johnson, Round 2

You are a sales representative of a specialized systems development group for a large, diversified multinational corporation. You do sales, interact with the engineering and design group, and provide some customer support for a number of custom-designed control systems. An individual sale is usually in the $20,000-$60,000 range. Three months ago, Pat Howard took over the Philadelphia office, and has been reasonably effective as manager. The office is way ahead of last year and seems on track for the yearly sales projections, except for the new HX11 control system. Pat has been able to address the turnover problem that the previous manager had. Two vacant positions have been filled and there is no more talk about people leaving.

You have been happy to have Pat as your manager. It has certainly been an improvement over the previous person, Leslie Little. The product line you sell is very complicated and "high-tech" (especially the new HX11). You have been trying really hard to keep up with the frequent changes in technology of the product line, but it is always a struggle. At least Pat has been willing to provide some guidance when you feel overwhelmed by a new product or technology. You've always been willing to accept authority, and you still think the sales group needs a better sense of direction. You often have felt that your success as a sales representative is more dependent on product design, pricing, and marketing plans (and economic conditions in general) than your own efforts. You want to do a good job, but on the other hand, you don't want to worry yourself into an early grave.

> You **struggle** to keep up with changes in the product line.

You are in the office this morning for the quarterly district sales meeting. You are expecting to have a few minutes to talk individually with Pat before the meeting.

40. The Leadership Self-Study Project[1]

Purpose:
To develop a comprehensive self-portrait that will be useful in understanding and developing yourself as a person and manager.

Time Required:
Much of this project is done outside of class. The instructor may choose to do some of the exercises in class as well.

Instructions

This project builds on the experiential learning that happens in the classroom by providing an opportunity for related self-study. The project has two parts. Your instructor may assign one or both parts.

Part A: Profile yourself as a person and manager

In this project, you have the opportunity to take an objective, comprehensive look at your own style, strengths, and challenges as a manager. Using this textbook, select and complete at least 10 self-testing instruments (see list provided) as the basis of your analysis. Also, integrate your analysis with any pertinent learnings from the course readings or classes.

Write a paper evaluating yourself with regard to some standard and/or goals you may have. For example, you may want to become an international manager for a large pharmaceutical firm. What would be the attributes of such a manager and how well do you really match up? Write a paper describing your findings. Your instructor will inform you as to the specifications of the paper.

Exercise #	Name	Page #
5	Red and Blue Instrument	13
6	Personality Assessment: Jung's Typology	16
7	Locus of Control	21
12	Teaching Interpersonal Skills to Subordinates	42
14	Learning Organizations	49
15	The Learning-Model Instrument	54
20	Manifest Needs	76
21	Job Involvement	82
25	Stress Management	99
26	Odyssey into Organizational Hope	109
35	Leadership Style Inventory	139
39	Path-Goal Leadership	159

---

[1]By Rae Andre, associate professor, organizational behavior, Northwestern University. Used with permission.

Part B: Assessing yourself in groups

How do you function in groups? In this project you will analyze your behavior as a group leader and group member, using three suggested group exercises from this textbook (see the list provided). Be sure to get data (written comments based on observations) from other group members in order to have some objective basis for your analysis.

Write a paper describing your findings.

For profiling group leadership and membership characteristics

Intergroup Exercises

Chapter 12

Interpersonal Communication

41. Listening Exercise[1]

> **Purpose:**
> To examine common means of disrupting communication through poor listening.
>
> **Group Size:**
> Any number of groups of four or five members.
>
> **Time Required:**
> 30 minutes.
>
> **Room Arrangement Requirements:**
> So it is possible for four to five members to sit facing one another.
>
> **Related Topics:**
> Interpersonal Relationships

[1]By Frederic E. Finch, Halsey R. Jones and Joseph A. Litterer, *Managing for Organizational Effectiveness: An Experiential Approach.* New York: McGraw-Hill, 1976, pp. 163-164. Used with permission.

Exercise Schedule

		Unit Time	Total Time

1.   Assign groups   **2 min**   **2 min**

Divide into groups of four to five members each. Any class members left over and not in a group can act as group observers.

2.   First round   **2 min**   **4 min**

One volunteer in each group will talk for two to three minutes on any topic. The task for the other three members in each group is to make irrelevant comments every time there is a break in the "speech." For example, if the speaker is describing a trip he or she took recently, the other group members intervene with statements like, "I had a hamburger for supper last night," or "Gee, you're nice." Members can also key their nonverbal behavior to this mode of response. One person can act as observer.

3.   Group discussion   **3 min**   **7 min**

Each group should discuss the experience within the group. In particular, the speaker should indicate how this kind of response made him or her feel. How many times have you had this kind of response happen to you, observed it, or done it to others? What impact does it have on the speaker?

4.   Class discussion (optional)   **3 min**

The instructor will lead a general class discussion to see whether different groups had different experiences. The observers can relate their observations at this time.

5.   Rounds 2-4   **15 min**   **22 min**

Steps 2, 3, and 4 will be repeated three more times. Another volunteer will speak each time, and the other group members will respond in the ways noted below.

a.   *Tangential responses:* The second task of the group members, whenever they can, is to make tangential responses – i.e., to move the focus of attention from the speaker to the person making the response. For example, if the speaker is talking about a recent trip, the respondent might break in and start describing a trip of his or her own, picking up something in the talk that enables the respondent to "butt in" and take over the conversation. This is a widely used technique which you all recognize. You will find that you can be very creative in moving the conversation back and forth between people. In your discussion you should note its impact on how people feel and on the organization of the interaction.

b.   *Interrogative responses:* As with tangential responses, you will proceed through Steps 2, 3, and 4 above. Another volunteer will be given a topic, and the task of the other three members is to make interrogative responses. With interrogative responses, you question the speaker. It may seem that you are interested in the speaker, but questioning limits the speaker and takes the conversation in directions dictated by the questioners. Interrogative responses are very useful in keeping the focus of the conversation on the speaker – sometimes in ways he or she does not intend. The respondent in this mode is really in control of the conversation. This response can be useful in clarifying misunderstandings, but it can also be used to manipulate the conversation.

c.   *Reflective responses:* Again a volunteer (some may volunteer twice – it is not necessary for each person to be a speaker) will speak on any topic. The task for the other three members is to make reflective responses. These should reflect both content and the feelings behind the content. (Reflective responses are described more fully in the section on "Non-Directive Interviewing" in the Appendix.) Try to match your nonverbal behavior to this mode of responding. You will probably feel uncomfortable using this mode (afterward check to see which responses you were most comfortable in using). Proceed through Steps 3 and 4.

6.   Class discussion   **8 min**   **30 min**

The instructor will lead a general discussion of the exercise.

42. First Impression/Best Impression[1]

Purpose:
1. To gain information on the first impression one makes.
2. To get feedback on the effectiveness of body language.
3. To learn the impact of voice upon others.
4. To illustrate the power of nonverbal and vocal communication in establishing power and credibility.

Group Size:
Any number of triads.

Time Required:
40 minutes.

Preparation Required:
Read the "Introduction" and "Background" below.

Room Arrangement Requirements:
Large room or break-out areas where triads can work in relative quiet.

Introduction

This exercise can help you manage the impression you want to make and will show you how to "read" other people. It will help you find answers to the four key questions that define a successful communicator:

What do I **look** like?

What do I **sound** like?

What do I **say**?

How well do I **listen**?

By answering these questions you will give a great deal of valuable information about how well or how ineffectively you communicate.

Knowing what kind of communicator you are is critical to success, for communication is what people – especially business people – do most:

✓ As much as 85 percent of your day may be spent in some form of communication – most of it speaking with and listening to others, according to a survey of business people conducted at Arizona State University's College of Business Administration.

---

[1]By Janet E. Elsea, Ph.D., from *The Four-Minute Sell: How to Make a Dynamic First Impression,* Simon and Schuster, 1984. Used with permission.

✓   The typical working American gives about a dozen "speeches" a year: oral presentations to staff, clients, community groups, labor unions, and professional associations.

✓   You spend two to four times as much time talking on the telephone as you do using any other technology, including computers and word processors. Executives spend about 14 percent of their days on the phone.

✓   Communication skills rate high as important factors in a business person's success.

Although nearly every waking moment is spent listening or speaking to someone or something, the truth is that most of us haven't the faintest notion of what we look like, how we sound, what we say, or whether we are good listeners. And yet scientific research verifies that when meeting someone for the first time, how you say something and what you look like when you say it are much more important than the words you actually speak.

If people aren't quickly attracted to you or don't like what they see and hear in those first two to four minutes, chances are they won't pay attention to all those words you believe are demonstrating your knowledge and authority.

They will find your client guilty, seek another doctor, buy another product, vote for your opponent, or hire someone else.

During your first few minutes of interaction with others, their attention span is at its greatest and their powers of retention highest: their eyes and ears focus on you and tell their brains what they see and hear. That process of creating first impressions is intriguing but somewhat predictable. Depending on the other person's background and expectations, as well as the context of the interaction, here is what experts tell us typically happens when you meet someone for the first time.

First, people tend to focus on what they can see, such as:

✓ gender	✓ appearance	✓ movement
✓ age	✓ facial expressions	✓ personal space
✓ eye contact	✓ touch	

So much meaning is conveyed by these eight components of nonverbal communication that a number of communication experts believe "what you look like" constitutes more than half the total message. An astonishing 55 percent of the meaning is conveyed by facial expressions and body language alone. And you haven't yet opened your mouth.

Next, people focus on what they can hear. When you speak, out comes a voice with additional characteristics, among them rate of speech, volume, pitch, tone, and articulation. These give the other person more information about you. Your voice – not including your actual words – may transmit as much as 38 percent of the meaning in face-to-face conversations; it conveys a great deal more information on the telephone, because the other person is deprived of your body language – facial expressions, gestures, eye contact, and all the rest.

Last, and certainly least in terms of those first few moments, the other person gets around to your words, which contribute a mere seven percent to the meaning.

It's not that your words are unimportant. But if others do not like what they see, or if they get past your body language only to be stopped by something in your voice, they may not care at all about what you say. Their minds may already be made up, their first impressions indelibly formed.

❏ Background

When you meet someone for the first time, you have but two to four minutes to make a positive or negative first impression. If that impression is positive, studies say you will be granted higher credibility and trust than if the first impression is negative. Additionally, it is difficult – perhaps impossible – to change a negative first impression unless you have time and opportunity to do so. Finally, when you can be seen (as opposed to, say, telephone communication), people take in information about you visually first. Thus, your nonverbal communication accounts for 55 percent of the meaning's message. Next, people process what their ears hear in your voice; hence, vocal variables of rate, volume, pitch, quality, and articulation are approximately 38 percent of meaning (and over 70 percent when telephoning). Thus, the words you use are worth only 7 percent of the meaning within the first few moments of a new interaction.

Exercise Schedule

1. **Preparation (pre-class)**
   Read the background on nonverbal communication.

	Unit Time	*Total Time*
Steps 2 and 3, setup	**5 min**	**5 min**

2. Divide into triads.

3. Move to your assigned locale (be it around the room or in another room).

Steps 4, 5, and 6, presentations	**15 min**	**20 min**

4. Person 1 stands and begins to speak for a minute about herself/himself; meanwhile, the others look, listen closely, and take notes using the check sheets on the following page.

5. Person sits down and the other triad members give feedback based on what they wrote on their check sheets.

6. Repeat steps 4 and 5, allowing Person 2 and then Person 3 to speak and receive feedback.

7. **Group discussion**	**10 min**	**30 min**

Answer the discussion questions below in your triads.

   a. What did you notice first about each other?

   b. When there was a contradiction between what people looked like, sounded like and/or said, which did you trust or believe?

   c. Was there any one thing that stood out about each person as they talked (appearance, facial expressions, tone of voice, rate of speech, and the like)?

   d. Did your first impressions change as you got to know the people in your trio?

   e. Note situations where first impressions are crucial.

   f. In which sorts of professions is appearance more important than body language, or the voice more crucial than what one looks like?

   g. When do words begin to play their part in the communication process?

8. **Class discussion**	**10 min**	**40 min**

With the whole class, the instructor wraps up with an overview on how crucial body language and vocal skills are to first impressions, after which generalizations and conclusions are discussed.

Appearance Checklist*

Characteristic	Person #1	Person #2
gender		
age		
appearance		
facial expression		
eye contact		
movement		
personal space		
touch		

Voice Checklist

Characteristic	Person #1	Person #2
rate		
pitch		
volume		
quality		
articulation		

*   Fill in boxes with comments on qualities you noticed for each characteristic –
     including strengths and weaknesses.

43. Feedback: Interpersonal Relationships in Groups[1]

Purpose:
1. To learn effective methods of interpersonal feedback.
2. To develop a cohesive group.

Group Size:
Small ongoing (intact) groups of four to six (or up to eight) members.

Time Required:
50 minutes (longer for larger subgroups).

Preparation Required:
Read "Giving and Receiving Feedback" in the Appendix of this book.

Room Arrangement Requirements:
Preferably a room large enough so that group members can give feedback in relative privacy.

Exercise Schedule

		Unit Time	Total Time
1.	**Introduction**	**5 min**	**5 min**

The exercise and purpose are discussed as a whole class.

2.	**Small groups give feedback**	**35 min**	**40 min**

The class is divided into groups of four to eight members. These should be groups which have worked together before. Each group member is to think about how to fill out the Feedback Statements/Questions below. You are to be as specific as possible and use other group members' names when responding. Next, you are to discuss your responses with all group members. Suggestion: One person at a time gives his/her answers to the statements and other group members give additional feedback.

3.	**Class discussion**	**10 min**	**50 min**

The instructor will lead a group discussion processing this exercise, discussing the importance of giving positive feedback and of resolving issues and conflicts in order for a group to function more efficiently.

---

[1]Original idea adapted from Brian Holleran, professor of speech communication, State University of New York, Oneonta. Used with permission.

Feedback Statements/Questions:

1. What I like most about this group is:

2. In this group, I have most difficulty in discussing the following topics:

    a.

    b.

3. Things that group members do that bother me the most are:

    a.

    b.

    c.

4. In this group, I would like to change:

5. I wish (_____) would:
    name(s)

6. If I could, I'd like to tell (_____) :
    name(s)

7. a. In this group, the person with whom I have the strongest relationship is:

    b. The strong relationship exists because:

8. I would like to ask (_____) how he/she sees me.
    name(s), or address to whole group

9. I would like to ask if (_____) is angry or upset with me.
    name(s)

10. I would like to ask (_____) what my best contribution to the group is.
    name(s)

11. I would like to ask (_____) if I have seemed to change since entering the group.
    name(s)

12. I would like to ask (_____) what he/she is confused about me and...
    name(s)

44. The 45-Second Punch[1]

Purpose:
To learn to communicate concisely and with strength.

Time Required:
45 minutes.

Group Size:
Any number of groups of three.

Preparation Required:
Read the "Background on Sound Bytes" and complete assignment at the end.

Exercise Schedule

		Unit Time	Total Time
1.	**Introduction**	5 min	5 min

Instructor goes over the main principles of getting one's message across in 45 seconds. Students discuss television commercials (most of which are 30 seconds) and comment on parts of the message given in each. What was said and how did they do it?

		Unit Time	Total Time
2.	**Practice presentations**	10 min	15 min

Students are put into groups of three. Person A gives a 45-second presentation. The instructor tells when the time is up. The other two group members have two minutes to give feedback to Person A. Following this, Persons B and C give their presentations using the same process as above.

		Unit Time	Total Time
3.	**Revise presentations**	10 min	25 min

Students are given 10 minutes to plan a revision of their presentation. They may ask advice of their group members.

		Unit Time	Total Time
4.	**Give presentations**	10 min	35 min

Person C gives a 45-second presentation with two-minute feedback from A and B. Then A and B do likewise.

		Unit Time
5.	**Class presentations (optional)**	20 min or more

Each person gives their 45-second presentation to the whole group. Each student gives feedback to the presenter on a small sheet of paper. One person goes around and collects these papers after each presentation and gives them to the appropriate person.

		Unit Time	Total Time
6.	**Class discussion**	10 min	45 min

The instructor leads a discussion on the importance of concise communication.

Background on Sound Bytes

The average adult's attention span is 45 seconds. We are used to listening to television and radio commercials of 30-60 seconds. Therefore, we listen to people for about 45 seconds before our minds wander. That is why we call 45 seconds a "sound byte," or a unit of time that we can expect to get attention from listeners.

Some of you may think that is too short a time to convey an important message. Think for a minute of all the 30-second television commercials and how much information is given in that half-minute.

When giving a message to someone, it is very important to get the gist of what you want to say in that 45-second time allotment. Anything you say after that should only re-emphasize the main message already stated. In order to make a strong impact with your 45-second message, keep the following points in mind:

1. Know your objective. Have a clear sense of purpose and what you are after. Ask yourself: What do I want out of this exchange? If you are not certain, the listener will be confused as well. Think of famous characters or historical figures who had clear objectives: Moses – get to the Promised Land; Dorothy in *The Wizard of Oz* (ditto), Gandhi – to free India.

2. Find the right person. Sometimes it may take a few phone calls to get the right person, but make sure you have that figured out. The right person is the individual who can get done what you need to happen. Another point to stress here is knowing that person. If you need to ask one of the clericals to help on an important rush job and you know she likes to be asked about her children, then do that! Don't rush in with your 45-second message before you prepare the way, as they say.

3. Choose the correct approach. If you are asking for something, put the request in terms of the listener's needs getting met – not yours. For example, when asking for a raise, avoid telling the boss your personal problems and why you need extra money. Instead, state it in terms of how hard you have worked and how you know the company wants to reward and motivate valuable workers. Try to see it from the other person's point of view and be less self-centered.

> **You don't have a second chance** to make a first impression.

4. Do your homework. Go prepared to answer questions, rather than having to tell the listener, "I don't know." And while preparing, know the subject. Act as if you are a reporter and answer the questions who, what, where, when, why, and how.

5. Grab the listener's interest. Find the most interesting, the most dramatic, unusual part of what you want to say. For example, if you are speaking to a group of managers about empowering their subordinates, which of the following grabs you more?

> "We need to delegate more to subordinates and include them in the decision-making process."

> "Every employee working for you wants to contribute to the well-being of the company. We just have to give them that chance."

6. Be concise. Delete superfluous information. Ask yourself: Does the listener really need to know this fact? Does the listener even care? Usually people are less interested in our pet projects than we are and we risk alienating others with too much detail.

7. Speak at the listener's level. Don't go over anyone's head and please do not talk down and patronize. This requires you to do homework on the listener.

8. Ask. Towards the end, you need to make your request. First, though, you must know what, precisely, you want from the listener.

9. Use visualization. Create imagery. Create pictures in the mind of the listener. Research in Bulgaria on "Superlearning" has shown that the more senses are used in a learning situation, the more likely the learner is to really learn the material. When you are speaking to someone, you want them to learn the message, so use imagery. Here's an example:

> "Imagine employees coming to work full of energy as they get out of their cars and briskly walk to their work areas. The adrenaline is pumping and their spirits are up."

10. Pay attention to first impressions. Remember, you don't have a second chance to make a first impression. Refer back to information given in "First Impression, Best Impression," on non-verbals, for those are crucial to making a good first impression, or later impressions, too. This is still a first impression for this message. Eye contact, gestures, voice modulation and speed, posture, body space, facial expressions/smile, and poise all have tremendous impact on your message. In addition, your appearance is important, too. Dress as if this meeting is really important to you. Show the listener you cared enough to make a special effort to look nice. This goes for clothes, hair, jewelry, etc. And you should always look professional, not like a model or a clothes horse.

Assignment:

Create a 45-second presentation, making a point on a topic of your choice. Use the principles listed in the background section. Practice it several times and be very careful not to exceed the 45-second limit. Be prepared to give this presentation to your classmates.

Feedback on 45-Second Presentations

How did the presenter do in terms of:

1. Objective?	6. Concise?
2. Knowing the right person?	7. Listener's level?
3. Right approach?	8. Asking?
4. Homework?	9. Visualization?
5. Grabbing interest?	10. First impressions and non-verbals?

References:

Elsea, Janet, Ph.D., from *The Four-Minute Sell: How to Make a Dynamic First Impression,* Simon and Schuster, 1984. Used with permission.

Frank, Milo O., *How to Get Your Point Across in 30 Seconds or Less,* New York, Pocket Books, 1986.

Chapter 13
Conflict and Negotiation

45. Peace Negotiations: A Conflict Resolution Simulation[1]

Purpose:
1. To examine the interaction of different levels of power.
2. To gain exposure to effective negotiation.
3. To understand the concept of leadership and its impact on decision-making.

Group Size:
15 to 24 players, in teams of three to five members.

Time Required:
One and a half to three hours, including 30 minutes for debriefing.

Context

War has been a daily reality in the Middle East for hundreds of years, but in its present form the conflict has been going on for over 70 years. Hundreds of thousands have lost their lives, and scarce resources that could be used to improve the economy of the region have been redirected to the war effort.

The four Middle Eastern nations below play major roles in the conflict. Historically, they have different political structures and approach the conflict with different leadership styles. The inherent differences among

---

[1]Adapted from "Shalom/Salaam: A Power-Simulation" by Gedaliahu H. Harel and Sandra Morgan, *Simulation and Gaming*, June 1994. Used with permission.

these countries will provide the participants with the opportunity to see the impact of leadership style on the negotiation process.

Israel	*Goal*: To maintain an independent Jewish homeland within secure borders that might include parts of occupied territories (the West Bank, the Gaza Strip, and the Golan Heights). To do so, it must negotiate peace with its neighbors.
Syria	*Goals*: To establish political and military leadership in the Middle East (including political and territorial influence in Lebanon), to regain the Golan Heights from Israel, and to resolve the dilemma of the Palestinians.
Jordan	*Goal:* To eliminate the threats to its sovereignty posed by the aggressive countries around it and by the large number of Palestinians living within it. It will agree to peace with Israel when the Palestinian issue is resolved in a way that both Palestinians and other Arab nations can agree upon.
Palestinians	*Goal*: To acquire an independent, recognized, and secure homeland on territory currently held by Israel, including, at the least, the West Bank – including East Jerusalem – and the Gaza Strip, which is now mainly populated by Palestinians. (Before Israel's 1948 War of Independence, Palestinians owned parts of the current state of Israel.)

Guidelines

Objective

The Arab teams must negotiate with the Israeli team in an attempt to come to a peace agreement.

Preparation

1. The facilitator divides participants into groups of three to five members (each group representing a nation), then chooses four independent observers and assigns each of them to a different team.

2. Each participant (except the observers) contributes an agreed amount to a pot held by the facilitator, thus giving everyone an equal stake in the negotiations. The pot will be redistributed among players at the end of the game, depending on the outcome of the negotiations.

3. A negotiator is chosen for each team, either by the teams themselves or by the facilitator (deciding who can best role-play the designated leadership style). The facilitator instructs each of the negotiators in their required team leadership style; before making agreements with any other team, they must make their decisions in the following way:

Israel:	Democratic style (decisions must be made by majority rule).
Syria:	Autocratic style (decisions must be made by the leader without consulting with other members).
Jordan:	Consultative style (decisions must be made by the leader after consulting separately with each member).
Palestinians:	Consensus style (decisions must be made by consulting all members of the team).

4. Refer to "What to Observe in Groups" in the Appendix.

Negotiations

1. There are three rounds of negotiations between Israel and each Arab nation:

Order of Negotiation	First Round	Second & Third Rounds
Syria/Israel	5 minutes	3 minutes
Palestinians/Israel	5 minutes	3 minutes
Jordan/Israel	5 minutes	3 minutes

2. Before negotiating, teams have 10 minutes to plan their strategies.

3. While two teams are negotiating, the other two must sit separately without communicating (they can, however, plan their strategy for the next round).

4. After the Third Round is completed, the teams go to separate locations to decide on one agreement they are willing to make and how to split up the payoff. They write this on the Agreement Form (in the Appendix) and give it to the facilitator in the negotiation room.

Resolution

1. Of the three possible agreements, only one can be chosen at the end of the negotiations. The facilitator compares Agreement Forms. If any two of them match, the pot is redivided between the two teams involved, according to the matrix below:

If Agreement is Made Between	Amount of Pot Distributed
Syria/Israel	70%
Palestinians/Israel	60%
Jordan/Israel	50%

(This roughly approximates the percentage of the Middle East conflict that each of these agreements could resolve.)

2. If none of the Agreement Forms match, the pot is not redistributed.

Forming Larger Coalitions

1. After a two-party agreement is made, the facilitator allows an additional five minutes of negotiation. The two teams in agreement can negotiate separately with the other two teams.

2. The teams in agreement can decide to bring an additional party into their agreement and divide the difference between the first and second payoff matrices among the three of them. In this case, the matrix below is used:

If Agreement is Made Between	Amount of Pot Distributed
Syria/Israel/Palestinians	90%
Syria/Israel/Jordan	80%
Jordan/Israel/Palestinians	70%

3. After three teams have agreed, they can decide to add the fourth party and divide 100 percent of the remaining money among all four of them.

4. If larger coalitions are formed, the facilitator pays out the additional money. Within each team, the members can work out how the money will be redistributed. If the teams cannot come to any agreement, or there is money left over, the facilitator allows the teams to designate a charity to which the money is given.

Discussion Questions

Leadership Style

How was the negotiator chosen in each team?

How did your negotiator make decisions? Give concrete examples.

What impact did his or her negotiating style (i.e., rigid, flexible, trusting, open) have on the outcome?

Was this style appropriate for the task? If yes, why? If no, what might have worked better?

How did the rest of the team participate in the group decisions?

Group Dynamics

What did negotiators do that encouraged or hurt the development of trust between teams?

What was the impact of team segregation on trust?

What were the communication patterns among members in each team?

Describe the climate in each team (e.g., trust level, openness, energy, anger, feelings).

What supportive behaviors were displayed on the team (e.g., empathy, questioning, freely expressed feelings, consideration, acceptance, providing data and opinions, active listening, all members participating)?

How satisfied were the team members with the process? With their chief negotiator? With their reward/outcome?

What unproductive behaviors were evident (e.g., distrust, guardedness, overpoliteness, defensiveness, fear of criticizing or being criticized)?

How did team members deal with conflict?

Power Differential and Negotiations

What was each team's initial strategy? Did this strategy change over time? If yes, in what direction did it change?

How did the power differential determined by the payoff matrix affect behavior in the negotiations? Team members' feelings about their status? The strategies?

Would you have liked to be on another team? Why or why not?

How can you transfer the learning about power to real-world situations?

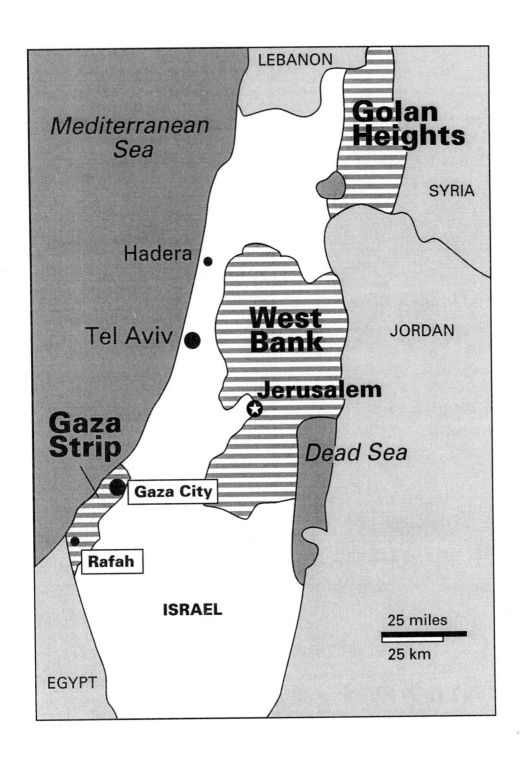

46. LazarRead Ltd.[1]

Purpose:
To explore various techniques in conflict resolution.

Group Size:
Any number.

Time Required:
20-40 minutes.

Other Topics:
Personality Style, Interpersonal Communication

Exercise Schedule

		Unit Time	Total Time
1.	**Pre-class** Students read case and answer questions.		
2.	**Small groups** Groups discuss answers to case questions.	10-20 min	10-20 min
3.	**Class discussion** Instructor leads discussion on issues in case study.	10-20 min	20-40 min

Case Study: _____

LazarRead Ltd.

LazarRead Ltd. (or LL) is a firm that manufactures and sells electronic scanners of various types. The scanners it sells are for a variety of commercial and research uses. The common element of all scanners made by LL is the use of laser technology. The firm was founded in 1977, in Oxnard, California, by Dr. Conrad Wurst, a noted physicist. The firm is a closely held corporation, with Wurst controlling 61 percent of the common stock. Dr. Wurst has many patents to his credit and it is through his creative genius that LL is as successful as it is. Wurst's energy, ambition, and intellect are attributes which help create competitive advantage for LL.

LL operates from three locations: Oxnard, California; Columbia, Missouri; and Wiley Ford, West Virginia. All administrative, marketing, personnel, and other "headquarters"-type functions are located at Oxnard. Manufacturing takes place at all three sites. The firm had sales of $212 million in 1992, and for the preceding nine years, even during periods of national economic recession, LL has earned healthy profits. The firm employs 511 persons, with 186 employed at the Wiley Ford facilities.

---

[1]By Paul Lyons, Frostburg State University. Used with permission.

The Electronic Scanning Equipment Industry

Internationally, there are 17 firms that manufacture electronic scanning equipment, and these firms account for about $1.5 billion in sales annually. This makes LL one of the larger actors in the industry. Only four of the firms use essentially the same basic technology as does LL, and these firms and LL account for about 80 percent of the total sales in the industry. The four firms are located in Austin (Texas), Stockholm, Osaka, and Cape Town. With the interest, world-wide, in quality assurance, inventory management, and information systems, the future for the industry seems bright. Technological breakthroughs are creating many more opportunities for the use of this equipment, as well.

The Wiley Ford, West Virginia, Site

LazarRead Limited's facilities in Wiley Ford were focused on research and design, pre-production engineering, and manufacturing of selected LL products. Of the 186 employees at the facilities, 37 were in the Research and Design Department, 15 were in the Pre-Production Engineering Department, and 134 were engaged in some aspect of manufacturing and inspection of products.

Each of the three areas was directed by a company vice-president. The Research and Design Department (RDD) was led by Eddy Perks. The RDD was sub-divided into three sections – Design, Research, and Development – and each section had a manager. The manager of the design section was Lydia Lakewood. Lydia was in her early 30s and was responsible for all designs of new products and product enhancements. Her section worked very closely with the other two sections, as their work and tasks were highly interdependent. However, the other two sections had members with more technical and advanced education than members of the design section, and they were paid more. Most of the people in the research and development sections were easy-going, reasonable people. They did seem to enjoy the status and prestige differences with regard to the Design section employees. Lydia had been with LL for six years. She had a Master's degree in industrial design from the University of Florida and was regarded by her boss, Perks, as a most capable manager and designer.

In early 1993, it was revealed that the Wiley Ford facilities were to be upgraded. In particular, the RDD was to have completely new facilities, work spaces, equipment, offices, state-of-the-art CAD/CAM, CIM, and furnishings. It was widely rumored throughout the facility that for this upgrade, "money was no object." Lydia was involved in several meetings over the next few months with VP Perks and the other two RDD managers regarding the new facilities. They discussed how tasks and equipment would be arranged, how much space to allocate for different tasks and functions, what specific equipment would be purchased, and the like. Their efforts had a cooperative tone; all seemed to understand the needs and special circumstances of the other parties. Perks gave the managers assurances that they would have the facilities they needed and wanted. Perks had first-hand knowledge of the RDD operations, as he once had been manager of the research section.

> All **seemed** to understand the needs and special circumstances of the other parties.

In addition to the general group meetings Lydia attended with her colleagues, she had a few meetings with the architect who was responsible for all of the detailed plans of the new facilities. Their meetings had been very productive, Lydia thought.

After a meeting in early June at which the architect presented the management group with the final plans and drawings, Lydia felt particularly good. Her section was going to have a lot of improvements in working conditions and in the work environment. She couldn't wait to get into the new facilities. Also, she felt pretty good about her role in this whole matter. She believed that she had been a worthy spokesperson for the nine employees in her section. She called a meeting of the section later in the day and told everyone about how their ideas and needs would be reflected in the new facilities.

About six weeks later, Lydia received a phone message from Eddy Perks' secretary, Binky Davis. Binky said that Eddy wanted each of the managers to come to his office sometime during the next few days, at their convenience, to review, for accuracy, the final, detailed blueprints of the facilities upgrade.

Two hours later Lydia went to the office to review the blueprints. No one else was around. She couldn't believe what she saw in the prints. The whole facility was intact, but her section's part of the facilities had been dramatically changed. The work spaces were smaller, the offices were smaller, some equipment was placed in less than desirable locations, and so on. Some storage spaces had been eliminated altogether. Interestingly, the other two sections seemed to have everything in place on the prints just as they had been discussed six weeks earlier. In fact, these sections had acquired the spaces that Lydia's section held earlier. She was furious. She had never been given any indication by anyone that the plans had changed.

Just at this moment, Eddy stepped into the office. As calmly as she could, Lydia said, "Eddy, these blueprints show that a great deal of space and other things have been cut from my section. What happened?" "Why, Lydia," he said, "you seem surprised. I told you we had to make some changes."

As calmly as she could, Lydia said, "Eddy... what happened?"

Discussion Questions

1. What are the emotions Lydia may experience at this time?

2. What is at stake for Lydia? For Eddy?

3. What should Lydia do?

4. Which conflict-resolution style would be effective? Which would likely be ineffective?

5. (optional) What are some of Lydia's personality characteristics?

6. (optional) How can Lydia's personality help or hurt her in this situation?

7. What principles of interpersonal communication are at work here?

47. Border Dispute[1]

Purpose:
To develop both competitive and collaborative behavior.

Group Size:
Any number of dyads.

Time Required:
50 minutes minimum, 90 minutes preferable.

Preparation Required:
Read the "Context" below.

Related Topics:
Dynamics Within Groups, Dynamics Between Groups

Exercise Schedule

		Unit Time	Total Time
1.	**Introduction**	**5 min**	**5 min**

Read the "Top Secret" Negotiation Information document. See the Appendix for this document and read only the one which applies to your country (i.e., Arak or Barkan).

2.	**Negotiate**	**30+ min**	**35 min**

The teacher will assign you a partner who is from the other country. You must negotiate a solution with your partner in the time period set by the instructor.

3.	**Record agreement**	**5 min**	**40 min**

a. Use treaty form in the Appendix to record your agreement.

b. Use scoring protocol in the Appendix to measure the quality of your agreement.

4.	**Class discussion**	**10+ min**	**50 min**

Instructor will lead a discussion based on the questions at the end of the exercise.

---

[1]By Gary Whitney. Used with permission.

Context: Arakian/Barkanian Border Dispute

There are two developing countries, Arak and Barkan, that have an unresolved border dispute. The result has been continuous squabbling over resource rights and political jurisdiction. The two countries have come together for one last chance at solving the dispute through negotiation. A failure to resolve the border dispute at this last conference will result in war between the two countries. To prevent war, the conference must end with a treaty agreed upon and signed in its entirety.

Background

You have been selected to represent your country at this conference because of your patriotism and grasp of the perilous situation which confronts your country. The future welfare of your country is at stake, and your countrymen are depending upon you to bring about a favorable and honorable solution to the dispute.

Negotiation

The negotiation is scheduled to last 30 minutes. As each minute of the negotiation passes, both of the countries are involved in a costly defense buildup for the possibility of war. If no agreement is reached after 30 minutes, then war will break out.

Treaty

A treaty form is in the Appendix. Complete all the necessary information. The negotiation is not over until the treaty is complete and signed by both negotiators. The treaty must include all details of the agreement.

The Disputed Region

The region is 50 miles wide and 180 miles long and divided into two areas of contention. The region is bounded in the north by Arak and in the south by Barkan. The Blue Ocean borders the region on the west and the nation of Cordan borders the region on the east. The two areas of dispute are:

Area I: Coastal Valley and Mountains

The history of Area I is tumultuous. Many small wars between Arak and Barkan have been waged over this area in the last 100 years because of its rich agricultural and natural resource potential. The area has been alternately owned by Arak and Barkan and as a result is populated by both Arakians and Barkanians. In addition to the valley near the coast, there is a mountainous region with peaks from 3,000 to 6,000 feet high that is heavily forested but sparsely inhabited.

The people who live in Area I have no particular allegiance to either Barkan or Arak, but they do have a strong allegiance to their township. For this reason, the townships shown on the map cannot be subdivided in any way. Presently, Area I is occupied by a United Nations peacekeeping force pending settlement of the negotiations between the two countries.

Area II: Desert Region

This is an arid, uninhabited region. The average annual rainfall is two inches and that comes in one or two storms in the winter.

Discussion Questions

1. How did your definition of the situation affect your behavior?

2. Did running short of time influence your negotiation tactics?

3. Can you be perceptive enough and flexible enough to recognize different kinds of issues and act appropriately?

4. What is the risk of sharing information during negotiations?

5. Would the outcome be different if you had collaborated on Area II before discussing Area I?

6. Can you see the parallels between these negotiations and "real-world" negotiations (e.g., in labor negotiations, wage is usually a competitive issue, while job enrichment is a potentially collaborative issue)?

48. Ugli Orange Case[1]

Purpose:
To practice negotiation skills in a conflict situation.

Group Size:
Any number of groups with three members.

Time Required:
40 minutes.

Related Topics:
Interpersonal Communication

Exercise Schedule

		Unit Time	Total Time
1.	**Groups form**	5 min	5 min

Form groups of three members. One person will be Dr. Roland, one will be Dr. Jones, and the third will be an observer.

		Unit Time	Total Time
2.	**Read roles**	5 min	10 min

Roland and Jones read only their own roles, while the observer reads both.

		Unit Time	Total Time
3.	**Role-play**	10 min	20 min

Instructor announces: "I am Mr./Ms. Cardoza, the owner of the remaining Ugli oranges. My fruit-export firm is based in South America. My country does not have diplomatic relations with your country, although we do have strong trade relations."

Groups spend about 10 minutes meeting with the other firm's representative and decide on a course of action. Be prepared to answer the following questions:

1. What do you plan to do?
2. If you want to buy the oranges, what price will you offer?
3. To whom and how will the oranges be delivered?

		Unit Time	Total Time
4.	**Observers report**	10+ min	30 min

Observers report the solutions reached. Groups describe decision-making process used.

		Unit Time	Total Time
5.	**Class discussion**	10 min	40 min

The instructor will lead a discussion on the exercise, addressing the following questions:

a. Which groups had the most trust? How did that influence behavior?
b. Which groups shared more information? Why?
c. How are trust and disclosure important in negotiations?

---

[1]By Dr. Robert House, University of Toronto. Used with permission.

Role Of "Dr. Jones"

You are Dr. J. W. Jones, a biological research scientist employed by a pharmaceutical firm. You have recently developed a synthetic chemical useful for curing and preventing Rudosen. Rudosen is a disease contracted by pregnant women. If not caught in the first four weeks of pregnancy, the disease causes serious brain, eye, and ear damage to the unborn child. Recently there has been an outbreak of Rudosen in your state, and several thousand women have contracted the disease. You have found, with volunteer patients, that your recently developed synthetic serum cures Rudosen in its early stages. Unfortunately, the serum is made from the juice of the Ugli orange, which is a very rare fruit. Only a small quantity (approximately 4,000) of these oranges were produced last season. No additional Ugli oranges will be available until next season, which will be too late to cure the present Rudosen victims.

You've demonstrated that your synthetic serum is in no way harmful to pregnant women. Consequently, there are no side effects. The Food and Drug Administration has approved production and distribution of the serum as a cure for Rudosen. Unfortunately, the present outbreak was unexpected, and your firm had not planned on having the compound serum available for six months. Your firm holds the patent on the synthetic serum, and it is expected to be a highly profitable product when it is generally available to the public.

You have recently been informed on good evidence that Mr./Ms. R. H. Cardoza, a South American fruit exporter, is in possession of 3,000 Ugli oranges in good condition. If you could obtain the juice of all 3,000, you would be able to both cure present victims and provide sufficient inoculation for the remaining pregnant women in the state. No other state currently has a Rudosen threat.

You have recently been informed that Dr. P. W. Roland is also urgently seeking Ugli oranges and is also aware of Cardoza's possession of the 3,000 available. Dr. Roland is employed by a competing pharmaceutical firm. S/he has been working on biological warfare research for the past several years. There is a great deal of industrial espionage in the pharmaceutical industry. Over the past several years, Dr. Roland's firm and yours have sued each other for infringement of patent rights and espionage law violations several times.

You've been authorized by your firm to approach Cardoza to purchase the 3,000 Ugli oranges. You have been told s/he will sell them to the highest bidder. Your firm has authorized you to bid as high as $250,000 to obtain the juice of the 3,000 available oranges.

You've been **authorized** to purchase the 3,000 Ugli oranges.

Role Of "Dr. Roland"

You are Dr. P. W. Roland. You work as a research biologist for a pharmaceutical firm. The firm is under contract with the government to do research on methods to combat enemy uses of biological warfare.

Recently several World War II experimental nerve gas bombs were moved from the United States to a small island just off the U.S. coast in the Pacific. In the process of transporting them, two of the bombs developed a leak. The leak is presently controlled by government scientists, who believe that the gas will permeate the bomb chambers within two weeks. They know of no method of preventing the gas from getting into the atmosphere and spreading to other islands, and very likely to the West Coast as well. If this occurs, it is likely that several thousand people will incur serious brain damage or die.

You've developed a synthetic vapor that will neutralize the nerve gas if it is injected into the bomb chamber before the gas leaks out. The vapor is made with a chemical taken from the rind of the Ugli orange, a very rare fruit. Unfortunately, only 4,000 of these oranges were produced this season.

You've been informed on good evidence that a Mr./Ms. R. H. Cardoza, a fruit exporter in South America, is in possession of 3,000 Ugli oranges. The chemicals from the rinds of all 3,000 oranges would be sufficient to neutralize the gas if the serum is developed and injected efficiently. You have been informed that the rinds of these oranges are in good condition.

You have also been informed that Dr. J. W. Jones is also urgently seeking purchase of Ugli oranges, and s/he is aware of Cardoza's possession of the 3,000 available. Dr. Jones works for a firm with which your firm is highly competitive. There is a great deal of industrial espionage in the pharmaceutical industry. Over the years, your firm and Dr. Jones' have sued each other for violations of industrial espionage laws and infringement of patent rights several times. Litigation on two suits is still in process.

The federal government has asked your firm for assistance. You've been authorized by your firm to approach Cardoza to purchase the 3,000 Ugli oranges. You have been told s/he will sell them to the highest bidder. Your firm has authorized you to bid as high as $250,000 to obtain the rinds of the oranges.

Before approaching Cardoza, you have decided to talk to Dr. Jones to influence him/her not to prevent you from purchasing the oranges.

You've been **authorized** to purchase the 3,000 Ugli oranges.

49. Management of Differences[1]

Purpose:
To determine which style of conflict resolution students use.

Group Size:
Any number of groups of four to six members.

Time Required:
45 minutes.

Preparation Required:
Complete the inventory.

Exercise Schedule

1.   Preparation (pre-class)
Complete inventory and answer questions in Part II.

		Unit Time	Total Time
2.	**Discussion**	**10 min**	**10 min**

In groups of four to six members, students discuss answers to questions.

3.	**Role-plays**	**20 min**	**30 min**

Groups do one or more role-plays, depending on time available.

4.	**Class discussion**	**15 min**	**45 min**

Instructor leads discussion on the Management of Differences Model and how it is useful in understanding behavior, as well as resolving conflicts. If more time is available, instructor may choose to have some groups perform their role-play for the whole class.

---

[1]From *Management of Differences Inventory (MODI)* by Herbert S. Kindler, Ph.D. May not be duplicated. Used with permission. Inventory booklets are available from Center for Management Effectiveness, P.O. Box 1202, Pacific Palisades, CA 90272. Telephone: 310/459-6052.

Part I

The Inventory

For each pair of statements on the following pages, allocate exactly three points between "a" and "b" to show how frequently you behave as described, using these guidelines:

    3 = very often   1 = occasionally

    2 = moderately often   0 = rarely or never

Use only whole numbers, not fractions. Each pair of scores must add up to 3 exactly.

Example:

In a disagreement, dispute, or difference of view with another:

0.   a. _3_ I set out to win the argument   a. _2_   a. _1_
                                              OR   OR
    b. _0_ I withdraw to check my facts   b. _1_   b. _2_

In a disagreement, dispute, or difference of view with another:

1.   a. __ I let emotions cool before taking decisive action.
    b. __ I find some formula or criteria we both agree on.

2.   a. __ I assert myself to gain what I am after.
    b. __ We jointly develop a mutually agreeable plan that merges both views.

3.   a. __ I continue to follow my view, and the other person continues his or her view.
    b. __ I yield on some points to get my way on others.

4.   a. __ I place more emphasis on similarities and less emphasis on differences.
    b. __ I find logical rules we both agree on as the basis for our decision.

5.   a. __ We take action that lets both parties retain their initial positions, at least on an interim basis.
    b. __ Within agreed-upon limits, I give control to the other person while providing encouragement and support.

6.   a. __ I gain agreement for my position by avoiding details on which we may disagree.
    b. __ I try solutions proposed by the other person.

7.   a. __ I push to have my approach or my ideas prevail.
    b. __ I accept the views of the other person.

8.   a. __ We work out a fair combination of losses and gains for both of us.
    b. __ I encourage both of us to get our concerns in the open, and we problem-solve together.

9.   a. __ I wait until I feel better prepared to take action.
    b. __ After stating my expectations, I encourage the other person to come up with the answer.

10.   a. __ I avoid highly emotional scenes that may detract from the point that I am making.
    b. __ We agree to disagree, at least for a while or on an experimental basis.

11. a. __ I ask the person who disagrees with me to accept my view
         by emphasizing its positive features.
     b. __ I fully express my ideas and feelings, and I urge the other person
         to do the same.

12. a. __ We find a formula to resolve our differences.
     b. __ I find solutions in which gains balance out losses for both parties.

13. a. __ I strive to get my ideas accepted.
     b. __ I express confidence in the other person by allowing him or her,
         within limits, to resolve our issue.

14. a. __ We mutually agree on rules or procedures to resolve our differences.
     b. __ I accommodate myself to the other person's views.

15. a. __ I convince the other person of the merit of my position.
     b. __ We acknowledge and allow each other's differences to exist
         until appropriate means for resolutions become clear.

16. a. __ I accept the views expressed by the other person.
     b. __ We work together to integrate ideas of both persons.

17. a. __ I avoid presenting information likely to hurt the other person's feelings.
     b. __ Within a given framework, I let the other person work out an issue
         while indicating confidence in him or her.

18. a. __ I hold back until the other person initiates the first action steps.
     b. __ We find mutually acceptable middle ground on which
         to resolve our differences.

19. a. __ I delay suggesting changes until I feel confident my views will be accepted.
     b. __ I don't resist complying with the views of the person.

20. a. __ We find mutually agreeable objective procedures (such as taking a vote,
         a lottery, or appropriate test).
     b. __ We find ways to jointly reframe our differences to satisfy both our needs.

21. a. __ I give in on some points if the other person is likely to reciprocate.
     b. __ I state my expectations and concerns and encourage the other person
         to work out a solution.

22. a. __ I show the other person that in the final analysis, our views really
         aren't very different.
     b. __ I give the other person a turn or concession if I believe he or she
         will do the same for me.

23. a. __ I find ways that allow each of us to pursue our individual viewpoints.
     b. __ We find solutions that take both our views fully into account.

24. a. __ I deal with differences only after waiting until I feel the time is right.
     b. __ I act in ways that advance my position.

25. a. __ We let mutually agreeable rules or procedures decide the issue.
     b. __ We find ways in which we can both pursue our respective points of view.

Management of Differences Inventory (cont'd)

26.   a. __ I find ways to accept the other person's views.
       b. __ Given acceptable boundaries, I am willing to have the other person
          deal with our differences while I provide support.

27.   a. __ I persuade the other person of the merit of my position.
       b. __ I establish an objective basis with the other person
          for resolving our differences.

28.   a. __ I place more emphasis on similarities and less emphasis on differences.
       b. __ I find logical rules we both agree on as the basis for our decision.

29.   a. __ We settle our differences by working out a compromise solution.
       b. __ I agree to follow the other person's approach.

30.   a. __ I point out that our differences aren't substantial enough to fight over.
       b. __ I oppose the other person's view.

31.   a. __ I defer making changes until I have adequate support to win my position.
       b. __ We find new perspectives that satisfy both our needs.

32.   a. __ I don't express all the negative possibilities.
       b. __ I get agreement from the other person to live with our differences
          at least for a period of time.

33.   a. __ We jointly agree to accept an objective criterion or the decision of a third party
          as the basis for resolving our differences.
       b. __ Within stated bounds, I encourage and support the other person to take
          the initiative in dealing with our differences.

34.   a. __ I play to win.
       b. __ I make adjustments only when the other person is willing to do the same.

35.   a. __ I urge the other person to take the initiative and, within defined limits,
          I support his or her decision.
       b. __ We integrate and harmonize the ideas expressed by both individuals.

36.   a. __ We agree to follow our separate paths until joint action seems feasible.
       b. __ I accept the other person's idea.

Scoring the Inventory

Total your scores for each dimension using the following guide, then transfer your scores to the appropriate spaces on the following pages to help you interpret them.

A1: Maintenance	1a + 9a + 10a + 18a + 19a + 24a + 28a + 31a	= _____
A2: Smoothing	4a + 6a + 11a + 17a + 22a + 28b + 30a + 32a	= _____
A3: Domination	2a + 7a + 13a + 15a + 24b + 27a + 30b + 34a	= _____
B1: Decision Rule	1b + 4b + 12a + 14a + 20a + 25a + 27b + 33a	= _____
B2: Coexistence	3a + 5a + 10b + 15b + 23a + 25b + 32b + 36a	= _____
B3: Bargaining	3b + 8a + 12b + 18b + 21a + 22b + 29a + 34b	= _____
C1: Non-Resistance	6b + 7b + 14b + 16a + 19b + 26a + 29b + 36b	= _____
C2: Supportive Release	5b + 9b + 13b + 17b + 21b + 26b + 33b + 35a	= _____
C3: Collaboration	2b + 8b + 11b + 16b + 20b + 23b + 31b + 35b	= _____

The inventory brings into focus the two critical dimensions that underlie the management of differences: viewpoint flexibility and interaction intensity. The nine management-of-differences styles indicated below relate to those two dimensions.

Scoring of Flexibility/Interaction Dimensions

If A3 + B3 + C3 is greater than 40, your behavior may be intrusive.

If A1 + B1 + C1 is greater than 40, your behavior may be too aloof.

If A3 + A2 + A1 is greater than 40, your behavior may be too rigid.

If C3 + C2 + C1 is greater than 40, your behavior may be too irresolute.

Understanding Your Scores

A *style* is an automatic reactive behavior. A *strategy* is a deliberate, consciously chosen plan of action. Your effectiveness in dealing with disagreement depends on choosing an appropriate approach from a comprehensive range of possibilities.

To determine if you are over- or under-using available strategies, compare your scores with the mean scores of 225 managers from industry, government, and nonprofit organizations. If any of your scores are 3 or more points below the mean, you may be under-utilizing this particular strategy. If your score is 3 or more points above the mean, you may be over-utilizing this strategy (suggesting an automatic response). If you have scores +/- 3 points (for the statistically minded respondent, one standard deviation is about 3 points), you'll find the following questions helpful in building self-awareness and broadening your repertoire.

Maintenance: Your score_____   **Manager Mean Score = 10.2**

> Low score (7 or less): Do you take enough time to collect vital information?
> High score (13 or more): Do you delay acting to where you're seen as risk-averse?

Smoothing: Your score_____   **Manager Mean Score = 11.6**

> Low score (8 or less): Do you have trouble selling good ideas to others?
> High score (15 or more): Are your selling tactics viewed as heavy-handed
>   or manipulative?

Domination: Your score_____   **Manager Mean Score = 10.7**

> Low score (8 or less): Are you seen as lacking conviction?
> High score (14 or more): Are you seen as pushy, or uncaring of other views?

Decision Rule: Your score_____   **Manager Mean Score = 12.3**

> Low score (9 or less): Do you get too personally involved, even on minor issues?
> High score (15 or more): Are you unwilling to take the heat of personal confrontation?

Coexistence: Your score_____   **Manager Mean Score = 11.9**

> Low score (9 or less): Can you tolerate keeping several balls in the air?
> High score (15 or more): Do you waste time with too many parallel experiments?

Bargaining: Your score_____   **Manager Mean Score = 13.7**

> Low score (11 or less): Are you getting the best deals available?
> High score (17 or more): Do people inflate needs, expecting you
>   to bargain them down?

Non-Resistance: Your score_____   **Manager Mean Score = 10.6**

> Low score (8 or less): Are you seen as uncooperative or not a team player?
> High score (14 or more): Are you overly concerned with ingratiating yourself?

Supportive Release: Your score_____   **Manager Mean Score = 12.2**

> Low score (9 or less): Are you adequately helping others develop their initiative?
> High score (15 or more): To help others mature, are you taking excessive risks?

Collaboration: Your score_____   **Manager Mean Score = 14.8**

> Low score (12 or less): Do you neglect views that diverge from your own?
> High score (18 or more): Do you waste too much time holding meetings?

Reflecting on these difficult questions will help you challenge your reactive patterns and seek strategies that fit the unique needs of each situation appropriately.

A1_____	**B3**_____	**C3**_____	Highly Involved
Domination	**Bargaining**	**Collaboration**	A3 + B3 + C3
You unilaterally induce, persuade, force compliance or resist.	You jointly seek means to split differences, set trade-offs, or take turns	You jointly problem-solve to integrate views.	
A2_____	**B2**_____	**C2**_____	Moderately Involved
Smoothing	**Coexistence**	**Support Release**	A2+B2+C2
You unilaterally accentuate similarities and downplay differences	You jointly establish a basis for both parties to maintain their differences	You unilaterally release the issue, stipulate any limits and provide needed support.	↕ Intensity of Interaction ↕
A1_____	**B1**_____	**C1**_____	Uninvolved
Maintenance	**Decision Rule**	**Non-Resistance**	A1+B1+C1
You unilaterally avoid confronting differences or delay making changes.	You jointly set objective rules that determine how differences will be handled.	You offer no resistance to the other party's views, blending your efforts with theirs.	

↔   Flexibility of Viewpoint   ↔

Firm	Moderately Flexible	Highly Flexible	Total = 108
A1+A2+A3	B1+B2+B3	C1+C2+C3	

Part II

Questions

1. Which was your most dominant style of conflict resolution?

2. Which one of the styles would you like to be able to use more effectively?

3. Think of two bosses you have had. What were their dominant styles?

4. Which styles do you think are most common in organizations?

Part III

Role-Plays

#1 The Troubled Employee

Pat is manager in a state agency and has been proud over the years of his/her ability to run an efficient office. Last year some real difficulties began when an employee from another agency was transferred to Pat's department (as a result of cutbacks in that agency). This new employee, Carl/Carla, goes from being bright and competent to having ideas which could only be described as "windy." To make matters worse, Carl/Carla has severe mood swings. Some days he/she is up and cheerful, and other days he/she is down in the dumps and does everything to bring others down as well. On those days, many employees run for cover, because no one wants to get in Carl/Carla's way and be the object of the usual verbal abuse. In short, Carl/Carla has disrupted the previously harmonious office climate. Carl/Carla has made an appointment with Pat to discuss a problem Carl/Carla is having with another employee, Bill, whom Carl/Carla feels is trying to take over Carl/Carla's job and make him/her look bad. Pat has been frustrated with Carl/Carla, but knows how difficult it is to fire someone. Pat plans to spend some time talking with his/her own boss, Michael, about the matter.

> *Assignment*: One person is assigned as Carl/Carla and three as Pat. The first person should play Pat using the smoothing style. The second person should play Pat using the domination style. The third should play Pat using the collaboration style.

◆

#2 The Performance Evaluation

Marvin/Marjorie is a middle manager who has just received a yearly evaluation, getting a "satisfactory" rating from his/her boss, Chris. This seems quite unfair to Marvin/Marjorie, because s/he has worked extremely hard during the last year and the department has surpassed a number of other departments in several key areas. Marvin/Marjorie has made an appointment with the boss to discuss this matter.

> *Assignment*: One person is assigned as Chris and three as Marvin/Marjorie, using the maintenance, bargaining, and collaboration styles.

◆

#3 The Overspent Budget

George/Georgann, director of sales, has been overspending on his/her voucher limit. Department heads are allowed to spend up to $750 without the boss's (Lyle or Lynn) approval, but the director of sales frequently spends more than that without clearing it with Lyle/Lynn. The sales department has been doing well in the past year, but also has been overspending its total budget. Lyle/Lynn has called the director of sales into his/her office.

> *Assignment*: One person to play George/Georgeann, and three to play Lyle/Lynn, using the non-resistance, domination, and collaboration styles.

◆

#4 The Efficient Secretary

Lou's hard-working and generally efficient secretary, Jan, has recently been bringing in resumes and cover letters to type for his/her unemployed spouse, who has been out of work for six weeks. This has caused the regular work to be backlogged somewhat. Lou has been concerned about this for several weeks but has been hesitant to bring it up because Jan frequently does personal favors for Lou, such as buying presents for the spouse and children, typing letters to personal friends, and picking up dry cleaning. This morning, though, two of Lou's subordinates, who also use Jan, stormed into Lou's office and demanded something be done to get work out faster. Lou called Jan in for a meeting.

> *Assignment*: One person to play Jan, and three to play Lou, using maintenance, bargaining, and collaboration styles.

Note:

Other members of the group not participating in the immediate role-play should act as observers, giving feedback. Look particularly at eye contact, gestures, posture, voice, etc.

Chapter 14
Organizational Culture

50. Organizational Culture Assessment

Purpose:
Option 1:
a. To identify campus norms students hold in common.
b. To identify norms in various organizations.
Option 2:
a. To diagnose organizational cultures in terms of corporate philosophy, valued performance, decision-making, reward system, communications, political system, etc.
b. To classify several organizations using a modified version of the organizational culture typology of Deal and Kennedy (1982).

Group Size:
Any number of groups of three to eight members.

Time Required:
Option 1: 45 minutes in class.
Option 2: 15-30 minutes advance preparation, several hours of preparation out of class, and one class period of at least 50 minutes for reporting and comparing findings.

Preparation Required:
Option 2: Read "Introduction II" and "Corporate Culture Assessment Instrument" below.

Related Topics:
Organization Structure, Values, Leadership

Option 1: Norms Exercise[1]

➤➤ Introduction I

Every organization or social group has a set of norms that help to determine people's behavior. A norm is an unwritten rule for behavior in a group. When it is broken, negative feedback (negative comments, stares, sarcastic statements) is given.

Exercise

As an individual, write down all the norms you can think of now in the following areas:

Dress	Classroom behavior	Dating: Who? How often?
Studying	Eating in cafeteria	Inter-racial? Students/faculty?
Weekend activities		

Option 2: Assessing Organizational Culture[2]

➤➤ Introduction II

Organizational culture is the collection of relatively uniform and enduring beliefs, values, customs, traditions, and practices shared by the organization's members and transmitted from one generation of employees to another. The expectations derived from culture create norms of acceptable behavior and ways of doing things in the organization. An organization's culture is analogous to an individual's personality. Like people, organizations can be described on trait continuum as conservative/experimenting, warm/cold, stable/dynamic, relaxed/tense, uncontrolled/controlled, practical/imaginative, etc. Culture influences the way members of the organization relate to each other as well as their relations with people outside the organization. Culture affects the kinds of goals the organization will pursue and how the organization will pursue them, as well as how workers will be motivated to work toward the goals. The amount, direction, and openness of communication is influenced by organizational culture, as is the style of leadership exercised by supervisors in the organization. The use of rules, standard procedures, and close supervision versus the exercise of individual autonomy in job performance is a function of the organization's culture. Over time, heroes, myths, and rituals that perpetuate the values of the culture emerge and serve to demonstrate and emphasize the way things are done in the organization. Thus behaviors like innovating, decision-making, communicating, organizing, measuring success, and rewarding achievement may vary considerably from organization to organization, and these differences are reflected in the organizational culture.

Organizational culture can be diagnosed by observing the behavior of people at work, by interviewing people inside and outside the organization, and by questionnaires. In this exercise, you will be asked to investigate the culture of your university or organization, to compare your findings to those of other investigators, and to classify the organization into one of four types, or a combination of the four types, identified by previous research.

To diagnose the culture of your chosen organization, you may observe people's behavior, ask questions, and administer questionnaires. The following list of questions may be useful in conducting your diagnosis.

---

[1] © 1985 by Dorothy Marcic. All rights reserved.
[2] By John E. Oliver. Used with permission.

Corporate Culture Assessment Instrument[3]

Ratings
1 – ??? Don't know
2 – Not a factor
3 – Low: Done infrequently, little recognition
4 – Some importance - in regularity or recognition
5 – Important: ingrained, valued or behavior guide

A. Common Elements

1. Corporate philosophy, policy
    Organization's tone or climate
    "Who we are" and "what we are
    are trying to do and
    what we stand for"
    Clarity of corporate mission
    or objectives

2. Valued performance features
    and behaviors
    Competitiveness, assertiveness,
    aggressiveness
    Demonstrated company loyalty, act
    of organizational commitment
    "Macho," stoic, "hanging-in"
    Productivity, performance
    ratings, workaholism
    Control of resources, information
    Valued departmental assignments

3. Decision-making
    Centralization/decentralization
    Factors considered
    Degree of support documentation
    Scope of participation

4. Organization's reward system
    Management by objectives,
    accomplishments
    Performance appraisal ratings
    Assessments of potential
    Wage/salary increases, bonuses
    Internal recognition
    (communications, ceremonials)

5. Sponsorship
    "Adoption" by power figure
    Expert guidance
    Having a home department

6. Mentoring
    Guidance/counseling by key person

7. Career ladders
    Knowledge of valued routes
    Qualifications to "enter"
    valued career routes
    How to navigate valued routes

---

[3]From Elmer Burack, *Creative Human Resource Planning and Application: A Strategic Approach.* Englewood Cliffs, N.J.: Prentice Hall, 1988. Used with permission.

Corporate Culture Assessment Instrument (cont'd)

8. Social networking
    Acquaintance with key, power,
    or in-group figure(s)
    Part of recognized "old boy" or
    "old girl" network
    Support of "favored" charities
    Participation in selected sports/
    recreation activities

9. Dress, mannerisms, personal
    features, education
    Type of dress
    Posturing that is recognized/valued
    Knowing when to take a position
    or to "back off" (be flexible)
    Age, physical size
    Education: type of degree, school

10. Political system
    Knowledge of the key "actors"
    and their areas of influence
    Who has the power and the basis for it
    How is the power asserted, what
    is its influence on decisions (e.g.,
    succession, recruiting, selection)

B.   Comprehensiveness and Social Integration

1. Extent to which the "common
    elements (A)" are identifiable by
    corporate leadership

2. Extent to which formal corporate
    communications feature regular,
    "cultural" elements

3. Extent to which informal corporate
    and organizational communications
    include culture elements

4. Consistency with which values and
    desired aspects of behavior have
    been transmitted to incoming and
    successive generations of managers
    and corporate leaders

5. Extent to which "culture" elements are seen
    as well as working (adequately) well

6. Consistency with which elements
    of supervisory and managerial
    decision/behavioral patterns
    reflect "culture" (elements) –
    thereby, serving as models of behavior

Exercise Schedule

		Unit Time	Total Time
1.	**Introduction**	**15+ min**	**15 min**

(15-30 minutes – at least one week in advance)

The group is divided into sub-groups of three to eight people. The "Introduction" and "Corporate Culture Assessment Instrument" are read and discussed.

2.   Approximately three hours outside of class

Participants must select an organization to diagnose. Depending on what the instructor assigns, it may be your university or it may be an organization in which a participant works or has worked.

Participants try to answer the questions on the "Corporate Culture Assessment Instrument" by observing and questioning the members and clients of the organization. The answers are then used to classify the organization into one or a combination of the four types described on the "Organizational Culture Profiles" at the end of the section.

		Unit Time	Total Time
3.	**Group presentations**	**50 min**	**50 min**

In class, the "Organizational Culture Profiles" are discussed and participants are asked to classify the organizational culture that they studied into one or a combination of the four types. Each sub-group is allowed five minutes to discuss their culture and its classification, giving examples to support their conclusions.

Discussion Questions

1. What internal forces cause organizations to develop unique cultures?

2. What external (environmental) forces cause organizations to develop unique cultures?

3. How does organizational culture affect the behavior of individuals in the organization?

4. What are the dangers of organizational cultures?

5. How might organizational culture affect an organization's ability to change?

6. How might organizational culture affect personnel selection and promotion?

Organizational Cultural Profiles[4]

Name of the culture	Driving	Outgoing	Specialist	Control
Type of risks that are assumed:	High	Low	High	Low
Type of feedback from decisions:	Fast	Fast	Slow	Slow
The ways survivors and/or heroes in this culture behave	They have a tough attitude. They are individualistic. They can tolerate all-or-nothing risks.	They are super salespeople. They are often friendly, hail-fellow-well-met types. They use a team approach to problem-solving. They are non-superstitious.	They can endure long-term ambiguity. They always double-check their decisions. They are technically competent. They have a strong respect for authority.	They are very cautious and protective of their own flank. They are orderly and punctual. They are good at attending to detail. They always follow set procedures.
Strengths of the personnel/culture	They can get things done in short order.	They are able to quickly produce a high volume of work.	They can generate high-quality inventions and major scientific breakthroughs.	They bring order and systems to the work place.
Weaknesses of the personnel/culture	They do not learn from past mistakes. Everything tends to be short-term in orientation. The virtues of cooperation are ignored.	They look for quick-fix solutions. They have short-term time perspective and are more committed to action than to problem-solving.	They are extremely slow in getting things done, are vulnerable to short-term economic fluctuations and often face cash-flow problems.	There is lots of red tape. Initiative is downplayed. They work long hours.
Habits of the survivors and/or heroes	They dress in fashion. They live in "in" places. They like one-on-one sports such as tennis. They enjoy scoring points off one another in verbal interaction.	They avoid extremes in dress. They live in neighborhoods. They prefer team sports such as football. They socialize together.	They dress according to their organizational rank. Their housing matches their hierarchical positions. They like sports such as golf, in which the outcome is unclear until the end of the game.	They dress according to hierarchical rank. They live in apartments or no-frills homes. They enjoy process sports like jogging and swimming. They like discussing systems.
Typical kinds of organizations that use this culture	Construction, cosmetics, television, radio, venture capitalism, management consulting.	Real estate, computer firms, auto distributors, door-to-door sales operations, retail stores, mass consumer sales.	Oil, aerospace, capital goods manufacturers, architectural firms, investment banks, mining and smelting firms, military.	Banks, insurance companies, utilities, pharmaceuticals, financial services firms, many agencies of the government.

[4]Adapted from Terrence E. Deal and Allen A. Kennedy, *Corporate Cultures: The Rites and Rituals of Corporate Life.* Reading, Mass.: Addison-Wesley, 1982, Chapter 6. Used with permission.

51. Caught Between Corporate Cultures[1]

Purpose:
To analyze organizational culture issues.

Group Size:
Any number of groups of five to eight members.

Time Required:
30 minutes or more.

Preparation Required:
Read the "Consolidated Life" case study and answer questions.

Related Topics:
Leadership, Communication, Power

Exercise Schedule

1. **Preparation (pre-class)**
   Read the case study and answer questions.

		Unit Time	Total Time
2.	**Group discussion**	**15+ min**	**15 min**
3.	**Class discussion**	**15+ min**	**30 min**

Case Study: _____

Consolidated Life: Part I

It all started so positively. Three days after graduating with his degree in business administration, Mike Wilson started his first day at a prestigious insurance company, Consolidated Life. He worked in the Policy Issue Department. The work of the department was mostly clerical and did not require a high degree of technical knowledge. Given the repetitive and mundane nature of the work, the successful worker had to be consistent and willing to grind out paperwork.

Rick Belkner was the division's vice-president, "the man in charge" at the time. Rick was an actuary by training, a technical professional whose leadership style was laissez-faire. He was described in the division as "the mirror of whomever was the strongest personality around him." It was also common knowledge that Rick made $60,000 a year while he spent his time doing crossword puzzles.

---

[1] Adapted from Terrence E. Deal and Allen A. Kennedy, *Corporate Cultures: The Rites and Rituals of Corporate Life,* © 1982 by Addison-Wesley Publishing Co. Reprinted by permission of Addison-Wesley Publishing Co., Reading, Mass.

Mike was hired as a management trainee and promised a supervisory assignment within a year. However, because of a management reorganization, it was only six weeks before he was placed in charge of an eight-person unit.

The reorganization was intended to streamline workflow, upgrade and combine the clerical jobs, and make greater use of the computer system. It was a drastic departure from the old way of doing things and created a great deal of animosity and anxiety among the clerical staff.

Management realized that a flexible supervisory style was necessary to pull off the reorganization without immense turnover, so they gave their supervisors a free hand to run their units as they saw fit. Mike used this latitude to implement group meetings and training classes in his unit. In addition, he assured all members raises if they worked hard to attain them. By working long hours, participating in the mundane tasks with his unit, and being flexible in his management style, he was able to increase productivity, reduce errors, and reduce lost time. Things improved so dramatically that he was noticed by upper management and earned a reputation as a "superstar," despite being viewed as free-spirited and unorthodox. The feeling was that his loose, people-oriented management style could be tolerated because his results were excellent.

> His style was tolerated because his **results were excellent.**

A Chance for Advancement. After a year, Mike received an offer from a different Consolidated Life division located across town. Mike was asked to manage an office in the marketing area. The pay was excellent and it offered an opportunity to turn around an office in disarray. The reorganization in his present division at Consolidated was almost complete, and most of his mentors and friends in management had moved on to other jobs. Mike decided to accept the offer.

In his exit interview he was assured that if he ever wanted to return, a position would be made for him. It was clear that he was held in high regard by management and staff alike. A huge party was thrown to send him off.

The new job was satisfying for a short time, but it became apparent to Mike that it did not have the long-term potential he was promised. After bringing on a new staff, computerizing the office, and auditing the books, he began looking for a position that would both challenge him and give him the autonomy he needed to be successful.

Eventually word got back to his former vice-president at Consolidated Life, Rick Belkner, that Mike was looking for another job. Rick offered Mike a position with the same pay he was now receiving and control over a 14-person unit in his old division. After considering other options, Mike decided to return to his old division, feeling that he would be able to progress steadily over the next several years.

Enter Jack Greely: Return Mike Wilson. Upon his return to Consolidated Life, Mike became aware of several changes that had taken place in the six months since his departure. The most important change was the hiring of a new divisional senior vice-president, Jack Greely. Jack had been given total authority to run the division. Rick Belkner now reported to Jack.

Jack's reputation was that he was tough but fair. It was necessary for people in Jack's division to do things his way and "get the work out."

Mike also found himself reporting to one of his former peers, Kathy Miller, who had been promoted to manager during the reorganization. Mike had always "hit it off" with Kathy and foresaw no problem in working with her.

After a week Mike realized the extent of the changes that had occurred. Gone was the loose, casual atmosphere that had marked his first tour in the division. Now, a stricter, task-oriented management doctrine was practiced. Morale of the supervisory staff had decreased to an alarming level. Jack Greely was the major topic of conversation in and around the division. People joked that MBO now meant "management by oppression."

Mike was greeted back with comments like "Welcome to prison!" and "Why would you come back here? You must be desperate!" It seemed like everyone was looking for new jobs or transfers. Their lack of desire was reflected in the poor quality of work being done.

Mike's Idea: Supervisor's Forum. Mike felt that a change in the management style of his boss was necessary in order to improve a frustrating situation. Realizing that it would be difficult to affect his style directly, Mike requested permission from Rick Belkner to form a Supervisor's Forum for all the managers on Mike's level in the division. Mike explained that the purpose would be to enhance the existing management-training program. The Forum would include weekly meetings, guest speakers, and discussions of topics relevant to the division and the industry. Mike thought the forum would show Greely that he was serious about both his job and improving morale in the division. Rick gave the okay for an initial meeting.

The meeting took place and 10 supervisors who were Mike's peers in the company eagerly took the opportunity to "Blue Sky" it. There was a euphoric attitude about the group as they drafted their statement of intent. It read as follows:

To: Rick Belkner
From: New Issue Services Supervisors
Subject: Supervisors' Forum

On Thursday, June 11, the Supervisors' Forum held its first meeting. The objective of the meeting was to identify common areas of concern among us and to determine topics that we might be interested in pursuing.

The first area addressed was the void that we perceive exists in the management-training program. As a result of conditions beyond anyone's control, many of us over the past year have held supervisory duties without the benefit of formal training or proper experience. Therefore, what we propose is that we utilize the Supervisors' Forum as a vehicle by which to enhance the existing management-training program. The areas that we hope to affect with this supplemental training are: a) morale/job satisfaction; b) quality of work and service; c) productivity; and d) management expertise as it relates to the life insurance industry. With these objectives in mind, we have outlined below a list of possible activities that we would like to pursue.

1. Further utilization of the existing "in-house" training programs provided for manager trainees and supervisors, i.e., Introduction to Supervision, E.E.O., and Coaching and Counseling.

2. A series of speakers from various sections in the company. This would help expose us to the technical aspects of their departments and their managerial style.

3. Invitations to outside speakers to address the Forum on management topics such as managerial development, organizational structure and behavior, business policy, and the insurance industry. Suggested speakers could be area college professors, consultants, and state insurance officials.

4. Outside training and visits to the field. This could include attendance at seminars concerning management theory and development relative to the insurance industry. Attached is a representative sample of a program we would like to have considered in the future.

In conclusion, we hope that this memo clearly illustrates what we are attempting to accomplish with this program. It is our hope that the above outline will be able to give the Forum credibility and establish it as an effective tool for all levels of management within New Issue. By supplementing our on-the-job training with a series of speakers and classes, we aim to develop prospective management personnel with a broad perspective of both the life insurance industry and management's role in it. Also, we would like to extend an invitation to the underwriters to attend any programs at which the topic of the speaker might be of interest to them.

cc: J. Greely
      Managers

The group felt the memo accurately and diplomatically stated their dissatisfaction with the current situation. However, they pondered what the results of their actions would be and what else they could have done.

Part II

An emergency management meeting was called by Rick Belkner at Jack Greely's request to address the "union" being formed by the supervisors. Four general managers, Rick Belkner, and Jack Greely were at that meeting. During the meeting it was suggested the Forum be disbanded to "put them in their place." However, Rick Belkner felt that if "guided" in the proper direction, the Forum could die from lack of interest. His stance was adopted but it was common knowledge that Jack Greely was strongly opposed to the group and wanted its founders dealt with. His comment was: "It's not a democracy and they're not a union. If they don't like it here, then they can leave." A campaign was directed by the managers to determine who the main authors of the memo were so they could be dealt with.

> "If they don't like it here, **then they can leave."**

About this time, Mike's unit had made a mistake on a case, which Jack Greely was embarrassed to admit to his boss. This embarrassment was more than Jack Greely cared to take from Mike Wilson. At the managers' staff meeting that day, Jack stormed in and declared that the next supervisor to "screw up" was out the door. He would permit no more embarrassments of his division and repeated his earlier statement about "people leaving if they didn't like it here." It was clear to Mike and everyone else present that Mike Wilson was a marked man.

Mike had always been a loose, amiable supervisor. The major reason his units had been successful was the attention he paid to each individual and how they interacted with the group. He had a reputation for fairness, was seen as an excellent judge of personnel for new positions, and was noted for his ability to turn around people who had been in trouble. He motivated people through a dynamic, personable style and was noted for his general lack of regard for rules. He treated rules as obstacles to management and usually used his own discretion as to what was important. His office had a sign saying: "Any fool can manage by rules. It takes an uncommon man to manage without any." It was an approach that flew in the face of company policy, but it had been overlooked in the past because of his results. However, because of Mike's actions with the Supervisor's Forum, he was now regarded as a thorn in the side, not a superstar, and his oddball style only made things worse.

Faced with the fact that he was rumored to be out the door, Mike appraised the situation.

Part III

Mike decided on the following course of action:

1.   Keep the Forum alive but moderate its tone so it didn't step on Jack Greely's toes.

2.   Don't panic. Simply outwork and outsmart the rest of the division. This plan included a massive retraining and remotivation of his personnel. He implemented weekly meetings, cross-training with other divisions, and a lot of interpersonal "stroking" to motivate the group.

3.   Evoke praise from vendors and customers through excellent service and direct that praise to Jack Greely.

The results after eight months were impressive. Mike's unit improved the speed of processing 60 percent and lowered errors 75 percent. His staff became the most highly trained in the division. Mike had a file of several letters to Jack Greely that praised the unit's excellent service. In addition, the Supervisor's Forum had grudgingly attained credibility, although the scope of activity was restricted. Mike had even improved to the point of submitting reports on time as a concession to management.

Mike was confident that the results would speak for themselves. However, one month before his scheduled promotion and one month after an excellent merit raise in recognition of his exceptional work record, he was called into his supervisor's, Kathy Miller's, office. She informed him that after long and careful consideration the decision had been made to deny his promotion because of his lack of attention to detail. This did not mean he was not a good supervisor, just that he needed to follow more instead of taking the lead. Mike was stunned and said so. But before he said anything else, he asked to see Rick Belkner and Jack Greely the next day.

The Showdown. Sitting face to face with Rick and Jack, Mike asked if they agreed with the appraisal Kathy had discussed with him. They both said they did. When asked if any other supervisor surpassed his ability and results, each stated Mike was one of the best – if not the best – they had. Then why, Mike asked, would they deny him a promotion when others of less ability were approved. The answer came from Jack: "It's nothing personal, but we just don't like you. We don't like your management style. You're an oddball. We can't run a division with 10 supervisors all doing different things. What kind of business do you think we're running here? We need people who conform to our style and methods so we can measure their results objectively. There is no room for subjective interpretation. It's our feeling that if you really put your mind to it, you can be an excellent manager. It's just that you now create trouble and rock the boat. We don't need that. It doesn't matter if you're the best now, sooner or later as you go up the ladder, you will be forced to pay more attention to administrative duties and you won't handle them well. If we correct your bad habits now, we think you can go far."

Mike was shocked. He turned to face Rick and blurted out nervously, "You mean it doesn't matter what my results are? All that matters is how I do things?" Rick leaned back in his chair and said in a casual tone, "In so many words, yes."

Mike left the office knowing that his career at Consolidated was over, and immediately started looking for a new job.

What went wrong?

> **"We don't like your management style.** You're an oddball.

Epilogue

After leaving Consolidated Life, Mike Wilson started his own insurance sales and consulting firm, which specialized in providing corporate-risk managers with insurance protection and claims-settlement strategies. He works with a staff assistant and one other associate. After three years, sales averaged over $7 million annually, netting approximately $125,000 to $175,000 before taxes to Mike Wilson.

During a return visit to Consolidated Life, three years after his departure, Mike found Rick Belkner and Jack Greely still in charge of the division in which Mike had worked. The division's size had shrunk by 50 percent. All of the members of the old Supervisor's Forum had left. The reason for the decrease in the division's size was that computerization had removed many of the people's tasks.

Discussion Questions

1. Describe the culture of Consolidated Life under Jack Greely.

2. What value conflicts existed between Wilson and Greely? Could these have been resolved?

3. Compare the leadership styles of Wilson and Greely. Which was most appropriate for the situation?

4. How could group dynamics help explain what happened in this case?

5. What were the power relationships between the major parties?

Chapter 15

Power and Political Behavior

52. Empowerment Questionnaires and Exercise

Purpose:
1. To measure levels of empowerment.
2. To apply French and Raven's power model.

Group Size:
Any number of groups of five to eight members.

Time Required:
15-55 minutes or more.

Preparation Required:
Complete questionnaires for Parts A and B.

Related Topics:
Assertiveness, Dynamics Within Groups, Interpersonal Relationships

Exercise Schedule

Parts A and B – Empowerment Questionnaires

1. **Preparation**

   Complete and score Empowerment (Others) and Empowerment (Self) Instruments (Parts A and B, below) and fill out checklists under "Empowerment" section. Read the analysis of scoring.

		Unit Time	*Total Time*
2.	**Class discussion**	**15 min**	**15 min**

The instructor will lead a discussion on the empowerment of individuals and how it is impacted by organizations.

Part A

IDEA – Identifying Dimensions for Empowering Actions[1]

IDEA gives you, as a manager, an opportunity to identify and examine your strengths and development needs in 16 new dimensions of management. It is not intended to measure behaviors which fall under traditional management functions. Instead, it concentrates on non-traditional management roles. These may be found in organizations which are redesigned to include more empowered workers, self-directed work teams, flatter organizational structures, etc.

The feedback from this instrument is completely self-assessed and self-generated. It will help you identify where you need to concentrate your efforts to become a more effective manager in an empowering organization.

Answer the questions honestly. Examine your own actual behavior before marking each question.

Instructions

1. Read the following sixteen skill dimensions and under each one, identify and record a specific activity or task from your job which illustrates it.

2. Once you have read each dimension and recorded an activity to the **IDEA** instrument, complete the left column by rating your current practice/proficiency in each dimension (5 = High : 1=Low).

3. Next, in the right hand column, rate the importance of these new dimensions to your organization (High, Medium, Low). Theory would suggest that all sixteen dimensions should be rated "High" in an empowering work environment. Please be realistic in your assessment of what dimensions your organization values. It may be helpful, with the organization's values and practices in mind, to review the examples you recorded under each dimension.

4. The **IDEA** instrument is designed to give you immediate feedback to help you create an action plan to become a more effective manager in a redesigned work environment. Empowering skill dimensions which need development can be determined by finding the dimensions with scores "to the right." If you selected "Highly important" to "Organization" but gave yourself a low practice/proficiency score, this would be a developmental dimension.

    Your developmental plan should:

    ✓   review current activities and behaviors.

    ✓   identify resources (people, money, projects) to help you.

    ✓   establish a timeline which incorporates monitoring checkpoints.

---

[1]© 1991 by Kent Wilson Jones Company. All rights reserved. Used with permission.

IDEA: 16 Skill Dimensions

Knows the Business

1. Facilitates management functions: Assigns responsibilities; delegates; empowers others to perform their responsibilities; provides resources and coordinates the management of those resources; removes anything in the way of getting the work done; coordinates the work of the team when necessary; monitors the progress of team members.

   job activity/behavior example: _____

2. Fosters common vision: Works with the team to develop a common vision; provides clear direction and assists in setting team priorities; clarifies roles and responsibilities of team members.

   job activity/behavior example: _____

3. Understands politics of the new organization: Understands what is important to others; gives and takes when working with others and develops effective and important relationships in the organization; knows which issues are critical to the group and when to take a stand; balances what is in the best interest of one's own group with the needs of the broader organization.

   job activity/behavior example: _____

4. Access resources: Technically and functionally knowledgeable about profession and industry; keeps technical/industry knowledge up-to-date; identifies, evaluates, uses other expert resources when necessary.

   job activity/behavior example: _____

5. Understands the industry/organization: Understands current issues relevant to the industry and broad organization; possesses broad range of knowledge.

   job activity/behavior example: _____

Leads and Facilitates Others

6. Leads with conviction: Is recognized as a courageous leader; addresses difficult issues and problems; defends points of view and does not back down when necessary.

   job activity/behavior example: _____

7. Advocates change: Challenges tradition and advocates as change agent; encourages, supports others in change; readies organization, paves way for positive change; implements change effectively.

   job activity/behavior example: _____

8. Demonstrates flexibility: Manages multiple demands, changing priorities, and unanticipated change; shows stability in adverse situations; demonstrates adaptability.

   job activity/behavior example: _____

Communicates Effectively

9. Influences others: Offers own ideas and influences others; gains commitment and support of others; creates an environment where others are mobilized to take action.

   job activity/behavior example: _____

10. Develops relationships: Builds relationships with others as a priority; expresses sincere interest in the problems and concerns of others; relates to others in a friendly, open and accepting way.

    job activity/behavior example: _____

11. Deals with adversity: Brings important, meaningful disagreements/conflicts into open with attempts to resolve non-adversarially; uses consensus in decision-making and problem-solving.

    job activity/behavior example: _____

12. Encourages open communication: Supports and facilitates the open expression of opinions and ideas; fosters an environment where high quality information is exchanged in a timely manner.

    job activity/behavior example: _____

IDEA: 16 Skill Dimensions (cont'd)

13. Practices effective listening: Attends to and conveys understanding of the conversations of others; listens as part of a group playing the appropriate role; responds to questions appropriately.
    job activity/behavior example: _____

Demonstrates Team Skills

14. Encourages collaboration: Fosters teamwork by building effective teams committed to the goals of the organization; champions collaborative relationships among team members and among teams; allows and encourages teams to address important issues.
    job activity/behavior example: _____

15. Creates atmosphere for excellence: Empowers others; encourages others to meet and exceed challenging performance standards, and feel ownership of the work and commitment to the organization as a whole.
    job activity/behavior example: _____

16. Helping others develop and grow: Accesses strengths and development needs of team members; gives specific feedback in a timely manner; provides challenging assignments and opportunities for personal growth and development; develops a helpful, supportive coaching style.
    job activity/behavior example: _____

IDEA   Identify Dimensions for Empowering Actions

SELF Practice/Proficiency		Skill Dimensions	ORGANIZATION Values/Importance		
5 4 3 2 1	1.	Facilitates Management Functions	Low	Medium	High
5 4 3 2 1	2.	Fosters Common Vision	Low	Medium	High
5 4 3 2 1	3.	Understands Politics of the New Organization	Low	Medium	High
5 4 3 2 1	4.	Accesses Resources	Low	Medium	High
5 4 3 2 1	5.	Understands the Industry/Org.	Low	Medium	High
5 4 3 2 1	6.	Leads with Conviction	Low	Medium	High
5 4 3 2 1	7.	Advocates Change	Low	Medium	High
5 4 3 2 1	8.	Demonstrates Flexibility	Low	Medium	High
5 4 3 2 1	9.	Influences Others	Low	Medium	High
5 4 3 2 1	10.	Develops Relationships	Low	Medium	High
5 4 3 2 1	11.	Deals with Adversity	Low	Medium	High
5 4 3 2 1	12.	Encourages Open Communication	Low	Medium	High
5 4 3 2 1	13.	Practices Effective Listening	Low	Medium	High
5 4 3 2 1	14.	Encourages Collaboration	Low	Medium	High
5 4 3 2 1	15.	Creates Atmosphere for Excellence	Low	Medium	High
5 4 3 2 1	16.	Helping Others Grow and Develop	Low	Medium	High

5 = High : 1 = Low

The IDEA Wheel

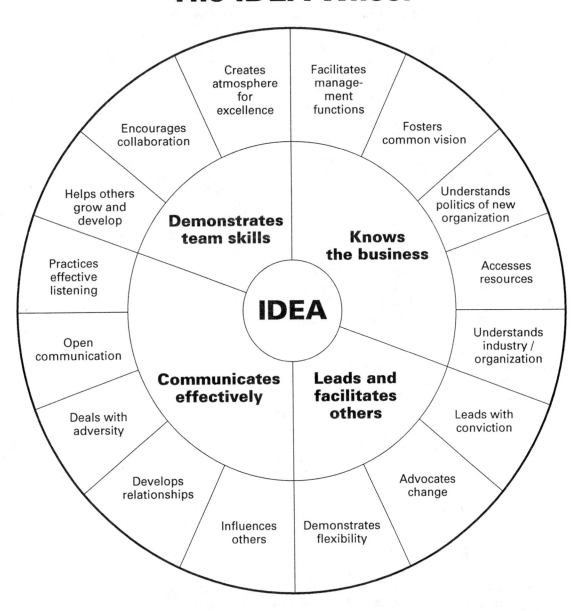

The Kent Wilson Jones Company

Part B

Empowerment (Self) Instrument[2]

Check either A or B to indicate how you usually are in these situations:

1.   If someone disagrees with me in a class or a meeting, I
     a. immediately back down.
     b. explain my position further.
2.   When I have an idea for a project I
     a. typically take a great deal of time to start it.
     b. get going on it fairly quickly.
3.   If my boss or teacher tells me to do something that I think is wrong I
     a. do it anyway, telling myself he or she is "the boss."
     b. ask for clarification and explain my position.
4.   When a complicated problem arises, I usually tell myself
     a. I can take care of it.
     b. I will not be able to solve it.
5.   When I am around people of higher authority, I often
     a. feel intimidated and defer to them.
     b. enjoy meeting important people.
6.   As I awake in the morning, I usually feel
     a. alert and ready to conquer almost anything.
     b. tired and have a hard time getting myself motivated.
7.   During an argument I
     a. put a great deal of energy into "winning."
     b. try to listen to the other side and see if we have any points of agreement.
8.   When I meet new people I
     a. always wonder what they are "really" up to.
     b. try to learn about them and give them the benefit of the doubt until they prove otherwise.
9.   During the day I often
     a. criticize myself on what I am doing or thinking.
     b. think positive thoughts about myself.
10. When someone else does a great job I
     a. find myself picking apart that person and looking for faults.
     b. often give a sincere compliment.
11. When I am working in a group, I try to
     a. do a better job than the others.
     b. help the group function more effectively.
12. If someone pays me a compliment I typically
     a. try not to appear boastful and I downplay the compliment.
     b. respond with a positive "thank you" or similar response.

---

13. I like to be around people who
    a. challenge me and make me question what I do.
    b. give me respect.
14. In love relationships I prefer the other person
    a. have his/her own selected interests.
    b. do pretty much what I do.
15. During a crisis I try to
    a. resolve the problem.
    b. find someone to blame.
16. After seeing a movie with friends I
    a. wait to see what they say before I decide whether I liked it.
    b. am ready to talk about my reactions right away.
17. When work deadlines are approaching I typically
    a. get flustered and worry about completion.
    b. buckle down and work until the job is done.
18. If a job comes up I am interested in I
    a. go for it and apply.
    b. tell myself I am not qualified enough.
19. When someone treats me unkindly or unfairly I
    a. try to rectify the situation.
    b. tell other people about the injustice.
20. If a difficult conflict situation or problem arises, I
    a. try not to think about it, hoping it will resolve itself.
    b. look at various options and may ask others for advice before I figure out what to do.

Scoring:

Score one point for each of the following circled:

1b, 2b, 3b, 4a, 5b, 6a, 7b, 8b, 9b, 10b, 11b, 12b, 13a, 14a, 15a, 16b, 17b, 18a, 19a, 20b

Analysis of Scoring

16-20 —You are a take-charge person and generally make the most of opportunities. When others tell you something cannot be done, you may take this as a challenge and do it anyway. You see the world as an oyster with many pearls to harvest.

11-15 — You try hard, but sometimes your negative attitude prevents you from getting involved in productive projects. Many times you take responsibility, but there are situations where you look to others to take care of problems.

0-10 — You complain too much and are usually focused on the "worst case scenario." To you the world is controlled by fate and no matter what you do it seems to get you nowhere, so you let other people develop opportunities. You need to start seeing the positive qualities in yourself and in others and see yourself as the "master of your fate."

Empowerment

A word that is more tuned into the teamwork concept is empowerment, since it does not assume dominance over others. Empowerment means that you feel more able to reach your goals and work with those around you. All of us can remember times when we felt extremely powerless and dependent. We hate situations that make us feel we are returning to that state. Along with a feeling of empowerment comes a sense of mastery over the tasks at hand and a sense of future success in interpersonal relationships.

Most of us can think of times when we felt on top of the world. Whatever was at hand, we could manage it. We could tough it out. That's what it feels like to be empowered.

Empowerment comes from the inside. It comes from self-confidence, liking yourself, and determination to get the job done. These are qualities that you can develop.

If you feel that your self-confidence is low, you can work on that. One way is to give yourself affirmations – to notice what is good about yourself. For a start, list below the ten thing you like best about yourself.

1.

2.

3.

4.

5.

6.

7.

8.

9.

10.

Did you find that hard to do? If asked to list ten things you *didn't* like about yourself, you probably would have had an easier time. That just shows how used we are to looking at ourselves negatively. And that only chips away at our self esteem and lessens our personal power.

Keep reminding yourself of your good qualities. It's not bragging or boasting: it's just appreciating yourself. And unless you like yourself, you're not going to be able to like other people, either.

People who feel secure within themselves and empowered have less need to dominate others and can cooperate more easily. Below is an exercise to help you understand under what conditions you feel powerful or powerless. Complete the sentences and then re-read your answers. Do you notice patterns?

While doing this inventory, keep your frame of mind in the workplace. It will be natural for some of you to focus on your personal relationships. You'll have a chance to do that in a later chapter. For now, though, think of your co-workers when you fill in the statements on the next few pages.

Answer the following questions/statements.

1. I feel powerless when _____ .

2. I feel powerful when_____ .

3. People I hold the most power or control over are_____ .

4. People who exert the most power or control over me are _____ .

5. I feel intimidated when _____ .

6. I am intimidating when _____ .

7. It's easy for me to cooperate with _____(name) and _____(name) when

    _____ .

8. I'm afraid of cooperation because _____ .

9. I don't trust _____(names) because _____

    _____ .

10. It's easy for me to trust _____(names) because _____

    _____ .

11. Trust breaks down when _____ .

12. I need to be careful around _____ (names).

13. I can encourage cooperation by_____ .

14. I become insecure when _____ .

15. I feel confident and secure when _____ .

List five things you can do to strengthen your own empowerment.

1.

2.

3.

4.

5.

If you are a manager, list four things you can do in your organization to increase trust and help your subordinates to feel more empowered.

1.

2.

3.

4.

Although cooperation is generally very important in the workplace, it also can be dangerous at times. When you're working in a hostile, distrustful environment, or interacting with a manipulative person, trying to cooperate will probably mean that you will be taken advantage of. In those cases you need to make some hard choices on whether you will stay in that job or not.

One organization had a lot of back-biting, and lies were spoken about people who weren't part of the central clique. In this environment it would be foolish to be honest and open with people because the clique would take advantage of you.

If you find yourself in a situation like that, you have three choices; one is to live with it the way it is, and make the best of it. Try not to store up a lot of resentment because it will only eat away at your own self-esteem and your own productivity.

Choice number two is to prove to the people in power that you are competent and trustworthy. That may take some time and determination.

Choice number three is to get a job elsewhere. Many people believe that they have no other career options where they live. Don't limit yourself. Maybe your job *is* the only one of its kind available there; then maybe it's time to start considering moving or a career change. An excellent book to read on this is *What Color Is Your Parachute* by Richard Booles. It helps you to look at what positive qualities and abilities you have and to discover where those might best fit.

Part C

An Exercise in Social Power[3]

Exercise Schedule

1.	**Introduction**		**5 min**	**5 min**

Divide the class into five groups of equal size, each of which is assigned one of the French and Raven power bases.

2.	**Influence plan**		**10+ min**	**15 min**

Read the following case and prepare an actual influence plan using the type of power that has been assigned to your group. When finished with your planning, select one member to play the role of instructor. Then, also choose from your own or another group a "student" who is to be the recipient of the "instructor's" attempt.

> You are an instructor in a college class and have become aware that a potentially good student is repeatedly absent from class and sometimes unprepared when he or she is there. S/he seems to be satisfied with the grade s/he is getting, but you would like to see him/her attend regularly, be better prepared, and thus do better in the class. You even feel that the student might get really turned on to pursuing a career in this field, which is an exciting one for you. You are respected and liked by your students, and it kind of irritates you that this person treats your dedicated teaching with such a cavalier attitude. You want to influence the student to start attending class regularly.

3.	**Role-playing**		**15+ min**	**30 min**

a.   Each group role-plays its influence plan, going in the following order: punishment, reward, referent, legitimate, expert.

b.   During the role-plays, members in other groups should think of themselves as the student being influenced. Fill out the "Reaction to Influence Questionnaire" at the end of the exercise for each role-play, including one for self.

4.	**Results and discussion**		**10+ min**	**40 min**

Tabulate the results of the questionnaire within your group. For each role-play determine how many people thought the power used was punishment, reward, etc. Then add up each member score for Item 2, doing the same for Items 3, 4, and 5.

a.   As a total class discuss which influence strategy is the most effective in compliance, long-lasting effect, acceptable attitude, and enhanced relationship.

b.   What are the likely side effects of each type of influence strategy?

---

[3]Adapted from Gib Akin from *Exchange*, Vol. 3(4), 1978, pp. 38-39. Used with permission.

Role-Play #1

	Role-Plays				
	1	2	3	4	5

1. Type of power used (mark one)

Punishment – ability to influence because of capacity
to coerce or punish

Reward – ability to influence because of potential reward

Referent – comes from admiration and liking

Legitimate – stems from formal position in organization

Expert – comes from superior knowledge or ability
to get things done or image of it

Information – because of having information others want

Fill in the number of each of the scales below which indicated in the grid the best statement completion for you. That is, think of yourself on the receiving end of the influence attempt described and record your own reaction.

	1	2	3	4	5

2. As a result of influence attempt I will...

definitely not   definitely
comply   comply

    1   2   3   4   5

3. Any change that does come about will be...

temporary   long lasting

    1   2   3   4   5

4. My own personal reaction is...

resistant   acceptant

    1   2   3   4   5

5. As a result of this influence attempt my relationships
with the professor will probably be...

worse   better

    1   2   3   4   5

53. A Simple – But Powerful – Power Simulation[1]

Purpose:
To understand some of the power dynamics in organizations at every level – from the individual to the systematic.

Group Size:
24-90 people.

Time Required:
60 minutes or more if time permits.

Materials:
Each student brings a dollar bill to class.

Room Arrangement Requirements:
A room large enough to accommodate two work groups and enough space in a hallway or corridor for a third group.

Related Topics:
Interpersonal Communications, Organizational Design

Exercise Schedule

Part A – Simulation

		Unit Time	*Total Time*
1.	**Divide groups**	**5 min**	**5 min**

Students turn in a dollar bill to the teacher and are divided into three groups based on criteria given by the instructor, assigned to their work places, and instructed to read the rules and tasks below. The money is divided into thirds, giving two-thirds of it to the top group, one-third to the middle group, and none to the bottom group.

2.	**Conduct simulation**	**30+ min**	**35 min**

Groups go to their assigned work places and complete their tasks.

---

[1]By Lee Bolman and Terrence E. Deal from *Exchange*, Vol 4(3), 1979, pp. 38-42. Used with permission.

Rules:

a. Members of the top group are free to enter the space of either of the other groups and to communicate whatever they wish, whenever they wish. Members of the middle group may enter the space of the lower group when they wish but must request permission to enter the top group's space (which the top group can refuse). Members of the lower group may not disturb the top group in any way unless specifically invited by the top. The lower group does have the right to knock on the door of the middle group and request permission to communicate with them (which can also be refused).

b. The members of the top group have the authority to make any change in the rules that they wish, at any time, with or without notice.

Tasks:

✓   Top Group: To be responsible for the overall effectiveness and learning from the simulation, and to decide how to use its money.

✓   Middle Group: To assist the Top Group in providing for the overall welfare of the organization, and to decide how to use its money.

✓   Bottom Group: To identify its resources and to decide how best to provide for learning and the overall effectiveness of the organization.

Part B – Debrief

1. **Representatives discuss**   **10+ min**   **45 min**
    Each of the three groups chooses two representatives to go to the front of the class and discuss the following questions with the instructor.

    a. What can we learn about power from this experience? Does it remind us of events we have seen in other organizations?

    b. What did each of us learn individually? How did we think about what power is? Were we satisfied with the amount of power we had? How did we try to exercise or to gain more power?

2. **Class discussion**   **15+ min**   **60 min**
    The instructor will lead a discussion on the following:

    a. Discuss what occurred within and between the three groups.

    b. What were the in-group, out-group dynamics?

    c. How did trust and mistrust figure into the simulation?

    d. What does this exercise say about structural injustice?

    e. What were some differences of being in the top group versus being in the bottom one?

54. Visibility/Credibility Inventory[1]

Purpose:
To measure visibility and credibility in groups.

Group Size:
Any number of groups of two to eight members.

Time Required:
10 minutes or more.

Preparation Required:
Complete and score the inventory prior to class.

Related Topics:
Dynamics Within Groups, Interpersonal Conversation

Exercise Schedule

1. **Preparation (pre-class)**
    Complete and score the inventory prior to class. This takes about 20 minutes.

		Unit Time	Total Time
2.	**Theory**	10 min	10 min

    Instructor gives a presentation on the theory behind the visibility/credibility inventory.

3. **Groups discuss (optional)**   **15+ min**
    Form groups of two to eight people. Members share and discuss their positions on the matrix, consider implications of these positions, and provide feedback about perceptions of behavior.

[1]Reproduced from *The 1988 Annual: Developing Human Resources* by J. William Pfeiffer, (Ed.).© 1988 by Pfeiffer & Company, San Diego, CA. Used with permission.

The Visibility/Credibility Inventory

Instructions:

Completing this instrument will give you an opportunity to learn about your power and influence in your group or team. Please answer each question candidly, recognizing that there are no right/wrong, good/bad answers. Base your responses on your initial reaction to your actual behavior, not what you wish your behavior to be. Circle one of the numbers next to each statement to indicate the degree to which that statement is true for you or is descriptive of you.

1 – Strongly disagree (very unlike me)   5 – Slightly agree (somewhat like me)
2 – Disagree (not like me)   6 – Agree (like me)
3 – Slightly disagree (somewhat unlike me)   7 – Strongly agree (very like me)
4 – Neither agree nor disagree (neither like nor unlike me)

1.	I am usually one of the more vocal members of the group.	1	2	3	4	5	6	7
2.	I frequently volunteer to lead the group.	1	2	3	4	5	6	7
3.	People in the group usually listen to what I have to say.	1	2	3	4	5	6	7
4.	I frequently find myself on "center stage."	1	2	3	4	5	6	7
5.	I am able to influence the decisions that the group makes.	1	2	3	4	5	6	7
6.	People often seek me out for advice.	1	2	3	4	5	6	7
7.	I feel that I am trusted by the group.	1	2	3	4	5	6	7
8.	I enjoy the role of being "up-front."	1	2	3	4	5	6	7
9.	My opinion is usually held in high regard by group members.	1	2	3	4	5	6	7
10.	I am often reluctant to lead the group.	1	2	3	4	5	6	7
11.	I receive much recognition for my ideas and contributions.	1	2	3	4	5	6	7
12.	I have a reputation for being believable.	1	2	3	4	5	6	7
13.	Group members typically influence what I have to say in the group.	1	2	3	4	5	6	7
14.	I would rather lead the group than be a participant.	1	2	3	4	5	6	7
15.	I do not like being in the limelight and avoid it whenever possible.	1	2	3	4	5	6	7
16.	My ideas are usually implemented.	1	2	3	4	5	6	7
17.	Group members frequently ask for my opinions and input.	1	2	3	4	5	6	7

18. I take the initiative in the group and am usually one of the first to speak out.   1 2 3 4 5 6 7

19. I usually volunteer my thoughts and ideas without hesitation.   1 2 3 4 5 6 7

20. I seem to blend into a crowd at parties.   1 2 3 4 5 6 7

21. During meetings I am alone in presenting my own point of view.   1 2 3 4 5 6 7

22. I wait to be asked for my opinion in meetings.   1 2 3 4 5 6 7

23. People seek out my advice.   1 2 3 4 5 6 7

24. During meetings my point of view is not joined by others.   1 2 3 4 5 6 7

25. People check with others about the advice I give to them.   1 2 3 4 5 6 7

26. I ask questions just to have something to say.   1 2 3 4 5 6 7

27. I often find myself in the role of scribe during meetings.   1 2 3 4 5 6 7

28. Group members usually "check out" data I give them.   1 2 3 4 5 6 7

29. Group members view me as an expert in my field.   1 2 3 4 5 6 7

30. I am in a highly visible race, ethnic, or gender group (for example, a woman in a predominantly male organization).   1 2 3 4 5 6 7

31. I am often asked to work at organizational levels higher than my own.   1 2 3 4 5 6 7

32. Group members usually consult me about important matters before they make a decision.   1 2 3 4 5 6 7

33. I try to dress well and/or differently from members of my group.   1 2 3 4 5 6 7

34. I usually try to sit at the head of the conference table at meetings.   1 2 3 4 5 6 7

35. Group members often refer to me in their statements.   1 2 3 4 5 6 7

36. I speak loudly during meetings.   1 2 3 4 5 6 7

37. I have noticed that group members often look at me even when not talking directly to me.   1 2 3 4 5 6 7

The Visibility/Credibility Inventory (cont'd)

1 – Strongly disagree (very unlike me)   5 – Slightly agree (somewhat like me)
2 – Disagree (not like me)   6 – Agree (like me)
3 – Slightly disagree (somewhat unlike me)   7 – Strongly agree (very like me)
4 – Neither agree nor disagree (neither like nor unlike me)

38.	I stand when I have something important to say.	1 2 3 4 5 6 7
39.	Sometimes I think group members do not know I am present.	1 2 3 4 5 6 7
40.	I am emotional when I speak.	1 2 3 4 5 6 7
41.	Following my absence from the group, I am not asked to explain where I was.	1 2 3 4 5 6 7
42.	The word "wisdom" has been used in reference to me.	1 2 3 4 5 6 7
43.	Group members come to me for gossip but not for "substance."	1 2 3 4 5 6 7
44.	I seem to have the "ear" of the group.	1 2 3 4 5
45.	I am very influential in my group.	1 2 3 4 5 6 7
46.	I clown around with group members.	1 2 3 4 5 6 7
47.	Group members do not like me to disagree with them.	1 2 3 4 5 6 7
48.	I jump right into whatever conflict the group members are dealing with.	1 2 3 4 5 6 7
49.	I like telling jokes and humorous stories in the group.	1 2 3 4 5 6 7
50.	My contributions to the group are not very important.	1 2 3 4 5 6 7

The Visibility/Credibility Inventory Scoring Sheet

Instructions:

Transfer the number you circled for each item onto the appropriate blank on this scoring sheet. Then add each column of numbers and write its total in blank provided.

Visibility		Credibility	
Item Number	My Score	Item Number	My Score
1.	_____	3.	_____
2.	_____	5.	_____
4.	_____	6.	_____
8.	_____	7.	_____
10.	_____*	9.	_____
14.	_____	11.	_____
15.	_____*	12.	_____
18.	_____	13.	_____*
19.	_____	16.	_____
20.	_____*	17.	_____
22.	_____*	21.	_____*
26.	_____	23.	_____
27.	_____	24.	_____*
30.	_____	25.	_____*
33.	_____	28.	_____*
34.	_____	29.	_____
36.	_____	31.	_____
38.	_____	32.	_____
39.	_____*	35.	_____
40.	_____	37.	_____
41.	_____*	42.	_____
43.	_____	44.	_____
46.	_____	45.	_____
48.	_____	47.	_____
49.	_____	50.	_____*
Total	_____	Total	_____

*Reverse-score item. Change your score according to the following scale and write the corrected number in the blank (1 = 7, 2 = 6, 3 = 5, 4 = 4, 5 = 3, 6 = 2, 7 = 1).

The Visibility/Credibility Inventory
Profile Sheet

Name _____ Date _____

Instructions:

Plot your position on the matrix below by finding the square at which your Visibility score and your Credibility score intersect. For example, if your Visibility score is 90 and your Credibility score is 120, find where 90 on the horizontal axis and 120 on the vertical axis intersect. Mark the spot by shading in that square.

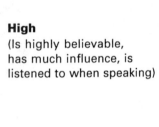

High
(Is highly believable,
has much influence, is
listened to when speaking)

CREDIBILITY

Low
(Is not believable,
has little influence, is
ignored when speaking)

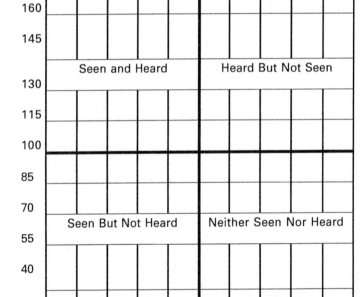

High
(Is visible,
"up-front,"
center stage)

VISIBILITY

Low
(Is in background,
one of the crowd,
not at all visible)

Theoretical Framework

The concept of power is important in organizational and group dynamics. However, behaviors called "power moves" or "plays" are often misinterpreted. In fact, most group members are not aware of the ways in which they use power and influence among themselves. Consequently, the authors have developed an instrument that assists group members in understanding their own and one another's functioning with regard to power within the group.

This instrument is based on two of the primary components of power: visibility and credibility. Visibility results from those behaviors that permit a person to be "up-front" and physically visible; the focus is on the person's visible, external attributes. Credibility results from those behaviors that give a person influence so that he or she is believed – and believed in – by others; the focus is on the person's credible internal attributes.

These two components are interactive, and an individual's behavior in a group can be rated along a visibility continuum as well as along a credibility continuum. The two continua thus form a matrix (see previous page) on which the individual's position with regard to visibility and credibility within a particular group can be plotted. For purposes of discussion, we focus on the more extreme or "pure" types that the matrix helps to identify.

1. High Visibility/High Credibility

People who fall in Quadrant I are both "seen and heard." They exhibit behaviors that permit them to be physically seen by others as well as to have influence on others. In large organizations these people are typically the upwardly mobile and young leaders, and they are often referred to as "water walkers" and "fast trackers."

2. Low Visibility/High Credibility

Quadrant II locates those who are "heard but not seen." These people are "behind-the-scenes" influences who are content to have power but wish to stay out of the limelight. In this quadrant is included the "sage" or the opinion leader whose sound input is sought before major decisions are made.

3. High Visibility/Low Credibility

Those "seen but not heard" reside in Quadrant III. This quadrant houses a wide range of organizational types who are visible but who have little credibility or influence. One of these people is the resident "gossip"; he or she may be well-known among colleagues but cannot be trusted and has little influence. Also included in this quadrant is the "yes man," who derives his or her visibility from another source, usually the boss. Also, it is unfortunately the case that in this quadrant we find tokens, that is, women and minorities whose gender, race, or position makes them highly visible but who have very little credibility because the formal power resides elsewhere.

4. Low Visibility/Low Credibility

In Quadrant IV we find those who are "neither seen nor heard." For whatever reasons, Quadrant IV people prefer or are placed in positions that offer little credibility or visibility. Although they may do their work, they rarely move up in the organization. Most often they remain unknown or are passed over.

Chapter 16

Management of Diversity

55. Becoming a Minority:
Being Exposed to Cultural Diversity[1]

Purpose:
1. To become exposed to cultural or ethnic differences.
2. To examine your feelings resulting from being a minority.

Group Size:
Any number.

Time Required:
Guidelines for Minority Exercise done outside of class.
In-class discussion – 45 minutes.

Preparation Required:
Complete "The Assignment."

Related Topics:
Interpersonal Communication, Interpersonal Relationships, Perception, Learning

---

[1]By Renate R. Mai-Dalton. In *The Organizational Behavior Teaching Review,* Vol. 9(3), 1984-85, pp. 76-82. Used with permission.

➡ Introduction

Because we are moving into more of a cosmopolitan world, it is important to understand and appreciate that people's backgrounds are different from your own. This is supported by continuing demands from both the business and academic communities to educate our students to become sensitive to foreign and diverse cultures, to become aware of and open to different value systems, and to develop an understanding of the social aspects of a pluralistic society (Neureiter, 1984; Nanus, 1984).

Exercise Schedule

1.   Preparation (pre-class)
Students complete assignment, as described below.

		Unit Time	*Total Time*
2.	**Divide groups**	**5 min**	**5 min**

After completing the papers, during class you will be divided into groups of four to seven members according to where you visited. Examples of possible group compositions are students who have visited:

     a. similar religious services (e.g., Catholic, Jewish, Protestant)

     b. different racial groups

     c. physically and/or mentally handicapped groups

     d. different ethnic groups

3.	**Group discussion**	**15+ min**	**20 min**

Groups discuss what they have experienced and record:

     a. similarities and

     b. differences of the experiences,

     c. advantages and

     d. disadvantages of the exercise.

4.	**Class discussion**	**20 min**	**45 min**

Each group reports on its conclusions of 3, a-d, above.

Assignment:

Guidelines for Minority Exercise

The following assignment exposes you to a new situation, requires you carefully to observe your surroundings, and asks you both to describe what you felt and what other individuals might feel to have you among them.

Your task is to go by yourself (you may not take anyone with you) to a place where you have not been before and to observe what you see. Then, from this experience, write a two-page paper that reports on the following:

1. Date and address of where the experience took place.

2. Length of time that you were there.

3. Brief description of the setting.

4. Your reaction to the situation in terms of your behavior and feelings.

5. The reaction of the other individuals toward you.

6. What this experience teaches you about being different from others in your environment.

7. How such an experience might influence your development if you were to live or work in such a setting all your life.

8. Concluding comments about the experience.

Whenever possible, relate your experience to the literature that we have covered in the course. To give you some ideas about possible places to visit, below are examples of previous students' choices:

a. Protestants visited a Catholic service and vice versa.

b. Caucasians visited Black churches and student organizations.

c. A Caucasian went to a Japanese birthday party.

d. A Caucasian visited a Croatian wedding.

e. People went to the School for the Deaf or the School for the Blind.

f. White-collar workers went to a blue-collar cafeteria.

g. Someone visited a body building club.

h. A younger person visited a nursing home.

i. A female went to a car auction with predominantly male customers.

j. A younger student sat in the Faculty Lounge.

There are, of course, many other possibilities. Think of situations that you have often wondered about and want to get to know. Do not choose a setting where you would feel like an intruder into someone's privacy. If in doubt, telephone ahead and inquire if your presence is acceptable to the group. Only choose a setting that you sincerely want to learn about. This will avoid your feeling of being an "undercover agent." Instead, your sincere wish to learn about a group, different from your own, will maintain your integrity and will justify your visit.

One word of caution: Use your good judgment. Do not place yourself into a situation that is physically dangerous to you. We shall discuss in class what you might have learned from this exercise.

References
Nanus, B. (1984) "Future Influences on Management Education." *Selections*, Spring, 15-18.
Neureiter, N.P. (1984) "Training for International Management." *International Management Newsletter*, Academy of Management, Vol. VII (2), pp. 1-2.

56. Freida Mae Jones: Racism in Organizations[1]

Purpose:
To examine issues of racism in organizations.

Group Size:
Any number of groups of five to eight members.

Time Required:
30 minutes or more.

Preparation Required:
Read "Freida Mae Jones" and answer the questions.

Related Topics:
Interpersonal Communication, Leadership, Women in Management

Exercise Schedule

1. **Preparation (pre-class)**
   Read the case and answer the questions.

		Unit Time	Total Time
2.	**Group discussion**	15+ min	15 min
	Groups discuss the questions at the end of the case.		
3.	**Class discussion**	15+ min	30 min
	The instructor leads a discussion on the case.		

Case Study: _____

Freida Mae Jones

Freida Mae Jones was born in her grandmother's Georgia farmhouse on June 1, 1949. She was the sixth of George and Ella Jones' ten children. Mr. and Mrs. Jones moved to New York City when Freida was four because they felt that the educational and career opportunities for their children would be better in the North. With the help of some cousins, they settled in a five-room apartment in the Bronx. George worked as a janitor at Lincoln Memorial Hospital, and Ella was a part-time housekeeper in a nearby neighborhood. George and Ella were conservative, strict parents. They kept a close watch on their children's activities and demanded they be home by a certain hour. The Joneses believed that because they were black, the children would have to

[1] © 1985 by Martin R. Moser, Ph.D., Associate Professor of Management, College of Management, University of Massachusetts at Lowell, Lowell, Mass. All names in this article are fictitious.

perform and behave better than their peers to be successful. They believed that their children's education would be the most important factor in their success as adults.

Freida entered Memorial High School, a racially integrated public school, in September 1963. Seventy percent of the student body was Caucasian, 20 percent black, and 10 percent Hispanic. About 60 percent of the graduates went on to college, of which 4 percent were black, Hispanic, and male. In her senior year, Freida was the top student in her class. Following school regulations, Freida met with her guidance counselor to discuss plans upon graduation. The counselor advised her to consider training in a "practical" field such as housekeeping, cooking, or sewing, so that she could find a job.

George and Ella Jones were furious when Freida told them what the counselor had advised. Ella said, "Don't they see what they are doing? Freida is the top-rated student in her whole class and they are telling her to become a manual worker. She showed that she has a fine mind and can work better than any of her classmates and still she is told not to become anybody in this world. It's really not any different in the North than back home in Georgia, except that they don't try to hide it down South. They want her to throw away her fine mind because she is a black girl and not a white boy. I'm going to go up to her school tomorrow and talk to the principal."

> "They want her to throw away her fine mind **because she is a black girl and not a white boy.**"

As a result of Mrs. Jones' visit to the principal, Freida was assisted in applying to ten Eastern colleges, each of which offered her full scholarships. In September 1966, Freida entered Werbley College, an exclusive private women's college in Massachusetts. In 1970, Freida graduated *summa cum laude* in history. She decided to return to New York to teach grade school in the city's public school system. Freida was unable to obtain a full-time position, so she substituted. She also enrolled as a part-time student in Columbia University's Graduate School of Education. In 1975 she had attained her Master of Arts degree in teaching from Columbia but could not find a permanent teaching job. New York City was laying off teachers and had instituted a hiring freeze because of the city's financial problems.

Feeling frustrated about her future as a teacher, Freida decided to get an MBA. She thought that there was more opportunity in business than in education. Churchill Business School, a small, prestigious school located in upstate New York, accepted Freida into its MBA program.

Freida completed her MBA in 1977 and accepted an entry-level position at the Industrialist World Bank of Boston in a fast-track management development program. The three-year program introduced her to all facets of bank operations, from telling to loan training and operations management. She was rotated to branch offices throughout New England. After completing the program she became an assistant manager for branch operations in the West Springfield branch office.

During her second year in the program, Freida had met James Walker, a black doctoral student in business administration at the University of Massachusetts. Her assignment to West Springfield precipitated their decision to get married. They originally anticipated that they would marry when James finished his doctorate and could move to Boston. Instead, they decided he would pursue a job in the Springfield-Hartford area.

Freida was not only the first black but also the first woman to hold an executive position in the West Springfield branch office. Throughout the training program Freida felt somewhat uneasy, although she did very well. There were six other blacks in the program, five men and one woman, and she found support and comfort in sharing her feelings with them. The group spent much of their free time together. Freida had hoped that she would be located near one or more of the group when she went out into the "real world." She felt that although she was able to share her feelings about work with James, he did not have the full appreciation or understanding of her co-workers. However, the nearest group member was located one hundred miles away.

Freida's boss in Springfield was Stan Luboda, a 55-year-old native New Englander. Freida felt that he treated her differently than he did the other trainees. He always tried to help her and took a lot of time (too much, according to Freida) explaining things to her. Freida felt that he was treating her like a child and not a like an intelligent and able professional.

"I'm really getting frustrated and angry about what is happening at the bank," Freida said to her husband. "The people don't even realize it, but their prejudice comes through all the time. I feel as if I have to fight all the time just to start off even. Luboda gives Paul Cohen more responsibility than me and we both started at the same time with the same amount of training. He's meeting customers alone and Luboda has accompanied me to each meeting I've had with a customer."

"I run into the same thing at school," said James. "The people don't even know that they are doing it. The other day I met with a professor on my dissertation committee. I've known and worked with him for over three years. He said he wanted to talk with me about a memo he had received. I asked him what it was about and he said that the records office wanted to know about my absence during the spring semester. He said that I had to sign some forms. He had me confused with Martin Jordan, another black student. Then he realized that it wasn't me, but Jordan he wanted. All I could think was that we all must look alike to him. I was angry. Maybe it was an honest mistake on his part, but whenever something like that happens – and it happens often – it gets me really angry."

"Something like that happened to me," said Freida. "I was using the copy machine, and Luboda's secretary was talking to someone in the hall. She had just gotten a haircut and was saying her hair was now like Freida's – short and kinky – and that she would have to talk to me about how to take care of it. Luckily, my back was to her. I bit my lip and went on with my business. Maybe she was trying to be cute, because I know she saw me standing there, but comments like that are not cute: they're racist."

"I don't know what to do," said James. "I try to keep things in perspective. Unless people interfere with my progress, I try to let it slide. I only have so much energy and it doesn't make sense to waste it on people who don't matter. But that doesn't make it any easier to function in a racist environment. People don't realize that they are being racist. But a lot of times their expectations of black people or women, or whatever, are different because of skin color or gender. They expect you to be different, although if you were to ask them they would say that they don't. In fact, they would be highly offended if you implied that they were racist or sexist. They don't see themselves that way."

"Luboda is interfering with my progress," said Freida. "The kinds of experiences I have now will have a direct effect on my career advancement. If decisions are being made because I am black or a woman, then they are racially and sexually biased. It's the same kind of attitude that the guidance counselor had when I was in high school, although not as blatant."

In September 1980, Freida decided to speak to Luboda about his treatment of her. She met with him in his office. "Mr. Luboda, there is something that I would like to discuss with you, and I feel a little uncomfortable because I'm not sure how you will respond to what I am going to say."

"I want you to feel that you can trust me," said Luboda. "I am anxious to help you in any way I can."

"I feel that you treat me differently than you treat other people around here," said Freida. "I feel you are over-cautious with me, that you always try to help me, and never let me do anything on my own."

"I always try to help the new people around here," answered Luboda. "I'm not treating you any differently than I treat any other person. I think that you are being a little too sensitive. Do you think that I treat you differently because you are black?"

"The thought had occurred to me," said Freida. "Paul Cohen started here the same time that I did and he has much more responsibility than I do." (Paul was already handling accounts on his own, while Freida had not yet been given that responsibility.)

"I feel that **you treat me differently** than you treat other people around here."

"Freida, I know you are not a naive person," said Luboda. "You know the way the world works. There are some things which need to be taken more slowly than others. There are some assignments for which Cohen has been given more responsibility than you, and there are some assignments for which you are given more responsibility than Cohen. I try to put you where you do the most good."

"What you are saying is that Cohen gets the more visible, customer contact assignments and I get the behind-the-scenes running of the operation assignments," said Freida. "I'm not naive, but I'm also not stupid either. Your decisions are unfair. Cohen's career will advance more quickly than mine because of the assignments that he gets."

"Freida, that is not true," said Luboda. "Your career will not be hurt because you are getting different responsibilities than Cohen. You both need the different kinds of experiences you are getting. And you have to face the reality of the banking business. We are in a conservative business. When we speak to customers we need to gain their confidence, and we put the best people for the job in the positions to achieve that end. If we don't get their confidence they can go down the street to our competitors and do business with them. Their services are no different than ours. It's a competitive business in which you need every edge you have. It's going to take time for people to change some of their attitudes about whom they borrow money from or where they put their money. I can't change the way people feel. I am running a business, but believe me I won't make any decisions that are detrimental to you or to the bank. There is an important place for you here at the bank. Remember, you have to use your skills to the best advantage of the bank as well as your career."

"So what you are saying is that all things being equal, except my gender and my race, that Cohen will get different treatment than me in terms of assignments," said Freida.

"You're making it sound like I am making a racist and sexist decision," said Luboda. "I'm making a business decision utilizing the resources at my disposal and the market situation in which I must operate. You know exactly what I am talking about. What would you do if you were in my position?"

"What would you do if you were in my position?"

Discussion Questions

1. Briefly summarize the case. What were Freida's concerns?

2. When Freida approached her manager, Mr. Luboda, he denied that he treated her unfairly. He suggested that she was too sensitive to the racial issue. Was Mr. Luboda being defensive, or was Freida highly sensitive to this issue? Support your position.

3. Were Freida's concerns justified? Why or why not?

4. What were Mr. Luboda's concerns? How do you evaluate his actions in light of those concerns?

5. Were Mr. Luboda's actions illegal under Title VII of the 1964 Civil Rights Act? Why or why not?

6. Suppose Freida had benefited from Mr. Luboda's actions (e.g., by gaining more accounts). How would that change your evaluation of the case?

7. If you were in Mr. Luboda's position what would you do differently, given the conservative nature of the bank's clients?

8. If you were Freida, how would you have approached Mr. Luboda? What could she have done to be more persuasive?

57. Problems and Issues Surrounding the Hiring of Protected Class Members[1]

Purpose:
To experience and understand the difficulties in making hiring decisions in an environment that is attempting to redress past discrimination and preclude future discrimination.

Group Size:
Three individuals in the roles of job candidates, three on a "panel group," and "observer groups" of four to six members.

Time Required:
One 50-minute session, with second 50-minute schedule optional.

Preparation:
Students who will play the roles of job candidates receive their resumés in advance.

➤➤ Introduction

One issue regarding diversity in organizations is the extent to which managers are willing to hire workers from "protected classes." Even though such workers have legal recourse if they are unjustly rejected, many do not. Furthermore, many managers do not even realize how deep and unconscious go their own prejudices towards these groups.

Exercise Schedule

1. **Pre-class**
    Instructor gives background material to students to read before coming to the next class session. Three students are chosen to be job applicants and those students only get their own resumés to read in order to prepare for their role-play.

		Unit Time	*Total Time*
2.	**Design criteria**	**10 min**	**10 min**

    A panel of three for the search committee is selected. Remaining students divide into observer groups of four to six members, who surround the search committee in a fish-bowl design (physical environment permitting). Search committee develops a list of criteria for position, as well as questions to ask during the interview. At the same time, observer groups also develop criteria and list of interview questions.

3.	**Read resumés**	**5-10 min**	**15+ min**

    Instructor passes out resumés of three candidates for committee and observers to read.

---

[1] By William P. Ferris, "Demonstrating the Problems and Issues Surrounding the Hiring of Protected Class Members." In W.A. Ward and E.G. Gomolka (Eds.), *Managing for Performance: Proceedings of the 26th Annual Meeting of the Eastern Academy of Management*, Portland, ME, May 1989. Used with permission.

4. Interviews   15-30 min   30+ min

One at a time, candidates are brought in and interviewed for 5-10 minutes each. After interview, each candidate is allowed to remain in the room for the remaining interviews.

5. Committee decision   10-15 min   40+ min

Candidates leave room and search committee discusses merits of each candidate, preparing public statement on who was hired and why. While this is going on, each observer group also develops a hiring decision.

6. Decision announced   5 min   40+ min

Candidates come back into room and hear the committee and observer statements.

7. Feedback   5-15 min   45+ min

Instructor gives specific feedback to search committee and to observer groups. In addition, observer groups give feedback to search committee on interview behaviors.

8. Further reading (optional)

Instructor may assign further materials for students to read.

Second session (optional)

                                                    Unit Time   *Total Time*

1. Assign roles   5 min   5 min

Instructor hands out materials to students for preparation on an upcoming case regarding protected class members. Students are assigned to become

- members of the OFCC board who will sit in on the case (at least some of the four to six should be protected class members themselves)
- plaintiffs (rejected candidates from first session)
- plaintiff's lawyer
- defendants (should be among original search committee and observer groups who rejected the plaintiffs)
- defendant's lawyer
- observers

2. Prepare roles   10-15 min   15+ min

Each person or group prepares its roles, its case, its defense, etc.

3. Hearing   15-25 min   30+ min

Hearing of case, with instructor as moderator.

4. Deliberations   10-15 min   40+ min

OFCC Board deliberates. The format here is for the board members to form a small circle with everyone else around them, fish-bowl style. Board deliberates in public, with participants allowed to watch, but not to comment. The board then announces a verdict.

5. Debrief   10-20 min   50+ min

Instructor gives feedback to the board members, after which other members comment on the process and what happened during the exercise.

☐ Background

Midwest Industrial is a fair-sized industrial company of about 200 employess. It is currently a non-union shop and wanting to stay that way. Located in St. Louis, Missouri, it is a supplier of industrial metal and rubber hoses for vacuum motors and pumps. Its main customers are plumbing supply houses, well drilling companies, and it is an OEM for several big-name pump manufacturing firms. By nature of its business, Midwest has employed a mostly male work force (88 percent), although there are several secretaries and clerks in payroll and billing who are female. Of the 24 managerial level employees, only the accounts receivable supervisor is a woman (her department consists of four female clerks). Ten minority members, including four blacks, three Hispanics, and two Asian-Americans, work for the company. Of the 200 employees, only 12 have college degrees or higher. All of these 12 are managerial level employees and include the comptroller, the company officers, and a few first-line shift supervisors.

Midwest's president realizes the company needs to be brought up to date on issues such as OSHA, modern training and development and motivational techniques, EAP's, keeping up with fringe benefits and compensation, etc. Additionally, he is concerned that hiring be more successful as the company grows and that managerial personnel work hard to keep unions away. The company didn't used to need a personnel function, but now it is getting too big and the laws are getting too complicated for it to afford the practice of having secretaries take care of personnel issues. Accordingly, the president appointed a personnel manager and now realizes that there is a need to give him an assistant.

HUMAN RESOURCE SPECIALIST NEEDED

POSITION: ASSISTANT MANAGER
HUMAN RESOURCES DEPARTMENT

The Human Resources Department of a growing industrial company located in the southern mid-west section of the country needs an assistant manager for its newly developing HR department. Successful candidate will have excellent interpersonal skills as well as managerial potential. Bachelor's degree, a minimum 3.0 GPA, and at least one year's experience in an HR department necessary. No line subordinates as yet, but department is slated for growth along with the company. If you know something about recruitment, compensation, training, and would like to be in on the ground floor, call 413-782-1629 immediately for a confidential interview. Salary: $24K.

Midwest Industrial
St. Louis, Missouri
"Affirmative Action/EEO Employer"

---

58. Managerial Decision-Making[1]

Purpose:
1. To practice making decisions in a managerial setting.
2. To explore organizational problems resulting from male/female differences.

Group Size:
Any number of mixed-sex groups of four to six members.

Time Required:
50 minutes or more.

Preparation Required:
1. Read the "Background" and "Introduction" below.
2. Read the memoranda (there are six cases).
3. Complete the "Response Sheet."

Related Topics:
Decision-Making

Exercise Schedule

		Unit Time	Total Time
1.	**Preparation (pre-class)**		
	Read the following memoranda and complete the "Response Sheet" before class.		
2.	**Group discussion**	**30+ min**	**30 min**
	In mixed-sex groups of four to six members, discuss your answers to the Response Sheet and the discussion questions at the end of Case #6.		
3.	**Class discussion**	**20 min**	**50 min**
	The instructor will lead a discussion focusing on the main issues brought out in each case.		

❏ Background

In the course of a busy workday, the typical manager is faced with a variety of decisions involving the behavior of other people. Some of these decisions involve personnel actions such as selection, promotion, training, and discipline. Other decisions involve more subtle questions of interpersonal influence, such as the choice of a leadership style or a motivational approach, or the resolution of various kinds of personal problems.

Although decisions of this sort must often be made under time pressures and on the basis of limited information, they have an important cumulative effect on managerial performance.

---

[1]Adapted from Dianne McKinney Kellogg, Duncan Spelman and Marcy Crary, from "Introducing Women in Management Issues in an OB Course." *The Organizational Behavior Teaching Review,* Vol. 9(3), 1984-1985, pp. 83-95. Used with permission.

You will find the questions framed as a series of "in-basket" organizational problems that could arise during the course of a normal workday. This approach has the advantage of greater realism than simply explaining situations. It asks you to assume a specific managerial role and to treat each questionnaire item as if it were a separate memo or letter in your in-basket, giving your evaluations and decisions. There are six "cases" for you to consider.

➡ Introduction

Try to put yourself in the following situation: You are the executive vice-president at Miller Clothing Company, which manufactures several lines of men's apparel and employs a work force of about 5,000. Recently, the decision was made to expand operations and put into production a new line of clothing and men's furnishings for casual living. In order to implement this expansion, the "Bennett Division" has been created and a new factory has been constructed.

You have been put in charge of the start-up phase of this new operation. Your major responsibility is to act as troubleshooter, resolving the daily problems and conflicts associated with a new operation of this sort. The president of the company has asked you to take complete charge, making your own decisions to the greatest extent possible. "Be decisive and I'll back you to the hilt – as long as you are right," he urged.

You are to assume the role of the executive vice-president and to go through the contents of this questionnaire, treating each item as if it were a separate memo or letter in your "in-basket," and indicating on the Response Sheet how you would evaluate and handle each situation.

Case 1 _____

MEMORANDUM

TO: Executive Vice-President

FROM: Richard Bell, Accounting Manager

SUBJECT: Request for Leave of Absence

Ruth Brown, an accountant in the main office, has requested one month's leave beginning next week. She has already taken her vacation this year. She wants the leave in order to take care of her three young children. The day care arrangements the Browns had made for the period covered by the request suddenly fell through, and they have been unable to make other arrangements satisfying their high standards. Ruth's husband is principal of the junior high school and he cannot possibly get time off during the next month.

The problem is that Ruth is the only person experienced in handling the "cost" section in the accounting department. We would either have to transfer an accountant with the same experience from the Richardson Division or else train a replacement for only one month's work. I have urged Ruth to reconsider this request, but she insists on going ahead with it.

I have also checked with the legal department and we do not have to hold the position open for Ruth if she insists on taking the whole month off.

I would appreciate it if you could give me your decision on this as soon as possible.

*Case 2*_____

MEMORANDUM

TO: Executive Vice-President

FROM: Joseph Schmidt, Computer Operations

As you know, Ronald Cooper is a computer operator in my section. He has played a key role in computerizing our inventory system. Recently, Ronald's wife was offered a very attractive managerial position with a large retail organization on the West Coast. They are seriously considering the move. I told Ronald that he has a very bright future with our organization and it would be a shame for him to pull out just as we are expanding our operations. I sure would hate to lose him now. What do you think we should do about the situation?

*Case 3*_____

MEMORANDUM

TO: Executive Vice-President

FROM: Mark Taylor, Corporate Personnel Office

SUBJECT: Promotion of Margaret Adams

We are at the point where we must make a decision on the promotion of Margaret Adams of our personnel staff. Margaret is one of the most competent employees in the corporate personnel office, and I am convinced that she is capable of handling even more responsibility as Bennett Division Personnel Director. However, I am not altogether certain that she is willing to subordinate time with her family to time on the job, to the extent that may be required with Bennett. I have had the opportunity to explore with her the general problem of family versus job, and she strongly believes in a healthy balance between them. She believes that she should very rarely stay late at the office or participate in weekend meetings.

She believes that her first duty is to her family, and that she should manage her time accordingly. This viewpoint has not affected her performance in the past, but it could be a problem in the more demanding position as head of personnel with the Bennett Division.

What do you think we should do?

*Case 4*_____

MEMORANDUM

TO: Executive Vice-President

FROM: Judy Garrison, Marketing Staff, Bennett Division

I appreciate the discussion we had the other evening. It was comforting to learn that the problem I am having with my husband is not unusual in managerial ranks. I have taken your suggestion and written up a recent conversation between me and my husband, for your use in your human-relations seminar in Chicago. This is, of course, with the understanding that the source of this case will not be revealed to anyone.

I would really appreciate it if you would let me know how you think this situation should be resolved. I'll also be looking forward to hearing from you about the discussion in Chicago.

I have entitled the attached case "The Cocktail Party."

The Cocktail Party

Jack and Judy Garrison have been married for three years. Judy is an aspiring business executive and Jack is a very successful free-lance writer. Below is a part of their conversation after attending a cocktail party at the home of an executive in Judy's division.

Jack: Oh boy, what a bunch of creeps! Do we have to go to these parties, honey?

Judy: Jack, honey, you know we have to. These things mean a lot to me. Tonight I had a chance to talk with Mr. Wilson. On the job it would take a week to get an appointment with him. I was able to get across two good ideas I had about our new sales campaign, and I think he was listening.

Jack: Is Wilson that fat slob who works in marketing, the one with the dull wife? I spent ten minutes with her and I nearly died! She's too much. Judy, the people there tonight were so dull I could have cried. Why did I major in English Lit, anyhow? I prefer to talk with people who know what is going on in the world, not a bunch of half-wits whose main interests are their new cars and spoiled kids. I tried to talk to one guy about Virginia Woolf and he didn't even know who she was. These people are incredible. Do we have to go to another cocktail party again next week? I'd like to see "Look Back in Anger" instead. I've got the tickets. One of my husbandly duties is to give you culture. What an uncouth bunch in the business world.

Judy: One of my wifely ambitions is to get ahead in the business world. You know that these parties are required for bright junior executives coming up in the organization. And I'm a bright junior executive. If we don't go, who knows which of the other junior execs will get to Wilson with their good ideas!

Jack: Can't you relax and work a 40-hour week? That's what they pay you for.

Judy: I guess I'm too ambitious to relax.

Jack: I'd still like to go to the play. At least we could think about real problems.

Judy: And I'd be a mediocre, lower-management nobody for the rest of my career.

Jack: I want you to be a success, Judy. But the idea of spending more evenings talking to idiots is too much!

Case 5

MEMORANDUM

TO: Executive Vice-President – CONFIDENTIAL

FROM: Frank Williams, Controller

I would like to get your advice on a matter of great sensitivity involving one of the junior executives in our organization. It has been brought to my attention by an unimpeachable source that Roger Holman, Assistant Comptroller in my division, is having an affair with a prominent young playgirl. I understand it has reached the point where any day now Roger's wife will publicly denounce the young playgirl as a homewrecker. I have been reluctant to bring this up, but I know that Roger's marital problems will hurt his work. I would appreciate any advice you could give me on this.

*Case 6*_____

MEMORANDUM

TO: Executive Vice-President

FROM: Production Manager

SUBJECT: Conference for Production Supervisors

I am pleased that we have the opportunity to send a representative to the Dunbar conference on production supervision. I know from personal experience that it is a high-quality conference, and it has developed such a favorable reputation in this area that it is considered an important form of recognition for those who are selected to attend.

I have reviewed our supervisory staff quite carefully and have narrowed the choice down to two people, both of whom I feel are qualified to attend. Unfortunately, we can send only one person, and I will leave the final selection up to you, depending on what you feel we want to emphasize. The two candidates are John Elms and Susan Adams.

Susan Adams is supervisor of Knitting Unit A. She is 25, married, and has no children. She has been employed by our company for three years. She is a college graduate with a general business degree, and we consider her to have good potential for higher-level positions.

John Elms is supervisor of Knitting Unit B. He is 43, married, and has two teen-age children. He has been employed by our company for 20 years. He is a high school graduate. He has been a steady, conscientious employee, advancing gradually from a helper's job to his present position, which may be as high as he will be able to go, judging from our assessment of the information in his file. Selection for this conference would mean a lot to John.

Response Sheet

1.   How appropriate is it for Ruth to request a leave of absence?

Highly Inappropriate	Moderately Inappropriate	Slightly Inappropriate	Slightly Appropriate	Moderately Appropriate	Highly Appropriate
_____	_____	_____	_____	_____	_____

Would you grant the leave (without pay)?   _____ Yes   _____ No

My rationale is:

2.   Please evaluate each of the following courses of action that Schmidt might take to influence Ronald Cooper's decision, checking either yes or no for *each* alternative.

	Yes	No	
a.	___	___	Try to convince Ronald to remain with the organization.
b.	___	___	Don't try to influence Ronald.
c.	___	___	Offer a raise as an incentive to stay.
d.	___	___	Find an attractive position in the organization for Ronald's wife.

My rationale is:

3.   Which of the following three actions would you recommend?

a.	_____	Do not promote Margaret.
b.	_____	Try to persuade Margaret to make a commitment before going ahead with the promotion.
c	_____	Promote Margaret based on past performance.

My rationale is:

4. Which of the following alternatives would you recommend to the Garrisons?

    a. _____ Jack should go to parties and stop making it an issue.

    b. _____ Judy should attend parties alone.

    c. _____ Judy should stop attending parties.

    My rationale is:

5. Evaluate each of the following methods of dealing with this situation, checking either yes or no for *each* alternative.

        Yes   No

    a. ____   ____   Confront Roger – tell him that he better terminate the affair or he will be fired.

    b. ____   ____   Advise Roger to see a marriage counselor before it is too late.

    c. ____   ____   Do nothing unless Roger brings it up.

    My rationale is:

6. Please indicate which candidate you would send to the conference.

    a. _____ John   b. _____ Susan

    My rationale is:

Discussion Questions

Case 1: Why are people more inclined to give a leave of absence for childcare to a woman than to a man? What can managers do to moderate their own bias in this area? Will the time ever come when men will feel as comfortable as women in asking for such a special consideration? What would the long-term costs and benefits be to the company of granting such a request?

Case 2: Why would people be more inclined to persuade a male to stay than a female, even if it could result in the loss of a valuable employee? To what extent should a company try to persuade an employee to stay if his or her spouse has an attractive offer in another city? What else could a company do to convince an employee to stay? How would or could dual career couples decide which career takes precedence at any given time?

Case 3: Why would people be more accepting of a man putting family first than a woman? To what extent should promotion decisions be based on guesses about future performance? Loyalty? Values and priorities of the employee? Does Margaret represent the manager of the future? If so, what will the costs and benefits be to the organizations such managers work for? What are your priorities and values regarding family vs. career?

Case 4: Why is the issue of participation in work-related social gatherings different for women than it is for men? Is this changing? To what extent is a spouse responsible for attending work-related social gatherings? How important are social gatherings to a person's career?

Case 5: Why would people be less likely to talk with a man about being involved in an affair than with a woman? How involved should companies get in the private lives of their employees? Should the boss's values about such behavior be a factor in whether or not to become involved?

Case 6: To what extent was the factor of age rather than sex a determinant of which employee was sent to the conference? In those cases where the younger employee was sent, why would people be more likely to choose the male than the female? What factors should a manager take into account when selecting an employee for training?

59. Gender Differences in Communication[1]

Purpose:
To see the differences in communication styles of men and women, and discuss the implications of these differences for the workplace.

Group Size:
Groups of five to six members.

Time Required:
50 minutes.

Exercise Schedule

		Unit Time	Total Time
1.	**Preparation**	**20 min**	**20 min**

Twelve students, evenly divided between males and females, are chosen from the class and sent out of the room. The remaining students (the observers) form groups of five to six students. The groups will develop guidelines for judging effective communication. They will be evaluating the role-plays, so they want to focus on what criteria they will use to determine which employees made the best presentations for a raise. There are role-play instructions for these students to give them ideas for the guidelines. The observers do not receive the set of facts that the employees and managers receive.

After the volunteers leave the classroom, they are divided into three groups of four: two employee groups and one management group. The management group must establish the criteria to determine whether or not to allocate the raise; the employee groups will determine how best to ask for the raise. Groups discuss the assignment with the instructor, and select representatives to role-play the parts.

At the end of the 20 minutes, everyone who is not going to be in the role-play returns to the classroom. The members from the employee groups should not sit together.

2.	**Role-play**	**15 min**	**35 min**

The manager sets up an office scene in front of the classroom, and the first employee comes to the office, where the role-play begins. The role-play should be executed in about five minutes. At the end of the first role-play, the second one begins. After the role-plays, students are to work in groups (management returns to their original group) while the employee groups should join individually with the other groups in the class. Students should determine who gave the best presentation for a raise, and justify their decision. Management should announce their judgment, followed by the other groups revealing their judgments.

3.	**Debriefing**	**15 min**	**50 min**

The instructor will lead a discussion of the following questions:

> What were the differences in how the request for a raise was communicated?

Do you think these differences were related to gender?

Did you find one style more convincing than the other? Why?

How did your perceptions of the "right way" to ask for a raise affect your interpretation of the role-play?

How might men and women communicate more effectively with each other?

Role-Play Instructions ONLY for Observers

Purpose

You will be watching two role-plays of employees asking for raises. At the end of the role-play, you will evaluate the persuasiveness of the person asking for a raise.

Task

Form groups of five to six students. Prior to the role-play, you need to decide the criteria you will use to assess the persuasiveness of the person asking for a raise. Below are some suggestions of things you might watch during the role-play. Use these to develop guidelines within your group for watching the role-play. For instance, some people might count the number of sentences that apply to each category. You might also consider the length of time for the discussion, or the tone used in the conversation. Following the role-play, you will use the guidelines you developed to decide who gave the most persuasive presentation.

Examples of things to consider when developing your guidelines:

To what extent did the person asking for the raise:

try to show friendliness with the boss?

try to emphasize personal needs?

try to emphasize work accomplishments?

try to emphasize their position in the organization?

try to show their power with respect to their employees?

ask directly for what they wanted?

hint about their needs, without being direct?

give the boss options for awarding the raise (e.g., make several suggestions)?

show politeness and respect to the boss?

make the boss feel comfortable before asking for the raise?

act businesslike in the approach?

raise their voice?

After the role-play

Using your group's guidelines, determine who made the most effective request for a raise. Be sure to consider the factors above, or any others that you thought might be important. Each group will be asked to report to the class their answers to the following questions:

1)   Who made the most effective request?

2)   How did you reach that conclusion?

Role-Play Instructions ONLY for Management

Purpose

You are the Dean of the Business School at Midwestern University. Your office manager has requested a meeting with you this morning. While you do not know the purpose of the meeting, you suspect that he/she intends to ask for a raise. You are inclined to grant the raise because you think this person is doing a good job. During the meeting you are expected to act reasonably friendly, but the office manager must convince you that his or her performance merits a raise.

Tasks

1. The group should determine who will play the role of the Dean during the role-play.

2. Prior to the actual role-play, as a group you should decide on the criteria that will most likely persuade you to grant the raise. This will allow you to evaluate the individual's request after the role-play.

3. During the role-play, the office manager will tell you about his or her performance during the past year. He or she may also tell you about family problems or developments. During the interview, make sure that you do all you can to encourage the manager to give you all information pertinent to a raise. That is, do not cut off the interview early. However, do not ask specific questions unless they directly pertain to a point that is made, as it is the office manager's responsibility to determine which facts he or she will present. When the interview is over, tell the office manager that you will consider the evidence and let him/her know about the raise in a few days. (*Note*: It's important that you engage in behavior that keeps the employee talking, so that the employee has the opportunity to reveal as much information as he or she sees fit. You should not try to steer the conversation in any way, however.)

Background information:

The office manager currently earns $25,000.

The highest-paid subordinate under the office manager earns $22,000.

The cost of living increase last year was 5 percent.

The office manager has not received a raise in 18 months.

All workers supervised by the office manager are unionized; they recently received an 8 percent salary increase.

Role-Play Instructions ONLY for Employees

Purpose

You are an office manager for the Business School at Midwestern University. You report directly to the Dean. As part of your job, you oversee 30 employees who serve in three different functions: some are department secretaries, some are word-processing specialists, and some provide technical help to the faculty (e.g., photocopying, audio-visuals, and computer support). You have worked in this position for five years, and during this time you have created quite a bit of commitment among the employees toward their jobs. In general, you believe that you have done a good job during the past year, and you intend to ask the Dean for a raise today. You have arranged for a meeting with the Dean, but have not given a reason for the meeting.

Tasks

1.   Decide on who will play the role of the office manager.

2.   Working together as a group, determine a strategy that the office manager should use to ask for the raise. Use the job description above and the following information in any way you choose. You are to assume that the Dean wants you to make the best possible case for a raise. Because you have not told the Dean the purpose of the meeting, you cannot expect that he or she will have reviewed your performance before the interview. You may use any techniques that you want to persuade the Dean of the need for a raise, but remember that you are a professional. Therefore, you should not threaten to quit your job.

Background Information

1.   The cost of living has increased 5 percent this year.

2.   You have not received a raise in 18 months.

3.   You have three children at home (all under 8 years).

4.   You typically stay late at least one night a week, and work for five hours on Saturday.

5.   In general, you are working about 50 hours a week.

6.   Your subordinates, all of whom are unionized, recently received a pay increase of 8 percent.

7.   The highest-paid subordinate is earning $22,000.

8.   You earn $25,000 a year.

9.   Your spouse is also employed full-time.

10.   You have a combined family income of $50,000.

11.   You are quite good at motivating your employees.

12.   You just bought a new house.

13.   You have worked at this job for five years.

14.   You have recently completed a leadership program designed to make people more effective managers. This program lasted eight weeks, and was held on Sunday afternoons.

60. Exploring Gender Conflict[1]

Purpose:
To create a humorous, participative environment in which to discuss sexism in the workplace.

Group Size:
Four groups of three people each (total 12 per group).

Time Required:
45 minutes, or more.

Materials:
Live microphone, video camera and monitor (optional).

Exercise Schedule

		Unit Time	Total Time
1.	**Groups share experiences (optional, pre-class)**	**10-20 min**	

Each person in a group of 12 shares an experience they've had with sexism in the workplace. The group then chooses four of the experiences from which to create short skits.

		Unit Time	Total Time
2.	**Subgroups write scripts (optional, pre-class)**	**10-20 min**	

Dividing into four subgroups of three, each subgroup is responsible for writing a short script depicting their event. The goal is to create an unresolved scenario that will generate audience discussion. The group must choose one person from the 12 to be the host of the show (the "personality").

		Unit Time	Total Time
3.	**Skit presentations**	**35-50 min**	**35-50 min**

The host introduces the overall topic, sets the scene for each skit, and facilitates discussion by asking the audience a provocative question at the end of each skit. *This is a critical role.* The host is responsible for creating participation and maintaining momentum.

		Unit Time	Total Time
4.	**Closing**	**10-15 min**	**45-60 min**

At the end of the final skit, the host summarizes the events of the show and reiterates the main points of discussion.

---

[1]By Robert Marx, Patricia Meny, Lisa Deschamp and Lucinda Berlew, University of Massachusetts. Used with permission.

61. Chris Jamison: Gender and Career Decisions[1]

Purpose:
To identify and examine important issues related to personal career decisions.

Group Size:
Four to six members.

Time Required:
25-50 minutes.

Exercise Schedule

		Unit Time	Total Time
1.	**Individuals read case**	**5-10 min**	**5-10 min**

Students individually read the case indicated by the instructor (either here or in the Appendix), then quickly decide the course of action the protagonist in the case should take. Be prepared to state the reasons supporting your decision.

		Unit Time	Total Time
2.	**Small groups discuss**	**10-20 min**	**15-30 min**

Small groups of four to six members discuss their responses to the case.

		Unit Time	Total Time
3.	**Class discussion**	**10-20 min**	**25-50 min**

Instructor leads class discussion on the issues, concerns, and problems that this exercise helps to identify.

---

[1] By Charles M. Vance and Ellen A. Ensher, *Journal of Management Education*, Vol. 18, No. 1, February 1994, pp. 98-104. © 1994 Sage Publications, Inc. Reprinted with permission.

Case Study: _____

Chris Jamison

Chris Jamison was sitting alone, deep in thought on Friday afternoon in June in the Phoenix branch office of the Big Six accounting firm, Arthur Andersen & Co. She has worked there in the tax audit division for the past six years and has done very well. She has worked hard in lower staff positions and has developed a strong reputation, both at the local office and recently, at Chicago headquarters, as a very competent professional who has great promise within the company.

Chris sat contemplating the conversation she had just had with her office manager and mentor, Jim Wilkins, about Chris' promotion to the position of tax audit manager within the firm. This promotion would involve Chris' relocating to a new branch office in Portland. The promotion would represent a personal and gratifying challenge Chris had wanted for some time now, and would serve as an outstanding opportunity leading to much higher management advancement within the firm.

> The promotion would represent **a personal and gratifying challenge**.

Despite this very positive news, Chris felt quite perplexed and anxious about how this career opportunity would affect her family. Her husband, Kim, was just finishing up his Ph.D. in English Literature at Arizona State University. Ever since their marriage eight years before, Kim had dreamed about teaching English literature at an Ivy League school back East. He also wanted to do professional writing on the side. University faculty positions in English Literature were very scarce throughout the country, and Kim had heretofore been looking for a position with very little success. Recently, however, he interviewed at Cornell University and was offered a one-year visiting assistant professor position beginning in September. Kim was very pleased with this opportunity which could possibly turn into a permanent position at Cornell. As Kim considered whether or not to accept the Cornell offer, he thought that even if a permanent position were not subsequently offered, he would have a much stronger chance at obtaining a permanent faculty position elsewhere with Cornell experience on his resumé.

Chris initially felt very pleased for Kim, but now she was feeling torn between supporting Kim in his career dream pursuit by moving to Cornell in the small town of Ithaca, New York, or accepting the very attractive career opportunity recently presented to her. Jim Wilkins indicated that he understood Chris' dilemma, but that she should know that such a tremendous opportunity within the firm occurs rarely. Besides, her turning down this career advancement offer might even, in fact, hurt her prospects for significant future advancement within the firm.

Chris had majored in accounting in college and had a solid B grade point average. She was a good student, but wasn't very excited about her coursework. After graduation she accepted a job with a small firm which helped support Kim through graduate school. A year later they had a child, David. Soon, Chris joined Arthur Andersen & Co. with a considerable salary increase; but more importantly to her, she became very pleased and excited about her new work and career opportunity. David was placed in day care during the time when Kim was occupied with his studies. Chris was glad that Kim was able to spend much of his study time at home with David, but she had feelings of regret and even guilt that she herself had so little time to spend with her precious child.

Chris thought about the conversation that she would soon have with Kim when she returned home. Her anxiety was heightened by Jim Wilkins' request for her to have a response to the promotion offer when she returned to work the following Monday morning.

Chapter 17
Organizational Design and Effectiveness

62. The Four-Frame Model: Analyzing the NASA Space Shuttle Disaster

Purpose:
1. To understand some dynamics that led to organizational disaster.
2. To analyze the NASA experience using Bolman and Deal's Four-Frame Model for understanding and managing organizations.

Group Size:
Any number of groups of five to eight members.

Time Required:
50 minutes or more.

Preparation:
1. Read the NASA case study.
2. Read "Background on the Four-Frame Model."

Related Topics:
Leadership, Dynamics Within Groups, Dynamics Between Groups, Organizational Structure

➡ Introduction

The Rogers Commission (appointed by the President to investigate the shuttle disaster) was largely rocket scientists and engineers who did not ask all the important questions necessary to get at the true problems of NASA. Your group will advise NASA on the merits and drawbacks of each of the four possible consulting groups.

Exercise Schedule[1]

		Unit Time	Total Time
1.	**Single groups**	**10 min**	**10 min**

Groups of three are assigned to each of the four possible frames. Discuss how issues in the case study relate to to that particular frame. In addition, discuss the advantages and disadvantages of hiring the consulting group that represents the assigned frame.

		Unit Time	Total Time
2.	**Pairs of groups**	**15 min**	**25 min**

Bring together pairs of groups with two different frames to try to come up with a common understanding of each other's position. Come up with some advice for the director of NASA on the advantages/disadvantages of the different frames.

		Unit Time	Total Time
3.	**Groups report**	**15 min**	**40 min**

Each group presents its results and recommendations to the whole class.

		Unit Time	Total Time
4.	**Class discussion**	**10 min**	**50 min**

The instructor leads a discussion on how the Four-Frame Model can be used to analyze the NASA shuttle disaster.

Case Study: _____

The Challenger Disaster: Why?[2]

"At the beginning all the decisions were made at the lowest possible level...It was simply inconceivable that one person could have thought something was wrong...and everyone else not know about it. People making the decisions are getting farther and farther away from the people who get their hands dirty."

These observations reflect the kind of changes in structure and in decision-making practices that had occurred at NASA – changes that were ultimately responsible for the tragic decision to launch the Challenger on January 28, 1986.

Changes in NASA's history included a strengthening of the headquarter team in order to better coordinate efforts among field centers in 1961, a decentralization in 1963, a recentralization to integrate decision-making in 1967 and, with reclassification of the shuttle program from developmental to operational, another reorganization in 1983. These shifts resulted not only from the internal workings of NASA, but reflected the goals and agendas of U.S. presidents and the degree of financial support that could be obtained.

A lot of support was provided through the Kennedy-Johnson Administration, and NASA responded to its own technological momentum without being overly concerned with externally developed goals. However,

---

[1] Exercise structure developed by Michal Čakrt, Czechoslovak Management Center.
[2] By Fiona Crofton, educator and educational change consultant, Simon Fraser University, Vancouver, B.C.

the Kennedy-Johnson Administration also opened NASA up to the public and moved NASA away from its concern for secrecy. An eager press followed and, with space flights becoming more common, new images of astronauts replaced the time-worn picture of astronauts as daredevils. Contractors, performing 80 to 90 percent of NASA's design and development work, could now publicly and more actively lobby to promote their interests.

With the Nixon Administration came a call for more practical goals and more tangible scientific, economic, and security benefits. This shift from a technical base for decision-making was followed by President Reagan's two 1982 policy priorities: to expand private-sector involvement and investment and to maintain U.S. leadership in space. No longer its own customer, NASA faced several new challenges – commercialization, meeting the needs of civilian and military agencies, developing private sector activities, and meeting customer commitments. Meeting the needs and priorities of the new network of primary stakeholders (including Congress, the Department of Defense, and private industry) resulted in more emphasis being placed on cost and schedule constraints. Safety issues were overshadowed as personnel were pushed beyond their limits to meet deadlines. This was no longer an organization dominated by scientists and engineers. The bureaucrats and administrators were now in charge.

> This was **no longer** an organization dominated by scientists and engineers.

Consensual decision-making and problem-solving based on technical issues had been the norm at NASA. However, by the mid-1980s, with the various internal and external changes, a distinction was made between engineering and program management decisions. Decisions that once were made at the lowest possible level were now moved upward through successive decision-making levels. The final decision to launch the Challenger required the coordination of hundreds of prior decisions – cargo space, crew training, flight plans, schedules, computer programming, rocket flight ability – made by various contractors, subcontractors, and three space centers. Each person along the line assessed increasingly reduced summaries, added their own perceptions, and passed their evaluations and decisions up to yet another level.

On the Challenger launch decision, the Mission Management Team was the last in the chain of command. They took over management 48 hours prior to the launch and encouraged officials at lower levels to report new problems or difficulties. However, the time when anyone along the line could call a halt based on some safety concern was a tradition of the past. Reports had to pass up through the chain of command and, like a game of "pass it on," the information can be distorted as it moves up the hierarchy and is filtered by the interests and agendas of decision-makers along the way. This, along with the distinction in decision-making responsibility and the resultant reduced decision-making authority of technical personnel, was ultimately responsible for the decision to launch that fateful January.

Engineers of Morton Thiokol Inc. (MTI was responsible for solid rocket motors) had concerns about seal integrity at particularly low temperatures. These concerns were presented at an evening telecon meeting between MTI, the Marshall Space Flight Center, and the Kennedy Space Center, hours before the Challenger launch. According to Roger Boisjoly, the senior engineer on the MTI project, the data supported a no-launch decision. At the end of the presentation, Mulloy of NASA asked those present for their launch decisions. Based on the engineering position, MTI did not support the launch. Hardy of NASA, while "appalled" by MTI's recommendation, would not support a launch over a contractor's objection. Mulloy presented his views and suggested the data was inconclusive.

Had NASA's early rules requiring contractors and themselves to prove flight safety been in effect, the inconclusiveness would have been enough to stop the flight. However, it is likely that Mulloy's statement prompted MTI Vice-President Kilminster to request an off-line caucus to re-evaluate the data. As soon as MTI was off-line, MTI General Manager Mason declared, "We have to make a management decision."

Two MTI engineers, Thompson and Boisjoly, were present at that off-line meeting. Concerned that executive level management would attempt to reverse the no-launch decision, they tried to make themselves heard as the managers began a discussion among themselves. None of the managers seemed to want to discuss the facts and, ignoring the engineers, they struggled to build a list of data that would support a launch decision. The 12-point launch rationale that the managers formulated included one statement that was a lie, one statement that was supportive but did not address the concerns raised, and one statement that was merely engineering fact. Beyond this, the rationale actually supported a no-launch decision.

The engineers were excluded from the discussion and the final vote poll indicated only the four senior executives present. Returning to the telecon, Kilminster read the rationale and recommended that the launch proceed as scheduled. The launch recommendation was accepted by NASA without discussion or question. Rather than requiring the contractor to prove it was safe to fly, NASA had asked them to prove it was not safe to fly. The consequences of NASA's decision reverberated on television screens and radio waves around the world on January 28, 1986, a vivid memory that will be long in fading.

The Consulting Firms for the Four-Frame Model

Structor Associates – A structural approach to organizations
   "We design management systems to meet tomorrow's needs."

Humanotics – A human resource approach to organizations
   "We emphasize people in high tech."

The Luyd Group – A political approach to organizations (pronounced Lloyd)
   "Carving coalitions for creative causes."

Northstar – A symbolic approach to organizations
   "Pointing the way with symbols since 1903."

Structor Associates

This consulting firm has been highly successful in solving problems in some of our nation's most prestigious and powerful public and private organizations. The key to their success has been a focus on structure. The staff of Structor Associates believe the primary goal of a smoothly running organization is to have clear goals and established policies and lines of authority that will lead to reaching or surpassing those goals. "The key thing is structure," stated one Structor executive recently. "When you have the right structure and the people understand it, the organization will function as it is supposed to." A Structor consultant stated that, "If the right procedures are in place at NASA, things will work. You don't need to worry about pressure from Congress or personalities in the system. Let's design a NASA where engineers can engineer, managers can manage, and astronauts fly."

Humanotics

This consulting firm has been highly successful in solving problems in some of our nation's most prestigious and powerful public and private organizations. The key to their success has been a focus on people. Humanotics feels that organizations are basically made up of people. When the organization is responsive to their needs and supports their goals, you can count on their loyalty and commitment. They believe that management that doesn't communicate effectively and "really listen" to their employees is risking the creation of a disenchanted and unmotivated workforce. In such work climates, problems simmer just beneath the surface and company support is for show.

One Humanotics consultant said, "The good old days where NASA was really a tightly-knit family of people who talked straight to one another and cared about each other is gone. Once one of the strong "people-type" managers left, morale dropped and bureaucracy crept in. People don't come first any more at NASA and it took the explosion of Challenger to make this public."

The Luyd Group

This consulting firm has been highly successful in solving problems in some of our nation's most prestigious and powerful public and private organizations. The key to their success has been a focus on political realities. The Luyd group believes that all organizations are coalitions of various interest groups, each having its own agenda. There are not enough resources to give everyone what he/she wants, so those who can anticipate and manage these inevitable conflicts will survive while the others will become extinct. The Luyd group has not only helped organizations handle internal political issues that can sap an organization of its vitality, but has helped organizations become more cohesive internally, thus enabling them to compete for scarce resources more effectively in the marketplace.

The Luyd group helps organizations negotiate differences and reach reasonable compromises while at the same time teaching them how to "line up your ducks." One Luyd representative put it this way: "NASA got creamed by the politics in D.C. They said launch, launch, launch, while cutting back their funds. That led to a lot of infighting over safety issues and manned/unmanned space flights. Teams were split. You can bet no heads in Congress are being chopped off by this disaster. The people on 'The Hill' know how to protect themselves."

Northstar

This consulting firm has been highly successful in solving problems in some of our nation's most prestigious and powerful public and private organizations. The key to their success has been a focus on the symbols and culture of an organization. Northstar believes that organizations have unique identities like people. They have stories, history, and rituals. Really getting to know the essence of an organization is crucial if you want to help it grow and change. You can't really learn much from an annual report to understand the essence of an organization. Northstar believes that the saga is always unfolding and changing and that new symbols and heroes and villains are being added to the legacy of the past. A shared vision and sense of mission that bonds people and helps them overcome obstacles is needed. A Northstar consultant stated that after Apollo landed on the moon, Kennedy's vision had been realized and the drama was over. The image of space pioneers cavorting on the moon in their high tech version of covered wagons had given way to the less glamorous image of space lab assistants who were forced to rely on gimmicks, such as flying foreigners, minorities, senators, and civilians, to gain national attention. "NASA has lost its magic. It can't make it on technology alone. There has to be a special feeling there, a commitment, a leader with vision, a '90s version of JFK."

Ranking

After reading the perspectives of these four companies indicate which company you think should get the NASA contract. Please rank order your most preferred company "1" and the rest of the companies in declining order to "4" for your least preferred.

_____ Structor Associates   _____ Humanotics   _____ The Luyd Group   _____ Northstar

Sources

Stubbart, Les, Virginia Traub, and Michael Cavanaugh, in the *Journal of Management Case Studies,* Vol. 3, 1987, pp. 300-318. Original source of material by Lee Bolman and Terry Deal, *Modern Approaches to Understanding and Managing Organizations.* San Francisco, Jossey-Bass, 1984.

Background on the Four-Frame Model

The explosion of space shuttle Challenger, Mission 51,-L on January 28, 1986, left the nation stunned and the space program in disarray. The Rogers Commission Report (1986) identified the cause of the accident as the "failure in the joint between the lower segments of the right solid rocket motor... specifically... the destruction of the seals that are intended to prevent hot gases from leaking through the joint during the propellent burn of the rocket motor." The technological detective work that fingered the infamous "O-rings" as the chief perpetrator of this tragic accident also pointed to collateral reasons for the loss of the Challenger and its crew. Testimony taken by the Rogers Commission identified policies and procedures originating in the history and culture of NASA's space shuttle program that contributed to its sluggish response to a faulty O-ring design – a problem right from the start. NASA's ability to react and respond to critical problems as they arose was found to be limited by the management systems that were in place.

And yet 24 Challenger launches had succeeded before the key combination of elements all lined up in the required manner to spell disaster. A test pilot has a 23 percent chance of dying in an accident over a 20-year career. Perhaps the odds inherent in this risky adventure finally caught up with NASA.

The Four-Frame Analysis

Many complex organizations experience their own version of the Challenger debacle. For most, however, the results are not as obvious, deadly, or as publicized. When things go wrong with a project, questions are asked. But in order to arrive at effective remedies, what should these questions be? How can an effective administrator make sense out of the available data? In the space shuttle case, what strategies represent the "right stuff" for understanding the causes of the problem and managing its solution?

A recent book by Lee Bolman and Terrence Deal (1984) entitled *Modern Approaches to Understanding and Managing Organizations* introduces a novel approach for making sense of the chaotic environment we call organizational life. They suggest that effective leaders are able to view organizational problems from multiple perspectives or what they call "frames." Briefly, these points of view include:

(a) A structural perspective – What is the most appropriate organizational structure to accomplish established goals?

(b) Based on rational system theory, a human resources perspective – How well does the organization meet human needs? Based on human resource theory.

(c) A political perspective – How does the organization handle conflict and distribute scarce resources? Based on political theory.

(d) A symbolic perspective – What are the shared values and symbols of the organization and the meaning of their work? Based on symbolic theories.

Core Assumptions

The Structural Approach _____

1. Organizations exist primarily to accomplish established goals.

2. For any organization, there is a structure appropriate to the goals, the environment, the technology, and the participants.

3. Organizations work most effectively when environmental turbulence and the personal preferences of participants are contained by norms of rationality.

4. Specialization permits higher levels of individual expertise and performance.

5. Coordination and control are accomplished best through the exercise of authority and impersonal rules.

6. Structure can be systematically designed and implemented.

7. Organizational problems usually reflect an inappropriate structure and can be resolved through redesign and reorganization.

The Human Resource Approach

1. Organizations exist to serve human needs (and humans do not exist to serve organizational needs).

2. Organizations and people need each other. Organizations need the ideas, energy, and talent that people provide, while people need the careers, salaries, and work opportunities that organizations provide.

3. When the fit between the individual and the organization is poor, one or both will suffer: The individual will be exploited or will seek to exploit the organization, or both.

4. When the fit is good between the individual and the organization, both benefit: Humans can do meaningful and satisfying work while providing the resources the organization needs to accomplish its mission.

The Political Approach

The political frame views organizations as "alive and screaming" political arenas that house a complex variety of individuals and interest groups. Five propositions summarize the political perspective:

1. Most of the important decisions in organizations involve the allocation of scarce resources.

2. Organizations are coalitions composed of a number of individuals and interest groups (for example, hierarchal levels, departments, professional groups, ethnic groups).

3. Individuals and interest groups differ in their values, preferences, beliefs, information, and perceptions of reality. Such differences are usually enduring and change slowly if at all.

4. Organizational goals and decisions emerge from ongoing processes of bargaining, negotiation, and jockeying for position among individuals and groups.

5. Because of scarce resources and enduring differences, power and conflict are central features of organizational life.

The Symbolic Approach

1. What is most important about any event is not what happened but the meaning of what happened.

2. The meaning of an event is determined not simply by what happened but by the ways that humans interpret what happened.

3. Many of the most significant events and processes in organizations are substantially ambiguous or uncertain. It is often difficult or impossible to know what happened, why it happened, or what will happen next.

4. Ambiguity and uncertainty undermine rational approaches to analysis, problem solving, and decision-making.

5. When faced with uncertainty and ambiguity, humans create symbols to reduce the ambiguity, resolve confusion, increase predictability, and provide direction. Events themselves may remain illogical, random, fluid, and meaningless, but human symbols make life meaningful. Improvements come through symbols, myth, and image.

Bolman and Deal offer the four frames as one way of organizing and making sense of large amounts of data. They want managers to be flexible in their diagnoses of events in organizational life so that managers can recognize and cope with a variety of problems. Unfortunately, many managers limit their effectiveness by seeing most problems as stemming from a single source.

63. Hospital Departmental Consolidation[1]

Purpose:
To apply concepts of Organizational Design through a hospital case study.

Group Size:
Any number.

Time Required:
30 minutes.

Preparation Required:
Read the case study below.

Related Topics:
Decision-Making, Goal-Setting

Exercise Schedule

1. **Preparation (pre-class)**
   Read the following hospital case study and answer the discussion questions.

		Unit Time	Total Time
2.	**Group discussion**	15+ min	15 min

In groups of four to six members, discuss the answers to the questions.

3.	**Class discussion**	15 min	30 min

As a total class, discuss the responses to the questions.

Case Study: _____

Hospital Departmental Consolidation

Janet Johns is the administrator of Suburban Memorial Hospital, a 275-bed hospital in an upper class suburb located in the western states.

Ms. Johns recently asked the new assistant administrator, Sam Donalds, to investigate whether a consolidation of the EKG, Pulmonary Function, and Cardio-Pulmonary Rehabilitation departments would result in a significant savings to the hospital.

---

[1] © 1988 by Dorothy Marcic and Richard C. Housley.

Background

The three departments do basically the same types of patient tests. As medicine has progressed, there has been a movement away from static (at rest) testing to dynamic (in-motion) testing. Dynamic testing is used in the EKG Department for tests on the heart, in the Pulmonary Function Department for lung tests, and in the Cardio-Pulmonary Rehabilitation Department for both heart and lung.

At present there is a duplication of services and equipment among the three departments at Suburban Memorial. In addition, three separate technicians are employed as well as three different part-time physicians who work on a percentage basis, according to the volume of work.

The EKG and Pulmonary Function Departments make a significant contribution to Suburban's revenue. The contribution margin of Pulmonary Function has been 80 percent (for every $100 earned, the hospital spends only $20 to earn it) and that of EKG has been 60 percent.

Revenues for each department have been:

Department	Annual Revenue	Contribution Margin
EKG	$460,000	60%
Pulmonary Function	$620,000	80%
Cardio-Pulmonary (new department, less than one year)	$180,000	unknown

The total annual revenue of Suburban Memorial is $21.4 million and the net income is $2.1 million. Mr. Donalds has calculated that a departmental consolidation could initially save the hospital $160,000 by selling duplicated equipment. In addition, the annual savings would amount to:

$ 74,000	personnel costs (fewer technicians needed, etc.)
25,000	ordering and supplies reduction (no duplication, less ordering)
175,000	reduced physician fees (only one physician would be needed)
26,000	plant and facilities (can lease out space not needed after consolidation)
$300,000	**Total**

Therefore, the annual savings, in essence additional revenue, would be $300,000 in addition to the initial $160,000 for the selling of equipment.

Physicians

Dr. Bartl, head of Pulmonary Function, is responsible for 80 percent of the pulmonary admissions to the hospital and about 4.7 percent of the total admissions. He is an extremely popular physician, attracting respiratory cases from well outside the normal service area of Suburban Memorial.

Dr. Neuman, head of EKG, controls 20 percent of the hospital's cardiac/internal medicine cases. She admits about 30 percent of the hospital's patients.

Finally, the head of the new Cardio-Pulmonary Rehabilitation Department, Dr. Hermann, controls 100 percent of those cases which at this point represent a negligible percentage of the hospital's patient revenue.

All three physicians have more or less equal support from the medical staff.

Ms. Johns is wondering what to do about the physicians if she decides to go through with the consolidation. One of the three physicians would have to be chosen (with a new reimbursement contract) to head this new department, or perhaps a new, salaried physician could be brought in. The combined workload would still be less than full-time.

However, Ms. Johns sees several problems with either of those two alternatives. First of all, the physicians who would be "excluded" from this new department might become resentful and start admitting their out-of-service-area patients to other hospitals. Ms. Johns and Mr. Donalds have estimated a 25 percent probability that the three physicians would do so, which would mean a possible loss to the hospital of 15 percent of these physicians' admissions.

Ms. Johns has asked Mr. Donalds to prepare a report of the situation, including his recommendations, which will be discussed at the next management council meeting.

Discussion Questions

1. If you were Mr. Donalds, what would you recommend? Prepare the type of report Ms. Johns has asked for, as if it were going to be presented to the management council.

2. Assuming the council votes for consolidation, prepare another report outlining your recommended strategy, which would result in the least amount of alienation and maximum cooperation.

3. Which organization design theorists would back up and which would disagree with your proposal?

64. Sociotechnical Systems on Old McDonald's Farm

Purpose:
To learn to integrate the social as well as technical systems in an organization.

Group Size:
Any number of groups of four to six members

Time Required:
40 minutes or more.

Preparation Required:
Read background and case study and answer questions

Exercise Schedule

1. **Preparation (pre-class)**
   Read background and case study and answer questions.

		Unit Time	*Total Time*
2.	**Groups discuss**	**20+ min**	**20 min**

   Groups of four to six members discuss Mr. McDonald's dilemma and how to solve it.

3.	**Presentation**	**20+ min**	**40 min**

   Each group presents its recommendations to Mr. McDonald. These recommendations should be specific, so that Mr. McDonald could implement them soon.

Background in Sociotechnical Systems[1]

Sociotechnical Systems (STS), a term originated by the research group at the Tavistock Institute in London, represents a specific application for General Systems Theory in work settings. It narrows the broad focus of General Systems Theory to the interface between two organizational subsystems: social/human and technical. Cooper and Foster (1971, p. 467) provide the following definition:

The concept of the sociotechnical system is based on the simple fact that any production system requires both a technology – machinery, plant layout, raw materials – and a work-relationship structure that relates the human operators both to the technology and to each other. The technology makes demands and places limits on the type of work structure possible, while the work structure itself has social and psychological properties that generate their own unique requirements with regard to the task to be done.

According to Cummings and Srivasta (1977, p. 49), the term "social system" refers to "...a relationship between people who interact with each other in a given environment for the basic purpose of achieving an agreed-upon

---

[1] Adapted from Karen Brown, "Integrating Sociotechnical Systems into the Organizational Behavior Curriculum: Discussion and Class Exercise," *OBTR*, Vol. XII(1), 1987-88, pp. 35-48. Used with permission.

task or goal." They suggest that this may include human-human interaction, as well as human-environment interaction. These authors go on to describe the technological system as consisting of "the tools, techniques, and methods of doing that are employed for task performance." They emphasize the importance of not just viewing technology in terms of tangibles such as tools and machinery, and they advocate including abstract factors such as procedures, ideas, and methods of production as well.

Sociotechnical Systems Principles

Cherus (1978) has systematized the writings of others in the field of sociotechnical systems to develop a list of principles for this paradigm. These are named and described (briefly) below.

Principle 1: Compatibility. The process of system design must be compatible with its objectives. That is, if an organization is to be prepared to continuously adapt to its environment, it must make full use of the creative capacities of its members through participation.

Principle 2: Minimal Critical Specification. This implies that organizations should specify as little as possible about how tasks should be performed and who should perform them. Instead, organizations should specify what is to be done without designing jobs so specifically as to rule out creative options for meeting objectives.

Principle 3: The Sociotechnical Criterion. Variances, or unplanned events that affect outcomes, should be controlled as closely as possible to their point of origin. Examples might include machine maintenance being performed by the person who uses the machine, or quality inspection being performed by the person producing the goods.

Principle 4: The Multifunctional Principle – Organism vs. Mechanism. Organizations will be more adaptive to changing demands imposed by the environment if they avoid fractionating the tasks of elements (e.g., members). Instead, elements should be capable of a range of functions which may be used and combined in various ways over time. For example, an organization that employs a rigid assembly line with narrowly-defined tasks will find it difficult to adapt quickly to a market-driven change in product lines.

Principle 5: Boundary Location. Here, Cherus suggests that intra-organizational boundaries based on technology are likely to be simple for a manager to control, but are less likely than other forms to be efficient. Division of a job shop by machine-type, for example, results in clusters of like-technology (e.g., lathes) performing portions of many jobs in large batches. These batches of partially completed jobs move rather sluggishly through the system because of all the time they must spend waiting for other batches of jobs to be processed within each of a series of technology clusters. The alternative, which is exemplified by "group technology" and "just-in-time" manufacturing, involves creating boundaries based on time. That is, certain operations tend to occur in sequence, so the technologies required may be grouped together into small, responsive clusters.

Principle 6: Information Flow. This principle is an important adjunct to Principle 3, regarding proximity of control. It suggests that information systems should provide information initially to those who are in the best position to act upon it (i.e., those who control the variance). For example, feedback about production quality or quantity should be first (and frequently) made available to those at the operating level. Cherus (1978, p. 68) indicates that most information systems provide operating performance data to top levels first, inciting "top management to intervene in the conduct of operations for which their subordinates are and should be responsible."

Principle 7: Support Congruence. According to Cherus (1978), "support" includes pay systems, selection, training, conflict resolution, measurement of work, performance evaluation, timekeeping, leave allocation, promotion, and separation. Principle 7 advocates consistency between these systems and the organization's design and general philosophy. Specifically, if an organization is to employ the "team" approach advocated by STS, then all of the aforementioned systems should be congruent with that design. For example, an individual incentive pay system, or promotion based on individual output, would be counter-productive in a team-based structure.

Principle 8: Design and Human Values. This principle has to do with quality of work life (QWL). It suggests that QWL for members is an important responsibility of the organization. Each member of an organization may define QWL somewhat differently, but in general, jobs should be designed so that they are reasonably demanding, and provide opportunities for learning, decision-making, and recognition. Additionally, they should meet an individual's needs for relating one's job to one's social life, and perceiving the job as moving one toward a desirable future (Cherus, 1978).

Principle 9: Incompletion. This final principle emphasizes that organization design, involving the simultaneous consideration of social/behavioral and technical systems, is an ongoing process. Evaluation and review must continue indefinitely.

References

Cherus, A.B. "The Principles of Sociotechnical Design." *Sociotechnical Systems: A Source Book.* W.A. Pasmore and J.J. Sherwood (eds.). LaJolla, Ca: University Associates, pp. 61-71.

Cooper, R., and M. Foster. "Sociotechnical Systems," *American Psychologist,* 26, 1971, pp. 467-474.

Cummings, T.G. and S. Srivasta. *Management of Work: A Sociotechnical Systems Approach.* Kent, Ohio: Comparative Administration Research Institute, Kent State University Press, 1977.

Case Study: _____

Old McDonald's Farm[2]

Let's start considering structure with a very simple case. Below, you will see an illustration of Old McDonald's farm. On this farm, he had no pigs, cows, or chickens. On this farm, he had only corn, planted in long rows that grew all year around. McDonald had a perfect environment for growing corn. The soil was rich and the climate was perfect, 12 months out of the year.

McDonald's rows of corn were so long that at one end of the row, the soil was being prepared for planting, while the next section on that row was being planted, the next section was growing, and the next was being harvested. McDonald had four of these long rows.

McDonald is a progressive and scientific farmer. He is concerned about both productivity and quality. He had an industrial engineer study the amount of effort required to complete the work in each function on each row. He found that two employees were required per section, on each row, fully employed in that function all year round. Therefore, he employed eight workers on each row. For the purpose of this case, assume that this is true.

Initially, Mr. McDonald had only four rows, A, B, C and D, and a total of 32 people. But recently he decided to expand, adding two more rows. This added 16 more workers. Now he had 48 employees. Until this time, he had only one supervisor responsible for directing the work of all 32 employees on the initial four rows. Now he decided that there was too much work for one supervisor. He added another.

Mr. McDonald now had to decide whether to reorganize the work of his managers and employees.

Mr. McDonald decided to talk to his two supervisors, Mr. Jones and Mr. Smith. He found that they had very different ideas.

---

[2] From *Design for Quality* by Lawrence M. Miller, pp. 157-158, © 1991. The Miller Consulting Group. Used with permission.

	Soil Prep	Planting	Growing	Harvesting
Row A				
Row B				
Row C				
Row D				
Row E				
Row F				

Mr. Jones insisted that the only intelligent way to organize was around the technical knowledge, the functional expertise. He argued that he should take responsibility for all employees working on the first two sections, soil preparation and planting, on all rows; while Mr. Smith, whom he acknowledged had greater expertise in growing and harvesting, would take responsibility for all employees in the last two sections. They would each have an equal number of employees.

Mr. Smith had an entirely different idea. He argued while there was some specialized knowledge needed, it was more important for the employee to take responsibility for the entire growing cycle. This way they could move down the row, seeing the progress of the corn. He argued for organizing them into teams by row.

Mr. McDonald has hired you as a consultant to help him build the best possible organization. You are now to design the basic organization from the bottom up. Answer the following questions.

Questions

A. How will you organize employees on Mr. McDonald's farm and how will you assign responsibility to Smith and Jones? You are free to make any assignment you like, as long as you don't change the assumptions of the case (numbers of employees required on each task).

B. What sociotechnical system principles support you decision? Why is your decision better than alternatives?

65. Quality and the New Management Paradigm

Purpose:
To examine new directions in management theories and practices.

Group Size:
Any number of groups of three to five members.

Time Required:
30-40 minutes, depending on options.

Preparation Required:
Depends on whether doing Option A, B, and/or C.

Exercise Schedule

Option A

		Unit Time
1.	**Presentation of group findings**	**10 min per group**
2.	**Class discussion**	**15 min per group**

Instructor leads discussion on the importance of each of the six characteristics of the New Management Paradigm. Is that list complete? Should any be removed? How did the organizations studied fare on the six characteristics?

Assignment:

In groups of three to five members, choose an organization to study. It may be the workplace of one member or it may be an organization members are interested in and would have access to information from employees.

On the following pages are listed 12 paradigm shifts. Rate the organization you are studying on each of the 12 items. Use the questions in "The Quality Culture Survey" as a basis for your evaluation. In order to gather the necessary data, you will need to interview employees and managers at various levels and in different units. Ask them about each of the 12 characteristics.

For your 10-minute presentation to the class, give the ratings for each characteristic, as well as reasons for that particular rating. Feel free to use appropriate charts, graphs, overheads, or handouts in your presentation.

Twelve Shifts and the New Manager's Role[1]

Another way to understand the new manager's role is to consider the following 12 paradigm shifts. These paradigms demonstrate the swift change in thinking and behavior that world-class organizations have made. Each of these shifts implies new priorities.

12 Paradigm Shifts to World-Class Quality

1. Control Management	➤➤	Commitment Leadership
2. Command Decisions	➤➤	Consensus Decisions
3. Individual Work	➤➤	Team Work
4. Task Focused	➤➤	Process and Customer Focused
5. Experts and Labor	➤➤	Experts All
6. Control Through Threats and Fear	➤➤	Control Through Positive Reinforcement
7. One Right Way	➤➤	Continuous Improvement
8. Recordkeeping	➤➤	Scorekeeping
9. Tall & Rigid Structure	➤➤	Flat & Flexible Structure
10. Unstated Values and Vision	➤➤	Shared Values and Vision
11. Tough on People	➤➤	Tough on Competition
12. Wealth-Exploiting	➤➤	Wealth-Creating

1. Control Management to Commitment Management

The culture of our organization is changing because the nature of work and workers is changing. In the past, work was controllable. On the assembly line, jobs were repetitive and required little thought. Performance could be measured simply and reward and punishment administered to provide control. The manager counted, controlled, and determined reward and punishment.

Today, however, the critical performance is thinking about better ways to get the job done, initiating action to improve, and creating new products, services, or methods. These are not so easily "controlled." They require innovative thinking, risk-taking, and autonomy.

[1]From *Managing Quality Through Teams* by Lawrence M. 2Miller and Jennifer Howard. © 1991. The Miller Consulting Group. Used with permission.

The manager must give up control to those who have their hands on the work. High control increases fear and reduces risk-taking, initiative, and creativity, and destroys the very performance that is key to today's success. High control requires high management overhead costs. Eliminating fear and unnecessary control increases commitment, creativity, and other discretionary effort.

Managers create commitment by sharing vision and values, involving employees in decision-making, facilitating knowledge of customers and performance, and helping to improve the process.

2. Task Focus to Process and Customer Focus

In the past, managers were responsible for defining employee responsibility in terms of specific tasks. Industrial engineers measured each movement and the manager's job was to cause employees to adhere to the task definition.

In today's work environment, the "right" task definition changes too frequently as methods and machinery are continuously improved. Highly specific definitions quickly become rigid and an obstacle to improvement.

To optimize quality, employees at all levels must understand who their customers are, their requirements, and they must be involved in efforts to improve their process to meet customer needs. A quality organization is a customer-focused organization. A customer-focused organization defines work in terms of responsibility for complete processes that serve customer needs.

Managers must know who their customers are. Even the president of the company has customers. Among those customers are the employees, stockholders, end-use customers, internal customers, and the community. The manager's job is conditioned by his understanding of the needs of his customers.

> A quality organization is a **customer-focused** organization.

3. Command to Consensus Decision-Making

Command decision-making has been the dominant, male, decision-making model for most of mankind's existence. In Henry Ford's factory, the workers were mostly uneducated and had little knowledge of the work process beyond their immediate station on the assembly line. Command decisions produced the conformity and uniformity that led to success in the highly repetitious work.

Things have changed. Rather than centralized command decision-making, we need commitment, involvement, and ownership, which leads to creativity and acceptance of responsibility. Even the President of the United States must consult with other leaders. The former Soviet Union is moving towards consensus decision-making. Corporate CEOs must consult with stockholders, analysts, and interest groups. The degree of system integration or interdependence between organizations and people dictates a consultative or consensus decision process.

Most managers are now struggling to find the boundaries that define the appropriate style of decision-making. It is very difficult to switch styles. We develop habits of decision-making which are hard to change. It is normal to be somewhat confused and to have difficulty making this transition. If you are experiencing this difficulty, you may take some comfort in knowing that you have lots of company.

4. Individual Work to Team Work

In the past, managers assigned tasks to individuals and then rewarded or punished them. This worked well as long as the tasks were simple and independent.

> Today, tasks are increasingly complex and interdependent, requiring greater teamwork. Teamwork requires decision-making by the employee and among employees. Today, in many team-based organizations, employees are making their own decisions about which tasks will be completed by whom. They may take turns rotating tasks, or they may choose to specialize in tasks.

> Now the manager helps the team make these decisions well and assures that the process is functioning well.

5. Experts and Labor to Experts All

Even in our laws, we have enshrined the class distinction of labor and management, salaried and hourly, thinkers and doers. Perhaps this class distinction made sense on the farm or in the primitive factory. It does not make sense today!

> Today, "workers" may operate multi-million-dollar pieces of complex, computer-controlled production machinery, which in itself represents a whole production process. Most employees today are "knowledge" workers, regardless of the color of their collar, whether they push paper or steel. Accepting and promoting all employees as experts in their process is critical to the thinking of a quality organization.

> Managers may still be expert in a particular technical area. Increasingly, the role of managers will be to advise and educate the team on techical matters and assist in the improvement of equipment and technical processes. However the team is also an expert team. They are expert on their process and it is the manager's role to assure their competence, to provide the training, coaching, and feedback that will allow them to succeed.

6. Punishment to Positive Reinforcement

On the sailing ships of the British navy, Lord Nelson and the other captains ruled by leadership and punishment. Specifications detailed the punishments for any offense, from flogging to the yard arm. The men expected – and the captain relied upon – strong punishment. The men were conscripts with few options and largely ignorant. The nature of the work and the workers was consistent with the use of punishment.

> In the modern organization, everything is changed. Little punishment is allowed and everyone seeks and expects recognition and reward. Behavior is a function of its consequences. You get that which is rewarded. Performance must be made to matter with positive reinforcement.

> Many mangers have a great deal of difficulty providing positive recognition. Praising others is uncomfortable. For years they have seen their role as enforcing proper discipline, assuring that people are doing their assigned tasks doing what they are "supposed" to do. If they are "supposed" to do it, they should not have to be praised for it. Right? Wrong!

> Today, it is the manager's responsibility to provide an environment in which employees are encouraged to make suggestions, think creatively, and become enthusiastic about their team's performance. This can only be accomplished if managers recognize good performance, are outspoken in their praise, and demonstrate that they truly value the initiative of their associates.

7. One Right Way to Continuous Improvement

Products and services, requirements, and work processes changed slowly in the past. These change overnight today. By the time the "right way" is discovered, a new way is required. We must adopt the "racing spirit." Like continuous improvement of race cars on the track, we must constantly be looking for a better way.

In the past, the manager was the authority on the right way to do things. If he did not know how it was supposed to be done, he was seen as weak. Therefore, he often acted like he knew the right answer, even when he did not. Now the manager is liberated from this dehumanzing assumption.

Now it is assumed that the "right way" is constantly moving forward. The new "best way" may come from the lowest-level employees who have their hands on the product. Now the manager is not judged by knowing the right way, but by helping to facilitate continuous improvement. Continuous improvement is only possible if everyone at every level and in every function, not just the manager, is involved and accepts responsibility for improving performance to customers.

8. Recordkeeping to Scorekeeping

In the past, managers kept the numbers to keep track of others. Managers kept track of employees. Customers kept track of their suppliers. Accounting kept track of everybody. The assumption was that people, fundamentally, could not be trusted.

The manager in the team-based organization assumes that people can be trusted, given the correct system. A part of that system is numbers that allow people to keep their own score, set their own objectives, and experience the game of business. The manager today helps to provide the numbers to the team. The manager helps to provide numbers to suppliers so they can improve their work.

The manager in a team-based organization is a coach. What do coaches do? They provide feedback to their team members. The best kind of feedback is facts, numbers, and scores on the performance of the team. The coach helps the team members by suggesting things they can do to improve the numbers. However, when possible, the coach allows the team members to decide on their own action.

> The manager in a team-based organization is a **coach**.

9. Tall and Rigid Structure to Flat and Flexible Structure

As civilizations and companies rise, the buildings grow in height and have increasingly specialized rooms, complex patterns, and decorations. The organization chart and the patterns in our minds follow suit.

Bureaucracies have many layers and become rigid. Bureaucracies create fiefdoms within – and internal warfare among – competing departments. The walls grow, isolating people and slowing the work process. Improvement becomes increasingly difficult.

The team-based organization is in motion, with experts working across functions or disciplines taking responsibility for the entire process that serves customers. Because people are trusted and work in self-managing teams, rigid structure and layers of management are not necessary.

This has tremendous implications for the manager. In the past, managers measured their success by their rank, by the number of rungs on the ladder they had climbed. In the future, there will be fewer layers of rank. If managers continue to measure their success based on rank, they will find themselves disappointed.

In the future, managers will measure their success based on genuine accomplishment – new products developed, new levels of performance achieved, new methods developed, and new customers served. These are the genuine accomplishments of business, not levels or ranks. Now, managers must be recognized and appreciated for these contributions. New systems of compensation and recognition must be developed to encourage managers to spend their time and energies on activities that add value to their true customers.

10. Unstated Values to Stated and Shared Values

In the past, the leaders were not accountable to those below and did not need to reveal their principles. They only answered to someone above. The United States Constitution established the pattern of an agreed-upon set of principles to which the governors and those governed would mutually adhere.

Likewise, quality organizations have clearly stated values that define desired behavior, ethics, and goals. When values are clearly stated and shared, they serve as a unifying force directing energy toward productive effort.

Stated and shared values create a problem for managers. They are expected not only to conform to these principles, but to be an example. If the organization values teamwork, managers are expected to model teamwork. If the organization values continued learning, managers are expected to model continued learning. This is a heavy burden for managers to bear.

11. Tough on People to Tough on Competition

One of the greatest misconceptions about leadership during the recent past is that leaders are tough on their own people. The world's greatest military leaders (Alexander the Great, Lord Nelson, Napoleon, etc.) all demonstrated great affection and affiliation, even tenderness, toward their own people. They were hard on their competition.

Many of our so-called "tough" bosses, such as Frank Lorenzo at Eastern Airlines, are tough on their own people and easy on their competition. Delta has thrived while Lorenzo has been "tough."

> **Napoleon** was tough on the competition.

12. Wealth-Consuming to Wealth-Creating

The quality organization fulfills the fundamental role of business organization in a free society by creating new products and services. This creates new jobs and adds to the collective wealth of the society.

Those of us in business organizations can feel good about our contribution to society. We fulfill a worthwhile and noble purpose. It is the business organization that creates jobs, goods, and services, and determines the wealth of the society. In poor countries, it is likely that the business institution is not fulfilling its purpose.

Within our organization, we have a responsibility to ensure that we spend our resources in a way that adds value and creates wealth. This can only be accomplished if managers see themselves as responsible for creating new products and services, improving products and services, making better use of all resources, and thereby creating new jobs. This is the wealth-creation process.

Quality Culture Survey[2]

	Control Mgmt.			Commitment Mgmt.	
	Disagree	Somewhat Agree		Agree	
1. Our management trusts that employees will do their best work without controlling supervision.	0	2.5	5	7.5	10
2. Employees generally feel a commitment to the goals of the organization and have knowledge of the organization's performance.	0	2.5	5	7.5	10
3. Employees are organized to manage their own work effort.	0	2.5	5	7.5	10
4. Employees are trusted to make decisions about their work process so that they can improve performance on the spot.	0	2.5	5	7.5	10

	Task Focused			Process & Customer Focused	
5. Employees have defined their customers and communicate directly with those customers.	0	2.5	5	7.5	10
6. Employees have defined their work process to meet their customers' need.	0	2.5	5	7.5	10
7. Employees are organized so teams can work together with the common objective of improving service to their customers.	0	2.5	5	7.5	10
8. Employees receive regular feedback from their customers.	0	2.5	5	7.5	10
9. Employees are organized for, and are expected to, give feedback to their suppliers.	0	2.5	5	7.5	10

	Command			Consensus	
10. There are few layers of management because all employees are involved in decision-making and take responsibility for their own work.	0	2.5	5	7.5	10
11. I am involved in important decisions that will affect the way we do our work.	0	2.5	5	7.5	10

[2] From *Design for Total Quality* by Lawrence M. Miller. © 1991. The Miller Consulting Group. Used with permission.

Quality Control Survey (cont'd)

12. Managers do not consider themselves to be the decision-makers, but those who help and facilitate decisions by those who have the most knowledge of the work.	0	2.5	5	7.5	10
13. Employees are organized into decision-making groups and know the boundaries within which they can make decisions.	0	2.5	5	7.5	10

	Individual Work			Team Work	
14. Information on performance, scores and feedback are based on the work of our team.	0	2.5	5	7.5	10
15. We do our work in a way that is based on teamwork, rather than individuals working alone	0	2.5	5	7.5	10
16. Our team is appraised as a team.	0	2.5	5	7.5	10
17. We are rewarded and held accountable as a team.	0	2.5	5	7.5	10

	Experts and Labor			Experts All	
18. All employees are considered experts in their work, rather than simply workers.	0	2.5	5	7.5	10
19. Our company invests in our skills because it knows that competence equals quality.	0	2.5	5	7.5	10
20. We are rewarded for developing our skills.	0	2.5	5	7.5	10

	Control With Punishment			Control With Reinforcement	
21. There is little fear of punishment or criticism, and we are more likely to anticipate recognition for good performance.	0	2.5	5	7.5	10
22. There is a system by which excellent performance of teams is rewarded.	0	2.5	5	7.5	10
23. There are opportunities for individuals to achieve recognition by superior effort and skill.	0	2.5	5	7.5	10
24. It is common for individual managers to recognize performance.	0	2.5	5	7.5	10

	One Right Way			Continuous Improvement	
25. It is our job to continually improve our work methods.	0	2.5	5	7.5	10
26. Managers are anxious to hear that employees have found a way to improve their own work.	0	2.5	5	7.5	10

27. We reward innovation in how we do things.   0   2.5   5   7.5   10

	Record-keeping		Scorekeeping	
28. Our team keeps our own scores on our performance.   0   2.5   5   7.5   10

29. Our scores are visualized graphically, so we can see the effect of our performance.   0   2.5   5   7.5   10

30. We are not concerned about someone else keeping track of us. Rather, we are concerned about improving our own score.   0   2.5   5   7.5   10

	Tall and Rigid Structure		Flat and Flexible Structure	
31. There are few layers of management, and the managers who make decisions that affect us are close to us.   0   2.5   5   7.5   10

32. It is common to create teams or other groups to work on problems, projects, customers or other issues that arise.   0   2.5   5   7.5   10

33. Our team is built around the work process so that employees can take responsibility for a whole work process.   0   2.5   5   7.5   10

	Unstated Values and Vision		Shared Values and Vision	
34. The organization has a clearly stated set of values that guides behavior.   0   2.5   5   7.5   10

35. We know the vision of senior management for the future of this organization and we share that vision.   0   2.5   5   7.5   10

36. The vision of our future is exciting.   0   2.5   5   7.5   10

	Tough on People		Tough on Competiton	
37. Managers never demean or insult their employees.   0   2.5   5   7.5   10

38. We are feared by our competitors for our innovation, speed, and quality.   0   2.5   5   7.5   10

	Wealth-Exploiting		Wealth-Creating	
39. This organization is creating new products and services, expanding our market.   0   2.5   5   7.5   10

40. This organization is creating jobs by developing better products and services and doing a superior job of meeting customer needs.   0   2.5   5   7.5   10

Option B

A Manager's Job[3]

Listed below are some statements a 37-year-old manager made about his job at a large and successful corporation. If your job had these characteristics, how would you react to them? After each statement are five letters, A-E. Circle the letter that best describes how you would react according to the following scale:

A. I would enjoy this very much; it's completely acceptable.
B. This would be enjoyable and acceptable most of the time.
C. I'd have no reaction one way or another, or it would be about equally
   enjoyable and unpleasant.
D. This feature would be somewhat unpleasant for me.
E. This feature would be very unpleasant for me.

1. I regularly spend 30-40 percent of my time in meetings.   A B C D E

2. A year-and-a-half ago, my job did not exist, and I have been
    essentially inventing it as I go along.   A B C D E

3. The responsibilities I either assume or am assigned consistently
    exceed the authority I have for discharging them.   A B C D E

4. At any given moment in my job, I average about a dozen phone calls
    to be returned.   A B C D E

5. There seems to be very little relation in my job between the quality
    of my performance and my actual pay and fringe benefits.   A B C D E

6. I need about two weeks of management training a year to stay
    current in my job.   A B C D E

7. Because we have very effective equal employment opportunity
    in my company and because it is thoroughly multi-national, my job
    consistently brings me into close contact at a professional level with
    people of many races, ethnic groups, and nationalities and of both sexes.   A B C D E

8. There is no objective way to measure my effectiveness.   A B C D E

9. I report to three different bosses for different aspects of my job,
    and each has an equal say in my performance appraisal.   A B C D E

10. On average, about a third of my time is spent dealing with
    unexpected emergencies that force all scheduled work to be postponed.   A B C D E

---

[3] By Peter B. Vaill in *Managing as a Performing Art: New Ideas for a World of Chaotic Change,* published by Jossey-Bass, 1989. Used with permission of the publisher.

11. When I need to meet with the people who report to me, it takes my secretary most of a day to find a time when we are all available, and even then I have yet to have a meeting where everyone is present for the entire meeting.   A B C D E

12. The college degree I earned in preparation for this type of work is now obsolete, and I probably should return for another degree.   A B C D E

13. My job requires that I absorb about 100-200 pages a week of technical material.   A B C D E

14. I am out of town overnight at least one night a week.   A B C D E

15. My department is so interdependent with several other departments in the company that all distinctions about which department is responsible for which tasks are quite arbitrary.   A B C D E

16. I will probably get a promotion in about a year to a job in another division that has most of these same characteristics.   A B C D E

17. During the period of my employment here, either the entire company or the division I worked in has been reorganized every year or so.   A B C D E

18. While I face several possible promotions, I have no real career path.   A B C D E

19. While there are several possible promotions I can see ahead of me, I think I have no realistic chance of getting to the top levels of the company.   A B C D E

20. While I have many ideas about how to make things work better, I have no direct influence on either the business policies or the personnel policies that govern my division.   A B C D E

21. My company has recently put in an "assessment center" where I and other managers must go through an extensive battery of psychological tests to assess our potential.   A B C D E

22. My company is a defendant in an antitrust suit, and if the case comes to trial, I will probably have to testify about some decisions that were made a few years ago.   A B C D E

23. Advanced computer and other electronic office technology is continually being introduced into my division, necessitating constant learning on my part.   A B C D E

24. The computer terminal and screen I have in my office can be monitored in my bosses' office without my knowledge.   A B C D E

Scoring:

4 points for each A	2 points for each C	0 points for E
3 points for each B	1 point for each D	

Compute the total, divide by 24, and round to one decimal place.

Exercise Schedule

Option C

		Unit Time	Total Time
1.	**Group discussion**	**20+ min**	**20 min**

Groups of three to five members discuss answers to case studies.

2.	**Class discussion**	**20+ min**	**40 min**

Instructor leads a discussion on the Honda plant and how it works toward quality. Students share their experiences with quality (or lack thereof).

Case Study: _____

The Honda Way: A Visit to Marysville[4]

It became a practice at Honda America Manufacturing in Marysville, Ohio, to use my book *American Spirit* as a management development text. This resulted in an invitation to visit and present to the Honda management group. I spent two days touring the plant, speaking with managers and production associates, sitting in on meetings, and asking lots of questions. Why is Honda so good? The answer is both simple and complex. There is little that Honda does that is completely unique. There is nothing that stands out as their secret to quality. The secret is – they do everything – and they do it as a team!

I find that in every healthy corporate culture there is a common understanding of philosophy, the values and visions upon which decisions and practices are based. The management practices, the structure, systems, skills, style, and symbols are consistent with the philosophy. At Honda there is clearly a "Team" culture.

Even before entering the building, the philosophy became evident. As we drove toward the plant I noticed lines of newly planted trees. I was told that they were planted by newly hired associates. Each new associate plants a tree "so they can grow with the company." All associates (the term used for all employees) know the company philosophy. They see it every day in a hundred ways. They hear it consistently from their leaders. There are no contradictions.

The president of Honda of America is Shoichiro Irimajiri, known as Mr. Iri by the associates. Earlier in his career, Mr. Iri was responsible for managing Honda's successful racing efforts, designing engines and managing production facilities in Japan. He frequently speaks of the "Racing Spirit." The Racing Spirit includes five principles:

1. Seek the challenger.
   2. Be ready on time.
      3. Teamwork.
         4. Quick Response.
            5. Winner Takes All!

Perhaps more instructive of the Honda philosophy is his story of one of his early racing efforts.

It was in 1965 when Mr. Iri was working on the Formula I racing engines. In the British Grand Prix of that year, the engine failed and it was torn down and examined by Mr. Honda himself.

Examining the failed piston he turned to Shoichiro Irimajiri and demanded, "Who designed this piston?" "I did," he acknowledged. After examining the engineering drawing Mr. Honda roared out, "You! Stupid! No

---

[4] From *Managing Quality Through Teams* by Lawrence M. Miller. © 1991. The Miller Consulting Group. Used with permission.

wonder the piston gets burned. You have changed the thickness here." After the young Irimajiri attempted to defend his design change with some data from previous engines, Mr. Honda roared again: "I hate college graduates! They use only their heads. Do you really think you can use such obsolete data obtained from old, low-performance engines? I have been making and designing pistons for several years. I am fully aware how critical half a millimeter is here. A company does not need people like you who use only their heads. Before you laid out this design, why didn't you listen to opinions of those experienced people in the shop? If you think academic study in college is everything, you are totally wrong. You will be useless in Honda unless you spend more time on the spot for many years to come."

> **"I hate college graduates! They use only their heads!"**

"You will go to the machining shop," Mr. Honda ordered the young engineer, "and you will apologize to every person there, for you have wasted their efforts." Mr. Honda followed him down the hall to make sure he did as directed. Mr. Iri recalls that he was only glad that he had no ambition of becoming president of the company. He was not even sure he would succeed as an engineer. He learned his lesson. He not only succeeded as an engineer, designing several successful racing engines, but he became the president of Honda of America, the first Japanese company to export cars back to Japan. Shoichiro Irimajiri still listens to those experienced people in the shop and he is not wasting their time.

The Honda philosophy stresses to be on the spot in the plant and see the problem, touch the part, and gain experience in the actual job, in order to effectively solve a problem. Engineers and management spend most of their time in the factory, in touch with their associates, the product, and the process.

The Honda philosophy is manifested in all of the management practices. In the symbols, structure, systems, skills, and style, the philosophy can be seen and experienced every day, by every employee, every hour.

Symbols: When I arrived I was given a uniform to wear in the plant. I was told that this wasn't given to all guests, only "honored guests." To cover my tie with the white smock with the Honda name, to look the same as every other associate, was an honor. I can assure you that by the time my visit was finished it felt like an honor. To be part of a proud group of people, to share their symbol of equality, caused me to feel a part, invested, in their shared goals.

All associates, from president to newest hired associate, eat in the same cafeteria, park in the same undesignated parking spaces, and managers sit at the same metal desks in open office areas. Most of the desks are arranged in blocks of six, often with paired Japanese and American managers sitting across from one another. All of the managers of the motorcycle plant sit at one block of six identical desks, the Japanese vice-president and the American plant manager sitting across from each other.

As I walked through the plant – the cleanest non-food manufacturing plant out of several hundred I have been in – I observed a vice-president stop and pick up a misplaced object on the floor. There is nothing on the floor. There are also no maintenance people to clean up! Everyone, every associate and manager, cleans his or her own area.

To many, these symbols will seem trivial. They would be if they stood alone, at odds with the behavior and attitudes of the people, or if the structure and systems stood in contradiction. However, they are one part of a total system, like a well-engineered engine with all components balanced and moving in unison.

Structure: Everyone is a member of a team. The team is the first level of organization. At 6:30 a.m. each day, every associate meets with his team and team leader. The day's work is discussed and feedback on the previous day's quality is given. Any problems, changes, or concerns are shared during this meeting.

A team is comprised of 15 to 20 associates who work in a common area. As I toured both the auto and motorcycle plant, I stood and watched the assembly line in operation. I asked which person was the team leader and which was the production coordinator, the second-level manager. It was very hard to find them or distinguish them. I watched as there was an apparent problem on the motorcycle line.

One employee, having difficulty getting a frame over an engine assembly, had stopped the line. He and another associate worked frantically to get the frame in place. It took about twenty seconds for the line to move again. I asked where the team leader was. The other associate, helping to form the frame, was the team leader. The production coordinator was at the next station on the assembly line helping another associate catch up on the placement of electrical wire assemblies. I watched for about fifteen minutes as the team leader and production coordinator (equivalent of first-line supervisor and department manager) worked on the line, smiling, joking, and working hard and fast with their associates.

Nowhere is there a private office for team leaders or production coordinators. They do not remove themselves from the work. They are on the spot, seeing and touching the product, gaining experience and solving problems. They are part of the working team.

All managers are organized into teams and solve problems together. The structure of the organization, as well as the physical arrangement of desks and offices, makes group problem-solving a natural and constant occurrence.

Participation in the constant improvement process is also structured through Quality Circles. NH Circles (NH stands for "Now Honda, New Honda, Next Honda") are similar to circles in many other companies. However, at Honda they are one component of a total involvement process which they call VIP (Voluntary Involvement Program).

> Nowhere is there a **private office** for team leaders or production coordinators.

VIP includes a suggestion system, quality awards, and safety awards. Twenty percent of all associates participate in circles. The rate of suggestions adoption is 59.4 percent, and 60 percent participate in some component of the VIP process. In speaking with several NH Circle members, I was impressed that they felt the responsibility to see that accepted recommendations for improvement were implemented. They also felt that their circles were different from those in other companies in that they are constantly looking for any improvement in the production process, large or small, and even small improvements are highly valued. They said that the success of Honda was the result of constantly finding small improvements, not just looking for major ones.

Systems: I expected to find systems of employee involvement at Marysville. However, I was somewhat surprised to see the amount of thought put into the positive reinforcement systems. Honda of America practices performance management. They have found ways to provide constant feedback, recognition, and tangible positive reinforcement for almost every form of desirable performance.

The NH Circle program, suggestion system, quality awards, and safety awards are all tied together with a point system. Every associatiate earns points by participating in any of these improvement processes. Awards include award certificates, gift certificates, Department Manager's Award, Plant Manager's Award, and President's Award. These also result in points accumulating over your career, and these points can earn a Honda Civic (that's for 2,500 points) and an Accord (5,000 points), plus two weeks off with pay and airplane tickets to anywhere in the world with spending money.

In addition to hourly or salaried compensation, all associates participate in profit sharing. This profit sharing is an innovation of Honda of America and is not part of the system in Japan. Ten percent of the gross profit generated by Honda Motor Company is shared with associates based on their relative compensation. Good attendance results in another bonus. The average bonus check for attendance in 1986 was $832. The average profit sharing check was $2,688.

Performance analysis and feedback is an important part of any total performance management system. In each of the open office areas and in each of the many conference rooms, all of the walls are literally covered with charts and graphs representing different quality and productivity performance variables. The graphs are of every possible variety, some employing Statistical Process Control methods and some simply reflecting historical data with means, trends, and goal lines. Frequently, along with the charts on the wall are lists of causes or solutions to problems. Diagrams of auto parts or production machinery with arrows pointing to sources of problems are also frequent. It is obvious that all of the managers at Honda are in touch with plant performance data.

Another system worthy of mention is the discipline system. There are some fairly traditional and sound procedures for gradual counseling and discipline. However, the unique part of the discipline process is the peer review provided for associates who are dismissed for poor conduct. If an associate wishes to appeal a termination, a peer review panel is formed by randomly selecting six or eight production associates. One senior manager also serves on the panel with equal vote. The panel hears both sides of the case and then decides to overturn or accept the management decision. Nine out of ten times the decisions are upheld by the associates.

Skills: The measure of skills is found in the work product. There is no question Honda has highly skilled engineering and quality personnel. Most engineers are Japanese. Hiring and training more Americans is a goal for coming years. Honda is an engineering company. Most of the Japanese senior managers have served as design engineers for engines, including racing engines, or other components.

Having worked at other auto companies, it soon became obvious to me that at Honda the most valued personnel are those with engineering and technical competence. At many other companies, it is the financial managers and management professionals who are most valued. Honda is in the business of making excellent cars. Many other companies are in the business of making money, and, only secondarily, making cars. Honda makes money and does not need layers of bureaucratic managers because they are passionately dedicated to their technology and products.

On the assembly line, there is a process of continual skill development. Associates are rotated from one position to another to broaden their skills and increase their flexibility. Even when applicants are interviewed for employment at Honda, they are asked questions to determine their flexibility. Flexibility and the development of broad-based skills is a central principle.

At Honda, it is assumed the production associates are intelligent, skilled, and dedicated. They can, therefore, be trusted to manage the quality process. Every associate is a quality control inspector. The assembly process at Honda is based on just-in-time (JIT) inventory and assumption of 100 percent quality parts. Each associate knows it is his or her job to inspect each part to assure conformance to requirements. Any associate can reject a part. If a manager wants the part used after the associate has rejected it, the burden is on the manager to explain to the associate why it should be used. There is a quality assurance department with a team of associates who will call the suppliers regarding any and every bad part. Every vendor is assigned to one associate, who knows exactly who to call, including home telephones, to provide immediate feedback on any deviation from quality requirements.

> Every associate is a **quality control** inspector.

All of the methods described above are held together by people with a sense of humor and a high level of people-to-people skills.

As I interviewed managers, I repeatedly asked them how they felt working for, or with, Japanese managers. I wanted to know if there was any resentment toward the Japanese. I could find absolutely none. I could only find the most sincere respect and friendship. There was no feeling of "us Americans" working for "them." The reason for this mutual respect became more clear the next morning.

Every morning the 10 or 12 managers of the motorcycle plant meet to review performance, solve problems, and make plans for the day. The Japanese vice-president responsible for the motorcycle operations sat at the end of the table. The meeting was led by a manager who was two levels down. There was a lively discussion about the handling of an "almost-in-time" inventory situation that had almost halted production the previous day. There were three or four Japanese managers and about eight Americans in the meeting. One of the Japanese managers was very vocal about how confusing the situation was and how it should have been handled better. Several others discussed what happened and how it was being resolved today. The vice-president sat quietly through a half hour of discussion, never saying anything until the meeting was coming to a conclusion. Only then did he speak out. He had two points. First, he wanted to thank everyone for their efforts yesterday, rising to meet the challenge presented by their problem. Second, he wanted to stress how important it was to meet another challenge that was coming up within the next week. His tone was calm and reassuring.

These incidents, and dozens of others like them, proved to me that the integration of cultures is working in Marysville. The Americans have adopted the Japanese patience and view things from a long-term perspective. The Japanese have adopted, or at least accepted, the American fun-loving familiarity and creativity.

The style at Honda is different than at other Japanese companies and this may be central to their success and initiative in manufacturing in the United States. The traditional Japanese company places a high value on age and seniority. Honda does not. Mr. Irimajiri is a young man excited by winning races and building racing engines. Mr. Honda has retired because he believes the company should be run by young men. The first principle of Honda management policy is: "Proceed always with ambition and youthfulness." The second is: "Respect sound theory, develop fresh ideas and make the most effective use of time." The third is: "Enjoy your work, and always brighten your working atmosphere."

Honda now employs 6,000 youthful-minded and creative Buckeye associates in Marysville. That number will be raised to over 8,000 as the second auto assembly plant is built nearby. The U.S.-manufactured content of the Honda Accord is now about 60 percent and will be increased to 75 percent. The Accord is more American than some GM, Ford, or Chrysler nameplates with higher imported content.

As I left Marysville, I didn't leave with the feeling that I had visited a "foreign" manufacturer. Rather, I had the feeling that I had visited something new. I had visited a world-embracing company, with a world-embracing philosophy, as much American as Japanese, perhaps the best of both worlds. I could also think of nothing that Honda was doing, no secret in either principle or practice, that could not be adopted by any company – if its senior managers were knowledgeable, committed, and would "proceed always with youthfulness."

Discussion Questions

1. What does Honda do differently from places where you've worked?

2. What makes the Marysville Honda site a world-class plant?

3. How could other organizations work toward a world-class status?

4. Which of the nine principles of socio-technical systems (see the previous exercise, "Old McDonald's Farm," for description of these principles) does Honda use?

66. Words-In-Sentences Company

Purpose:
To design an organization for a particular task and carry through to production; to compare design elements with effectiveness.

Group Size:
Any number of groups of six to 14 persons.

Time Required:
50-90 minutes.

Related Topics:
Dynamics Within Groups, Work Motivation

❑ Background

You are a small company that manufactures words and then packages them in meaningful English-language sentences. Market research has established that sentences of at least three words but not more than six words are in demand. Therefore, packaging, distribution, and sales should be set up for three- to six-word sentences.

The "words-in-sentences" industry is highly competitive; several new firms have recently entered what appears to be an expanding market. Since raw materials, technology, and pricing are all standard for the industry, your ability to compete depends on two factors: (1) volume, and (2) quality.

Your Task

Your group must design and participate in running a WIS company. You should design your organization to be as efficient as possible during each ten-minute production run. After the first production run, you will have an opportunity to reorganize your company if you want.

Raw Materials

For each production you will be given a "raw material word or phrase." The letters found in the word or phrase serve as raw materials available to produce new words in sentences. For example, if the raw material word is "organization," you could produce the words and sentence: "Nat ran to a zoo."

Production Standards

There are several rules that have to be followed in producing "words-in-sentences." If these rules are not followed, your output will not meet production specifications and will not pass quality-control inspection.

1. The same letter may appear only as often in a manufactured word as it appears in the raw material word or phrase: for example, "organization" has two o's. Thus "zoo" is legitimate, but not "zoonosis." It has too many o's and s's.

2. Raw material letters can be used again in different manufactured words.

3. A manufactured word may be used only once in a sentence and in only one sentence during a production run; if a word – for example, "a" – is used once in a sentence, it is out of stock.

4. A new word may not be made by adding "s" to form the plural of an already manufactured word.

5. A word is defined by its spelling, not its meaning.

6. Nonsense words or nonsense sentences are unacceptable.

7. All words must be in the English language.

8. Names and places are acceptable.

9. Slang is not acceptable.

Measuring Performance

The output of your WIS company is measured by the total number of acceptable words that are packaged in sentences. The sentences must be legible, listed on no more than two sheets of paper, and handed to the Quality Control Review Board at the completion of each production run.

Delivery

Delivery must be made to the Quality Control Review Board thirty seconds after the end of each production run, or else all points are lost.

Quality Control

If any word in a sentence does not meet the standards set forth above, all the words in the sentence will be rejected. The Quality Control Review Board (composed of one member from each company) is the final arbiter of acceptability. In the event of a tie on the Review Board, a coin toss will determine the outcome.

Exercise Schedule

		Unit Time	*Total Time*
1.	**Form groups, organizations, and assign workplaces**	**2-5 min**	**2-5 min**

Groups should have between six and fourteen members (if there are more than 11-12 persons in a group, assign one or two observers). Each group is a company.

2.	**Read "Background"**	**5 min**	**7-10 min**

Ask the instructor about any points which need clarification.

3.	**Design organizations**	**7-15 min**	**14-25 min**

Design your organizations using as many members as you see fit to produce your "words-in-sentences."

You may want to consider the following:

    a. What is your objective?

    b. What type of task and environment do you have?

    c. What technology would work here?

    d. What type of division of labor is effective?

Assign one member of your group to serve on the Quality Review Board. This person may also take part in production runs.

4.   **Production Run #1**   **7-10 min**   **21-35 min**

The instructor will hand each WIS company a sheet with a raw material word or phrase. When the instructor announces "Begin production," you are to manufacture as many words as possible and package them in sentences for delivery to the Quality Control Review Board. You will have ten minutes. When the instructor announces "Stop production," you will have 30 seconds to deliver your output to the Quality Control Review Board. Output received after 30 seconds does not meet the delivery schedule and will not be counted.

5.   **Quality Review Board meets, evaluates output**   **5-10 min**   **26-45 min**

While that is going on, groups discuss what happened during the previous production run.

6.   **Companies evaluate performance and type of organization**   **5-10 min**   **31-55 min**

Groups may choose to restructure and reorganize for the next production run.

7.   **Production Run #2 (same as Production Run #1)**   **7-10 min**   **38-65 min**

8.   **Quality Review Board meets**   **5-10 min**   **43-75 min**

Quality Review Board evaluates output while groups draw their organization charts (for Runs #1 and #2) on the board.

9.   **Class discussion**   **7-15 min**   **50-90 min**

Instructor leads discussion of exercise as a whole. Discuss the following questions:

a.   What were the companies' scores for Runs #1 and #2?

b.   What type of structure did the "winning" company have? Did it reorganize for Run #2?

c.   What type of task was there? Technology? Environment?

d.   What would Joan Woodward, Henry Mintzberg, Frederick Taylor, Lawrence and Lorsch, or Burns and Stalker say about WIS Company organization?

Chapter 18
Organizational Decision-Making

67. Group Dynamics: Consultation[1]

Purpose:
To learn new skills in group problem-solving.

Group Size:
Any number.

Time required:
30 minutes or more.

➤➤ Introduction

Good ideas can wither from the ambience of the organization itself, for without trust and support, people are less likely to share ideas. In a risk-adverse environment, threat of punishment prevents ideas from ever being generated.

Even under the worst of conditions, though, some will have new ideas. There will always be the Edisons, the Fords, etc. However, in these turbulent times, organizations must look to involve as many people as possible in the innovation process, so that the maximum number of ideas come forth. The survival of the organization is at stake.

---

[1]This section was adapted by Dorothy Marcic from the article "Principles of Consultation Applied to the Process of Innovation in a Corporate Environment," by Robert B. Rosenfeld and Michael Winger-Bearskin, of Idea Connection Systems. Some parts are excerpted with permission from the authors. © 1994.

Exercise Schedule

		Unit Time	*Total Time*

1. **Class ideas on groups** — 10 min — 10 min

The instructor asks the class to list reasons why task groups don't work, and writes these on the board.

2. **Class ideas on how groups can be better** — 10 min — 20 min

The instructor asks the students, "What behaviors would a group have if it would be successful in its tasks or in problem-solving?" and writes their ideas on the board.

3. **Consultation** — 10-15 min — 30-35 min

The instructor goes over the main ideas of the consultation methodology. The class discusses how this group technique would work in practice.

4. **Role-play (optional)** — 20 min

The instructor assigns students to act in two role-playing exercises. In the first one, the group uses a less effective group technique. In the second, it uses consultation. The class observes and later discusses differences between the two.

How Can One Manage Diversity?

George Bernard Shaw once remarked that the worst block to communication is the assumption that it has already been made. Thinking we have the answer, we stop asking. Tending to accept miscommunication as a normal part of human interaction, we often think it is easier to maintain a pattern of misreading than struggling to grasp a different way of viewing the world. Yet it is that different view that could save us from countless misunderstandings.

Within corporations, one must communicate, and communicate effectively, to survive. Effective communication can be significantly enhanced through the process of consultation, a means by which a group can have true dialogue. In his new book, *The Fifth Discipline*, Peter Senge lists five requirements for organizational success in the future. One is team dialogue, the sharing of ideas. He contrasts that with discussion, which comes from the root words concussion and percussion, basically meaning to throw ideas at one another. In this new post-industrial age, merely having a series of individual monologues in meetings will not be sufficient.

Consultation

Consultation is a method of communication that is solution-driven, as opposed to power-oriented. Its goal is investigating truth. Anyone who speaks must do so *not* with an attitude of correctness, but rather with the idea of contributing to consensus. While listening, each person needs to carefully consider the merits of what is being put forth, rather than automatically thinking of ways to oppose or undermine the argument. If another idea seems worthy, the listener should accept it and not willfully hold on to his/her own.

> "If he finds that a previously expressed opinion is more true and worthy, he should accept it immediately and not willfully hold to an opinion of his own."   — 'Abdu'l-Bahá

"But before the majority...comes to a decision, it is not only the right but the...obligation of every member to express freely and openly his views, without being afraid of displeasing or alienating his fellow members. [Members] should give up the method of asking other members to voice your opinion and suggestions. This indirect way of expressing your views...creates an atmosphere of secrecy [and] would also lead to many misunderstandings and complications." — *Shoghi Effendi Rabbani*

Consultation has three main features:

- Meeting group goals

- Utilizing diversity in order to discover the truth

- Respect of others' ideas, so that no one is ever belittled

Principles underlying this process are:

- Purity of motive

- Truth-seeking

- Patience and courtesy

- Unity

Consultation requires group members to value contributions from all members without invoking hierarchy in the decision-making process. Striving to make one's opinions dominant is too often the case in normal discussions, where leadership gets confused with domination.

"[They] must learn to forget personalities and to overcome the desire – so natural in people – to take sides and fight about it." — *Shoghi Effendi Rabbani*

Consultation requires full participation of all members, and leadership is expressed in service to the group. This idea, interestingly, is similar to Janet Hagberg's in *Real Power,* where she defines the highest form of power as that of service to others. It also parallels the concepts in the Tao of Leadership, where the one in charge is most effective when helping the group.

True respect is shown by word and deed, by the way people talk to one another, the tone of voice, and by the manner of interaction. Without respect, there can be no trust, and without trust, it is not possible to capitalize on human diversity. Intimidation silences the meek, and disrespect antagonizes the proud. Groups cannot afford such silences if their aim is to solve problems larger than themselves – larger than their need to intimidate, larger than their pride, greater than their desire to dominate or be "right."

"Through the clash of personal opinions...the spark of truth is often ignited. [They] should therefore not feel discouraged at the differences of opinion that may prevail...for these...fulfill a valuable function in all...deliberations...." — *Shoghi Effendi Rabbani*

Consultation is propelled by goals that are formed by the sincere collective will of individuals and made successful by the integration of differences within a framework of unity. This is consultation's key element – unity of thought and action emerge from an acceptance of difference, not its negation.

The three principles of

meeting group goals, utilizing diversity and maintaining respect

are all central to innovation in an organization. Consultation as a process can soften the rigidity of a corporate structure, allowing ideas to navigate successfully through a complex system.

Consultation: Turning Conjecture Into Certainty

Purpose:

• Create team commitment, trust among diverse participants

• Identify opportunities and solve problems

• Determine the best course of action

Ten Principles for Success

1. Respect each participant and appreciate each other's diversity. This is the prime requisite for consultation.

2. Value and consider all contributions. Belittle none. Withhold evaluation until sufficient information has been gathered.

3. Contribute and express opinions with complete freedom.

4. Carefully consider the views of others – if a valid point of view has been offered, accept it as your own.

5. Keep to the mission at hand. Extraneous conversation may be important to team-building, but it is not consultation, which is solution-driven.

6. Share in the group's unified purpose – desire for success of the mission.

7. Expect the truth to emerge from the clash of differing opinions. Optimum solutions emerge from diversity of opinion.

8. Once stated, let go of opinions. Don't try to "defend" your position, but rather let it go. Ownership causes disharmony among the team and almost always gets in the way of finding the truth.

9. Contribute to maintaining a friendly atmosphere by speaking with courtesy, dignity, care, and moderation. This will promote unity and openness.

10. Seek consensus. But if consensus is impossible, let the majority rule. Remember, though, that decisions, once made, become the decision of every participant. After the group has decided, dissenting opinions are destructive to the success of the mission. When decisions are undertaken with total group support, wrong decisions can be more fully observed and corrected.

Additional Quotations on Consultation from 'Abdu'l-Bahá...

The members thereof must take counsel together in such wise that no occasion for ill-feeling or discord may arise. This can be attained when every member expresseth with absolute freedom his own opinion and setteth forth his argument.

Man should weigh his opinions with the utmost serenity, calmness, and composure. Before expressing his own views, he should carefully consider the views already advanced by others.

Should any one oppose, he must on no account feel hurt, for not until matters are fully discussed can the right way be revealed. The shining spark of truth cometh forth only after the clash of differing opinions.

He who expresseth an opinion should not voice it as correct and right, but set it forth as a contribution to the consensus of opinion; for the light of reality becometh apparent when two opinions coincide.

68. Casual Togs, Inc.[1]

Purpose:
To integrate various concepts from the organizational behavior class.

Group Size:
Four to six members.

Time Required:
10-20 minutes or more

Preparation Required:
Read case study and answer questions.

Exercise Schedule

		Unit Time	Total Time
1.	**Pre-class** Read case study and do assignment.		
2.	**Small groups (optional)** Groups of four to six members come to a consensus on possible solutions.	10-20 min	
3.	**Groups report (optional)** Each group gives a brief summary of its solutions.	10-20 min	
4.	**Class discussion** Instructor leads a discussion on possible solutions.	10-20 min	10-20 min

Assignment:

Assume you are an outside consultant making a report to the Board of Directors who, as a group, are unhappy with sales and profits over the last five years, i.e. both have been decreasing (profits more than sales) at an increasing rate. The only Board member presently content is Judy Geldmark; she and other members have a hostile, adversarial relationship. She owns 12 percent of outstanding common stock, vs. 80 percent by Cy Geldmark and eight percent by other board members.

---

[1]By Paul J. Wolff II, professor, Oxford, MD. Used with permission.

Case Study: _____

Casual Togs, Inc.

Casual Togs is a 20-year-old firm producing moderately priced women's apparel, headquartered in a midwestern city. About 80 percent of production is sold to large and middle-sized department stores in cities throughout the country. The remaining 20 percent is sold to small women's specialty shops. All clothes carry the firm's well-known brand label. Products are principally shirts and blouses, with some knit dresses making up the balance.

The owner and principal stockholder, Cy Geldmark, is an entrepreneur. Cy served a long apprenticeship in the New York garment district and saved part of his meager wages until he could open his own firm, staffed primarily with relatives and friends. An innovator, Cy pioneered in the "mix and/or match" coordinate idea of fashion ensembles whereby a customer of moderate means could build a complete wardrobe of work and casual clothes. Designers with trend-setting styles and above-average quality (considering the semi-mass-production methods employed) helped propel Casual Togs to a prominent position in the industry.

However, the mix-and-match coordinate idea was not patented and intense fashion competition has now developed from larger firms as well as from new, smaller companies with fresh fashion ideas. In Cy's words, price competition is "deadly." The company has rapidly expanded in the last five years, setting up production plants in seven southern states as well as one in Arkansas to capitalize on low wage rates in these areas.

All facilities in these states are leased. Notwithstanding the use of the latest in large-capacity cutters and high-speed sewing machines, production hinges on a great expenditure of careful, personal effort by the individual worker. Many quality checks are necessary before a garment is finished.

In an attempt to coordinate production and delivery, the company is constructing a new multi-million-dollar central distribution plant at the present home office location, where all administrative and some production functions are performed. All production runs will be shipped to this new facility and then be dispatched by a computer-programmed delivery-inventory scheduling method. This facility is planned to help cope with an increasingly serious problem of merchandise returned from customers who refuse acceptance because delivery is later than promised.

The industry is characterized by five distinct selling fashion "seasons;" consequently garments must be ordered, produced, and delivered within a relatively short time period. This five-season cycle produces unusual production and forecasting problems. Based on pilot sales during the first two weeks of each season, forecasts are developed regarding the quantity and styles to be produced for the entire season. Once the bolts of cloth are cut into a particular season's patterns, there is no turning back. If pilot sales are not indicative of the rest of the season or if the sales forecast is in error, the company is saddled with stock that can be disposed of only through "off-price" outlets, usually at a loss.

In an effort to increase the accuracy of sales forecasting and to pinpoint specific reasons for late deliveries, Cy instituted a computer printout of each day's sales, as reported by telephone by field salesmen. This printout was, initially, distributed to the president, the vice-president of sales, the sales forecast manager, the treasurer, the production manager, and the eight regional sales managers. All of these people were located at the firm's headquarters offices. The printout was voluminous, often running 100 or more pages.

> Cy relied a great deal on his **"feel of the situation"** for making decisions.

Cy relied a great deal on his "feel of the situation" for making decisions. Although he made all final important operating and policy decisions, he said that all department heads should feel free to act as "you see fit;" he said that he would back any decisions made without consultation with him. Despite Cy's exhortations that he need not be consulted, almost all vice-presidents and departmental managers conferred daily with him, usually regarding the progress of the then current fashion season's products. During each fashion season, many style modifications and quantity level changes were made. With rare exceptions, Cy made all important daily decisions in these matters.

These daily decision sessions were marked by emotional outbursts by various management personnel. The meetings were informal and nonscheduled and different groups would meet at different times with Cy. The groups were not formal or even based on functional problem lines. If one individual felt that a daily printout indicated change "X," regardless of whether or not it affected his department, he would go to the president asking that the change be effected. If another department manager or even a vice-president were present and disagreed, inevitably a shouting match developed in the president's office. Usually Cy remained impassive during these interchanges, giving his decision after all participants had finished.

Some management personnel said that Cy was "too lenient" and should curb these emotionally charged sessions because they were disruptive and led to erroneous decisions. These same critics pointed to Cy's reputation as an easy mark for suppliers, e.g., if a supplier had some previous tie from the old days or was remotely related to someone in Cy's family, he would be assured of at least some orders, despite the fact that his prices were higher than those of competing suppliers.

Often the president's sister, Judy, who was vice-president in charge of administration, would wander into these daily decision sessions. She would often object to proposed changes on the grounds that they had been proposed by "imbeciles" or were "too damned expensive." Judy was everywhere, initiating changes herself in every department. Her decisions affected everything from copier paper to salesmen's commissions to rest period schedules for the clerical help. She often countermanded a department manager's instructions and would hire and fire personnel without the manager's knowledge. Judy's personality was judged abrasive by all who contacted her; she was given to using profanity publicly at a "longshoreman's quality level." When speaking "normally," she could be heard for some distance. Cy always backed Judy's decisions once they were made.

> Judy was everywhere, **initiating changes herself** in every department.

Although the formal organizational chart depicted Judy and the treasurer as being on the same level, the treasurer, Stan Seeburg (Cy's nephew), was not allowed to approve any expenditure over $1,000 without Judy's informal approval. Judy was one of the original founders, owned 12 percent of the firm's stock, was unmarried, and of middle age. From time to time Cy tried, by his own admission, to calm her down, with a notable lack of success. But several sources reported that if Judy and her brother had an argument in private, Judy always deferred to her brother's decisions.

For many years Cy's chief source of sales data and forecast was Andy Johnson, sales forecast/budget manager. Andy prepared daily, handwritten recaps from telephone reports in the earlier years and from the printout in more recent years. Using intuition and a very thorough knowledge of the garment industry, Andy would prepare the season's forecasts and modify them as the actual sales started coming in. He had a rapport with Cy and was quite proud of the clearly evident esteem that the president had for him.

This rapport was important to Andy for more than reasons of self-esteem. Andy had been with the firm for 15 years, but despite his knowledge had never been promoted. He resented this keenly and attributed his lack of success to the fact that he was not a relative or of the same nationality as the other managers. "At least," said Andy once, "Cy listens to me more than to these shirt-tail relatives." Andy was one of the very few people who called the president by his first name in public.

In a recent change in office location, Andy and his former co-worker, Sol Green, were moved from one large, shared office, which housed subordinates as well, to individual glass-partitioned offices. The subordinates were now located adjacent to Andy's and Sol's offices. After this move, Sol was promoted to manager/internal accounting and sales, and was given control over all subordinates who previously had worked collectively for Andy and Sol.

Andy was given one new man to help with sales forecasts and budgets; the new man had an M.B.A. and was trained in statistical analysis. Andy held a bachelor's degree in business. Bill Smith, the new man, suggested several new methods of collating and analyzing the daily printout to Andy, who abruptly rejected the ideas, saying, "Cy isn't used to getting data in that form; he would be confused by a change."

As the daily printouts began to be more detailed and more widely distributed, Andy became more critical of them than usual. He said that they didn't "really" show what styles were leading, and that there were many errors. Andy quoted personal conversations with field salesmen to prove his points. When Bill cited several new styles in what had previously been one category, Andy replied that he was using horse sense to report data in a way that Cy and others would best understand. Andy was away from his desk for long periods during this time, attending numerous management meetings that the president called. The pattern of these meetings was as before, or worse; there were loud, emotional arguments punctuated by fist-pounding and door-slamming.

> "Cy isn't used to getting data in that form; **he would be confused by a change."**

The problem of returns was now most acute; on average, 40 percent of all shipments were being returned. Although all management personnel agreed that the reason for returns was late deliveries, some managers argued that forecasting by style lines was inaccurate and resulted in erroneous production scheduling, and others said that there was no coordinating between the nine production centers and the shipping department, which was located at the home office site. Still others said that shipping and/or production methods were not efficient. The production manager said that there was a disparity between the delivery dates given by customers and those in the salesmen's orders, which served as the basis of a production run. The sales manager maintained that poor quality was the real reason for returns: customers did not want to become embroiled in arguments with home office personnel over quality questions and therefore they wrote "late delivery" on sub-standard merchandise because it was simpler.

In an effort to solve the dilemma, Cy hired an experienced market analyst, Stan Levine, who had a strong computer-oriented background. Stan was given a private office and the authority to effect any changes he deemed necessary. Several events happened immediately; a supplemental recap of the printout was published every day by Stan — in addition to Andy's handwritten recap; the printout format was changed. Sol objected violently to the new format, saying that it did not provide accounting with the categorizations necessary for their work. Andy began a "war" with Stan, "to show up this egotistical, snot-nosed kid."

At this same time, several new designers were hired, salesmen's commission schedules were changed, many regional vice-presidents were put on the road "temporarily," and Andy, backed by Cy, cut all departments' budgets by 15 percent (the company was in the middle of a 12-month budget period).

Approximately four weeks after all these changes had occurred, the following events transpired: returns had increased to an even higher level; many old customers had stopped ordering, saying that poor quality and late deliveries made Casual Togs too undependable; the distribution center construction was halted at midpoint "because the company could not find a qualified individual to fill the job of supervisor;" the nine plant centers fell, on average, 15 percent under previously established production goals; two of the new designers resigned; Judy fired the new vice-president of industrial relations after he had been on the job four weeks (he held a three-year management contract for $30,000 per year); neither Andy Johnson, Sol Green, nor Stan Levine would speak to each other; Andy began distributing two daily sales recap reports to a select, small group of top management; and the computer services department complained directly to Cy that their new workload was too great because Stan now required them to produce a daily selling forecast, by week, month, and season.

Discussion Questions

1. What are the major problems facing this firm?

2. What led to these problems?

3. By area, e.g. Marketing, Production, etc.:

   a) develop/formulate a strategic plan for dealing with these problems

   b) show the stages, or steps, or phases, through which your plan should evolve –
      i.e., a time line with sequences and your rationale for using these stages

4. What strategy/tactic would you employ to persuade Cy to change his ways? Why?

5. For the company as a whole, to prevent future problems and help ensure adequate responses
   to the dynamics of the women's fashion industry (that segment comprising the middle-to-upper
   middle-to-lower-upper price level), one highlighted by rapid changes in consumer tastes,
   what initiatives should the company take in areas of:

   a) management information systems?

   b) management practices?

   c) structural changes (align with strategy suggested in 3 above)?

   d) responses to changes in:
      (1) environment?

      (2) competitive situation?

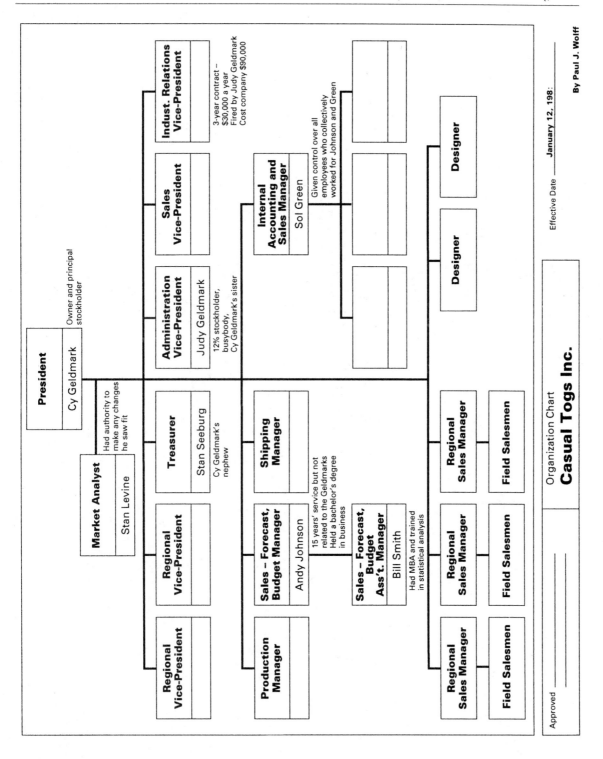

President

Cy Geldmark

Owner and principal stockholder

Market Analyst

Stan Levine

Had authority to make any changes he saw fit

Indust. Relations Vice-President

3-year contract – $30,000 a year
Fired by Judy Geldmark
Cost company $90,000

Sales Vice-President

Administration Vice-President

Judy Geldmark

12% stockholder, busybody, Cy Geldmark's sister

Internal Accounting and Sales Manager

Sol Green

Given control over all employees who collectively worked for Johnson and Green

Treasurer

Stan Seeburg

Cy Geldmark's nephew

Regional Vice-President

Sales – Forecast, Budget Manager

Andy Johnson

15 years' service but not related to the Geldmarks
Held a bachelor's degree in business

Shipping Manager

Sales – Forecast, Budget Ass't. Manager

Bill Smith

Had MBA and trained in statistical analysis

Regional Vice-President

Production Manager

Regional Sales Manager

Regional Sales Manager

Regional Sales Manager

Field Salesmen

Field Salesmen

Field Salesmen

Designer

Designer

Designer

Approved _____

Organization Chart

Casual Togs Inc.

Effective Date _____ **January 12, 198:**

By Paul J. Wolff

Chapter 19
Nature of Planned Organizational Change

69. Downsizing: Merger at LocalBank[1]

Purpose:
To discuss change issues regarding mergers and downsizing.

Group Size:
Groups of four to six members.

Time:
20-40 minutes or more.

Exercise Schedule

1. **Pre-class**
   Read case study and answer questions.

	Unit Time	Total Time
2. **Groups prepare report**	10-20 min	10-20 min

   Groups answer questions and prepare presentation or written report.

3. **Groups present (optional)**   **10-20 min**
    Each group briefly presents the main points and issues.

4. **Class discussion**   **10-20 min**   **20-40 min**
    Instructor leads discussion of main issues.

Case Study: _____

Merger at LocalBank

LocalBank is a large regional bank with over 100 branches in the metropolitan area. It has been known throughout its history for stability, conservatism, and strong community ties. Mary Johnson is the regional manager responsible for six branches in a suburban area. Each branch has the following staff: a branch manager, 10-15 tellers, and one assistant branch manager. Mary has been with LocalBank since 1986. Her branch managers have between one and 25 years of service.

Mary joined LocalBank after graduating from Loyola College with her MBA in Finance. She started as a Marketing Analyst and was promoted to her present position about six months ago. She has a good relationship with her staff, although she does not believe that she knows them very well as yet.

The six branch managers are profiled below:

Robert – Age 45, 15 years of service with the bank. Good performer. Previously served in the military before joining the bank. Has a wife who was recently laid off after her company merged and then downsized its staff.

Millicent – Age 32, 10 years of service with the bank. Above-average performer. This is her only employer. Single. Is planning a month-long trip to South America in three months.

Paul – Age 61, 25 years of service. Good performer. Spouse recently retired for health reasons from the federal government. Needs one more year of service to retire, but has recently mentioned his intention to stay until age 65 so that he can keep full health benefits for his wife.

Calvin – Age 27, one year of service. Good performer. This is his third employer. The last two banks he worked for each merged and then downsized staff. Calvin had the least seniority and was laid off. He is married and has one young child.

Renee – Age 28, three years of service. Exceptional performer. Also a Loyola MBA graduate. Married for eight years to an artist whose work is just beginning to sell.

Florence – Age 58, 23 years of service. Exceptional performer. Started with the bank after raising her children. Does not have her degree and is attending college part-time.

The tellers range in age from 21 to 62. Most are women and many have been with the bank for several years. It is a relatively stable workforce, since the bank is known for its generous benefits and competitive salaries. Also, tellers can receive bonuses for exemplary customer service, accuracy, and sales of bank services.

Merger Announced

Last Monday, at the monthly staff meeting, Mary Johnson's boss announced that the rumors were true: LocalBank was going to merge with a large regional bank with branches in the Baltimore, Washington, and northern Virginia markets. (The acquiring organization is run by a CEO who previously was with American Express. This organization has been aggressively making acquisitions and using mass marketing techniques to promote its products.) Mary's manager did not have any further information, but was certain that it would mean at least a 10 percent cut in branches and staff at *all* levels in the bank (i.e., one branch totally closed, others reduced). He advised each manager that during the next 90 days, they must achieve the following:

> **It would mean at least a 10% cut at all levels in the bank.**

(1) Begin preparing staff for the merger – changes in procedures, processes, job descriptions, and the other thousands of details. He noted that specific information would be coming daily and would then have to be disseminated to staff quickly and efficiently.

(2) Prepare a personnel evaluation document ranking each employee on performance. This document would be used to prepare a layoff listing.

Mary's boss also told his staff to announce the merger and the downsizing plan. In addition, he stated that each regional manager had to maintain customer service and morale in the branches. He also noted that an Organizational Development consultant would be available to assist each branch manager with organizational issues, communication to staff, etc.

On Tuesday, last week, Mary met with her six branch managers to announce the merger and downsizing plans. Each branch manager then returned to his/her branch and made announcements. Tomorrow, Mary will meet with the OD consultant for the first time.

Case Questions

In your team, please prepare a brief presentation (or written report) on the following:

1. What are the general issues in this case?

2. What reactions can Mary expect from her staff? Customers?

3. Teacher may write Mintzberg's managerial roles on the board. Based on these, outline some specific actions that you would recommend to Mary as she acts in each role. (Note: Your group may decide that all the roles are not applicable – be prepared to defend why.) What are the expected outcomes of the actions you recommend?

4. Which two roles do you think will be most critical during the coming months? Why?

5. How should Mary be rewarded for exemplary performance over the coming months?

6. Should Mary stay with this organization or immediately look for another position? Why or why not? Defend your answer.

70. Force Field Analysis

Purpose:
To apply Lewin's Force Field Analysis Model to a problem in your life.

Group Size:
Any number of groups of three to four members.

Time Required:
35 minutes or more.

Preparation Required:
Read the "Introduction."

Exercise Schedule

		Unit Time	Total Time
1.	**Preparation (pre-class, optional)**	10 min	
	Complete the Problem Analysis section and fill in the model.		
2.	**Group discussion**	20 min	20 min
	In groups of three to four members, discuss the driving and restraining forces in each person's problem.		
3.	**Class discussion**	15 min	35 min
	The instructor will lead a discussion on Force Field Analysis.		

a. Why is it useful to break up a problem situation into driving and restraining forces?

b. Would the model be used any differently whether applied to an individual or organizational problem?

➠ Introduction

A Force Field Analysis is one way to assess what is happening in an organization. This concept reflects the forces – driving and restraining – at work at a particular time. It helps to assess organizational strengths and to select forces to add or remove in order to create change. The theory of change suggested by Kurt Lewin, who developed the Force Field Analysis, is that while driving forces may be more easily affected, shifting them could increase opposition (tension and/or conflict) within the organization and add restraining forces. Therefore, it may be more effective to remove restraining forces to create change.

The use of the Force Field Analysis will demonstrate the range of forces pressing on an organization at a particular time. This analysis can increase the organization's optimism that it is possible to strategize and plan for change.

Example: Trying to increase student participation in student governance

Driving Forces	Restraining Forces
More money allocated for Student Government activities. ——>	<—— High emphasis on grades– a need to study more.
Better publicity and public relations programs for Student Government. ——>	<—— Time needed for work, family.
Student Gov. representatives go to classes and explain positive effects of Student Government. ——>	<—— Other activities – cultural, social, sports – divert interest.
Special career programs offered for Student Government participants. ——>	<—— Not much public relations work in the past.
	<—— Students do not see Student Government as effective or helping them finish degree or get a job.

Present
Balance
Point

Problem Analysis

1. Think of a problem you are now experiencing. It could be work-related or from your personal life. Describe the problem in a few words.

    Describe in a few words how you would want it to improve.

2. A list of forces driving toward change would include:

    a.

    b.

    c.

    d.

    e.

    f.

3.   A list of forces restraining change would include:

a.

b.

c.

d.

e.

f.

4.   Put the driving and restraining forces of the problem on the force field analysis below, according to their degree of impact on change.

Force Field Analysis

Driving Forces   Restraining Forces

Low extreme –   High extreme –
try to avoid   try to attain

Present
balance
point

71. An Ancient Tale[1]

Purpose:
To analyze issues of organization, boundary, membership, and responsibility for change.

Group Size:
Any number of groups of three to four members.

Time Required:
40 minutes.

Preparation Required:
Read the introduction and case study, and complete questions.

Exercise Schedule

1. **Preparation (pre-class)**
   Read the introduction and case study and answer the questions.

		Unit Time	Total Time
2.	**Group discussion**	20 min	20 min
	In groups of three to four members, discuss your answers.		
3.	**Class discussion**	20+ min	40 min
	Groups report to the whole class and the instructor leads a discussion on the issues raised.		

➤ Introduction

To understand, analyze, and improve organizations, we must carefully think through the issue of who is responsible for what activities in different organizational settings. Often we hold responsible someone who has no control over the outcome, or we fail to teach or train someone who could make the vital difference.

To explore this issue, the following exercise could be conducted on either an individual or group basis. It provides an opportunity to see how different individuals assign responsibility for an event. It is also a good opportunity to discuss the concept of organizational boundaries (what is the organization, who is in or out, etc.)

You should read the short story and respond quickly to the first three questions. Then take a little more time on Questions 4-6. The results, criteria, and implications could then be discussed in groups.

---

[1] By J.B. Ritchie and Paul Thompson. Reprinted with permission from *Organization and People: Readings, Cases and Exercises in Organizational Behavior.* © 1980 by West Publishing, pp. 68-70. All rights reserved.

Case Study: _____

An Ancient Tale

Long ago in an ancient kingdom there lived a princess who was very young and very beautiful. The princess, recently married, lived in a large and luxurious castle with her husband, a powerful and wealthy lord. The young princess was not content, however, to sit and eat strawberries by herself while her husband took frequent and long journeys to neighboring kingdoms. She felt neglected and soon became quite unhappy. One day, while she was alone in the castle gardens, a handsome vagabond rode out of the forest bordering the castle. He spied the beautiful princess, quickly won her heart, and carried her away with him.

Following a day of dalliance, the young princess found herself ruthlessly abandoned by the vagabond. She then discovered that the only way back to the castle led through the bewitched forest of the wicked sorcerer. Fearing to venture into the forest alone, she sought out her kind and wise godfather. She explained her plight, begged forgiveness of the godfather, and asked his assistance in returning home before her husband returned. The godfather, however, surprised and shocked at her behavior, refused forgiveness and denied her any assistance. Discouraged but still determined, the princess disguised her identity and sought the help of the most noble of all the kingdom's knights. After hearing the sad story, the knight pledged his unfailing aid – for a modest fee. But alas, the princess had no money and the knight rode away to save other damsels.

The beautiful princess had no one else from whom she might seek help, and decided to brave the great peril alone. She followed the safest path she knew, but when she was almost through the forest, the wicked sorcerer spied her and caused her to be devoured by the fire-breathing dragon.

Discussion Questions

1. Who was inside the organization and who was outside? Where were the boundaries?

2. Who is most responsible for the death of the beautiful princess?

3. Who is next most responsible? Least responsible?

4. What is your criterion for the above decisions?

5. What interventions would you suggest to prevent a recurrence?

6. What are the implications for organizational development and change?

	Most Responsible	Next Most Responsible	Least Responsible
Princess			
Husband			
Vagabond			
Godfather			
Knight			
Sorcerer			

Check one character in each column.

72. Organizational Assessment of Campus[1]

Purpose:
To apply organizational development concepts.

Group Size:
Any number of groups of four to eight members.

Time Required:
50 minutes.

Exercise Schedule

		Unit Time	Total Time
1.	**Evaluation**	20 min	20 min

Groups form and evaluate strengths and weaknesses of university, using Campus Profile Assessment. Prepare recommendations for interventions.

2.	**Group presentations**	20+ min	40 min

Each group presents its assessment of strengths and weaknesses, and its recommendations.

3.	**Class discussion**	10+ min	50 min

Instructor leads a discussion on organizational development concepts applied on campus.

Project Option

Instead of an in-class exercise, this may be assigned as a project. Each group would go and "collect" data from students, faculty, and administrators and present the data analysis to the class along with recommended interactions. *Optional*: The instructor may assign a paper in conjunction with the presentation.

➤➤ Introduction

One of the first steps in organization development is doing an organizational assessment to evaluate the strengths and weaknesses of the organization. You and your team have been hired as a consulting group by the university to assess the strengths and weaknesses of the university. You are to collect data from your group members in these five areas:

1. Academics and scholarly environment

2. Quality of teaching on campus

3. Campus social life

4. Cultural events on campus

5. Management by the university administration

After you have gathered the data, evaluate the strengths and weaknesses and make recommendations for intervention. These recommendations must be very specific so the university administration could implement them tomorrow without any more explanation. Avoid saying things like, "Teachers need to lecture better." Be specific by saying things such as, "We found 10 percent of the teachers didn't talk loud enough in class" or "50 percent of teachers get off the subject too frequently."

Campus Profile and Assessment

Not true 1 2 3 4 5 Very true

I. Academics

1 2 3 4 5   1. There is a wide range of courses to choose from.

1 2 3 4 5   2. Classroom standards are too easy.

1 2 3 4 5   3. The library is adequate.

1 2 3 4 5   4. Textbooks are helpful.

II. Teachers

1 2 3 4 5   1. Teachers here are committed to quality instruction.

1 2 3 4 5   2. We have a high-quality faculty.

1 2 3 4 5   3. Teachers have a good balance between theory and practice.

III. Social

1 2 3 4 5   1. Students are friendly to one another.

1 2 3 4 5   2. It's difficult to make friends.

1 2 3 4 5   3. Faculty get involved in student activities.

1 2 3 4 5   4. Too much energy goes into drinking and goofing off.

IV. Cultural Events

1 2 3 4 5   1. There are ample activities on campus.

1 2 3 4 5   2. Student activities are boring.

1 2 3 4 5   3. The administration places a high value on student activities.

1 2 3 4 5   4. Too much emphasis is placed on sports.

1 2 3 4 5   5. We need more "cultural" activities.

V. Organizational/Management

1 2 3 4 5   1. Decision-making is shared at all levels of the organization.

1 2 3 4 5   2. There is unity and cohesiveness between departments and units.

1 2 3 4 5   3. Too many departmental clashes hamper the organization's
                  effectiveness.

1 2 3 4 5   4. Students have a say in many decisions.

1 2 3 4 5   5. The budgeting process seems fair.

1 2 3 4 5   6. Recruiting and staffing are handled thoughtfully
                  with student needs in mind.

Identify Organization's Strengths

1. In Academics:

2. In Teaching:

3. In Social:

4. In Cultural Activities:

5. In Campus Management:

Identify Organization's Weaknesses

1. In Academics:

2. In Teaching:

3. In Social:

4. In Cultural Activities:

5. In Campus Management:

What interventions (in each of the five areas) would you recommend to resolve weaknesses and build on strengths?

1. In Academics:
a.

b.

2. In Teaching:
a.

b.

3. In Social:
a.

b.

4. In Cultural Activities:
a.

b.

5. In Campus Management:
a.

b.

Chapter 20
International Cross-Cultural Management

73. What If...?: Motivation in Diverse Applications[1]

Purpose:
To consider the implications of different cultural values and to evaluate a content area in terms of its cultural universality and applicability.

Group Size:
Any number of groups of three to six members each.

Time Required:
70-90 minutes (35-45 minutes each for Parts I and II).

Preparation Required:
None specifically, but helpful to have some knowledge of the content area to be discussed (in this example, "motivation").

Materials Required:
Index cards each containing one of the exercise statements with enough index cards for two cards for each group.

Related Topics:
Organizational Diversity, Multicultural Issues

[1]Prepared for this edition by Christopher Taylor, University of Arizona.

Exercise Schedule

Part I

	Unit Time	Total Time

1. Overview   5 min   5 min

Instructor/facilitator gives a brief overview of the impact of differences (diversity variables) on values and behavior. Any questions of clarification are answered, but a complete discussion of the topic is delayed.

2. Divide into groups   5 min   10 min

A brief discussion is held concerning how the larger group is going to be divided into subgroups. If the facilitator already has a plan for division, this step is omitted. Avoiding friends (or having friends in the same group); bypassing convenience of "next-to," or letting groups just form; promoting a great deal of diversity or very little diversity in groupings, either or both; using intact functional groupings or cross-functional assignment – these are just some of the possibilities.

3. Group work   20 min   30 min

Two index cards are handed to each group. Each group is to elect a scribe to take notes for later presentation of their efforts. The group is to choose one of the situations and brainstorm "what such a society would be like if..." In their discussion they are to:

   a. describe some of their images.

   b. address implications for organizational functioning and managerial policies/practices.

   c. share their reactions and have some fun.

4. Reports and discussion   15-20 min   45-50 min

After first reading the statement *not chosen* and commenting on why not, each group reports out the results of their efforts, allowing a brief discussion.

Part II

	Unit Time	Total Time

1. Create matrix   15 min   15 min

The chosen content area is highlighted in a brief presentation, with brief discussion. Then cultural/diversity issues are presented, again with brief discussion. A two-by-two matrix of the content components and of the diversity aspects is created on a flip chart or on the blackboard.

2. Groups discuss implications 10-20 min   25-35 min

Each group is assigned one or two cells of the matrix to consider. How are the two variables compatible? How are they not compatible? What are the implications for organizational concerns/policies/practices? What research is suggested? What insights have been gained?

3. Groups report   5 min   30-40 min

One or two groups report on some aspect of their analysis/discussion.

4. Summary comments   5 min   35-45 min

Summary comments are solicited to provide a wrap-up.

Application Matrix

	Focus	Control	Status	Style	Strategy
Need					
Reinforcement					
Social Learning					
Expectancy					
Equity					
Goal-Setting					

74. The Owl: Cross-Cultural Sensitivity[1]

Purpose:
To experience and understand how cultural values influence behavior and relationships.

Group Size:
Any number of groups of five to seven members.

Time Required:
50 minutes or more.

Preparation Required:
In a previous class session, roles need to be assigned: three X-ians and two Americans/Westerners per group. Larger classes may have one or two observers per group. X-ians must meet for about an hour prior to class to prepare for the role-playing. Americans/Westerners meet for no more than 15 minutes before the role-play begins.

Room Arrangement Requirements:
Circles of five chairs set up in various places around the room.

Exercise Schedule

1. **Preparation (pre-class)**
   X-ians, Americans/Westerners, and observers roles are assigned. Each group reads only its role sheet. Observers read both role sheets.

		Unit Time	*Total Time*
2.	**Role-play, Part 1**	**15 min**	**15 min**

X-ians take their places in groups of chairs and wait for the American/Western couple to arrive. Then the conversation begins.

3.	**Time out**	**5 min**	**20 min**

The instructor signals time up and the American/Western couple leaves the room while X-ians remain.

4.	**Role-play, Part 2**	**25 min**	**25 min**

The Americans/Westerners return and make their request. X-ians give a "yes" or "no" reply.

5.	**Class discussion**	**25+ min**	**50 min**

The instructor will lead a discussion on the exercise covering the following areas:

a. Which groups got a "yes"? Which ones got a "no"?

b. What were the reasons for the "success" or "failure"?

c. What did the Americans/Westerners understand about Culture X?

d. How does this exercise relate to stereotyping?

---

[1]Theodore Gochenour's "The Owl" reprinted with permission of Intercultural Press, Inc., Yarmouth, ME. © 1993.

Role Sheet for "The Owl"

Briefing Sheet #1 – To be read ONLY by X-ians.

You are a member of Country X, an ancient land of high culture which has, in the course of the centuries, tended to develop along somewhat isolationist lines. X-ians have a deep and complete acceptance of a way of life that no outside influence has altered in any appreciable way for many years due to the sense of perfection and harmony of life that each X-ian derives from her/his culture.

In Country X, women are the natural leaders, administrators, heads of households, principal artistic creators, owners of wealth through whom inheritance functions, and rulers of the state. Men rarely work outside the home – where they keep house, cook, mind children, etc. – and then only in menial positions where heavy labor is required. Among X-ian women, education is important, with a high percentage going on to the university level. Among men, there is little interest and no encouragement to go beyond basic literacy. In all respects, women know themselves to be superior to men, and are acknowledged to be superior by the men, both in individual attitudes and as expressed institutionally. There is a well-known expression, for example, which goes, "Don't send a man on a woman's errand."

Knowing much of the outside world – and rendered somewhat uncomfortable by what they know of male-female relationships in many other countries – X-ians have tended to withdraw into themselves. In Country X, marriage is between two women, forming what is known as the Bond. The two women (the Bond) then may wish to receive jointly a man into their household, for purposes of creating children, for tending the home, etc. Two women in the Bond are equal in all respects, jointly agree in all decisions, and mutually have responsibility for a man, should he be affiliated with them. Relating to a Bond, a man is legally regarded as an entity, having protection from the Bond. The man is considered "cherished" by the Bond. The women are "married"; his relationship is to the Bond, whereby he is "cherished." A state of being "cherished" is considered very desirable among men.

Knowing much of the outside world, **X-ians have tended to withdraw into themselves.**

The artistic powers of X-ian women are famous, particularly in having developed the design and care of gardens into a unique art form. In Country X, the Queen's Garden is open once a year on her birthday to the women of the country (no men allowed) in celebration of the natural processes of growth and rebirth. No foreigners have been able, so far, to observe this Queen's Garden Festival, though there is no law to the contrary that would prevent it from happening.

X-ians share with some cultures of the world a marked discomfort with prolonged eye contact. They, of course, look at another person with brief, polite glances when they are in conversation, but do not hold another person's eyes with their own. In Country X, one is very careful not to "stare," since it is very impolite, and considered to be the worst kind of aggressiveness.

You are an X-ian Bond, Ms. Alef and Ms. Beh, with your Cherished Man Peh. Ms. Alef holds an important position in the Ministry of Foreign Affairs as Directress of Cultural Affairs. Ms. Beh holds a position, also in the Ministry of Foreign Affairs, as Special Assistant to the Minister. Both women are distantly related to the Queen. Cherished Man Peh has been taken along by the two women of the Bond on one of their official trips outside Country X. The three of you are now in a restaurant in Athens, and have been spotted by an American/Western couple whom you have met once before but do not know very well.

When speaking with the Americans/Westerners, you must limit your vocabulary to words of only one or two syllables. The purposes for this are: (1) your native language is that of Country X, and thus it is quite natural for you to be limited in your command of English, and (2) by making you conscious of your language, it is an easy way to prevent a use of vocabulary and concepts that people rarely use except as sociologists and anthropologists.

This American/Western couple will attempt to gain your help in getting permission to observe the next Queen's Garden Festival. They will talk with you for about fifteen minutes. At that time, on some pretext, the American/Western couple will excuse themselves for a few minutes, then return to the three of you. At that time they will ask you for your help.

You must decide whether to say "yes" or "no." Basically, you should decide "yes" if, in your judgment, the Americans/Westerners have shown cultural sensitivity to what X-ians like. This means looking for and considering three main things:

1. The American/Western woman must be the one asking for permission, and she must ask the X-ian Bond (not Peh). The men in the role play (both the American/Western man and Peh) must not be involved in the request.

2. You must decide how thoughtful the Americans/Westerners have been about your limitations in use of English. They should not just rattle on when it is obvious by your speech that you may not understand them very well. If they show sensitivity in this, it will be one factor toward saying "yes."

3. The Americans/Westerners must also show sensitivity to your customs in eye contact. If they continue to "stare" at you during the conversation (and the request), then your answer would be "no."

Role Sheet for "The Owl"

Briefing Sheet #2 – to be read ONLY by the Americans/Westerners

You are two Americans/Westerners, male and female, both of you well-known journalists.

Both of you have master's degrees in journalism from recognized schools, and have spent several years in international travel and reporting on political, cultural, and artistic subjects in a number of countries.

Never at a loss to detect a possible "story," you are pleased to encounter three people in a restaurant in Athens whom you have met once before briefly. You do not remember their names, but do remember that they are from Country X, a rather exotic and unusual place not often visited by foreigners. Country X is one of those places in the world about which there are more legends than facts. It is known, however, to be a society with highly developed arts, literature, and gardens (which are apparently some kind of art form), with an atmosphere of being inaccessible and not too interested in getting into the world tourism business. One of the intriguing things about which speculation sometimes appears in the Sunday Supplements is the X-ian Queen's Garden Festival, which takes place apparently once a year, and which no one has ever visited or photographed. To do so, especially to be the first, would be a true journalistic "coup."

> You remember they are from Country X, **an exotic and unusual place.**

In this exercise, you will approach the X-ians at their restaurant table and ask to join them. Talk with them for about 15 minutes. Then, find a pretext and leave the table for two or three minutes and decide together what would be the best way to approach your real subject: Can you get permission to observe the next Queen's Garden Festival and do a story with pictures?

Try not to let your conversation run on too long. After you return from your two or three minutes of conferring, make your request to the X-ians. You will get a "yes" or "no" answer. At that point, the exercise is over, and you then excuse yourselves again and leave.

75. Work Values Around the World[1]

Purpose:
To understand how work-related values can be different around the world.

Group Size:
Any number of groups of four to six members.

Time Required:
50 minutes.

Preparation Required:
a. Read "Background on Work Values."
b. Rank order the ten countries on the four value dimensions.

Related Topics:
Dynamics Within Groups, Values

Exercise Schedule

1. **Background (pre-class)**

   Read the "Background on Work Values" and rank order the ten countries on the four value dimensions, using "Rank Ordering Work Values" table. *Optional:* Groups or individuals may be assigned to read about the various countries, in order to answer questions more accurately.

	Unit Time	*Total Time*
2. **Groups rank**	**15 min**	**15 min**

   Groups of five to eight members (with optional observers) rank order one of the dimensions as assigned by the instructor. If time permits, groups may be assigned two or more dimensions to rank.

3. **Presentations**	**15 min**	**35 min**

   Groups present their rankings to the class.

4. **Discussion**	**15 min**	**50 min**

   Instructor leads a discussion on work values and the differences from country to country.

---

[1]© 1992 by Dorothy Marcic. Based on Geert Hofstede's *Culture's Consequences* (Sage Publications, 1984) and *Cultures and Organizations: Software of the Mind* (McGraw-Hill, 1991). Used with permission.

Background on Work Values

Geert Hofstede examined international differences in work-related values and came up with the four dimensions of power distance, uncertainty avoidance, individualism, and masculinity. Below are some brief definitions of each of the four dimensions.

Power Distance (PD) measures human inequality in organizations, looking at the boss's decision-making style, employees' fear of disagreeing with the superior, and how subordinates prefer a boss to make decisions. Power Distance assesses the interpersonal power or influence between lower- and higher-ranking employees, as perceived by the less powerful one. What it essentially looks at is how less powerful people validate the power structure. Cultures with a low score tend to respect individuals, strive for equality, and value happiness, while those with a high score look to servitude and tact of lesser individuals, while allowing great privileges to those with influence. Other characteristics of low scored cultures are that managers tend to consult subordinates when making decisions, there is a stronger perceived work ethic, close supervision is evaluated negatively by subordinates, and employees are cooperative. High scorers are less likely to have managers consult subordinates; there is a weaker perceived work ethic, close supervision is seen positively by subordinates, and employees are reluctant to trust each other.

Uncertainty Avoidance (UA) explains each society's Search for Truth, and how anxious people become in situations with conflicting values or unstructured outcomes. Cultures with high Uncertainty Avoidance try to minimize the anxiety with a thorough set of strict laws and behavioral norms. To ease the discomfort on the philosophical level, there is a belief in One Truth, the One Way. Low Uncertainty Avoidance cultures tend to have fewer rules and more acceptance of diversity of thought and behavior. Organizations, too, try to avoid uncertainty by creating rules, rituals, and technology which give the illusion of predictability, at least. However, even group decision-making can be a means of avoiding risk, for no one individual then is accountable. Countries that have low UA tend to have a less emotional resistance to change, a stronger achievement motivation, a preference for managerial career over specialist, and hope for success. On the other hand, countries with high UA tend to have more emotional resistance to change, weaker achievement motivation, a preference for a specialist career over managerial, and fear of failure.

Individualism (I) looks at the degree to which people are part of groups or on their own. In collective societies, everyone is born into a strong clan of uncles, aunts, cousins (even third and fourth), and so on, who are part of one unit. Each person contributes to the group and is at some time taken care of by the group. Loyalties are to the group above everything else. In more individualistic societies, people are more or less on their own and are expected to take care of themselves and their immediate family. In collective countries (with a low I score) there is often an emotional dependence on the company, managers aspire to conformity and orderliness, group decisions are considered better than individual ones, and managers value security in their work. In societies with a high I score, though, there is more emotional independence from the company, managers aspire to leadership and variety, managers seek input from others, but individual decisions are still seen as better, and managers value autonomy in their work.

Masculinity (M) versus its opposite, femininity, examines how roles are distributed between the sexes. The predominant pattern of socialization worldwide is for men to be more assertive and women to be more nurturing. In countries with high M scores, the successful manager is seen as more male – aggressive, competitive, just, and tough – not as feminine: soft, yielding, intuitive, and emotional (as the stereotypes define it). In countries with high M scores, earnings, recognition, and advancement are important to employees, work is more central to people's lives, achievement is defined in terms of wealth and professional success, people prefer more salary rather than fewer working hours, "Theory X" gets some acceptance, and there is higher job stress. In societies with low M scores, on the other hand, cooperation and security are valued by employees, work is less central to people's lives, achievement is defined in terms of human interactions, people prefer fewer working hours rather than more salary, "Theory X" is less accepted, and there is lower job stress.

Rank Ordering Work Values

Below are listed ten countries and the four value dimensions. Rank order each country four times, once for each of the dimensions. When you rank order, use a "1" for the country that would have the highest score and a "10" for the country you feel would have the lowest score on that dimension.

Country	Power Distance	Uncertainty Avoidance	Individualism	Masculinity
Australia	____	____	____	____
Costa Rica	____	____	____	____
France	____	____	____	____
Germany	____	____	____	____
India	____	____	____	____
Japan	____	____	____	____
Mexico	____	____	____	____
Sweden	____	____	____	____
Thailand	____	____	____	____
U.S.A.	____	____	____	____

Chapter 21

Career Planning and Development

76. Ryan Brook Assessment of Employment Awareness[1]

Purpose:
To assess awareness on questions of employment, including recruitment, selection, and interviews.

Group Size:
Any size.

Time Required:
15-20 minutes to discuss assessment instrument.

[1] © 1994 by David M. Leuser, Ph.D., Plymouth State College of the University System of New Hampshire. Used with permission.

Ryan Brook Assessment of Employment Awareness

Directions: Read each item carefully and consider whether the item is generally true or false for the average American middle manager or professional. Indicate your response by circling the letter "T" or "F" in the response column.

Section I: General Employment Outlook

T   F   1. Job opportunities in certain industries are likely to be much better than those in other industries for some time to come.

T   F   2. After a decade or more of service, it is relatively easy for an employee to switch industries.

T   F   3. Accomplishments will be more important than titles during the 1990s.

T   F   4. Middle managers are being replaced by computers.

T   F   5. Employees have as much job security nowadays as they ever had.

T   F   6. An unemployed worker may be more likely to find suitable employment by moving to another region of the country.

T   F   7. Employers prefer to hire unemployed managers and professionals, since they are frequently willing to work for a lower salary.

T   F   8. Moonlighting is likely to hurt your long-term employment prospects.

T   F   9. Loyalty and long service to an organization are increasingly important nowadays.

T   F   10. A job hunter is more likely to find employment in a small business than in a large corporation.

Section II: Recruitment and Selection

T   F   11. Resumés are becoming less important in the employment screening process.

T   F   12. References from former employers are becoming more important in the employment screening process.

T   F   13. It is a good idea to return to school at the mid-career stage (between the ages of 35 and 45).

T   F   14. It is a good idea to participate actively in many professional organizations.

T   F   15. Women are less likely than men to be promoted into middle management positions.

T   F   16. A bad credit record may hurt a person's chances for employment.

T   F   17. It is not a good idea for an unemployed manager or professional to accept temporary employment.

T   F   18. Networking is becoming more important to both employment and career development.

T   F   19. One of the best job hunting strategies is to review the "Help Wanted" advertisements weekly in a regional newspaper such as *The Boston Globe.*

T   F   20. It is a good idea for an unemployed manager or professional to "cold call" potential hiring managers that they have never met and ask for advice on the job market.

Section III: The Employment Interview

T   F   21. The hiring manager is likely to be the first to interview the job applicant.

T   F   22. The applicant who has researched the potential employer has a significant competitive advantage over the applicant who has not.

T   F   23. It is important for the job applicant to ask the interviewer questions about the position and the company.

T   F   24. If the interviewer asks the applicant about salary requirements, it is important for the applicant to be honest about his or her desired salary.

T   F   25. An interview by a human resource professional is likely to be more objective and systematic than one done by a hiring manager.

T   F   26. If a firing or a layoff was the result of a "personality conflict" with a boss who treated you badly or unfairly, it is a good idea to explain the circumstances in detail.

T   F   27. A good strategy in any job interview is to "mirror" the interviewer's behavior.

T   F   28. When asked about weaknesses, it is a good idea to say that you are a "workaholic."

T   F   29. If the interviewer asks you an illegal question (such as, "What is your religious affiliation?"), the best thing to do is to refuse to answer it on the grounds that it would be legally inappropriate for you to do so.

T   F   30. While waiting to be called into the interviewer's office, it is a good idea to make small talk with the secretary or receptionist.

77. Ryan Brook Assessment of Resumé Writing Skills[1]

Purpose:
To provoke dialogue and exploration of issues related to resumé writing.

Group Size:
Any number.

Time Required:
15-20 minutes to discuss assessment instrument.

Ryan Brook Assessment of Resumé Writing Skills

Directions: Read each item carefully and indicate your response by circling either the letter "T" or "F" in the response column.

T	F	1.	A resumé should never be longer than one page.
T	F	2.	A paragraph format is more desirable than an outline format in a resumé, since more information can be included in the same space.
T	F	3.	During the initial review of job applicants, the average resumé is screened within 30 seconds to one minute.
T	F	4.	There is general agreement on what constitutes an ideal resumé.
T	F	5.	Regardless of experience or education, a resumé should begin with a clear job objective.
T	F	6.	Names, addresses, and telephone numbers of two to three references should be listed on every resumé.
T	F	7.	The functional resumé format is often viewed with suspicion by human resource professionals.
T	F	8.	It is okay to "embellish" your resumé (e.g. list a "Minor in Business Administration," even though you never completed the last two required courses), as long as you don't flagrantly lie.
T	F	9.	The best resumé is a generic one that could conceivably be applied to a broad array of positions.
T	F	10.	The chronological format is usually the best resumé format for the new college grad.
T	F	11.	A resumé should always contain a "Personal" section, including marital status, number of children, health, interests, and hobbies.
T	F	12.	It is more important to list "skills and accomplishments" than "duties and responsibilities" in the employment history section of the resumé.

---

[1] © 1994 by David M. Leuser, Ph.D., Plymouth State College of the University System of New Hampshire. Used with permission.

T F 13. The best resumés are always professionally typeset and printed.

T F 14. A single erasure or typographical error frequently leads to the rejection of a resumé.

T F 15. The best resumé should list every job held since graduation from high school.

T F 16. It is a good idea to print your resumé on colored paper and use novel typefaces and layout in order to make it stand out from the hundreds of other resumés that an employer may receive.

T F 17. It is a good idea to ask as many people as possible to critique your resumé.

T F 18. Every resumé should be updated annually.

T F 19. If possible, you should bypass the human resources department and send your resumé directly to the hiring manager.

T F 20. For the individual with over ten years of employment experience, the "Background Summary" section of the resumé is irrelevant, since the chronological listing of employment history will cover this.

T F 21. For a recent college graduate, "Education" should appear near the beginning of the resumé.

T F 22. For the seasoned manager, "Education" should appear near the end of the resumé, unless an advanced degree has been earned recently.

T F 23. Extracurricular activities are a very important component of the new college graduate's resumé.

T F 24. There is neither a need nor a mechanism for respondents to "blind ads" to identify the advertising organization or the requirements of the job.

T F 25. The best resumé is "targeted," that is, written explicitly to match the requirements of the job and hiring organization.

78. Career/Life Expectations Inventory[1]

Purpose:
To explore career, life, and marriage expectations.

Group Size:
Any number of groups of four to six members.

Time Required:
35 minutes.

Preparation Required:
Complete one of the questionnaires (and sentence completions) before class.

Related Topics:
Interpersonal Communication

Exercise Schedule

		Unit Time	*Total Time*
1.	**Group discussion**	**20+ min**	**20 min**

Meet in mixed-sex groups of four to six members, and discuss responses.

Questions:

a. Which items had the most disagreement?

b. What was learned about your career, life, and marriage expectations?

2.	**Group reports**	**15 min**	**35 min**

Groups will report to the whole class on items of most disagreement.

Career/Life Expectations Inventory
Female Form

Strongly Agree   Neutral   Strongly Disagree

    1   2   3   4   5

_____ 1. I prefer my husband to have at least as much or more education than I do.

_____ 2. I expect to fully develop my career and for my husband to encourage me.

_____ 3. If I am not employed, I will do all the housework; if I am employed, I will expect my husband to help somewhat.

_____ 4. I expect to stay home full-time with our children.

_____ 5. It is preferable for my husband to make most of the financial decisions, regardless of whether (and how much) income I would bring to the household.

_____ 6. Weekends will be time for my husband to relax, watch TV, etc., and I will strive to keep distractions (i.e., visitors, children) to a minimum for him.

_____ 7. Substitute mothers can do an excellent job and will take care of our children while I work.

_____ 8. I expect to have the major responsibility of raising our children, regardless of whether I am employed.

_____ 9. If there is a disagreement that we cannot resolve, I think the wife should most often give in to the husband.

_____ 10. I expect to take some vacations either a) by myself, or b) with my husband, but no children.

_____ 11. I may not want children, since I want to develop my career.

_____ 12. I expect to be able to continue my education if I wish, even if we have children.

_____ 13. I expect to be able to go out in the evening with my friends.

_____ 14. Yard work and fix-it tasks will mainly be done by my husband.

_____ 15. If my husband gets an excellent job offer elsewhere, I will expect to pick up and move to the new place. Therefore, his career will be more important than mine.

_____ 16. I expect that my husband will at some times have to put his career before our family, but I will not.

Career/Life Expectations Inventory
Male Form

Strongly Agree		Neutral		Strongly Disagree
1	2	3	4	5

_____ 1. I prefer to have at least as much or more education than my wife.

_____ 2. I expect my wife to fully develop her career and I will encourage her.

_____ 3. If my wife is not employed, I will expect her to do all the housework; if she is employed I will help a great deal.

_____ 4. I expect my wife to stay home full-time with our children.

_____ 5. It is preferable for me to make most of the financial decisions, regardless of whether (and how much) income is brought to the household by my wife.

_____ 6. Weekends will be time for me to relax, watch TV, etc., and I expect my wife to keep distractions (i.e., visitors, children) to a minimum for me.

_____ 7. Substitute mothers can do an excellent job and will take care of our children while my wife works.

_____ 8. I expect my wife to have the major responsibility for raising our children, regardless of whether she is employed.

_____ 9. If there is a disagreement that we cannot resolve, I think the wife should most often give in to the husband.

_____ 10. I expect to take some vacations either a) by myself, or b) with my wife, but no children.

_____ 11. We may not want children since I expect my wife to develop her career.

_____ 12. I expect my wife to be able to continue her education if she wishes, even if we have children.

_____ 13. I expect my wife to go out in the evening with her friends, as I do with mine.

_____ 14. Yard work and fix-it tasks will mainly be done by me.

_____ 15. If I get an excellent job offer elsewhere, I will expect my wife to pick up and move to the new place. Therefore, my career will be more important than hers.

_____ 16. I expect at some times to put my career before our family, but my wife will not.

Sentence Completions

1. My career goals are...

2. What I hope to be doing ten years from now is...

3. My goals for my personal life include...

4. I expect my spouse/partner to...

5. What I don't want to be doing ten years from now is...

6. How I intend to balance career and family life is...

7. One thing that would really upset me is if my spouse...

8. I would expect my spouse to be understanding about...

79. Professional Skills Assessment[1]

Purpose:
To assess your professional skills.

Group Size:
Any number of groups of two to three members.

Time Required:
55 minutes or more.

Preparation Required:
1. Read the "Introduction" below.
2. Complete the Professional Skills Assessment Questionnaire before class.

Materials:
15 pieces of paper or 15 index cards per person.

Related Topics:
Goal-setting

➡ Introduction

Any job you have or career you choose should provide an opportunity for both success and enjoyment. The following instrument is designed to help you identify the professional skills that you both enjoy using and have in the past had some success using.

Discovering these skills can be important to your future planning. A career built not only on your strengths, but on the strengths (or skills) you enjoy using is a career that can promise you greater satisfaction.

The following process for identifying the professional skills you use successfully and enjoy using is an enlightening one. Have fun with it!

Exercise Schedule

1. **Preparation (pre-class)**
   Complete Parts A and B before class

	Unit Time	Total Time

2. **Group discussion**   20+ min   20 min

   In groups of two to three, discuss the responses on the questionnaire and the table. You may exchange questionnaires, compare results, and help each other analyze findings.

   a. What is the most important thing you learned about yourself from this exercise?

---

[1]By Fernando Bartolome and Diane McKinney Kellogg. Used with permission.

b. For which career areas would your skills be appropriate?

3. **Class discussion** **15+ min** **35 min**

The instructor will lead a class discussion covering the areas of skill assessment and goal-setting.

Part A (pre-class, takes 15-30 min)

Think about achievements in your life since you graduated from high school. Remember that an achievement is defined as a task or activity that you completed that you both enjoyed and excelled at. As a task or activity it should be somewhat specific and discreet. For example, becoming more self-confident is certainly an accomplishment, but using your self-confidence to negotiate a raise would be an achievement. It can be in a work or non-work setting. Other people may or not have recognized it as an achievement, but to you it was a successful and enjoyable undertaking.

- ✔ On 15 different pieces of paper or index cards, list the 15 most prominent achievements. If you get stuck, leave them for awhile, but do return to complete 15. (If you list more, feel free to do so.)

- ✔ Sort the 15 achievements in descending order from most important to least.

- ✔ List the first 10 achievements in the 10 columns on the following pages of this book.

- ✔ Taking each achievement one at a time, go down the column of the 14 professional skills listed and check each of those you used in completing that particular achievement.

- ✔ After completing this process for all ten achievements, total the check-marks across and record in the Skill Total column the total number of times you checked each professional skill.

- ✔ To summarize your findings, list the seven professional skills you checked most often (in rank order from most to least) under "Summary." These are the skills you most enjoy using, and perhaps are most motivated to use.

Questionnaire

Write on top of each column a single word or phrase to describe each achievement.

	1	2	3	4	5	6	7	8	9	10	Skill total
1. Analytical Skills Comparing, evaluating and understanding complex problems or situations.											
2. Interpersonal Communication Skills Speaking with clarity, addressing both thoughts and feelings, clarifying misunderstandings, and listening effectively, through use of questions, reflecting skills, and attention to non-verbal cues.											
3. Making Presentations Presenting ideas to groups of people, with attention to audience response as well as effectively structuring presentation of information.											
4. Writing Skills Writing with clarity, conciseness, good logic, with appropriate attention to creativity if called for.											
5. Manipulating Data and Numbers Processing information and numbers skillfully, planning and administering budgets, preparing statistical reports.											
6. Entrepreneurial Skills and Innovation Recognizing and seizing opportunities for new ideas or products, creating new services or processes or products.											
7. Leading and Managing Others Inspiring others, assessing other's abilities, delegating effectively, motivating others to achieve a set of goals, setting priorities.											
8. Learning Skills Grasping new information quickly, using common sense to deal with new situations, using feedback from others to increase effectiveness.											

Questionnaire

Write on top of each column a single word or phrase to describe each achievement.

		1	2	3	4	5	6	7	8	9	10	Skill total
9.	**Team Membership Skills** Working well on committees, incorporating a variety of perspectives toward a common goal.											
10.	**Human Conflict Resolution Skills** Dealing with differences of personality and/or opinion, confronting others effectively, taking responsibility for my "share" of the conflict.											
11.	**Developing, Helping, Teaching, Training Others** Encouraging, guiding, and evaluating others; explaining and/or demonstrating new ideas or skills, creating an environment for learning and growth.											
12.	**Technical Competence** Demonstrating skill in specific functional areas; i.e., engineering, marketing, financial analysis or whatever.											
	Add below any additional skills that you saw manifested in your accomplishments.											
13.												
14.												
15.												

Summary: Motivated Skills

List the seven professional skills you have most often used (from most to least).

1.

2.

3.

4.

5.

6.

7.

Part B – (Pre-class, takes 20 minutes)

Complete "Analyzing Your Current Job Against Your Ideal" if you are currently or recently employed. This will help you analyze the extent to which your current or recent job gives you the opportunity to use the professional skills you most enjoy using.

Analyzing Your Current Job Against Your Ideal

1. Assuming your list of seven skills accurately reflects the skills you would most enjoy using, you might consider this to be a list of skills you would have the opportunity to use in your ideal job. List the seven skills in Column A below, adding others that you feel belong there.

   In Column B, evaluate the extent to which you use each skill in doing your current job. Use this scale:

There are plenty of opportunities to use this skill	7	6	5	4	3	2	1	No opportunities to use this skill at all

In Column C, evaluate the extent to which you could realistically reshape your current job to give you more opportunities to use this skill. Use this scale:

Extremely easy   7   6   5   4   3   2   1   Impossible
to add to   to add to
my current job   my current job.

2. If your present job is too far away from your ideal, and too difficult to reshape, begin thinking about other jobs that might come closer to your ideal job – providing more opportunities for you to do the things you do well and enjoy!

(A) Skills I enjoy using	(B) Opportunities for using this skill in my job	(C) Potential for reshaping my job
1.		
2.		
3.		
4.		
5.		
6.		
7.		
8.		
9.		
10.		

Chapter 22
Values and Ethics

80. Moral Dilemmas

Purpose:
To discuss the ethics of making certain decisions.

Group Size:
Any number of groups with five to eight members.

Time Required:
45 minutes or more.

Preparation Required:
Read the background and case studies and decide on a course of action.

Exercise Schedule

Part I: Case Studies [1]

1. **Preparation (pre-class)**
   Students read the background and moral dilemmas below and decide how they would act or react.

		Unit Time	*Total Time*
2.	**Group discussion**	**20+ min**	**20 min**

   Groups of five to eight members discuss what would be the most ethical decision in each case.

3. **Class discussion**   **25+ min**   **45 min**
   Facilitator goes through cases one by one, getting responses from each group on group outcomes.

Background on Moral Development

Lawrence Kohlberg (1981) is one of the most renowned experts on stages of moral development. Basically what he says is that moral reasoning is developmental. People move from the more basic, primary stages to higher levels. Not everyone reaches the higher levels, however, for some people do not develop the capabilities to involve themselves in the more difficult moral reasoning of the advanced stages.

His three levels of development translate into six stages of progression starting with individual need as preeminent – **stages one and two** (Rich and DeVitis, 1985). In these two stages, people only see their own needs in a conflict situation. These are the levels children are at when they think they *must* have whatever they want whenever they want it. Unfortunately, some adults are stuck in that level throughout their lives. Such people are seen by others as self-centered (although sometimes what others think is self-centeredness may only be a healthy awareness of ones needs – it is a matter of balance).

Kohlberg's second level (stages three and four) is an idea of fairness based on society's definition of fairness. Here the person is looking at how the collective group of people (society) have determined what is right and good. Moral judgments are based on such things as "That's the way I was brought up."

The final level (stages five and six) is a principled understanding of fairness based on an individual conception of equality and reciprocity. In this last level, which many never achieve (some writers have questioned whether anyone can get to level six), moral judgments are based on a thoughtful and analytical process which the person has cultivated over a long period.

More recent work by Carol Gilligan (1982) has shown that women, in fact, have a different type of moral development, neither better nor worse than men's – only different. She says that because young boys have to separate from their primary caretaker (mother) in order to truly develop their masculine sides, their moral reasoning has a quality of detachment to it where abstract reasoning is important. For females, though, who were always able to feel connected to their primary caretaker, their moral decisions are based on being connected and on a sense of relationship. Before Gilligan's work, some moral philosophers believed men were superior to women in moral development. Since then, however, the belief is common that women's development is neither superior nor inferior, just of a different nature.

Maturity helps bring about moral development, although some never reach the higher levels. Kohlberg says that by involving people in discussions of moral problems, it will help them develop better moral reasoning skills and aid in moral development.

---

*Case Studies:*_____

Moral Dilemmas

1. You are a manager with a six-year employee who did a fairly decent job the first two years. His quality of work was above average during that time period. After that, though, he started to slip. Year three was average, year four below average. In that two-year period, Joe kept promising to improve and he actually would for short periods. But it never lasted very long. During the past 12 months Joe's quality has slipped even further. Realizing Joe probably should have been fired last year, you decide to terminate him. The day you start the appropriate paperwork you learn that Joe's wife has recently been diagnosed as having a terminal disease and has been given two years to live.

> *What do you do?*

2. You have a job as department head of a fairly large unit. One of the people who reports to you is Bill – a superstar performer in whom you have a great deal of trust and confidence. This week, though, you were informed that one of Bill's subordinates has been accusing Bill of sexual harassment. Bill denies any wrongdoing and asks you a favor as he sits in your office: "Look, Bob, you and I have been very close for the past five years and you know me. I would never do this. The problem is it is so hard to prove this. My lawyer says to get evidence that Patsy was seductive and therefore always has sex on her mind. In other words, it is likely she created this whole thing in her imagination. As department head, would you be willing to testify that she dressed suggestively and sometimes made inappropriate remarks?"

Patsy is a secretary in your unit who has average performance. She gets her job done, but does not make any outstanding contributions. She does wear skirts shorter than other employees, but they are not lewd, and she does occasionally tell a dirty joke with the guys, but not very often. You also remember a rumor that circulated six years ago, before Bill worked in your department, that he was having an affair with his secretary, who subsequently left.

> *What do you do?*

3. Kathy is a good friend. You socialize frequently, your kids play together and you think she has a lot to offer your organization. As a senior manager in your division, you participate in staff meetings to discuss the performance and potential opportunities for individuals in that division. At those meetings it is apparent that your peers, including Kathy's boss, think that Kathy's performance is okay, but don't see her as having potential to move any higher in the organization. As Kathy's friend, you know her better and believe they are wrong. You have expressed your point of view in the staff meetings, but the rest of the staff suggests that your evaluation is influenced by your friendship and they stick to their opinion.

You have an opening in your department that would be a promotion for Kathy. Your peers believe you should put Karla in that job because she is evaluated as having greater potential, yet you know if you don't promote Kathy, she will not have any other opportunity to get ahead in the company.

> *What do you do?*

4. You have an open position on your staff and you are trying to decide which person to promote into that job. Sue, a white woman, is someone you always wanted to have in your department. She is a person with whom you are very comfortable, and you know that she would "fit" well with the rest of your staff. Alina is an African-American woman with whom you have worked a few times and with whom you feel socially uncomfortable. Both women are technically competent and qualified for the job. At this time you have no minorities in your department and the company has issued statements stressing the importance of affirmative action.

> *What do you do?*

5. Jack is a loyal, dependable, and productive member of your staff. Unfortunately he has recently fallen on hard times. His house caught fire and destroyed most of the family belongings for which Jack was under-insured. Right on the heels of that, two of Jack's four kids suffered accidents, resulting in very high medical bills, and one of them will need long-term, expensive care. You recently returned from a business trip with Jack and he has submitted his expense report. As you review the report and prepare to sign it, it appears that Jack has included $100 of false expenses. It was done is such a way that no one else in the company would ever catch it – in fact, it almost slipped by you. You recall that during the trip Jack mentioned that his youngest daughter's fifth birthday was coming up next week. She had asked for a new bicycle and Jack was feeling bad because he couldn't afford to get it for her.

What do you do?

6. You manage a research group and are under pressure to come up with something new and innovative. One of your bright young engineers bursts into your office and excitedly tells you that he has found a unique process that would enable your organization to create some innovative product. As you question Sam, you discover that he "found" this technology by talking with an engineer from another company while they were both at a conference. That engineer was complaining that his company's bureaucracy would keep them from applying for a patent on this technology for at least a month or so. Sam is confident that he can duplicate the technology in less time so your organization can apply for the patent first.

What do you do?

References

Gilligan, Carol. *In a Different Voice.* Cambridge: Harvard University Press, 1982.

Kohlberg, Lawrence. *The Philosophy of Moral Development.* San Francisco: Harper & Row, 1981.

Rich, John Martin and Joseph L. DeVitis. *Theories of Moral Development.* Springfield, IL: Charles C. Thomas Pub., 1985.

Exercise Schedule

Part II: The Social Responsibility Committee[2]

1.   **Preparation (pre-class)**

Instructor assigns roles to class members. Two options exist. The first is to assign the six roles to six people who will do the role-play in front of the class, while other class members evaluate one role-play member each. The other option is to break into smaller groups and have each group run the role-play, preferably with observers.

		Unit Time	*Total Time*
2.	**Role-play, Part 1**	**20 min**	**20 min**

All members have three minutes to name their preferred recipient and to state their position.

3.	**Role-play, Part 2**	**20 min**	**40 min**

Members discuss the issues and *must* arrive at a consensus on which group to give the $100,000. If the committee does not reach a decision, the president of the company will make the decision himself.

---

[2] By Dorothy Marcic and Earl Bolick. © 1992 by Dorothy Marcic. All rights reserved.

4.   Observers report (optional)   **10 min**

Observers, either from small groups or the class as a whole, report on how the role play members performed.

5.   Debrief   **10+ min**   **50 min**

Instructor leads a discussion on the role of values in group decision-making.

The Social Responsibility Committee

The Parkinson Company designated six people as members of its social responsibility committee, currently charged with determining the only recipient of their annual $100,000 donation. Below are listed six proposals for funding, all of which are from well-known groups with proven success in past similar endeavors:

1. Funding for development of a children's theatre, since the previous one closed its doors last year.

2. Start-up funds for jobs program for minority youth.

3. Abortion Clinic, which is requesting funding for prevention of teenage pregnancy.

4. The Benevolent Clinic wants to start two half-way homes for drug addicts.

5. Funding for AIDS education in local high schools.

6. Housing funds for homeless people.

Roles:

Jim Stanford, union president, who is a member of a minority group and lives in an integrated neighborhood with a large number of teenagers.

Marjorie Witherton, production supervisor. She is a member of the board of directors of two local arts organizations, as well as one of the more active people on her church council.

Janice Jeston, personnel coordinator, who has served on committees in the past for sex education in the schools and is an ardent supporter of more information for young people. She is a founding member of the Feminist Council.

Bill Wallace, engineer, who has a brother dying of AIDS and has been giving talks on the subject at different organizations.

Warren Pearson, accountant, a recovering alcoholic (sober for 12 years) who regularly attends AA meetings.

Cheryl Beyerly, cafeteria supervisor. In her off-hours, Cheryl is the volunteer chairperson of Meals on Wheels and she also coordinates the Golden Agers group for her church.

81. Ethics in International Business

Purpose:
To examine ethical foundations of bribery in an international setting.

Group Size:
Any number of groups of six to eight members.

Time Required:
50 minutes.

Preparation Required:
1. Read the case study and answer the questions before class.
2. Preferably have some background on the Foreign Corrupt Practices Act.

Related Topics:
Decision-making

Exercise Schedule

1. **Pre-class**
   Read the case study "A Different Situation."

	Unit Time	Total Time
2. **Small groups**	20 min	20 min

   In groups of six to eight members, discuss the following questions:

   a. Is there a difference between the legal and the ethical in business practice?

   b. Does American law (e.g., Corrupt Practices Act) say anything relevant to the situation Jane finds herself in?

   c. How responsive should Americans be to cultural differences that may approve of or even encourage business practices that would be frowned upon or outlawed in the U.S.?

   d. How does a person resolve conflicts between personal values held by the individual and "commonly accepted practices"?

   e. Would the situation be any different if something other than money were requested?

	Unit Time	Total Time
3. **Groups report**	20 min	40 min

   Groups report major points of their discussion to the whole class.

	Unit Time	Total Time
4. **Class discussion**	10 min	50 min

   The instructor leads a discussion on the case study examining values, ethics, and conflicts present in this case.

Case Study: _____

A Different Situation[1]

While Jane Welch was growing up in Texas, she was an excellent student. Her parents and teachers thought of her as "college capable"; in fact, she never seriously considered any option other than college. She chose to major in marketing because one of her goals was, in her own words, "not to get stuck in civil service like my dad did. Private industry is the place for me where I have more of an opportunity to be promoted on my own merits and not necessarily on seniority." Jane entered college and, as usual, did well scholastically.

As college graduation neared, Jane began to interview with a number of companies. The college placement counselor advised Jane to make a list of aspects that she would find desirable or undesirable in a job. One of the items on her list was that the company and its product or goal had to be socially justifiable. This item had come to mind because many of her classmates were going to work for oil companies. Jane believed that in spite of the oil companies' slightly higher pay scale, she would not want to work for a company that made its money selling a non-renewable resource.

Another of the items on her list was that she wanted to travel in her job. Her family had traveled in the U.S. on vacations when she was a child and she had been to Mexico and Canada, but she wanted to see something of other parts of the world. Although Jane did not care to live in another country, she did think that a job that took her periodically to other countries for short trips would be desirable.

One day during the spring semester of her senior year, Jane talked with one of her marketing professors, Dr. Mayfield, about her career goals, and Dr. Mayfield suggested that perhaps Jane should look into the exporting business. Dr. Mayfield said he had a friend in Memphis who was a vice-president in a cotton exporting firm, Cotton Belt Exporting. Things fell into place and Jane received and accepted an offer of a job in the firm.

For the first couple of years, Jane's responsibilities included traveling throughout the southern U.S. and California buying cotton from farmers and gins, but the company promised that once she had proven herself in a couple of positions she would be promoted into a position where she would be dealing directly with people in foreign countries. After about six years and two positions in the firm, she was promoted to Manager of Export Sales to Japan.

It took Jane some time to become accustomed to dealing with Japanese businesspeople, but in doing so she became fascinated by the differences in customs. She learned to understand that just because Mr. Tanaka said "yes" while Jane was talking to him, he did not mean that he agreed to what was being said – instead, he meant merely that he understood what was being said. Each trip to Japan was a learning experience.

Jane also became acquainted with the mechanics of selling cotton to Japan. She learned that disagreements between cotton sellers in the U.S. and cotton buyers in Japan were arbitrated to a large degree by two associations, one in the U.S. (the American Cotton Shipping Association) and one in Japan (the Cotton Trade Association). The two associations agreed on many rules for trade but when their rules conflicted, the cotton contracts themselves specified which rules would apply.

> She became fascinated by the **differences in customs**.

On one trip to Japan, Jane heard rumors from importers that the Cotton Trade Association was contemplating some rule changes in the near future that could affect her company's ability to trade with Japan. She paid a visit to the Association but her usual contact was on vacation in Hawaii, so she had to see another gentleman, Mr. Kodama. Mr. Kodama said that he knew little about the pending changes but he intimated that, although he was a busy man, for a small fee he could probably find out "many" details. Jane left the office promising to get back to Mr. Kodama.

---

[1]By Paul N. Keaton and Patricia A. Watson-Kuentz. Used with permission.

Jane considered her options. She decided that although she had never approved of paying to obtain such information, the urgency of the situation and the probable need for immediate action dictated that she should make the payment. The next day she returned to Mr. Kodama's office with an envelope containing 10,000 yen (equivalent to about $100 U.S.) which was, from her experience, the going rate for such payments.

Mr. Kodama told Jane that a middle-level government official, Mr. Nakamura, was pressuring the cotton importing people to diversify their source of cotton in order to reduce Japan's dependency on one country. The Association reacted by considering rule changes that would encourage importers to buy from sources other than their largest ones. Since the U.S. was the largest supplier of cotton to Japan, this action was certain to reduce the total amount of cotton it could sell to Japan.

Jane checked with her company, and her boss approved Jane's suggestion that she do some lobbying while she was in Japan. After obtaining the appropriate introductions, Jane arranged to have lunch with Mr. Nakamura. At the restaurant, Jane explained her company's situation, giving Mr. Nakamura facts about the promise of larger crops in the U.S., reduced prices because of technological advances in production, improved strains of cotton, etc. After much discussion, Mr. Nakamura indicated that, having given some thought to the specifics of the problem, he believed he might be able to see Jane's side of the argument.

> He intimated that **financial aid** to his son might make him see the situation more clearly...

Later in the conversation, Mr. Nakamura began to discuss the increasing cost of living, especially since his son had been admitted to Harvard in the U.S. He wondered if Jane's company might see fit to give the boy some type of scholarship – according to the Harvard catalog, his son would need about $20,000 per year to attend school. Mr. Nakamura subtly (but unmistakably) intimated that financial aid to his son might help him see the cotton situation more clearly.

Jane found herself in a dilemma. She had rationalized the payments for information, but somehow this situation seemed different...

82. Holier Than Thou: Attitudes Toward Profits[1]

Purpose:
To develop a macro-oriented perspective on ethical issues.

Group Size:
Groups of four to six members.

Time Required:
40 minutes or more.

➡ Introduction

When business organizations are found to be engaging in financially profitable but morally dubious practices, it is commonplace for individuals outside the organization to adopt a holier-than-thou attitude. Such an attitude, whether explicit or implicit, involves the assertion: "If I had been in charge, I never would have allowed those unscrupulous actions to take place!" This belief is generally quite resistant to change and is often expressed with considerable emotion.

Exercise Schedule

1. **Rank items (pre-class)**

   a. Consider yourself the director of a top management team in a hypothetical corporation. Rank the items in Table 1 below in order of importance, according to your own beliefs.

   b. Rank-order the items again, this time according to the priorities which you believe are actually assigned to the values in the business world, rather than your personal view.

   Unit Time   *Total Time*

2. **Groups rank**   **20-40 min**   **20+ min**

   In groups of four to six members, play the role of the top decision-making team in a large corporation. Come up with consensual rankings based on the personal sentiments and values of the group's members, not perceptions of how businesses actually operate.

3. **Class discussion**   **20-40 min**   **40+ min**

   Discuss the results of the rankings generated by all three phases of the rank-ordering.

---

[1] Adapted from an exercise by Michael Morris, professor of psychology, University of New Haven, West Haven, CT. Used with permission.

Table 1
Values in Business Items

1. Career development of employees

2. Concern for employees as people

3. Efficiency

4. Integrity

5. Managerial and organization effectiveness

6. Profit-making

7. Customer orientation

8. High quality of products and services

9. Social responsibility

10. Other[2]

---

[2] Adapted from James B. Lau, *Behavior in Organizations: An Experimental Approach,* Homewood, IL: Richard D. Irwin, 1979.

Chapter 23
Creativity

83. How Creative Are You?[1]

Purpose:
To measure different aspects of creativity.

Time Required:
10-20 minutes.

Preparation Required:
Complete and score the Creativity Inventory.

Related Topics:
Learning and Reinforcement

Exercise Schedule

1. **Pre-class**
Complete and score the inventory.

		Unit Time	Total Time
2.	**Class discussion**	10-20 min	10-20 min

Instructor gives some background on creativity and the class discusses its various aspects.

---

[1] Adapted from Eugene Raudsepp, *How Creative Are You?* New York: G.P. Putnam, 1981. Used with permission.

The Creativity Inventory

After each statement, indicate with a letter the degree or extent to which you agree or disagree with it: A = strongly agree, B = agree, C = in between or don't know, D = disagree, E = strongly disagree. Mark your answers as accurately and as frankly as possible. Try not to "second guess" how a creative person might respond to each statement.

1. I always work with a great deal of certainty that I'm following the correct procedures for solving a particular problem. _____
2. It would be a waste of time for me to ask questions if I had no hope of obtaining answers. _____
3. I feel that a logical, step-by-step method is best for solving problems. _____
4. I occasionally voice opinions in groups that seem to turn some people off. _____
5. I spend a great deal of time thinking about what others think of me. _____
6. I feel that I may have a special contribution to give the world. _____
7. It is more important for me to do what I believe to be right than to try to win the approval of others. _____
8. People who seem unsure and uncertain about things lose my respect. _____
9. I am able to stick with difficult problems over extended periods of time. _____
10. On occasion I get overly enthusiastic about things. _____
11. I often get my best ideas when doing nothing in particular. _____
12. I rely on intuitive hunches and the feeling of "rightness" or "wrongness" when moving toward the solution of a problem. _____
13. When problem-solving, I work faster analyzing the problem and slower when synthesizing the information I've gathered. _____
14. I like hobbies which involve collecting things. _____
15. Daydreaming has provided the impetus for many of my more important projects. _____
16. If I had to choose from two occupations other than the one I now have, I would rather be a physician than an explorer. _____
17. I can get along more easily with people if they belong to about the same social and business class as myself. _____
18. I have a high degree of aesthetic sensitivity. _____
19. Intuitive hunches are unreliable guides in problem-solving. _____
20. I am much more interested in coming up with new ideas than I am in trying to sell them to others. _____
21. I tend to avoid situations in which I might feel inferior. _____
22. In evaluating information, the source of it is more important to me than the content. _____
23. I like people who follow the rule "business before pleasure." _____
24. One's own self-respect is much more important than the respect of others. _____
25. I feel that people who strive for perfection are unwise. _____
26. I like work in which I must influence others. _____
27. It is important for me to have a place for everything and everything in its place. _____
28. People who are willing to entertain "crackpot" ideas are impractical. _____

29. I rather enjoy fooling around with new ideas, even if there is no practical pay-off. _____

30. When a certain approach to a problem doesn't work, I can quickly re-orient my thinking. _____

31. I don't like to ask questions that show my ignorance. _____

32. I am able to more easily change my interests to pursue a job or career than change a job to pursue my interests. _____

33. Inability to solve a problem is frequently due to asking the wrong questions. _____

34. I can frequently anticipate the solution to my problems. _____

35. It is a waste of time to analyze one's failures. _____

36. Only fuzzy thinkers resort to metaphors and analogies. _____

37. At times I have so enjoyed the ingenuity of a crook that I hoped he or she would get off scot-free. _____

38. I frequently begin work on a problem which I can only dimly sense and not yet express. _____

39. I frequently tend to forget things such as names of people, streets, highways, small towns, etc. _____

40. I feel that hard work is the basic factor in success. _____

41. To be regarded as a good team member is important to me. _____

42. I know how to keep my inner impulses in check. _____

43. I am a thoroughly dependable and responsible person. _____

44. I resent things being uncertain and unpredictable. _____

45. I prefer to work with others in a team effort rather than solo. _____

46. The trouble with many people is that they take things too seriously. _____

47. I am frequently haunted by my problems and cannot let go of them. _____

48. I can easily give up immediate gain or comfort to reach the goals I have set. _____

49. If I were a college professor, I would rather teach factual courses than those involving theory. _____

50. I'm attracted to the mystery of life. _____

Scoring Instructions

To compute your percentage score, circle and add up the values assigned to each item.

	A Strongly Agree	B Agree	C In-Between or Don't Know	D Disagree	E Strongly Disagree
1.	-2	-1	0	+1	+2
2.	-2	-1	0	+1	+2
3.	-2	-1	0	+1	+2
4.	+2	+1	0	-1	-2
5.	-2	-1	0	+1	+2
6.	+2	+1	0	-1	-2
7.	+2	+1	0	-1	-2
8.	-2	-1	0	+1	+2
9.	+2	+1	0	-1	-2
10.	+2	+1	0	-1	-2
11.	+2	+1	0	-1	-2
12.	+2	+1	0	-1	-2
13.	-2	-1	0	+1	+2
14.	-2	-1	0	+1	+2
15.	+2	+1	0	-1	-2
16.	-2	-1	0	+1	+2
17.	-2	-1	0	+1	+2
18.	+2	+1	0	-1	-2
19.	-2	-1	0	+1	+2
20.	+2	+1	0	-1	-2
21.	-2	-1	0	+1	+2
22.	-2	-1	0	+1	+2
23.	-2	-1	0	+1	+2
24.	+2	+1	0	-1	-2
25.	-2	-1	0	+1	+2
26.	-2	-1	0	+1	+2
27.	-2	-1	0	+1	+2
28.	-2	-1	0	+1	+2
29.	+2	+1	0	-1	-2
30.	+2	+1	0	-1	-2
31.	-2	-1	0	+1	+2
32.	-2	-1	0	+1	+2
33.	+2	+1	0	-1	-2
34.	+2	+1	0	-1	-2
35.	-2	-1	0	+1	+2
36.	-2	-1	0	+1	+2
37.	+2	+1	0	-1	-2
38.	+2	+1	0	-1	-2
39.	+2	+1	0	-1	-2
40.	+2	+1	0	-1	-2
41.	-2	-1	0	+1	+2
42.	-2	-1	0	+1	+2
43.	-2	-1	0	+1	+2
44.	-2	-1	0	+1	+2
45.	-2	-1	0	+1	+2
46.	+2	+1	0	-1	-2
47.	+2	+1	0	-1	-2
48.	+2	+1	0	-1	-2
49.	-2	-1	0	+1	+2
50.	+2	+1	0	-1	-2

Total Score _____

Interpreting the Score

80-100	Very Creative
60-79	Above Average
40-59	Average
20-39	Below Average
-100-19	Non-Creative

84. Creative Thinking: The Search for Different Ways of Looking at Things[1]

Purpose:
1. To unlock conventional ways of thinking.
2. To practice creative, divergent ways of looking at opportunities and problems.

Groups:
Up to eight groups of four to seven members.

Time Required:
Depends entirely on how the exercises are used and the number of participants: anything from 30 minutes to several days.

Preparation Required:
Reading the background information before starting the exercises is helpful but not essential.

Materials:
A flip chart and flip chart pens for each group.

Room Arrangement:
A table and chairs for each group.

Exercise Schedule

	Group Work	Plenary Session
1. Brainstorming using objects, pictures and words		
Each group will be given an object and/or picture and/or newspaper headline.	**10-15 min** per object, picture or headline	**Up to 5 min** per object, picture or headline

How many uses can you think of for, and how many connections can you make with, the object you have been given? How many explanations can you think of for, and how many connections can you make with, the picture/headline you have been given? Write the ideas on a flip chart.

Note: When brainstorming, use your imagination and sense of humor. Include every idea – do not censor any of them. You may be as absurd as you like, but you must keep the ideas coming until time is up.

Plenary session to share ideas and humor.

---

[1] By Philippa Börzsöny, organizational development and learning consultant. Used with permission.

2. **Similes and analogies**

What are the feelings, tastes, sounds, sights, and smells you associate with the element, phenomenon, experience, or event you have been given?	**10-15 min** per element, event, etc.	**Up to 5 min** per element, event, etc.

Note: To make sure you use similes or analogies (as opposed to literal descriptions), it is helpful to begin phrases with, "It feels/looks/tastes/sounds/smells like..." or "It seems as if/as though..." Include every idea – do not censor any of them. Be imaginative and use humor as appropriate.

Plenary session: Each group describes these feelings/phenomena for other groups to guess, and then add to.

3. **Solving imaginary problems**

Solving imaginary problems using brainstorming, similes, analogies, and humor.	**20-30 min** per problem	**Up to 10 min** per problem

Personal problem. You have just landed the job of your dreams. It is the opportunity of a lifetime. However, it requires you to work from an office about 400 miles from where you now live, and it involves a lot of traveling. Neither you nor your partner expected you to get the job, and you know that s/he will be delighted for you. On the other hand, s/he is enjoying his/her job and expects to be promoted in the near future. You know s/he does not want to move and does not like you to be away from home for any length of time. As a group, produce as many options as you can for solving this conflict of interests.

Organizational problem. You are the Passenger Transport Executive of a large bus company, which operates double decker buses in a big city. Your buses are operated by drivers, who also collect the fares. Late evening and night buses going to particular parts of town are being vandalized, mainly by drunks. More important, your drivers, who have repeatedly complained about being verbally and physically assaulted, are now threatening industrial action unless something is done to protect them. You cannot withdraw the evening and night services without endangering your license to operate at other times in the rest of the city. As a group, produce as many options as you can for solving these problems.

Plenary session to share ideas.

4. **Solving real problems**

Solving real problems using brainstorming, similes, analogies, and humor.	**20-30 min** per problem	**10 min** per problem

Each individual spends up to five minutes explaining a real personal or organizational problem/issue s/he is currently experiencing, using as many similes and analogies, and as much humor, as possible. The rest of the group then uses brainstorming and humor to create as many options as possible.

Plenary session to share ideas and learning gained from the experience.

5. **Applying logical thinking**

Applying logical, rational thinking to creative ideas.	**Negotiable**	**Negotiable**

Once the group has created ideas and generated options, they can be grouped into common areas and criticially evaluated to see which ones stand up to the rigors of logic and rationality.

Plenary session to explain outcomes and the thinking behind them.

Background Information

Logical, rational thinking...

Logical, linear thinking (A, therefore B, therefore C) is essential for evaluating ideas and for making rational decisions. On the other hand, it is easy to become "locked in" to thinking this way. If we rely on rationality as the only or main way of thinking, we:

- stop searching for alternative explanations.

- do not reinterpret evidence in the light of new information.

- use the direction best signposted from where we are at the moment, although better solutions might lie in the opposite direction.

- tend to define everything rigidly.

- have to base decisions largely on experience, which is in itself limiting and can be plain wrong.

- have to be right at every stage of the process (A, therefore B, therefore C). With lateral, divergent thinking, only the final conclusion needs to be correct.

The purpose of logical thinking is not so much to find the solution as to make sure a solution is sound.

The search for different ways of looking at things...

The search for different ways of looking at things requires a conscious effort. There are a number of techniques which can help. Three are explained below.

Brainstorming
This term is used to describe the generation of ideas and/or solutions by suspending all criticism and evaluation. It emphasises the quantity and quality of ideas: the larger and more diverse they are, the higher the probability of getting a winner.

Similes and analogies
By deliberately using similes, thereby employing all five senses, and creating analogies, which encourage imagination, we can see ideas and problems from a wider range of perspectives.

Humor
Anarchic, "off the wall," freeflowing humor encourages different ways of looking at things. Expressions like, "Many a true word spoken in jest" and "I can see the funny side of it now" reflect the fact that we value humor in everyday life. It can offer similar benefits at work, enabling us to see things in very different lights.

85. Tolerance for Ambiguity[1]

Purpose:
To measure level of tolerance for ambiguity.

Group Size:
Any number.

Time Required:
10-15 minutes for discussion.

Preparation Required:
Complete and score the inventory.

❏ Background

Literature on creativity and innovation suggest that tolerance for ambiguity is correlated with higher levels of creativity. Complete the inventory and then compare with the norms.

Tolerance for Ambiguity Survey Form

Please read each of the following statements carefully. Then rate each of them in terms of the extent to which you either agree or disagree with the statement using the following scale:

Completely Disagree		Neither Agree Nor Disagree				Completely Agree
1	2	3	4	5	6	7

Place the number which best describes your degree of agreement or disagreement in the blank to the left of each statement.

_____ 1. An expert who doesn't come up with a definite answer probably doesn't know too much.

_____ 2. I would like to live in a foreign country for a while.

_____ 3. The sooner we all acquire similar values and ideals the better.

_____ 4. A good teacher is one who makes you wonder about your way of looking at things.

_____ 5. I like parties where I know most of the people more than ones where all or most of the people are complete strangers.

_____ 6. Teachers or supervisors who hand out vague assignments give a chance for one to show initiative and originality.

[1] Adapted from Paul Nutt. Used with permission.

_____ 7.   A person who leads an even, regular life, in which few surprises or unexpected happenings arise, really has a lot to be grateful for.

_____ 8.   Many of our most important decisions are based upon insufficient information.

_____ 9.   There is really no such thing as a problem that can't be solved.

_____ 10. People who fit their lives to a schedule probably miss most of the joy of living.

_____ 11. A good job is one where what is to be done and how it is to be done are always clear.

_____ 12. It is more fun to tackle a complicated problem than to solve a simple one.

_____ 13. In the long run, it is possible to get more done by tackling small, simple problems rather than large and complicated ones.

_____ 14. Often the most interesting and stimulating people are those who don't mind being different and original.

_____ 15. What we are used to is always preferable to what is unfamiliar.

Scoring: For odd-numbered questions, add the total points.
For even-numbered questions, use reverse scoring (7 minus the score) and add the total points.
Your score is the total of the even- and odd-numbered questions.

Norms Using the Tolerance of Ambiguity Scale

Source: The Tolerance for Ambiguity Scale

Basis: The survey asks 15 questions about personal and work-oriented situations with ambiguity. You were asked to rate each situation on a scale from one to seven. (Alternating questions have the response scale reversed.) The index scores the items. A perfectly tolerant person would score 15 and perfectly intolerant person 105. Scores between 20 and 80 are reported with means of 45. The responses to the even-numbered questions with 7 minus the score are added to the response for the odd-numbered questions.

The Scale:

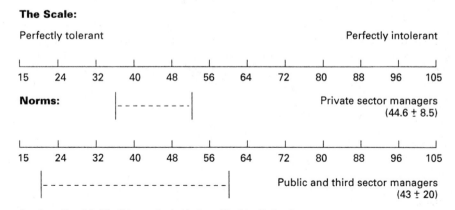

Data from: Nutt, P.C. "The Tolerance for Ambiguity and Decision Making." The Ohio State University College of Bu Working Paper Series, WP88-291, March 1988.

86. Adaptors and Innovators

Purpose:
To learn another way of defining creativity.

Group Size:
Any number.

Time Required:
50 minutes.

Preparation Required:
Complete the assessment and answer the questions.

Related Topics:
Communications

Exercise Schedule

1. **Preparation (pre-class)**
   Complete the creative style assessment. Then read the background on A-I Theory and answer the questions at the end of that section.

	Unit Time	Total Time

2. **Divide groups** — 5 min — 5 min

   Based on assessment scores, instructor divides class into groups of four to eight persons based on their A-I score. Students will be grouped with those of similar range on the A-I scale.

3. **Group assignment** — 20 min — 25 min

   Each group completes the following assignment:

   Develop a two- or three-minute presentation (depending on the number of groups – if there are more groups, the two-minute limit may be reasonable) for a product or process which would make some major improvement in the world or for some company. This may be an organization where one of your members works, or it may be a fictitious organization. This is all of the instruction you will receive on this assignment.

4. **Presentations** — 15+ min — 40 min

   Each group gives its presentation to the class.

5. **Class discussion** — 10 min — 50 min

   Instructor leads a discussion on adaptors and innovators and the differences, as well as how the various groups exhibited characteristics of their style.

Creative Style Assessment

Circle a or b, depending on which answer is generally more descriptive of your behavior.

1.   When I am working on a task, I tend to
     a. go along with a consistent level of work.
     b. work with high energy at times, with periods of low energy.

2.   If there is a problem, I usually am the one who thinks of
     a. a number of solutions, some of which are unusual.
     b. one or two solutions that are methods other people would generally accept.

3.   When keeping records, I tend to
     a. be very careful about documentation.
     b. be more haphazard about documentation.

4.   In meetings, I am often seen as one who
     a. keeps the group functioning well and maintains order.
     b. challenges ideas or authority.

5.   My thinking style could be most accurately described as
     a. linear thinker, going from A to B to C.
     b. thinking like a grasshopper, going from one idea to another.

6.   If I have to run a group or a project, I
     a. have the general idea and let people figure out how to do the tasks.
     b. try to figure out goals, time lines, and expected outcomes.

7.   If there are rules to follow, I tend to
     a. generally follow them.
     b. question whether those rules are meaningful or not.

8.   I like to be around people who are
     a. stable and solid.
     b. bright, stimulating, and change frequently.

9.   In my office or home, things are
     a. here and there in various piles.
     b. laid out neatly or at least in a reasonable order.

10. I usually feel the way people have done things in the past
     a. must have some merit and comes from accumulated wisdom.
     b. can almost always be improved upon.

Scoring

Score one point for "I" and "A" as follows:

I	A
1b	1a
2a	2b
3b	3a
4b	4a
5b	5a
6a	6b
7b	7a
8b	8a
9a	9b
10b	10a

Total for I	Total for A

Circle I or A below, depending on which score is higher.

If A is higher, you are adaptive (A).

If I is higher, you are innovative (I).

Subtract I from A.

Take the absolute value and place it here: _____

Scoring Styles:

If you are I or A and the difference between A and I is 1 or less, you are a MID I/A STYLE.

If you are A and the difference between A and I is 2-4, you are a MODERATE A STYLE.

If you are A and the difference between the two is 5-7, you are a MID-RANGE A STYLE.

If you are A and the difference between A and I is 8-10, you are a STRONG A STYLE.

If you are an I and the difference between I and I is 2-4, you are a MODERATE I STYLE.

If you are an I and the difference is 5-7, you are a MID-RANGE I STYLE.

If you are an I and the difference is 8-10, you are a STRONG I STYLE.

Background on A-I Theory

A-I theory measures creative style. Until recently, most work on creativity defined it as one type of behavior – that of a preponderance of many new and unusual ideas. However, Kirton (1976) developed an instrument to measure two styles of creativity – adaptive and innovative. Those with an adaptive style work within the situation as it is given and try to make it more efficient, reliable, and precise. People with the innovative style, though, are paradigm-breakers and are always looking for a new way to do something. As a result, they often rock the boat and may have more difficulty being part of an on-going team.

Therefore, both adaptors and innovators are creative, only in different ways, with different styles. Adaptors ask the question, "How can I make this better?' while innovators ask the question, "How can I make this different?"

Below are listed some characteristics of adaptors and innovators. See if the characteristics match how you see yourself and others.

Behavior Descriptions of Adaptors and Innovators[1]

Adaptors	Innovators
Characterized by precision, reliability, efficiency, methodicalness, prudence, discipline, conformity.	Seen as undisciplined, thinking tangentially, approaching tasks from unsuspected angles.
Concerned with resolving problems rather than finding them. Seeks solutions in tried and understood ways.	Could be said to discover problems and discover avenues of solution.
Reduces problems by improvement, greater efficiency, with maximum continuity, stability.	Queries problems' concomitant assumptions: manipulates problems.
Seen as sound, conforming, safe, dependable.	Is catalyst to settled groups, irreverent of their consensual views; seen as abrasive, creating dissonance.
Liable to make goals of means.	In pursuit of goals, treats accepted means with little regard.
Seems impervious to boredom, seems able to maintain routine (systems maintenance) high accuracy in long spells of detailed work.	Capable of detailed work only for short bursts. Quick to delegate routine tasks.
Is an authority within given structures.	Tends to take control in unstructured situations.
Challenges rules rarely, cautiously when assured strong support.	Often challenges rules, has little respect for customs.
Tends to have self-doubt. Needs consensus to maintain certitude and authority; compliant. Vulnerable to social pressure.	Appears to have low self-doubt when generating ideas, not outwardly conforming.
Is essential in the functioning of the institution all the time, but occasionally needs to be "dug out."	In the institution, is ideal in unscheduled crises, or better still to help avoid them if s/he can be controlled.
When collaborating with innovators, supplies stability and order.	When collaborating with adaptors, supplies task orientations, continuity to the partnership.
Sensitive to people, maintains group cohesion and cooperation.	Insensitive to people, often threatens group cohesion and cooperation.
Provides a safe base for the innovator's riskier operations.	Provides the dynamics to bring about periodic radical change, without which institutions tend to ossify.

[1] From Michael J. Kirton, "Adaptors and Innovators: A Description and Measure," *Journal of Applied Psychology*, Vol. 61:5, p. 623. © 1976 by the American Psychological Association. Reprinted with permission.

Chapter 24
Integrating Cases

87. Minute Memos[1]

Purpose:
To look at problems in management, organization and human behavior.

Group Size:
Three to six members.

Time Required:
10 or more minutes in class.

Preparation Required:
Complete the memos assigned by your instructor.

➤ Introduction

The most important thing about a minute memo is the opportunity it offers to address a business situation using what you have learned in different segments of this course. The situations are *ambiguous*, which is not an excuse or a reason to be surprised. There will not be enough information to determine the "right" answer. You should, however, have enough information to determine which questions need to be asked and to make suggestions regarding how the resulting information should be used.

Minute memos are designed to make you think about the material you have covered. This is one reason to do them in groups, and to limit the papers' length. You have to decide what is important: what additional information your friend should obtain, and what of the information already available should be used.

Optional: The instructor may assign the memos do be done individually.

---

[1]By Martin M. Greller, University of Wyoming, Laramie, WY. Used with permission.

Assignment

- The instructor will assign some of the following caselets.

- Your memo would take the form of a series of "If-Then" statements. It could take the form of questions you feel should be raised with this friend. In all likelihood it will be a combination of the two.

- There is no need to make a recommendation in a minute memo. Past experience indicates that many students will choose to make recommendations, and that is fine. But the quality of the analysis is what counts, not the recommended course of action.

- Each memo should be no more than two typed, double-spaced pages long (450-500 words).

Exercise Schedule

1.   **Pre-class**
     Complete the assignment.

		Unit Time	Total Time
2.	**Class discussion**	**10-30 min**	**10-30 min**

The instructor will lead a class discussion on some of the caselets.

Minute Memo 1A _____

Uncle Bernie's Legacy

You have a friend who is just graduating from the University of Wyoming. He had not solidified his career plans, so it was no surprise to see him looking distressed. But, when you asked, it turned out that the things worrying him were not what you had thought.

His Uncle Bernie had died. Bernie had run a printing business in a small Montana town for many years before his illness forced him to close the shop about six months ago. The business had been quite successful because (1) Bernie had developed strong relationships with the business people in this town, (2) Bernie was a capable printer, but had an artistic flair which caused people to come to him rather than to go to other printers, and (3) Bernie had accumulated a unique set of printing equipment over the years which allowed him to do jobs no one else in the state was properly equipped to tackle. Your friend's uncle has left all the equipment to him.

Your friend now needs to make a choice. The owner of the building in which Bernie had his shop has informed your friend that he has a potential tenant who would want the shop in two months. If your friend wants to continue the business in Montana, the landlord is willing to give him a lease on the same terms he gave to Bernie. He is also willing to crate the equipment so your friend can move it. But he needs to know what your friend wants to do by the beginning of next week. A machinery broker (who evaluated the equipment for the estate) says he is willing to buy the equipment or take it on consignment if your friend stores it. He will pay $25,000 for the equipment, although he is confident that it would eventually sell for $50,000 to $75,000. The problem is that it would sell very slowly, as the pieces are unique and meet a very specialized demand.

Your friend has discussed the situation with a number of people. One, the owner of a Laramie stationery store in which your friend works part-time, suggested that he open a printing business in Laramie, using his uncle's equipment and extra space the store owner had in the back of his building. The owner would make the space available for 5 percent of revenue and a wholesale rate on work channeled through the store. The owner has made the offer out of friendship, but says he wants to make sure your friend is serious if he takes up the offer.

As your friend sees it, he has three alternatives: (1) take over the business and run it in Montana; (2) sell the equipment to or through the broker; or (3) start a printing business in Laramie.

What factors does he need to consider in making this decision? Are there specific circumstances which would alter the attractiveness of these alternatives? What questions should your friend be asking himself?

Minute Memo 1B

Growth of a Printing Business

Your friend chose to open his printing business in Laramie. Following Uncle Bernie's lead, he exploited niches in the market where his equipment gave him a unique advantage. The businesses he first entered were small-volume engraving-like work for invitations and announcements, and printing and folding very heavy paper, such as that used for in-store displays and menus. These specialty markets proved profitable, but were limited, so he sought other specialty areas which he could enter, leveraging off the existing businesses.

He found a niche for mailing-list services for small businesses. Computers are used to customize mailings based on a client's past purchasing patterns. This business is operated by some sharp students hired part-time, working out of a computer store in town. Another business he developed specializes in flyers for realtors, which describe a property and are delivered to potential clients. Initially, these flyers were mailed, but your friend (ever searching for new specialty niches) offered another service delivering the flyers to businesses and homes. This formed the basis of yet another venture, delivering coupons and flyers for local businesses direct to homes in select parts of Laramie. This business competes with the *Boomerang* and operates out of the back of an auto-parts store in West Laramie, hiring casual workers to make the deliveries. A fourth business was based on restaurants and other businesses which used the heavy stock promotional displays with return reply tear-off cards. These might be requests for more information or surveys on customer satisfaction. Your friend uses the PCs (required for the mailing list) to compile statistical summaries of surveys and create mailing lists of people who requested information.

Certainly, business seems good. Early on, your friend stopped trying to be a printer (although he felt he was doing an acceptable job) and hired two printers on a part-time basis. One works for the university and is generally available in the evenings. The other works for the *Boomerang* and is generally available days. Your friend concentrates on selling the services of each of the businesses – a task which becomes easier as each establishes a clientele – and on managing the businesses, particularly reviewing month-end financial performance and deciding what changes need to be made for the next month.

But while the business seems to be going well, your friend confides he is going crazy. He never has any time. And, he says, he feels he spends most of his days preventing near-disasters. He gives you a couple of examples. In one instance, he had just landed a big printing job for a new customer when both part-time printers informed him they would not be available because they had to work overtime for their primary employers. On two occasions, return reply cards had been received by the computer people from a point-of-sale display when they had no idea what they were supposed to do with them. Last month, the flyers for two realtors were confused such that the wrong realtor was identified with each property. A small number had been distributed before the mistake was realized, and they had to be retrieved. The very morning you spoke to him, your friend had been informed by the auto-parts store that his distribution operation would have to move out in two weeks, because they needed the space for storage.

Minute Memo 1C

Cousins and Colleagues

Your friend's business in Laramie seems to have straightened out. He now has more time and he is trying to fulfill one of his Uncle Bernie's deathbed requests.

Bernie had come from a Central European country which was until recently under Soviet control. Several cousins remained, and during the Soviet period they had operated an underground newspaper which contributed to the overthrow of the government. Bernie always wanted to help them in their efforts, but was not able to do much for them during his lifetime. Your friend feels an obligation to offer some help.

However, since the Soviet-backed government's overthrow, things have changed for the cousins. They were able to get into the secret police's headquarters and secure some very interesting documents, both on previous government leaders and business people. The information and some naughty pictures of the government leaders were published in their (now above-ground) newspaper. This prevented these politicians from running under the banners of supposedly non-Communist parties and embarrassed several off the public stage entirely. It also more firmly established the reputation of their newspaper.

With the business people, they felt compelled to do something quite different. They have refrained from publishing anything, as long as these people offer them favorable contracts or preferred access to resources. Your friend has talked to the cousins about this, and they say they do not like to use information in this way but they feel they must. For example, if they had not had some power over the newsprint cartel's managing director, they never would have had enough paper to run the stories which kept the old Communists from sneaking back into power.

Paper and ink is now becoming still scarcer. They can only be bought from outside the country. The cousins' personal wealth and the assets of the paper are quite limited. However, with your friend's help, they believe they can work around this problem. They are in a position to "influence" key people in the fine china and beer manufacturing industries (using information from the secret police). They can cause these people to sign contracts with your friend which would enable him to export these high-quality goods from their country to Western Europe or North America, where they could be converted into local currency at a great profit. The cousins would not be able to export these goods – only the factories can sell overseas. But your friend could receive the goods.

In exchange for setting up this deal, the cousins want 50 percent of the profit – which they will use to buy paper, ink, and new press equipment from the West. This will allow them to survive the current shortage of these resources and continue to serve the needs of their emerging nation. When your friend expressed his concern with what they proposed, they indicated that they too were uncomfortable, but that there would be no paper if they did not do this. The Communist Party paper, under a new name, was the only one that had the resources to keep publishing, and would be the only national paper in a few months unless the cousins took action. They also observed that they had labored underground for years. Their presses had been stolen by the government twice. Another cousin had been tortured by the secret police and blinded so he could not work as a reporter. The old government and its industries owe their business a debt for the assets and opportunities they took away. This short-term strategy is both necessary and just, they argue. They will only need to do this for a few months and then normal supplies should be available. Besides, under the limited commercial code of their nation, such transactions are not explicitly illegal.

Your friend feels a tremendous obligation to Uncle Bernie and would like to fulfill the man's last wish. He has also been contacted by the U.S. State Department, which has encouraged him to give any assistance he can to these cousins, as the U.S. government believes their newspaper will play a key role in stabilizing the country's new, more democratic government.

If your friend is to do this, he would have to use his company, as financing would be required up front. This might be easy to arrange, as he was planning to import additional printing equipment for his company's use. However, the situation is complicated by the fact that he now has several investors in his company. While your friend owns more than 50 percent of the stock and is the CEO, such a venture would be quite different from anything the firm has proposed doing before.

Based on what you've studied in this course, how could you advise your friend? Keep in mind that he feels strong obligations to his uncle.

Minute Memo 2A _____

Supporting a Community Hospital

The mayor has asked for your assistance. She is concerned that the health-care situation in your community will soon deteriorate to the point that it will adversely affect economic development; specifically, she fears businesses will leave town. She is looking for ideas that would allow the community to avoid such losses.

The city is a small county seat with a population of 7,600. The county's population is 9,800. Geographically, the county looks like a 200-mile by 180-mile square with the county seat located in the middle. The county is served by a 20-bed hospital located in your city. There are two physicians practicing in town (one of whom is 64 years old and talks about retiring), a dentist, and a psychiatric social worker. Two other physicians are paid by the county to work one day per week at the hospital, where they offer a clinic.

The hospital has just been reviewed for re-accreditation, which is necessary to be licensed and to be reimbursed by insurers. It was told it must make considerable improvements to be re-accredited: about $500,000 in new equipment, another $500,000 in building renovations (much of it having to do with ventilation and sanitary facilities), and added nursing staff (costing $40,000 per year). The State Health Department has taken the position that there is a more substantial hospital three hours away (in the next county) and that consolidating the two would make a financially stronger hospital. Unfortunately, the three-hour drive can take seven to 12 hours in the winter. There is also reason to believe that the younger of the two doctors would move if the hospital closed. Several of the large companies with offices in town say they would relocate to another town if the hospital closed. Facts about employment:

type employer	% of work force	insured	not insured
self-employed persons	20%	10%	10%
small employers	40%	18%	22%
local businesses, 10 to 25	30%	20%	10%
local offices of large companies	10%	9%	1%
Totals	100%	57%	43%

The original hospital was built by the owner of a local mine in 1927. In 1955, the mine was bought by a large company which rebuilt the hospital as part of its emergency response plan. This was the last major improvement in the hospital. Since that time, the hospital has received a contribution each year from the city, the county has paid consulting physicians two days per week, there have been small private contributions, and the hospital receives fees for services.

The mayor had hoped to wait the situation out and that national health-care reform would take care of the problem. Now it appears that without the hospital, the county will be overlooked under most of the proposed plans. The hospital will close in six months unless an acceptable plan is presented to the accrediting agency. Following the review three years earlier (which produced a warning), the city government and local health-care providers met to discuss hospital improvements. No agreement was reached. The past mayor described the health-care providers as greedy and exploitative. They proposed improvements which required annual funding of $150,000 and a $1.3 million bond for capital improvements. The health-care providers described the past mayor as mean-spirited, unwilling to pay for the benefits the city receives. They pointed to the fact that the city would not fund 15 percent of a third physician's salary when 85 percent would have been paid by federal funds.

The mayor wants to know what do to. She does not expect you to have the right answer, but given your experience (including this class) she looks to you for guidance on the issues to be considered and the best way to proceed.

Minute Memo 2B _____

Challenge in a Community Hospital

While the broader issues of the hospital and its accreditation are being worked out, you have been asked to help with another question.

The staff seems to be demoralized. It is not as productive as management would like it to be. Efforts by the administrator to encourage increased work have been less than successful. In fact, several of the staff threatened to start a union.

The hospital reports to a volunteer board of directors, composed of a local physician, several political leaders, and several business leaders. The chief administrator of the hospital works on a part-time basis. She had been the controller for a large urban hospital before her husband was transferred to this town, and she has an excellent understanding of legal reporting and billing requirements.

The hospital is divided into four departments, all reporting to the administrator. The billing department (which also does inventory, scheduling, and personnel administration) consists of one full-time clerk and one who works part-time (from 4 p.m. to midnight). The nursing department makes sure there is one registered nurse (RN) on duty at all times and arranges for additional nurses to staff surgery. This means two RNs are typically on duty for two of the three shifts each day. There are actually 15 nurses who work different shifts and days each week. Several of these also work in the medical center in the next county. Finally, there is the custodial staff, which is responsible for cleaning not only rooms but the surgery area and kitchen, as well. (Meals are prepared at a local restaurant, but the dishes must be collected and cleaned before they are returned.) Typically, from three to seven people are on duty at any one time. Because of the range of things that must be done, they all need to pitch in to do whatever is needed at the moment.

The administrator started working at the hospital eight months ago. She helped the hospital improve its record-keeping, increased collections from insurance, and tried to put the hospital in administrative order. She introduced a computer program that helps in scheduling, offering the nurses greater certainty of when they will work. She also introduced incentives so that those nurses who are willing to work when called receive higher pay than those whose availability is limited.

The board is particularly pleased with her efforts to increase controls. This is particularly evident in the area of financial controls. She has reduced the inventory the hospital carries. Now things are ordered when needed with a form describing the purpose for the item(s). She has asked the nurse on duty to act as shift supervisor so that there is clear accountability. She also has instituted a check-in procedure, so that all employees note the exact time they arrive at and leave work. (The employees were subject to provisions of the wage and hour law, but there was not precise accounting for their time.)

Unfortunately, there has been a reduction in productivity. Whereas the hospital could get by with one or two nurses before, now it seems they need three on most shifts. The physicians have complained about lack of services and the "not my job" attitude of many of the staff. While everyone does pull together in an emergency, it seems to take something like a five-car accident to generate cooperation. Staff members refer to the administrator as "the old battle-ax." Several have said they would quit if her hours were increased from the current 12 per week. Her response has been that this is the normal reaction when people have been under-performing and acting without management. She says the sour grapes should disappear shortly – but these grapes have stayed the same for the last six months.

Minute Memo 2C _____

Growth in a Machine Parts Company

Your friend, the mayor, has to spend some time looking after her business. She owns a small manufacturing firm that fabricates metal parts. Her workers mold, cut, and chemically etch these parts to customer specifications.

The mayor's grandfather won the machinery used to start the business in a poker game. He moved to this town because the mine required a constant supply of metal parts. The company has never been one of the biggest employers, but it has enjoyed a very good reputation. For three generations the mayor's family has provided steady work, good wages and benefits, and respect for its employees. The mayor's family itself has always been active in community affairs. These activities have not always been entirely positive. The same grandfather who started the business also led the town when the Chinese people who remained after the railroad construction was completed were run off.

Maintaining a competitive business for three generations has required many adjustments. The rough-cut machining of the grandfather's day would not be acceptable today. Typical customers are manufacturers of computer peripheral devices or medical equipment, whose specifications have become ever more precise over the years. This has required state-of-the-art technology. Laser printer manufacturers have indicated that even finer tolerances will be required in the future as the speed of the printers increases.

A recent opportunity could move the company into the next century in technology. A Korean company has developed laser technology which not only permits extremely precise cutting, but does so at such cool temperatures that one can work very closer to microprocessors without damaging them. This could open whole new areas of work. The Korean company is willing to grant your friend's company the right to use the technology and will even provide a loan to finance the purchase of the required equipment, if the mayor's company will enter into a joint venture for those parts of the business using the technology. The Koreans see this as a window through which they can enter the North American market. The quality of the mayor's company and its traditional customer base made this deal attractive to them even without NAFTA.

This would certainly change the character of the business. Most of the growth would be in the joint venture, and it would consume most of the capital and attention your friend can contribute to the business. While the business would only be half-owned by your friend, she believes its potential size is more than twice that of the business at present, so it would be a gain for her. Besides, she cannot access this technology in any other way.

There will be changes in the work force. Some of her more senior workers do not have the skills that will be required to use the new equipment. But she believes many of them would willingly retire. This would help address another concern she has: some of the people who worked with etching chemicals in the 1950s may have developed a sensitivity which makes them react more strongly to chemicals and risks their health. The joint venture would also allow her to address benefits costs. The firm has provided health coverage since World War II, but between a high incidence rate for employees and generally increasing insurance rates, the firm's labor costs are becoming prohibitively high. By establishing the joint venture as a legally separate entity, she believes she could cease offering some of the more expensive benefits to new employees and gradually reduce her cost of labor relative to the competition. If she could retire some of the more senior employees in the original business, this, too, would reduce average labor cost.

She is quite excited about this opportunity, but has asked you for your ideas.

88. Mega Manufacturing[1]

Purpose:
To integrate several concepts from the Organizational Behavior class.

Group Size:
Four to six members.

Time Required:
35-50 minutes.

Preparation Required:
Read the case study and answer the questions.

Exercise Schedule

		Unit Time	Total Time
1.	**Preparation (pre-class)** Students read the case study and answer the questions.		
2.	**Group discussion** Groups of four to six members discuss their answers to the questions.	**15-20 min**	**15-20 min**
3.	**Class discussion** Instructor leads a class discussion on the issues raised by the case.	**20-30 min**	**35-50 min**

Case Study: _____

Mega Manufacturing

Susan Shoshoni walked into her new office in the fall of 1994. She felt proud to be the new CEO at Mega Manufacturing, an Israeli producer of upscale sports shoes for men and women. During the past few weeks, as she prepared to return to living in Israel from the U.S., she had spent a great deal of time reviewing company documents and information on various performance standards.

One of her first tasks was to call in the Head of Industrial Engineering and say, "Shlomo, I have just read the report on the high volume of wastage we have in the cutting department. We must do something about this wastage. It is hurting our earnings. And I probably don't have to tell you there are more and more competitors in this business every day. If we can't be more efficient and keep our costs down, we'll be out of business soon."

After this meeting, Shlomo called in a well-known Tel Aviv management consultant, David Nowall. After some initial meetings with Shlomo and Shoshoni, Nowall met with the cutting department foreman and staff,

---

[1] © 1994 by Gedaliahu Harel, Technion University, Haifa, Israel, and Dorothy Marcic.

a total of 12 people. These type of cutters are the most skilled workers in the factory and in the shoe industry in general.

Nowall spent some time with unfreezing and brainstorming and was, as a result, able to identify one major area of material wastage. It resulted from the method of cutting fabric for the top of the shoe, which involved using twelve different die-cut patterns to cut the 12 parts used to assemble the top part of the shoe (die-cuts were, of course, different for different shoe sizes). Ten layers of shoe fabric were piled on top of each other on a 10-meter-long table, at the end of which stood the cutter. An employee would take one die-cut at a time, place it down on the fabric pile, reach up to push the button, and the press would come down on top of the die-cut, which would then cut through the 10 layers of fabric in the desired form. After this, the cutter would take a different die-cut and go through the same process.

Wastage. Where the second and subsequent die-cuts were put were of prime importance. If they were put too far away from the other previously cut places, there would be fabric wastage. But if it was put too close and even a fraction of a millimeter was over the line of the other cut, the whole piece would have to be thrown out, as it could not be used at all.

Efficiency. Since the die-cuts were single pieces, it took a great deal of time to align them and use the press for each piece. Because workers were paid by how many pieces they cut per hour, they tended to be less careful on how they placed the die-cuts, for they were not rewarded on reducing wastage. As a result, speed and wastage were both high. In order to increase efficiency and productivity, Nowall determined wastage must be reduced without hindering the rate of production .

Nowall discussed with the cutters techniques for reducing wastage. They suggested soldering the 12 pieces together to make one large die-cut, which would serve to reduce wastage of material, the time required to align the knives, and the number of times needed to use the press to cut. Within a day, the cutters had designed the new large die-cut, but it took two months for it to be manufactured by another tool and die maker.

When it arrived, Nowall took it hopefully to the cutters and watched them position it on the press. They all held their breath as the press went down. Gasps were then heard, as the cracking of the metal indicated the die-cut had broken.

> If this didn't work, **how could they possibly** increase efficiency?

Nowall felt crushed. His hopes of the past two months were now dashed. If this didn't work, how could they possibly increase efficiency? What could he tell Susan Shoshoni?

Still disappointed, Nowall visited the chief engineer and told him about the problem. Peter Begin sat and listened, his chair tilted back as far as it could go and his legs up on the large wooden desk.

"Mr. Nowall, we tried this same thing 15 years ago and it didn't work then either. On the first try, the die-cut broke. In fact, we had four different cuts made and none of them worked. They all broke."

Now even more despondent, Nowall went back to the cutters and asked them if they had any other ideas and if they knew why this new die-cut kept breaking. Job Fisher, the foreman, took Nowall to the lunch area and put two shekels into the vending machine. As they stood there watching the coffee pour into the plastic cups, Nowall told him about his discussion with Begin. After sitting down at the formica table, Fisher said:

"Look, Mr. Nowall, we know how to make this new die-cut work, but what's in it for us? If we work the machine so the die-cut doesn't break (and, yes, we know how to do it), then the productivity standards go up for us without us getting any benefit from it. Why should we?"

Discussion Questions

1. If you were Nowall, what would you do now?

2. Using the list of motivational theories below, which theories explain the behavior of the cutters? Of the engineer? Of Susan Shoshoni?

3. Refer back to Vroom and Yetton's model (in Chapter 11) and determine which decision-making style Nowall (or Shoshoni) should use to solve this problem.

4. Using principles of TQM (at the end of the next exercise, "The Pleasure Boat Shipyard"), what would you suggest to do next?

5. Use goal-setting theory to explain the behavior of the engineer.

Applied Motivation Theories

Maslow: A hierarchy of needs, going from (a) basic survival needs (food, water, shelter); up to (b) safety; (c) love or belonging to a group; (d) esteem; and, finally, (e) self-actualization, where something is done for inner joy and satisfaction, not for external rewards.

Herzberg: A two-factor theory of higher and lower order needs, called dissatisfiers or hygiene factors – pay, benefits, working conditions, supervision, interpersonal relations – and satisfiers or motivators – recognition, achievement, the work itself, opportunities for advancement.

McClelland: Focuses on three types of needs – need for affiliation, need for achievement, need for power. All exist in each person, but at different levels.

Skinner: Theory of reinforcement and behavior modification. Through positive feedback for desirable behavior (and generally ignoring poor behavior), modification towards the desired behavior will occur.

Adam's Equity: People will equalize their work according to what equity rewards they see themselves and others get. For example, if someone is working hard and gets the same reward as slower workers, that person will tend to also work more slowly.

Vroom's Expectancy Theory: The amount of work put into a job will depend on the outcome or reward a person expects. For example, if a worker thinks she will get promoted if she works overtime, she is more likely to put in extra hours.

Festinzer: A source of motivation is the desire to remove any dissonance, either by avoiding uncomfortable situations or by trying to change those situations.

Mega Manufacturing

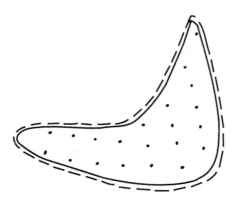

A. One of 12 individual die-cuts currently in use

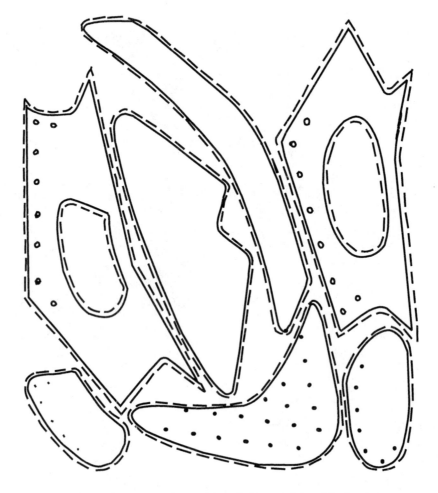

B. Design of proposed combined die-cut for athletic shoes

89. The Pleasure Boat Shipyard[1]

Purpose:
To examine work design, TQM principles, goal-setting, and group process.

Group Size:
Any number of teams consisting of up to six members.

Materials Required:
An ample number of sheets of plain 8-1/2" x 11" or 8" x 10-1/2" paper, which will be supplied by the instructor.

Preparation Required:
Preferably some previous discussion of effectiveness and efficiency, TQM and Deming's principles, self-managed work teams.

Related Topics:
Organizational Design, Self-Managed Work Teams, Re-Engineering

Exercise Schedule

		Unit Time	Total Time
1.	**Introduction**	5 min	5 min

Instructor explains exercise, groups are created, and members read relevant roles.

		Unit Time	Total Time
2.	**Team planning**	10 min	15 min

Teams plan the production process.

		Unit Time	Total Time
3.	**Production**	20 min	35 min

Performance of the production task.

		Unit Time	Total Time
4.	**Class discussion**	20 min	55 min

The instructor leads the discussion of the exercise about the differing effects of the two different work designs on effectiveness and efficiency, about the effects of continuous self-inspection of quality versus back-end quality inspection, and the implications for productivity.

---

[1]By Gedaliahu Harel, Technion University, Haifa, Israel. Used with permission.

☐ Background

You are working in a shipyard that produces pleasure boats for the nouveau riche market. These boats are sold in a very competitive market, thus customer satisfaction with the quality of the product is of major concern to everyone in the company.

Instructions for the assembly of the boat are provided at the end of the exercise. Your facilitator will act as the buyer for the major distributor of these boats, and will inspect them to ensure that they meet the expected quality standards (adherence to technical specifications, cleanliness, esthetics).

Measuring Performance

Each completed boat will be inspected by the buyer and, if accepted, the appropriate reward will be given. If it is not accepted, it will be returned for rework in the shipyard. Teams will compete with each other to sell the largest number of boats to the buyer.

Instructions for Self-Managed Teams

Groups of six members that represent self-managed teams select their own work flow design, obtain the necessary materials, and decide on the strategy to conduct the production and the quality inspections.

Instructions for Traditionally Managed Teams

The instructor appoints one person of a six-member team to be the manager.

Manager's Role

- appoints the quality inspector

- appoints the work force, determines the production flow, and assigns tasks

- supervises the work of the unit (does not do any of the assembly work)

- obtains the necessary materials

Quality Inspector's Role

- inspects production and finished products according to specifications

- determines when the product is ready to be sent to the market, or if it needs reworking

- does not participate in the assembly work itself

Employee's Role

- assembles the pleasure boats according to the written specifications

- follows any other guidelines given by the manager and the quality inspector

Instructions for the Assembly of the Pleasure Boat

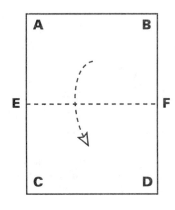

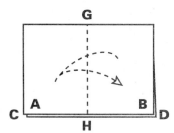

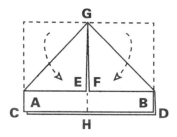

1. Fold the paper in half from top to bottom along line EF, so that corners A and B coincide with C and D.

2. Fold the paper in half again along line GH, and open.

3. Fold corners E and F to the middle so they meet at line GH.

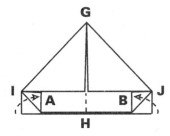

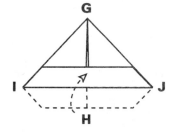

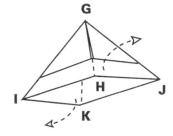

4. Fold up corners A and B to meet line IJ. Turn over and repeat fold from the bottom edge with the second layer of paper.

5. Fold up the bottom edge of the topmost layer of paper along line IJ. Turn over and repeat fold from the bottom edge with the second layer of paper.

6. Hold the triangle in the middle of the bottom leg of each side, at H and K. Pull open and flatten the triangle, so that points I and J coincide, thus forming a diamond.

Instructions for the Assembly of the Pleasure Boat, continued

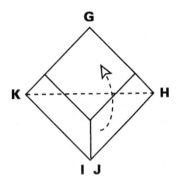

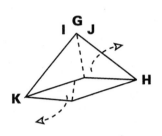

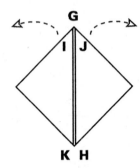

7. Fold up bottom corner I, along line KH, to coincide with G. Turn around and repeat the same step with corner J, resulting in a triangle.

8. Hold the triangle at the middle of the bottom leg of each side. Pull open the base and flatten the triangle so that points H and K coincide, thus forming a diamond.

9. Pull top points I and J out to the sides and flatten to form a boat shape.

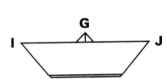

10. Open the base of the boat slightly so that it will stand upright

11. Fold in about one-third of the top edge of each side of the boat, gradually decreasing the fold towards the end points, to form a slightly curved deck.

Total Quality Management

Deming's 14 Points

1. Create constancy of purpose for improvement of product and service.

2. Adopt the new philosophy.

3. Cease dependence on mass inspection.

4. End the practice of awarding business on price tag alone.

5. Constantly and forever improve the system of production and service.

6. Institute modern methods of training on the job.

7. Institute modern methods of supervising.

8. Break down fear.

9. Break down barriers between departments.

10. Eliminate numerical goals for the work force.

11. Eliminate work standards and numerical quotas.

12. Remove barriers that hinder the hourly workers.

13. Institute a vigorous program of education and training.

14. Create a structure in top management that will push every day on the above 13 points.

90. Synthesis: Would You Hire Bob and Nancy?[1]

Purpose:
To apply concepts studied earlier in the course.

Time:
Varies.

Exercise Schedule

1. **Teams prepare (pre-class or optional in class)**   **20-30 min**

   Teams of three to four persons are each assigned characters from case studies/role-plays elsewhere in the course. Choices may be from other sources as well as this book. From this text, the following may be assigned:

Naomi in *A Case of Personality?*	ex. 9
Sue Davis in *The United Chemical Company*	ex. 29
Bob or Nancy in *What to Do With Bob and Nancy?*	ex. 37
John/Joan Ward in *The President's Decision*	ex. 38
Mike Wilson in *Consolidated Life*	ex. 51
Freida Mae Jones in case study of same name	ex. 56
Cy Geldmark in *Casual Togs*	ex. 68

   Groups assess how their character would react to a job offer from either

   United Chemical Co. (see ex. #29)
   NASA (see ex. #62)
   Honda (see ex. #65)

   or from another company studied in class or relevant in the news, i.e., IBM, Southwest Airlines, The Body Shop, Ben & Jerry's, etc.

2. **Groups present**   **3-5 min per group**

   Groups present their assessment to the class.

3. **Class discussion**   **10-20 min**

   Instructor leads a discussion on the issues raised during the presentations.

---

[1] © 1994 by Carole Y. Lyles, Loyola College. Used with permission.

Scenario Instructions:

Final Case Presentation

Your team has been assigned _____ from the _____.
                                       (name of character)   (name of case)

Your character has been offered a new job with _____ and is in the process of deciding
                                                   (name of company)
whether or not to accept.

Fortunately, your character has some sources to draw upon. Prior to his/her interviews, your character read several news articles. Now your character has decided to talk with a friend (or friends) currently employed at that company to get an unbiased perspective on the organization.

Your team must prepare a three- to five-minute presentation in which you will analyze the scenario. Following your presentation, you will be asked to respond to questions from the rest of the class and the instructor. Each member of your team must have a proportional role/task in the presentation.

Your challenge as a team is to make this presentation as realistic and as interesting as possible. Your character's actions and concerns must be linked to the details of the original case where s/he appeared — that case will provide ample evidence of the character's motivation, typical behavior, and likely future action. While you must use your imagination, the key to this exercise is critical thinking, use of relevant management and motivational theories, and close analysis of both cases.

The instructor will inform you how long you have to prepare your presentation. Any presentation format or style can be used.

Key questions that you should address in your presentation:

1.   What strengths does your character bring to the company?

2.   What issues or opportunities is s/he likely to face?

3.   What questions should s/he ask his/her friends?

4.   What are the critical decision points? What should be considered before accepting or rejecting this offer?

5.   What elements of the company's culture will support or sustain your character? Why?

6.   What must the company do to ensure a successful entry or orientation into the organization for this person?

7.   Was the decision by the company to offer this position a sound one? Why or why not?

8.   What advice would you give your character about this decision? Why?

Appendices

Group Developmental Theories: A Composite[1]

Stage	Themes & Group Behavior	Leader Behavior
Stage 1: Inclusion or Pre-Affiliation or "Forming"	Theme: What's this group for? Am I/should I be a member of this group? (These questions recycle at deeper levels throughout the lifetime of the group.) Defining the purpose of the group. There may or may not be agreement on a common purpose. Members may bring mindsets from the past that do not fit the present group (e.g., projections, assumptions, expectations). Am I in or out? What do I need to do to be a member of this group? Is it worth it? Approach-avoidance behavior is possible. Drop-out possibility high. Preliminary commitment only from some members. Members dependent on leader. Non-intimate relationships, politeness likely. Logistics need to be sorted out (time, place, frequency, resources, etc.).	Take initiative. Structure is important at this stage. Define purpose of group to larger picture (e.g. to organization, new policies). Introductions. The explicit inclusion of members is important. Share identities as much as possible. Begin setting facilitative norms. Begin establishing trust. Address confidentiality, if it's an issue. Allow member dependency on the group leader. Allow distance; allow members to join or not, be supportive of their choice (if it fits the purpose). Explore ambivalence re: who's in and who's out.

[1]by Susan H. Taft, associate professor, Kent State University, Kent, OH 44242. Based on material presented at the Organizational Behavior Teaching Conference in Windsor, Ontario, Canada, June 22-25, 1994. Based in part on the work of Schutz, Whittaker, and Tuckman, and on the ideas developed with several peers in the doctoral program in Organizational Behavior, 1981-86, Case Western Reserve University. For references, see J.P. Wanous, A.E. Reichers & S.D. Malik (1984), "Organizational Socialization and Group Development: Toward and Integrative Perspective." *Academy of Management Review,* 9(4), pp. 670-83.

Stage 2: Power and Control, Influence or "Storming"	Theme: Status jockeying, struggle for power or influence; competition; "top or bottom" issues. Am I "up" or am I "down?" Who's dominant? What skills, abilities, or resources does the group value, and do I have these? Testing each others' strengths, authority in the group. Testing of the leader likely. Fluid status structure. Unrest, conflict. Autonomy vs. group membership – ambivalence here is likely. Continued drop-out possibility by members; fight or flight. Dyads, cliques, and/or factions form; may be unstable. Rebellion, or member ejection, are possible. Some formalization of group rules likely.	Protect all members as needed – make the group a safe place for all. Clarify issues underlying conflict; use an even-handed process to clarify issues. Continued norm-setting: – Legitimize conflict as OK (assuming levels of conflict are healthy); set norm that conflict is necessary in order for group to be most effective (give permission). – Identify types of conflict or aggressive behaviors that are unacceptable. – Allow testing of leader's strength and authority. (Hint: let yourself be someone who is allowed to make some mistakes!) – Share/show your strengths, invite members to use strengths. Leader may be subject of transferences re: authority figures; discriminate between personal attacks and attacks on leader role and/or authority.
Stage 3: Intimacy, Closeness, or "Norming"	Theme: Increased "connection" among the members; sense of commonality, shared destiny. Familial. Honeymoon period. Am I "near" or "far?" Intensified interpersonal involvement. More emotions shared openly, a desire for group attention. Self-disclosure. Members relatively dependent on each other and/or group leader. Increasing trust and commitment. Group experience and membership becoming important. Well-established norms. Group rules, roles, and standards increasingly widely shared. Sense of universality. Intermittent appearance of old sibling rivalries. Growing capability to plan and carry out group task(s) effectively. Continued clarification of "what this group is for," at a deeper level.	Continued norm setting, clarifying, adjusting. Clarify group's growth by noting behavior change and group development. Positive feedback. Support group through acknowledgment. Be aware of individual differences, support comment on observed identities – e.g., members' abilities, strengths, foibles, eccentricities. Light joking and joshing OK, facilitative. Clarify feelings, positive or negative. Watch for confluence, a false sense of closeness, togetherness, being "all in the same boat." Differences lie right under the surface of the group process. A danger of "groupthink." The "warm fuzzy" stage of group development, often short-lived.

Stage 4: Differentiation or "Performing"	Theme: Increased cohesion, acceptance, mutual support for each other – "warts and all" (and the group knows where to find them!). "We've been through a lot together." Sense of this group as "special." Storming was necessary to get to this point. Acceptance of individual differences. Identities of members relatively known in group. Members can "be themselves"; to a great extent, leader can too. Authentic humor present. Most disagreement and conflict is OK, often creative and/or constructive. High level of authentic communication. Group structure, hierarchy, roles, norms are relatively established and accepted. Heightened focus on task, productivity. Teamwork promotes the utilization of varying strengths from the group.	Manage interface: group/external reality. Help the group run itself. Relinquish most of leader's directiveness. Provide guidance as the group and task require it. Continue to facilitate the management of differences in points of view within the group. Observe and "read" group humor, which should be authentic, often involves members' kidding of each other. Will reveal trust levels, and also suggest areas of tension. Watch for cycling through the other stages periodically, especially as tasks or membership evolve and change. Support development of group traditions, customs, celebrations. Facilitate the group's evaluation of its own effectiveness.
Stage 5: Separation or Termination	Theme: Disinvest, reinvest in new experience. Looking back, looking ahead. Holding on vs. letting go; some possible nostalgia or regret. Ambivalence may be present, or resistance to termination, or denial. Pride in accomplishments. Review of difficulties or failures. Appreciation. Reflection on learning. "Positive" flight. Potential excitement about future. Investments outside of group. Saying good-bye and moving on.	Facilitate group's self-evaluation. Support and encourage a review of the past and a look forward to the future. Facilitate celebration of "great moments in group!" and accomplishments. Tie up loose ends. Support closure of unsettling issues. Identify times of reunion or reconnection. Look for continuity of group experience into members' future lives, but don't deny the group's end. Help members let go.

Appendix B

Effective Group Participant Peer Evaluation (BARS Format)[1]

Ratee's Name (first, last) _____   Date _____

Names of Ratee's Group Members (first names only) _____

For each dimension, please circle the appropriate number or supply an in-between number of your own and circle it.

1.   **Willingness to volunteer**

This participant could be expected to:

100   Initiate group discussion; volunteer in every class.

75   Volunteer ideas most of the time; comment on others' ideas.

50   Comment willingly when asked; offer ideas when asked.

25   Comment reluctantly after being asked; occasionally volunteer ideas or encourage others to volunteer rather than volunteering himself/herself.

0   Refuse to volunteer under any situation or sit back silently.

2.   **Ability to communicate verbally**

This participant could be expected to:

100   Convey ideas and information in an understandable manner; accurately relay messages and report information using correct English; check to make sure others were heard correctly; ask questions when information is not understood; give only relevant information.

75   Speak in a calm, clear voice; convey ideas and information but be occasionally misunderstood; sometimes use lengthy sentences to convey simple ideas.

50   Fail to ask questions when subject matter is not understood; speak frequently without offering new information or ideas; ask same question repeatedly.

25   Report inaccurate information; use incorrect English; dominate discussion, barring input of ideas from others.

0   Refuse to offer ideas; not comment on other group members' ideas, or disrupt group activities with non-class related comments.

3.   **Listening/Attentiveness**

100   The student actively comprehends, interprets, clarifies the ideas conveyed by the group and demonstrates understanding through paraphrasing. The individual responds with appropriate eye contact, leans forward, receptive posture, nods acceptance, and encourages participation by his/her nonverbal gestures.

75   The student understands messages and responds with appropriate eye contact, leans forward, maintains good posture, nods acceptance, and contributes to the discussion.

---

[1]Used by permission of William P. Ferris, Western New England College.

50   The student accepts messages conveyed by the group, shows attentiveness by periodic eye contact and receptive posture, and actively participates in group discussions.

25   The student shows passive interest in the activities of the group, minor eye contact; comments are generally not applicable to the discussion.

0   This student is disinterested in the activities of the group, makes no eye contact, slouches in chair, and does not always acknowledge comments directed to him/her.

4.   Preparation

100   This student obtains additional outside reading material, identifies and shares outside experiences which relate to the subject matter under discussion, is prompt, well-organized, and committed to his/her role in the group.

75   This student reads material, relates it to outside experience, and actively and completely prepares for classes.

50   This student attends class, reads most required assignments, almost always has all required materials on hand, and is usually organized.

25   This student is sometimes disorganized, reads assignments intermittently, often fails to have required materials on hand.

0   This student is tardy, disorganized, does not read the assignments, does not come to class or have required materials on hand.

5.   Ability to work toward consensus

100   Always willing to compromise and work towards common goal of the group without violating integrity of own ideas. Comments are constructive and appropriate to the discussion. Does not dominate the group. Always works within time frame set for the group. Willing to modify ideas to attain goals of group. Volunteers for tasks that help further group goals.

75   Works towards the common goal of the group, but will support own ideas against group consensus if he/she feels his/her point is important enough. Will work within time frame of group but not willing to enforce time limits if discussion continues overtime. Sometimes volunteers for tasks that help further group goals.

50   Works towards common goal of group when in agreement with the goal.

25   Stresses own ideas over those of the group. Seldom agrees with the group consensus. Talks beyond time frame but will stop when group indicates to stop.

0   Argues against group consensus. Continues discussion beyond time frame despite indication from group to stop.

6. **Courtesy, Tact, Sense of Humor**

    100   Allows others to express ideas. Relieves tension in conflict situations. Recognizes humor in tense situation. Laughs at self when appropriate. Attentive when others speak. Actively works toward development of interpersonal skills with co-workers.

    75   Usually attentive when others speak and able to sense the needs of the situation. Accepts criticism. Allows tense situations to develop, but will try to relieve tension when situation gets extreme.

    50   Friendly and responsive to group members. Accepts criticism but is sometimes defensive. Defensive when object of group humor.

    25   Non-responsive to other group members' ideas. Intimidates other group members to stress own point. Creates tension in the group. Defensive when own ideas are challenged. Makes jokes at others' expense.

    0   Interrupts other group members. Dominates group discussion. Fails to recognize humor. Talks to other members of group when someone has the floor. Makes fun of other group members and/or their ideas.

7. **Open-mindedness**

    100   Takes initiative to encourage and accept others' opinions and ideas by directly asking them to elaborate and reinforcing the value of the ideas to the contributors.

    75   Accepts the ideas and opinions of others but will not actively seek them out.

    50   Occasionally considers ideas and opinions of others when asked to.

    25   Tends to verbally discourage ideas and opinions of others with sarcastic and intimidating remarks.

    0   Vehemently rejects any ideas and opinions from others, usually insisting on his/her own.

8. **Ability to offer/accept constructive criticism**

    100   Consistently offers specific, timely, and appropriate feedback. Actively seeks and accepts all feedback; verbally and non-verbally assents to validity of feedback and makes appropriate changes.

    75   Readily accepts constructive criticism and provides meaningful suggestions to others.

    50   Usually offers/accepts constructive criticism.

    25   Offers little or no valid criticism and sulks or pouts when any is offered.

    0   Becomes argumentative when criticized and denies validity. Offers only sarcastic and destructive criticism.

Effective Participator Assessment Form

Ratee's Name (first, last)_____ Date_____

Names of Ratee's Group Members (first names only)_____

Please use this sheet in tandem with the three-page master Peer Evaluation Form by placing eight appropriate numbers in the proper spaces.

1. _____ Willingness to Volunteer

2. _____ Ability to Communicate Verbally

3. _____ Listening/Attentiveness

4. _____ Preparation

5. _____ Ability to Work Towards Consensus

6. _____ Courtesy, Tact, Sense of Humor

7. _____ Open-mindedness

8. _____ Ability to Offer/Accept Constructive Criticism

_____ Total Points Achieved

General Comments: If you wish, please write any general comments that you think may be helpful in any way.

Appendix C

Instructions to New Groups[1]

This sheet is for new class groups. Its purpose is to (1) explain why groups are used as a part of the learning process, and (2) identify steps group members must take to work effectively together.

Businesses form around tasks that are too large for one person to carry out. Consequently, it is necessary for businesspeople to master the skills needed in working together. Many students who have not held positions of responsibility in business believe that these skills are easily mastered. However, students seldom have coped with the kinds of situations that businesspeople face. People in business commonly must deal with "people" situations involving leadership, exercise of power and authority, motivation, face-to-face work skills, persuasion, communication, empathy, work group effectiveness, management of conflict, ambiguity, establishing relations with superiors, politics, and networks. We know that when a person takes on a position of responsibility in business, his or her appreciation of and need for skills in working with others rises dramatically.

A primary purpose for using groups in class is to provide students with the opportunity to learn and practice "people" skills involved in working on a common task.

Many students are reluctant to join groups. The most commonly given reason is that they have been in groups before which have not worked well. Many students cite instances of past groups with bad experiences. Many people wound up doing all the work, while the rest did nothing. If the failures of these groups are analyzed, virtually all can be traced to one of two causes. The first is that the group was given insufficient power over outcomes important to its members. In many courses, groups are not given the authority to allocate group scores to members, and cannot hire or fire members. Consequently, they are unable to motivate group members to carry out the group's work. The second is that the group did have control over important rewards, but failed to exercise this power effectively. For example, groups always have control over the social approval and acceptance which members give to others in the group. In many groups, however, approval and acceptance is not given to members for good performance. Again, even when a group has control over score allocation and hiring and firing, it may back off from using this power.

Let's look now at how these two causes for group failure can be avoided.

Control over important rewards

Many students have had the experience of being assigned to a group project, with no say as to who was to be in the group or how scores earned by the group are to be distributed. A group of this design is an invitation to disaster, since some students are quick to realize they don't have to do anything: since everyone gets the same grade, they can rely on the more concerned students in the group to carry them. Sometimes a low-performing member can be brought around by pressure from others, but often low-performing members don't care very much how they are regarded by others. This has led to intense resentment by many group members, and failure of others to learn anything from the group project.

In the class you are now in, groups may have control over at least three types of member rewards. The first is the scores which members receive upon completion of a group assignment. Groups are expected to allocate earned points to members in proportion to their contribution to the assignment. The second reward is membership. Groups may recruit new members or discharge current members who are not meeting their standards. Similarly, an individual may move out of a group if it does not meet his or her standards. (*Note*: If any changes in membership are being considered, contact the instructor for procedures.) The third reward is

---

[1]By John Bigelow. Used with permission.

approval and acceptance of members by the group. It is very important for many people to feel they are accepted by their group and that they are seen as doing good work.

Taking responsibility

In order for a group to work, members must not only have power over important rewards – they must also use this power to motivate group members. It is all too common for a beginning group to start out with some statement like, "we're all equals here – we know everyone will do their share." This is an invitation to disaster. Very often it is discovered later that someone is not pulling his or her share of the load. If explicit expectations had not been set, it then becomes difficult either to penalize this person for not performing, or to avoid penalizing the other group members who are hurt by the low performer.

In order for a group to be effective, members must receive important rewards only when they are performing up to expectations. While this is easy to say, it takes some work to realize it in practice. The following guidelines are recommended during the course of their group life:

1. Take time at the start to find out about who the people in your group are: what they are looking for and the resources they bring to your group.

2. Involve everyone in group decisions which affect them. Don't let people sit back and let others do the deciding. Involvement in making decisions is an important way of motivating people to carry them out.

3. Develop clear expectations as to what people need to do to stay in the group and to get their share of group rewards. Don't wait until people screw up to set these expectations.

4. When delegating work to individuals, be triple sure you have the means to pull their work back together again into an integrated group product. Usually, assigning someone to edit the pieces is not enough.

5. Don't assume that agreement at the start of the course will carry through to the end. Be ready to renegotiate as the group develops.

6. Recognize that taking responsibility for one's group requires courage, patience, and skill. A significant amount of time must be scheduled for this purpose, and unpleasant or difficult issues may have to be dealt with. You will have to learn from your mistakes. The outcome (both in class and in business), however, is worth the effort: an effectively functioning, high-morale group, of which one can be proud to be a member.

Appendix D

An Introduction to Cases[1]

Management instruction involves the development of a set of philosophies, approaches, skills, knowledge, and techniques. Lectures and readings are a highly efficient way of acquiring knowledge and becoming informed about techniques. Exercises or problem sets are excellent beginning tools for learning about the application and limitations of techniques. But the development of philosophies, approaches, and skills is best served by the case method – a teaching approach that also helps provide knowledge and experience with techniques. Thus, the case method becomes a part of a broad-gauge approach to management education and development. Cases also help you gain institutional knowledge and develop your attitude toward managerial work.

Most students and executive program participants who come to our school are quite familiar with lectures, readings, and exercises, but the case method is often new to them. This material is designed to help those of you who haven't been exposed to the case method yet.

The case method is built around the concepts of *metaphors* and *simulation*. Each case is typically a description of a real business situation and serves as a metaphor for a particular set of problems and/or managerial tasks. As case studies cut across a range of organizations and situations, they provide, for any one student, an exposure far greater than one is likely to experience in day-to-day routine. Even though each particular situation may differ from the metaphors portrayed in the classroom cases, taken together, they provide a useful and relevant set of metaphors that can be applied to most management situations. They permit building knowledge across a range of management subjects, by dealing selectively and intensively with problems and issues in each field. You come to recognize that the situations managers face are not, to a large extent, unique to one organization, or even to a system of organizations, and you come to develop a more professional sense of management. In other words, the situations analyzed and skills developed are applicable to almost all management situations, from marketing to manufacturing to finance and so on.

Cases, and the related case discussions in class, presentations or other teaching designs provide a focal point where your experience, expertise, observations, and rules of thumb which have developed through years of on-the-job operation are brought to bear. What each of you brings to identifying the central issues of the case, analyzing them, and proposing solutions to them, is as important as the content of the case itself. It all helps the method of instruction based on the belief that management is a *skill* rather than a collection of techniques and concepts. The best way to learn a skill is to practice in a simulation-type process. Just as the swimmer learns to swim by swimming, the pianist learns piano by playing, and the figure skater learns by skating, so, too, the skills of management are learned by actively participating in an activity as close to managing as possible. Because it is impractical to have a student manage a company, the case provides a vehicle for *simulation*. Perhaps the most important benefit of using cases is that they help managers learn how to ask relevant and, hopefully, the right, questions.

While there is no "one ideal way to approach a case," some generalities can be drawn. You gain the most by immersing yourself in the case and actively playing the role of the protagonist. By actively studying the case, you begin to learn how to analyze a management situation and develop a plan of action, and then to defend and back up that plan against those in your classroom whose experiences and attitudes, gained by working elsewhere, may be quite different. By participating in an involved manner in the case discussion or in a presentation, you also learn to commit yourself to a position and to express that position articulately. Many argue that the core of management decision-making consists of these processes: analysis, choice, and persuasion.

There is another process that can be developed during the case discussion: generalization. The smart manager steps back from each situation he or she has experienced and asks, "What did I learn?" or "How do this situation

---

[1]Michal Čakrt, Czechoslovak Management Center. Used with permission.

and the lessons relate to my whole experience?" We all know, however, that this approach does not come naturally. It needs to be developed and the case method provides an excellent framework for this. An important part of the process is to relate the cases to the assigned reading material. The readings usually provide the structure and techniques – the tools to handle this or that problem; the case provides the simulated experience in the application of that structure or that tool. Consistent use of cases helps to develop a generalized approach to business situations, as well as a set of philosophies.

For those of you who have worked for a company and already have some managerial experience, there is one final benefit to be achieved by using cases: it renews the sense of fun and excitement which comes from being a manager. You will see in some cases problems which you did not have to face in real life, so you find that you were better off than some others. Other problems you will recognize from firsthand experience. You are encouraged to share that experience with your classmates. They also should come to sense that being a manager is a great challenge – intellectually, politically, and socially.

How to Prepare a Case

As I said above, in case preparation there is no single way that works for everyone. What I offer here are some general guidelines, and you can adapt them to the method that works best for you.

1. Go through the case *almost* as fast as you can turn pages, asking yourself, "What, broadly, is the case about and what types of information am I being given to analyze?"

2. Read the case very carefully, underlining or marking the key facts or phrases as you go. Then ask yourself: "What are the basic issues and tasks this/these manager/s has/have to resolve?" Try hard to put yourself in the position of a manager in the case. Develop a sense of *involvement* and *responsibility* for those problems. *Remember*, the case writer may not always have been on your side; the case might have been developed for a different setting or application and, as in real life, it may contain a lot of information that you do not need. Read to gain a thorough understanding of the *facts* of the case. You are not urged to disagree with facts that are presented as such. Rather, read between the lines and examine the opinions and judgments of people portrayed or quoted in the text. Assess all information, including such things as the attitude and tone of the actors, for its bearing on the situation.

3. Note the key issues on scratch paper. Then go through the case again, sorting out the relevant considerations for each problem area. Make your own judgment about what the real problem or opportunity is, and what is behind it. Do not assume automatically that the "problems," as described and interpreted by the characters in the case, are the real causes of the situations in question. Remember that anyone who presents his or her view *always*, intentionally or subconsciously, pursues their own interests.

4. Make your own decision about the "real" underlying problem or opportunity in the case. You are trying to answer the question "What's going on here and why?" Wherever possible, apply the concepts discussed in class or in the readings to your analysis of the case. The concepts are specifically designed to aid in ferreting out real difficulties and suggesting solutions.
    Do not assume that "problems" identified by actors are necessarily facts to work with. Be very careful not to confuse symptoms with the real causes. Do not be afraid to make some reasonable assumptions if specific information or data are not available. Make an assumption that is sensible, *state it clearly* as an assumption, and proceed. You will often find that your overall analysis of the case is not terribly sensitive to the assumption.

5. After you have identified what you believe is the real underlying difficulty or opportunity, outline a clear statement of your *analysis* of the overall situation that leads to this particular conclusion. Exactly why is the situation occurring and/or what are the key elements of the opportunity that is faced?
    Note: Problem identification and analysis are obviously intertwined. Ideally, problem identification

follows analysis. Often, however, you may be tempted to make a good and intuitive "leap" to problem identification. Regardless of how sure you are about your assessment of the situation, it is critical that you conduct a formal analysis. If you are in any way confused about the nature of the true difficulty, then formal analysis is probably the only route to successful evaluation.

Your analysis of factors (e.g., people, events, structures, relationships, etc.) that underlie the problem or create the opportunity constitute *the single most important step* in case preparation. Your recommendations will have to flow directly from the analysis.

6.   Develop a set of recommendations that address the problem, task, or opportunity at hand, supported by your *analysis* of the case facts. Your recommendations will have to flow directly from the analysis. Be sure to explore alternatives. A complete analysis is not one-sided. Recommendations are rarely credible unless couched in some discussion of the pros and cons of alternatives. You must, however, choose a specific course of *action*. You may decide, in some cases, that there is an important sequencing or timing for implementation of the recommendations: spell this out, as well.

Finally, you may believe that the effectiveness of certain portions of the recommendations depends critically on gathering additional information. Feel free to make information-gathering an important part of your recommendation. You should then be specific about *what* information you need and *how* it should be obtained. Describe and discuss possible changes in your recommendations depending on the results of the data-gathering. *Do not*, however, use a recommendation for "further study" as an excuse for not grappling with the situation now or fully analyzing the data and information you already have. Managers make important decisions under conditions of extreme uncertainty. If you have all the information, it is likely that your competitor has it, too!

A typical request at the end of the class case discussion is "What is the answer?" Let me emphasize here that the case method of learning does not provide the one and only *right answer*. Rather, several viable "answers" will be developed and supported by various participants with the total class.

Business is not – at least not yet – an exact science. There is no single, demonstrably right answer to a business problem. For the student or business person, it cannot be a matter of peeking in the back of a book to see if he has arrived at the right solution. In every business situation, there is always a reasonable possibility that the best answer has not yet been found – even by teachers![2]

Remember, although there is rarely a single "right" answer or solution to a case, there are always many *dumb* solutions. The quality of *your* analysis will make the distinction.

Learning results from rigorous discussion and controversy. Each member of the class – and the instructor – assumes a responsibility for preparing the case and for contributing ideas to the case discussion. Discussing things with others is also a very real-world occurrence. The rewards for these responsibilities are a series of highly exciting, practically oriented educational experiences which bring out a wide range of topics and viewpoints. The result of this very complex and complicated process that creates insight into the issue is usually a very simple and very brilliant idea.

I wish you plenty of those.

References

Gabarro, John J. (1983) Teaching and Using Cases. In *Instructor's Manual to Accompany Managing Behavior in Organizations: Text Cases, Readings*, Schlesinger, Phyllis F., Schlesinger, Leonard A., Eccles, Robert G. and Gabarro, John J., eds. New York, NY: McGraw-Hill, pp. 3-9.

Hammond, John S., *Learning by the Case Method*, Harvard Business School Case No. 9-376-241.

Pearce, Jone L. *Guidelines for Case Analysis*. Unpublished material. Graduate School Management, University of California, Irvine.

Shapiro, Benson P. (1984) *An Introduction to Cases*. A teaching note 9-584-097. Harvard Business School, Publishing Division.

----

[2]Craigg, Charles I., *Because Wisdom Can't Be Told*, Harvard Business School Case No. 9-451-005.

Appendix E

On Using the Classroom as an Organization[1]

Advice to Students

The organizational simulation you will be taking part in reflects some of the issues which you will have to confront in any organization you work for. In order to help understand the purpose of this simulation and to prepare you for some of the experiences involved, you should read the information below carefully.

Groups

Groups are a basic element of organizations. One of the most difficult things that students find on entering full-time work is developing the kinds of interaction that enable them to deal with this new environment. You should look out for how differences in background factors, personal interaction styles, and motivation affect how your group works. Remember, how well you do in this simulation, as in the real world, depends on your group – not just you. All groups experience problems during their development and while becoming cohesive. Try to understand what is going on both intuitively and by using formal models. Try out different strategies to deal with issues. Most of all, consider what you are doing as a member of your group.

Performance

Your group performance will be assessed by other groups in the organization, and they will be allocating resources to your group manager. Remember that your group is going to be viewed as a unit, so not only does your own performance count, but also the performance of other individuals in the group. You have a responsibility for the overall group performance. The manager will allocate rewards individually, and part of the manager's responsibility will be to ensure that rewards are equitable. Often in this simulation, managers over-allocate rewards and the manager's perceptions may differ from those of the groups that are evaluating you. You will need to deal with these conflicts in a constructive way.

Interactions

You will be dealing with what has been called "tacit knowledge" in this class. There appear to be three important elements that distinguish good performers from bad performers. These are:

1. Managing self – Knowledge about self-motivation and self-organizational aspects of performance, e.g., procrastination.

2. Managing tasks – Knowledge about how to do work-related tasks well.

3. Managing others – Interaction with peers.

These are important management tasks and you will be faced with a number of situations where the development of these skills will be important.

Remember, you are working in an organization, so things may not be structured as you want them. You will be presented with problems so that you can develop strategies to deal with them. Your performance is going, in part, to be dependent on other people, and there will be times when you will be frustrated and make mistakes. Learning to deal with these issues is an important part of this simulation and will be a large part of what you will be learning. Keeping a journal during this simulation will help you with this learning. Write down your experiences, how you dealt with issues, and your reactions to events. By writing these down you will be making your thoughts concrete, and you will also find as you read back over your journal that you will gain a perspective on yourself that will help you understand the kinds of interaction you will face in this class. What you learn and how well you do in this class is, in part, going to be a function of whether you are able to deal effectively with a changing environment, and your ability to use your intellectual and emotional resources in this environment.

---

[1] By John Betton. Used with permission.

Appendix F

Giving and Receiving Feedback[1]

Effective and Ineffective Feedback Behaviors

Effective Feedback	Ineffective Feedback
1. Describes the behavior which led to the feedback: "You are finishing my sentences for me."	Uses evaluative/judgmental statements: "You're being rude." Or generalized ones: "You're trying to control the conversation."
2. Comes as soon as appropriate after the behavior – immediately if possible, later if events make that difficult (something more important going on, you need time to "cool down," the person has other feedback to deal with, etc.).	Is delayed, saved up, and "dumped." Also known as "gunny-sacking" or ambushing. The more time that passes, the "safer" it is to give the feedback. Induces guilt and anger in the receiver, because after time has passed, there's usually not much she or he can do about it.
3. Is direct, from sender to receiver.	Indirect: ricocheted ("Tom, how do you feel when Jim cracks his knuckles?") – also known as "let's you and him fight."
4. Is "owned" by the sender, who uses "I messages" and takes responsibility for his or her thoughts, feelings, reactions.	"Ownership" is transferred to "people," "the book," "upper management," "everybody," "we," etc.
5. Includes the sender's real feelings about the behavior, insofar as they are relevant to the feedback: "I get frustrated when I'm trying to make a point and you keep finishing my sentences."	Feelings are concealed, denied, misrepresented, distorted. One way to do this is to "transfer ownership (see #4)." Another way is to smuggle the feelings into the interaction by being sarcastic, sulking, competing to see who's "right," etc. Other indicators: speculations on the receiver's intentions, motivations, or psychological "problems": "You're trying to drive me nuts." "You're just trying to see how much you can get away with." "You have a need to get even with the world."
6. Is checked for clarity, to ensure that the receiver fully understands the message conveyed: "Do you understand what I mean when I say you seem to be sending me a double message?"	Not checked. Sender either assumes clarity or – fairly often – is not interested in whether receiver understands fully: "Stop interrupting me with 'Yes, buts!'"

[1]Reprinted with permission from NTL Institute, "Giving and Receiving Feedback: It Will Never Be Easy, But It Can Be Better," by Lawrence Porter, pp. 42-45, *Reading Book for Human Relations Training*, edited by Lawrence Porter and Bernard Mohr. © 1982.

Effective Feedback	**Ineffective Feedback**
7. Asks relevant questions which seek information (has a problem-solving quality), with the receiver knowing information is sought and having a clear sense that the sender does not know the answer.	Asks questions which are really statements ("Do you think I'm going to let you get away with that?") or which sound like traps ("How many times have you been late this week?"). Experts at the "question game" can easily combine the two ("How do you think that makes me feel?" or "Do you behave that way at home, too?").[2]
8. Is solicited or at least to some extent desired by the receiver.[3]	Is imposed on the receiver, often for her or his "own good."
9. Refers to behaviors about which the receiver could do something ("Wish you'd stop interrupting me.") if he/she wants to.	Refers to behaviors over which the receiver has little or no control, if she or he is to remain authentic: "I wish you'd laugh at my jokes."
10. Affirms the receiver's existence and worth by acknowledging his or her "right" to have the reactions she or he has, whatever they may be, and by being willing to work through issues in a game-free way.	Denies or discounts the receiver by using statistics, abstractions, averages, or by refusing to accept his/her feelings: "Oh, you're just being paranoid." "Come on! You're over-reacting." "You're not really as angry as you say you are."[4]

[2] Most people can make significant improvements in their feedback skills by not asking any questions!

[3] Since the condition doesn't exist that often, you may wonder how you can ever give feedback. Keep two things in mind: 1) Not all the criteria have to be met all the time; and 2) If you have to impose it on the recipient, it's likely to be helpful to the process if you'll keep that in mind and take it into account as you interact.

[4] These may be accurate interpretations, of course, but the sender is not likely to "reach" the receiver by being "right" in these instances. In some significant human interactions, there are often more important things than being that kind of "right."

Appendix G

What to Observe in a Group[1]

Group Observation Table

Behavior in the group can be seen from the point of view of what its purpose or function seems to be. When a member says something, is s/he primarily trying to get the group task accomplished (task), to improve or patch up some relationships among members (maintenance), or to meet some personal need or goal without regard to the group's problems (self-oriented)?

Description of Behavior	Name of Individuals Observed				
Task – Types of behavior relevant to the group's task fulfillment.					
1) Initiator – proposes tasks or goals; defines a problem; suggests ways to solve problems.					
2) Information or opinion seeker – asks for facts, ideas, or suggestions; seeks relevant information about group concern; solicits expressions of values.					
3) Information or opinion giver – offers facts; states belief or opinion.					
4) Clarifier and elaborator – interprets ideas or suggestions; clears up confusions; defines terms; indicates alternatives and issues for the group.					
5) Summarizer – pulls together related ideas; restates suggestions; offers a decision or conclusion for acceptance or rejection.					
6) Consensus tester – asks to see whether the group is nearing a decision; sends up a trial balloon to test a possible conclusion.					

---

[1]Reprinted with permission from NTL Institute, "What to Observe in a Group," by Edgar H. Schein, pp. 72-75, *Reading Book for Human Relations Training,* edited by Lawrence Porter and Bernard Mohr, © 1982.

Description of Behavior	Names of Individuals Observed				
Maintenance – types of behavior relevant to the group remaining in good working order, having a good task work climate, and good relationships that permit maximum use of member resources.					
1) Harmonizer – mediates differences; relieves tension in conflict situations; gets people to explore differences.					
2) Gatekeeper – keeps communication open; facilitates the participation of others; suggests procedures for sharing information.					.
3) Encourager – friendly and responsive to others; offers praise; accepts others' points of view.					
4) Compromiser – when own idea is involved in conflict, offers compromise and admits error; keeps group cohesion.					
5) Standard-setter and tester – tests whether group is satisfied with its procedures; points out explicit or implicit norms to test.					
Self-Oriented – behavior that interferes with group work.					
1) Aggressor – attacks, deflates; sarcastic.					
2) Blocker – resists beyond reason; stops group movement by using hidden items.					
3) Dominator – interrupts; asserts authority; over-participates to the point of interference with others.					
4) Avoider – prevents group from facing controversy; stays off subject to avoid commitment.					
5) Abandoner – makes obvious display of lack of involvement.					

Questions

1. Who talks the most?

2. Who talks the least?

3. Who is listened to the most?

4. Who is listened to the least?

5. Who is the informal leader? (Look for the person who is looked at most when members speak.)

6. Leadership style?   autocratic   _____

    democratic   _____

    laissez-faire   _____

7. How is conflict resolved?

8. Are there any subgroups?

9. Are members withdrawn? What happened?

10. What are the group's norms? (i.e., voting or discussion, joking, interrupting, etc.)

11. How is expertise established and used?

Appendix H

Analysis of Team or Group Effectiveness[1]

Goals and Direction

No clear idea of direction,
confusion on goals

Purpose and direction
well understood

|
0   5   10

Lack of agreement on goals,
different directions in group

Strong agreement on goals,
common direction accepted

|
0   5   10

Climate of Group Atmosphere

Oppressive, doesn't want
to be part of group,
negative atmosphere

Exciting, congenial,
people look forward to group

|
0   5   10

Trust Factors

Very low trust, highly
suspicious attitudes

High trust,
acceptance of each other

|
0   5   10

Communications

Very closed, secretive,
guarded and cautious

Open, sharing, valid
information shared

|
0   5   10

---

[1]By Kenneth L. Murrell. Department of Management, University of West Florida, Pensacola. Used with permission.

No one listens, can't   Active listening
hear anyone but self   and high interest in
                                          what others are saying

_____

                              |
0   5   10

Conflict

Not dealt with openly,   Open discussion,
repressed, under-the-table   managed in order
                                       to use it to help the group

_____

                              |
0   5   10

Resources

Time and material resources   Managed time and other
not used well,   resources well in order
wasted and not managed   to get job done

_____

                              |
0   5   10

Members' Contributions

No one felt they worked   Individuals felt like
well or contributed   they "gave it their all"

_____

                              |
0   5   10

Control and Structure

No controls – just chaos,   Internal controls
no agreed upon or accepted   worked well,
structure   structure very appropriate

_____

                              |
0   5   10

Goal Accomplishments

We don't accomplish   All of our goals were met
anything we want
to get done

_____

                              |
0   5   10

Appendix I

Jung's Personality Typology[1]

Theory of Personality

Jung's personality typology, as operationalized in the Myers-Briggs Type Indicator, provides the theoretical basis for some of the exercises in Chapter 2. Jung observed that people's behavior, rather than being individually unique, fits into patterns, and that much of the seemingly random differences in human behavior are actually orderly and consistent, being explained by differences in psychological attitudes and functions. These differences were termed preferences, because people actually prefer one type of functioning over another (Myers, 1962).

Two of these preferences concern the person's attitude toward the world. It can be one of extraversion or introversion.

The introvert is interested in exploring and analyzing the inner world and is introspective, withdrawn, very preoccupied with his or her own thoughts and reflections and tends to be distrustful (Jung, 1971). What is happening inside the introvert's head is much more interesting than what is outside; the inner world is rich, fascinating, and engrossing. Therefore, the introvert seems to be in continuous retreat from the outer world, holding aloof from external happenings, feeling lonely and lost in large gatherings. This type may often appear awkward and inhibited because the best qualities are kept only for a few close people. Mistrust and self-will characterize the introvert; however, this apprehensiveness of the objective world is not due to fear but because the outer world seems negative, demanding, and overpowering. The introvert's best work is done by self-initiative without interference from others and not influenced by majority views or public opinion. In work situations, introverted managers tend to "like quiet for concentration, be careful with details, like to think a lot before they act, and work contentedly alone" (Myer, 1962).

The extravert, on the other hand, is characterized by an interest in the outer world, by responsiveness to and a willing and ready acceptance of external events, by desire to influence and be influenced by events, a need to join in, the capacity to endure, the actual enjoyment of all kinds of noise and bustle, by a constant attention to environment, the cultivation of friends and acquaintances (none too carefully selected), and, finally, by the great importance associated with the image one projects and therefore a strong tendency to make a show of oneself. As a result, the extravert's philosophy and morals tend to be highly collective with a strong streak of altruism, while moral misgivings result when "other people know." At work, extraverted managers "like variety and action, tend to be faster," "dislike complicated procedures," are often impatient with long, slow jobs, are interested in the results of their job, often act quickly (sometimes without thinking), and usually "communicate well" (Myers, 1962).

No one is a "pure" type. We are all in a state of balance between extraversion (E) and introversion (I), using one type more naturally and more frequently. Earlier research indicates a disproportionate number of extraverted managers. Since a manager is often required to work with and through other people, some extraversion would be useful. But too much can be counterproductive, with the real threat of getting "sucked" into external demands and becoming completely lost in them as well as losing identity and becoming submerged in conformist herd psychology.

Psychological Functions

Jung described four psychological functions which exist along two continua: the perception dimension, with sensing at one end and intuition at the other, and the judgement dimension, with thinking at one end and feeling at the other. According to Jung, one of these four functions will tend to dominate the personality of the individual. For example, a person may be a sensation-thinking, an intuition-thinking, a sensation-feeling, or an intuition-feeling type.

No one is a "pure" type, but we all strive to achieve a state of balance.

The perception dimension of sensation vs. intuition relates to the ways in which a person becomes aware of ideas, facts, occurrences. When using sensing, perception occurs literally through the use of the five senses (Jung, 1971). As a result, this type is very much present-oriented, interested in practical matters, and prefers things to be orderly, precise, and unambiguous. They typically work steadily, like established routine, seldom make errors of fact, and rarely trust their inspirations (Myers, 1962).

Perceiving by intuition, alternatively, cannot be traced back to a conscious sensory experience but rather it is a subconscious process, with ideas or hunches coming "out of the blue," yielding the hidden possibilities of a situation. The intuitive is future-oriented (Myers, 1962), always looking ahead and inspiring others with innovations. By the time everyone else catches up, the intuitive is off on another idea. In fact, the intuitive finds it difficult to tolerate performance of routine tasks; as soon as one is mastered, another is started. Intuitives also "like solving new problems, work in bursts of energy, frequently jump to conclusions, are impatient with complicated situations, dislike taking time for precision, and follow their inspirations, good or bad" (Myers, 1962, p. 50).

Just as there are two ways of perceiving the world, there are two ways of making judgments about one's perceptions: namely, by thinking or by feeling. Thinking is a logical and analytical process, searching for the impersonal, true vs. false, correct vs. incorrect. Principles are more important to the thinker than are people (Myers, 1962), and the thinker often has a difficult time adapting to situations which cannot be understood intellectually (Jung, 1971). Other characteristics of this type are: they "are relatively unemotional and uninterested in people's feelings, may hurt people's feelings without knowing it, like analysis and putting things into logical order, can get along without harmony, need to be treated fairly, are able to reprimand people or fire them when necessary, and may seem hard-hearted" (Myers, 1962, p. 80).

Alternatively, feeling is a personal, subjective process, seeking a good vs. bad or like vs. dislike judgment. Whereas thinking occurs using objective criteria, feeling occurs on the basis of personal values and, in this sense, is different from emotion since feeling judgments are mental evaluations and not emotional reactions. The feeling type lives according to such subjective judgments based on a value system which is either related to society's values, as in the case of the extravert, or personal values, as in the introvert.

Dominant Process

The remaining preference determines which function is the principal or dominant one, i.e., whether perceiving or judging is the primary mode. For instance, when a person follows explanations open-mindedly, then perception (P) is being used; if, on the other hand, one's mind is rather quickly made up as to agreement or disagreement, then judgment (J) is preferred.

A fundamental difference in these two preferences is manifested in terms of which process is turned off or ignored. In order for judging to take place, perception must stop; all the facts are in, so a decision can be made. On the other hand, in order for perception to continue, judgments are put off for the time being, as there is not enough data, new developments may occur.

Basically, the preference shows the difference between the perceptive types who *live* their lives as opposed to the judging types who *run* theirs. Each type is useful, but works better if the person can switch to the other mode when necessary. A pure perceptive type is like a ship with all sail and no rudder, while a pure judging type is all form and no content (Myers, 1962).

As mentioned above, the perception-judgment (P-J) preference determines the principal function. For instance, an ST who prefers perceiving would have sensation, that is, the perceiving function, as his or her principal functions. The principal function of an NF who prefers judging would be feeling, the judging function.

However, in the case of the introvert, the dominant process is turned inward and his or her auxiliary or secondary function is shown to the world. Hence, the best side is kept for self or very close friends. The M-B indicator measures the principal function that is used on the outside world; in the case of the introvert, this is actually the auxiliary function.

Shadow Side

The unconscious and less developed side of a person's personality Jung calls the "shadow side." For example, if a person is primarily a thinking type, the shadow will be feeling, will compensate, at times, for the thinking process, and may show itself at unexpected times (Jung, 1971).

Perception-Judgment Combinations

The four functional types are a means to comprehend the world. Sensation tells us something exists, thinking tells us what that something is, feeling enables us to make value judgments on this object, and intuition gives us the ability to see the inherent possibilities (Mann, et al., 1968).

In each person, one of the perception dimensions and one of the judgment dimensions are favored, so that we all prefer one of the following: 1) sensation with thinking; 2) intuition with thinking; 3) sensation with feeling; or 4) intuition with feeling.

Sensation with Thinking (ST)

This type is usually practical, impersonal, and down-to-earth, being interested in facts, data, and statistics and wanting everything to be orderly, precise, and unambiguous. The ST's tend to value efficiency, production, and clear lines of authority. In problem-solving, the ST analyzes the facts through step-by-step logic, focusing on short-term problems and using standard procedures to find solutions (Hellriegel and Slocum, 1975).

Intuition with Thinking (NT)

NT's are inventive and concept-oriented and are likely to see the possibilities in a situation through impersonal analysis, though sometimes their conceptualizations confuse the other types. Flow charts, graphs, PERT, etc., all are tools that NT's feel comfortable with. These people are innovators of new ideas, frequently spark enthusiasm in others, and when solving problems, will often rely on hunches which they attempt to analyze later.

Sensation with Feeling (SF)

Individuals who are SF's tend to be practical, yet also sociable and gregarious. Like the ST's they are interested in facts, but SF's are more interested in facts about people; and they, too, dislike ambiguity.

SF's would strive to create an open, trusting environment where people care for one another and communicate well (Kilmann, 1975).

Although concerned with people's welfare, SF's have no time or inclination for global reflections on problems, but rather look at small aspects of problems and try to solve these (Hellriegel and Slocum, 1975).

Intuition with Feeling (NF)

Creativity, imagination, and personal warmth are valued by the NF, who is enthusiastic and insightful, generally seeing possibilities in and for people. Their goals are proud and general, often encompassing world problems. Their ideal organization is a decentralized one that has no strict hierarchy, few rules, policies, and procedures, and encourages flexibility and open communication (Kilmann, 1975). It is very important to NF's to be committed to organizational goals. They may seem to be "dreamers" when solving problems, since theirs is, at times, an idealistic view of the world and its difficulties; but they are persistent and committed (Hellriegel and Slocum, 1975).

To summarize, then, Jung's Personality Typology is shown in Figure 1.

Figure 1

Jung's Personality Typology (The Four Preferences) – as Operationalized by Myers and Briggs

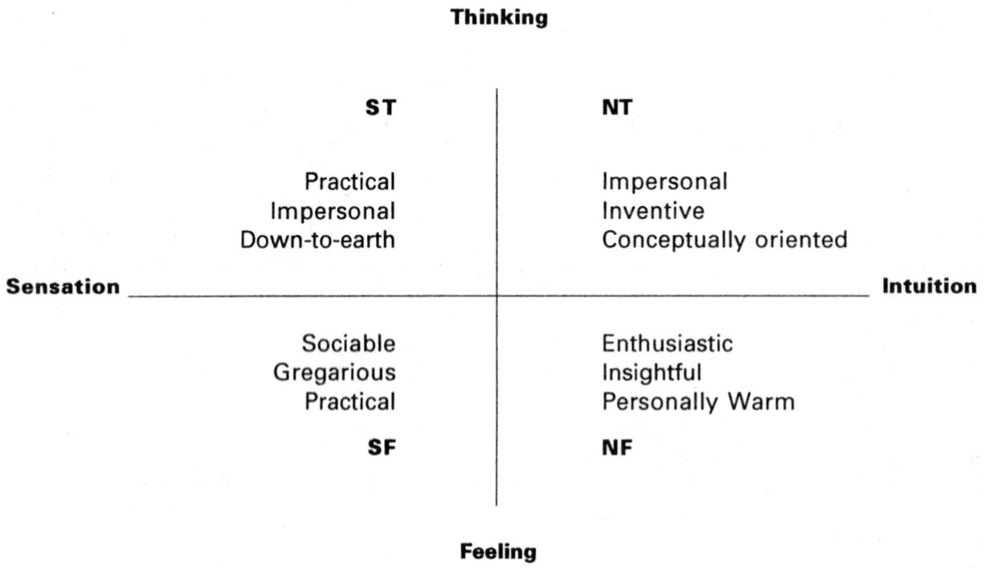

Thinking

	ST		NT	
	Practical		Impersonal	
	Impersonal		Inventive	
	Down-to-earth		Conceptually oriented	
Sensation				**Intuition**
	Sociable		Enthusiastic	
	Gregarious		Insightful	
	Practical		Personally Warm	
	SF		NF	

Feeling

References

Hellriegel, Don, and John W. Slocum, Jr. "Managerial Problem-Solving Styles." *Business Horizons,* December, 1975, pp. 29-37.

Jung, Carl. *Psychological Types.* Princeton, New Jersey: Princeton University Press, 1971.

Mann, Harriett, Miriam Siegler, and Humphrey Osmond. "The Many Worlds of Time." *Journal of Analytical Psychology,* 13, 1 (1968), pp. 33-56.

Myers, Isabel B. *The Myers-Briggs Type Indicator Manual.* Princeton, New Jersey: Education Testing Service, 1962.

Kilmann, R. "Stories Managers Tell: A New Tool for Organizational Problem Solving," *Management Review,* (July 1975) pp. 18-28.

Effects of the Combination of All Four Preferences[1]

SENSING TYPES

WITH THINKING	WITH FEELING

INTROVERTS

JUDGING

ISTJ

Serious, quiet, earn success by concentration and thoroughness. Practical, orderly, matter-of-fact, logical, realistic, and dependable. See to it that everything is well organized. Take responsibility. Make up their own minds as to what should be accomplished and work toward it steadily, regardless of protests or distractions.

Live their outer life more with thinking, inner more with sensing.

ISFJ

Quiet, friendly, responsible, and conscientious. Work devotedly to meet their obligations and serve their friends and school. Thorough, painstaking, accurate. May need time to master technical subjects, as their interests are not often technical. Patient with detail and routine. Loyal, considerate, concerned with how other people feel.

Live their outer life more with feeling, inner more with sensing.

PERCEPTIVE

ISTP

Cool onlookers, quiet, reserved, observing and analyzing life with detached curiosity and unexpected flashes of original humor. Usually interested in impersonal principles, cause and effect, or how and why mechanical things work. Exert themselves no more than they think necessary, because any waste of energy would be inefficient.

Live their outer life more with sensing, inner more with thinking.

ISFP

Retiring, quietly friendly, sensitive, modest about their abilities. Shun disagreements, do not force their opinions or values on others. Usually do not care to lead, but are often loyal followers. May be rather relaxed about assignments or getting things done, because they enjoy the present moment and do not want to spoil it by undue haste or exertion.

Live their outer life more with sensing, inner more with feeling.

EXTRAVERTS

PERCEPTIVE

ESTP

Matter-of-fact, do not worry or hurry, enjoy whatever comes along. Tend to like mechanical things and sports, with friends on the side. May be a bit blunt or insensitive. Can do math or science when they see the need. Dislike long explanations. Are best with real things that can be worked, handled, taken apart or put back together.

Live their outer life more with sensing, inner more with thinking.

ESFP

Outgoing, easygoing, accepting, friendly, fond of a good time. Like sports and making things. Know what's going on and join in eagerly. Find remembering facts easier than mastering theories. Are best in situations that need sound common sense and practical ability with people as well as with things.

Live their outer life more with sensing, inner more with feeling.

JUDGING

ESTJ

Practical realists, matter-of-fact, with a natural head for business or mechanics. Not interested in subjects they see no use for, but can apply themselves when necessary. Like to organize and run activities. Tend to run things well, especially if they remember to consider other people's feelings and points of view when making their decisions.

Live their outer life more with thinking, inner more with sensing.

ESFJ

Warm-hearted, talkative, popular, conscientious, born cooperators, active committee members. Always doing something nice for someone. Work best with plenty of encouragement and praise. Little interest in abstract thinking or technical subjects. Main interest is in things that directly and visibly affect people's lives.

Live their outer life more with feeling, inner more with sensing.

[1]Reprinted by permission of the publisher from *Manual for the Myers-Briggs Type Indicator* by Isabel Briggs Myers, © 1962 by Consulting Psychologists Press.

INTUITIVES

WITH FEELING   WITH THINKING

INFJ

Succeed by perseverance, originality, and desire to do whatever is needed or wanted. Put their best efforts into their work. Quietly forceful, conscientious, concerned for others. Respected for their firm principles. Likely to be honored and followed for their clear convictions as to how best to serve the common good.

Live their outer life more with feeling, inner more with intuition.

INTJ

Have original minds and great drive which they use only for their own purposes. In fields that appeal to them, they have a fine power to organize a job and carry it through with or without help. Skeptical, critical, independent, determined, often stubborn. Must learn to yield less important points in order to win the most important.

Live their outer life more with thinking, inner more with intuition.

INFP

Full of enthusiasm and loyalties, but seldom talk of these until they know you well. Care about learning, ideas, language, and independent projects of their own. Apt to be on yearbook staff, perhaps as editor. Tend to undertake too much, then somehow get it done. Friendly, but often too absorbed in what they are doing to be sociable or notice much.

Live their outer life more with intuition, inner more with feeling.

INTP

Quiet, reserved, brilliant in exams, especially in theoretical or scientific subjects. Logical to the point of hair-splitting. Interested mainly in ideas, with little liking for parties or small talk. Tend to have very sharply defined interests. Need to choose careers where some strong interest of theirs can be used and useful.

Live their outer life more with intuition, inner more with thinking.

ENFP

Warmly enthusiastic, high-spirited, ingenious, imaginative. Able to do almost anything that interests them. Quick with a solution for any difficulty and ready to help anyone with a problem. Often rely on their ability to improvise instead of preparing in advance. Can always find compelling reasons for whatever they want.

Live their outer life more with intuition, inner more with feeling.

ENTP

Quick, ingenious, good at many things. Stimulating company, alert and outspoken, argue for fun on either side of a question. Resourceful in solving new and challenging problems, but may neglect routine assignments. Turn to one new interest after another. Can always find logical reasons for whatever they want.

Live their outer life more with intuition, inner more with thinking.

ENFJ

Responsive and responsible. Feel real concern for what others think and want, and try to handle things with due regard for other people's feelings. Can present a proposal or lead a group discussion with ease and tact. Sociable, popular, active in school affairs, but put time enough on their studies to do good work.

Live their outer life more with feeling, inner more with intuition.

ENTJ

Hearty, frank, able in studies, leaders in activities. Usually good in anything that requires reasoning and intelligent talk, such as public speaking. Are well-informed and keep adding to their fund of knowledge. May sometimes be more positive and confident than their experience in an area warrants.

 Live their outer life more with thinking, inner more with intuition.

INTROVERTS   JUDGING

PERCEPTIVE

EXTRAVERTS   PERCEPTIVE

JUDGING

Appendix J

What Is the Most Important Feature of an Ideal Job?[1]

Auburn Freshmen

ISTJ	ISFJ	INFJ	INTJ
	A Stable and Secure Future	Use My Special Abilities	Be Creative and Original
ISTP	**ISFP**	**INFP**	**INTP**
A Stable and Secure Future		Be Creative and Original	Use My Special Abilities Earn a Lot of Money
ESTP	**ESFP**	**ENFP**	**ENTP**
	A Stable and Secure Future	Be Creative and Original	Be Creative and Original
ESTJ	**ESFJ**	**ENFJ**	**ENTJ**
A Stable and Secure Future	Be of Service to Others	Use My Special Abilities	

[1] Auburn University, W. Harold Grant, *Behavior of MBTI Types*, 1965, © 1962 by Isabel Briggs Myers
Using the Myers-Briggs Type Indicator in Organizations: A Resource Book © 1985 by Consulting Psychologists Press, Inc.

Appendix K

Role Description for "The President's Decision"

Role Sheet:

John/Joan Ward, President

You are president of the ABCO Manufacturing Company and have held this position for the past two years. In your previous position as controller, you advised the president on fiscal and policy matters and gained a close knowledge of the inner workings of the company. As president, your duties are much broader and more complex. You now have final responsibility for policy formulation and execution in such diverse fields as procurement, manufacturing, sales, finance, product development, personnel, public relations, and various other aspects of business operation. To a large extent, the progress of the company and your own success or failure as president depends on you making wise decisions. You get a certain amount of credit when things go well, but you also take the blame when they go wrong.

One of the most difficult problems you have been dealing with since becoming president is whether to expand operations. Within the company and among close business associates, there are conflicting views on the matter. Those opposed to expansion contend that real estate and building values are seriously inflated and that the cost of new equipment is out of line. A further argument is that the television and other electronics sales are highly sensitive to economic conditions. Since company reserves are low, you would have to obtain the necessary funds through stock sales or mortgage loans, and the company's present financial condition does not place it in an advantageous position for such financing. Furthermore, it would be some time before returns from expansion would begin to pay off to any great extent, and an early business slump could wreck the company.

While there are a number of people in the company who favor immediate expansion, all of them tend to see things in terms of their own particular area of the business and none are in a position to have a broad, overall perspective. Nevertheless, in casual discussion of the matter, they have come up with some impressive facts and arguments in favor of setting up a new plant. One contention, for example, is that the present four-story, thirty-year-old building is not adapted for modern straight-line production methods. Not only is it expensive to heat and light, but it lacks the flexibility needed for efficient changeovers to meet production requirements. In addition, it has been necessary to turn down two or three large orders in the past because of insufficient capacity to meet production deadlines. Then there is the contention that a lack of growth is damaging to morale and that good people tend to become discouraged and leave to go with larger or faster growing companies where opportunities are greater.

During the past several months, you tried to keep an open mind to both points of view and, despite the risks, were becoming convinced that on a long-term basis, expansion was the better course to follow. You have been making headway toward getting the company back on its feet, but, as things are, it is a slow, uphill struggle. Nevertheless, given the unfavorable circumstances, you think satisfactory progress has been made.

Despite your best efforts over the past two years, the board of directors informed you late yesterday that it had voted to give you one more year in which to show some results or else resign. You knew that certain members of the board were becoming impatient. However, this action was a shocker. Obviously, expansion is out of the question if results have to be shown within a year. It would take longer than that to make the necessary financial and other arrangements to construct a new plant and get it into operation. The only possible course of action is to play it safe and hope for the best. With a few good breaks and strict belt-tightening throughout the organization, it may be possible to demonstrate the desired results within the deadline set by the board. Certainly this is not the time to take chances. Your decision not to expand must be announced immediately. As a first step you have called a meeting of your three vice-presidents for 3 p.m. Your purpose is to check with them to see whether anything has been overlooked in arriving at your decision. It is now three o'clock and time to begin.

Role Sheet:

William/Wanda Carson, Vice-President, Manufacturing and Product Development

You are vice-president in charge of manufacturing and product development of the ABCO Company. When you moved into this job from that of plant superintendent two years ago, you had high hopes of streamlining operations and you have been able to accomplish a good deal. For years, the previous management had refused to spend money on manufacturing facilities, following a penny-pinching practice of patching and fixing and making you do the best you could with inferior, outmoded equipment and methods. Through your influence with Ward, you have been able to make a number of changes in layout and methods. By carefully shopping around, you have been able to get good buys on several pieces of second-hand but fairly modern equipment. In addition, you have set up a new product-development laboratory. This is a must if the company is to compete with the larger companies and their staff of research people, both in bringing out new products and in working out designs to simplify production. The company is slowly getting back on its feet and, in large part, this is due to the reduced unit costs you have been able to achieve in manufacturing.

However, you have gone just about as far as you can in this direction, and what is needed now is a new, modern plant. The present four-story building was satisfactory for its purpose thirty years ago, but with newer, integrated assembly-line procedures, all operations should be on one floor. The layout of the present building is awkward for moving things along from one process to the next and creates a lot of needless delay in changeovers when you have new orders to fill. It is also costly to light and to heat, and the construction on the upper floor is not strong enough to support some of the new heavy equipment where you could use it to the best advantage. You have urged Ward repeatedly to expand into a modern building and purchase new equipment; although Ward has always given you a fair hearing, you cannot get a commitment concerning your plan. Ward is a good accountant but doesn't know the manufacturing end of the business very well and seems to be a fence straddler. This may be because Ward was not experienced in administrative work before becoming president. As controller, Ward learned company operations from a fiscal angle, but merely advised the former president and did not have to make the final decisions. Now that Ward is on the firing line and has to stand or fall on his/her own judgment, he/she seems to have difficulty in making up his/her mind about things. You have given Ward the best advice you can and you want to help move things along faster, but Ward has to make up his/her mind to expand or else the company will no longer be able to meet competition.

Ward has called a meeting with you and the other two vice-presidents in the office for three o'clock today. Ward has these meetings at fairly frequent intervals. You don't know what he/she has in mind but you hope he/she has finally agreed to go ahead with the new plant. Almost anything would be an improvement over the one the company is in now.

Role Sheet:

James/Jane Jackson, Vice-President, Sales

You are vice-president in charge of sales and came to the ABCO Company five years ago. Before that, you were one of the assistant sales managers of a division of one of the large electrical manufacturing companies. Stepping into the vice-presidency of the ABCO Company meant quite an increase in salary and responsibility, and it seemed that there was a real opportunity to do a good job and make a name for yourself. Five years ago, the company had no real sales organization and was losing ground rapidly. One of your first moves was to try recapturing the market and to expand. This took a lot of work and you had a struggle to win the old management over to your ideas. Now there are sales offices in most of the principal Eastern cities where ABCO products are in demand by manufacturers, and a fairly strong organization has been built up. The reorganization two years ago had its advantages in that Ward gave you more freedom to operate than you had enjoyed previously. Ward is doing a fair job as president in some ways, but seems to be rather unimaginative. Ward always gives your ideas a fair hearing, but in the end he/she seems to shy away from new advertising campaigns. During the past two years, Ward has taken the steam out of some of your best promotional ideas simply by delaying action on them until too late. One of the things you have been pushing, for example, is an expansion of plant facilities. In the past year you have lost several big orders when Carson said he/she couldn't possibly meet the deadline set by the customers. There may have been something to what Carson calls "unreasonable deadlines" in one or two instances; however, it begins to look more and more as though Carson isn't fast enough on his/her feet to make the necessary changeovers in manufacturing and Ward refuses to push him/her. Carson seems to be Ward's fair-haired person. With a new modern plant, there could be no more excuses and you could take advantage of the breaks when big orders come in. It would help a lot, too, if those in charge of product development would get to work. They have been set up for two years now and despite the ideas for new things that your salesmen have been funneling in to them, they haven't shown any progress. A small company like this must have new and better products to offer if it is to compete for new markets. That way the newspapers and trade journals give you a lot of free publicity, and the salesmen have a chance to get a foot in the door of potential customers. The main thing, however, is to get a new plant so that larger orders can be handled. Turning down the big ones – as you had to do several times in the past – is what hurts. It demoralizes your sales force.

Ward has been receptive to your arguments for expansion, and there has been increasing evidence lately that he/she is ready to take action. Today at three o'clock there is to be a meeting in Ward's office with you and the other two vice-presidents. Apparently Ward is about to announce plans for the new plant, because his/her secretary told you over the phone that Ward wanted you to review in your mind, prior to the meeting, all the pros and cons on the matter of expansion. You are on your way to Ward's office now.

Role Sheet:

Russell/Rita Haney, Vice-President, Personnel and Industrial Relations

You are vice-president in charge of personnel and industrial relations, and have held this position since you moved up from the job of personnel director a year and a half ago. All the usual personnel services such as recruitment, hiring, promotions, training, and contract negotiations are handled through your office. On a policy basis, you have set up your office to serve three main functions. One is to prevent as many personnel problems as possible and assist the supervisors with those that arise. Second, you advise the president, Ward, on personnel matters. Third, you are responsible for maintaining a competent work force in which the employees get along well with each other and do a good job.

One of the things you were able to get underway as personnel director was an individualized program of training and work experience for promising young college recruits. Even though the conservatism of the previous management stymied their progress in many ways, you were able to obtain a few good people each year. Then, when the reorganization took place two years ago, a considerable number of these graduates were able to move up a notch. This left a number of vacancies at the trainee level that you were able to fill by going out to the colleges. However, you are now faced with the same problem you had previously: the company isn't growing and many of the people you brought in a few years ago who were not ready to move up during the reorganization are becoming impatient. You cannot hold out much promise to new college graduates because there just isn't any place for them to move up in the company, and there won't be any new opportunities unless the company expands its operations. Meanwhile, other companies are picking them off, one by one. If this is allowed to continue, the management at the middle and lower levels will be second-rate again in a few years. Unless the company can offer good people some inducements to stay, there will be crippling losses in many key positions. The company simply cannot afford that and still stay in competition. As far as you can see, expansion is absolutely essential if the company is to keep these employees.

Ward has sent word that there is to be a meeting at three o'clock in his/her office and that Carson and Jackson are also to be there. Because Carson is in charge of manufacturing and Jackson in charge of sales, it looks as though Ward may be ready to announce plans for the new plant.

Agreement Form for "Peace Negotiations"

Agreement Form

_____ Team and _____ Team

have agreed to split **70 / 60 / 50 percent** of the total "pot" of **$**____

(circle the correct %, based on the payoff matrix)

in the following manner:

Available for distribution: ____ % x **$**_____ ("pot") = **$**____ (**A**)

_____ Team receives ____ % of (**A**)

____ % x **$**_____ (**A**) = **$**_____ (**B**)

_____ Team receives ____ % of (**A**)

____ % x **$**_____ (**A**) = **$**_____ (**C**)

B+C must total A

_____, _____ Team

Signature of Chief Negotiator

Appendix M

TOP SECRET: ARAK
Negotiation Information

Preface

This document contains the information that you as a negotiator will need for the conference. It describes the scoring system, security, and goals of Arak for each area.

Scoring

You are to represent Arak in the negotiations over the disputed zone. Naturally the government of Arak expects you to do the best you can for the citizens. To assist you in meeting the desires of the citizens, the government has designed a point system that indicates the value of the issues as accurately as they can be estimated. Your goal is to maximize the total number of points for the whole negotiations.

Security

The disclosure of TOP SECRET information from the "Goal" sections that follow is left to your discretion during the negotiations. The following Area discussions are divided into three sections: Descriptions, Goals, and Intelligence.

Descriptions: All description are common knowledge.

> *Goals*: All goal sections are TOP SECRET. These are the intentions and priorities of Arak. They also provide additional information which is not available or known to Barkan.

> *Intelligence*: These sections are the result of espionage which has been conducted. Information about Barkan is presented that may be useful during negotiations.

Area I

Description: This is a choice food producing area, forest products resources area, and a potential source of bauxite (aluminum ore). The area is 50 miles wide and approximately 90 miles long.

> *Goal:* Ownership of this area can help overcome several major problems faced by Arak. They are: insufficient food for Arakians, a balance of payments deficit, and a diminishing supply of timber for the house building industry. In addition, it could provide a source of raw material for the country's developing industrial base.

> There have been severe shortages in three of the last ten years resulting in malnutrition of approximately three million school-age children. Naturally the solution to this problem is a high priority for Arak.

The second problem is the balance of payments deficit. Because of the recent food shortages, Arak has run up a large deficit and its credit rating is quite poor in the worldwide monetary market. It is crucial that Arak overcome this deficit by developing an export business.

The townships in the central part of Area I are particularly well suited to potato production, although potatoes can be grown successfully anywhere in the valley. Potatoes are central in the diet of Arakians. Other food crops can be grown at various places throughout the area. It is very important to obtain as much land as possible to alleviate the threat of malnutrition to Arakian school children.

Arak is well known for its pure grape juice which it exports when Area I is in its possession. Export of this juice brings in substantial revenue and adds immensely to the prestige of the country. Much of Area I is ideally suited for highly profitable production of both juice and table grapes.

Arak is attempting to provide housing for all of its population but it is facing a diminishing supply of timber within its present borders. If you can gain control of most of the forest land, you can assure adequate housing for Arakians. Without a sufficient supply of timber, many Arakians will remain in substandard housing.

The Ministry of Agriculture and Natural Resources has assigned a point value to each of the townships to indicate the relative value of each in solving Arak's problems. These are indicated in the TOP SECRET map. The Ministry estimates that if you gain control of any combination of townships worth 140 to 160 of the 248 points, then Arak will be free of food shortages, will be able to export juice, and will be able to adequately house the population.

Based on these estimates the Prime Minister has instructed you to try to obtain the maximum number of points you can for your country.

Intelligence: Because of the highly productive and useful nature of this area, you can expect Barkan to be very interested in this area, or at least very resistant to the idea of giving up all or part of this area.

Area II

Description: This is a very arid region which, until recently, was largely unknown. Because of the remoteness of this region, little development has taken place. The area is 50 miles wide and 90 miles long. Ten years ago, Cordan erected Steeltown about 25 miles outside this region. Cordan has never made any move to take over this region and remains friendly to both Arak and Barkan.

Goal: Arak has been put in a very difficult position in recent years. The need for steel has been acute in the past 10 years. Production of farm machinery, heavy equipment for construction, and defense weapons has depended on a regular supply of quality steel in Trade City, 50 miles north of Area II.

Since the erection of Steeltown in Cordan, Arak has traded vigorously for the steel produced. This has been marginally satisfactory in the past, but it presents Arak with two problems: unpredictable quality steel and a balance of payments deficit with Cordan.

Historically, 15 percent of the steel shipped from Steeltown has not passed the quality inspections. This occurs because Steeltown is operating over capacity and so cannot monitor adequately.

The trade has been secured primarily through the mining of a small iron ore deposit northeast of Trade City, about 75 miles from Steeltown. Ore is sold to Steeltown from this deposit at $5 per ton, and steel is purchased for $25 per ton. This has caused a serious balance of payments problem and the rapid depletion of this small ore deposit. It is estimated by the Ministry of Agriculture and Natural Resources that at current rates of mining, this deposit will be depleted at the end of two years. Consequently, an intensive search was made for a new ore deposit. An extremely large deposit was located. However, it is 100 miles south of Trade City, right on the border of Barkan. Knowledge of this deposit has been kept TOP SECRET and it is known that Barkan is not aware of this important resource. If this deposit could be obtained, trade with Cordan would continue and the balance of payments problem could be resolved.

Arak has long desired to produce its own steel, but it has not had all the necessary factors of production. It does have an ore deposit 900 miles north (not on map) but it can not exploit it because the iron ore and coal must be within 150 miles of each other to be economically useful. The Ministry of Industry advises that due to slowdowns in other fields, Arak has an abundance of skilled workers who could man a steel plant, but there is a serious question whether Arak has the technical skills to build a steel plant.

The Ministry of Industry found it impossible to anticipate all the solutions you, as a negotiator, might devise. But to help you weigh the issues in Area II, the Ministry advises that:

1. A solution that *almost certainly* will provide for reliable delivery of steel for the long run (20 years) is worth 100 points.

2. A solution that probably will provide long-term reliable delivery of steel is worth 70 points.

3. A solution that reduces the deficit with Cordan is worth 40 points.

4. No solution is worth zero points.

> *Intelligence*: The goals and priorities of Barkan are not known. However, it is known that Barkan receives at least some of its steel from Cordan. Also, it is estimated that steel is important to the welfare of Barkan, as it is with most developing countries.

Time for the Conference

The conference is scheduled to last thirty minutes. A treaty must be completed and signed by both negotiators by the end of the conference to prevent war between Arak and Barkan. Failure to prevent this war will result in no points for you as a negotiator.

For Arak Only

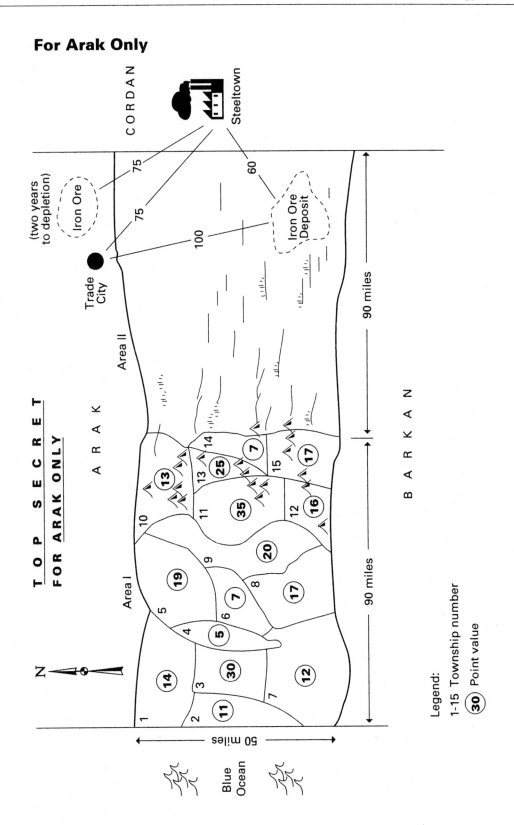

T O P S E C R E T
FOR ARAK ONLY

N

A R A K

Area I

Area II

CORDAN

(two years
to depletion)
Iron Ore

75

75

100

60

Trade
City

Iron Ore
Deposit

Steeltown

1
14
2
3
11
30
5
4
12
9
5
7
19
6
8
7
20
17
10
13
11
35
14
13
25
15
12
16
7
17

90 miles

90 miles

50 miles

Blue
Ocean

B A R K A N

Legend:

1-15 Township number

(30) Point value

Appendix N

TOP SECRET: BARKAN
Negotiation Information

Preface

This document contains the information that you as a negotiator will need for the conference. It describes the scoring system, security, and goals of Barkan for each area.

Scoring

You are to represent Barkan in the negotiations over the disputed zone. Naturally the government of Barkan expects you to do the best you can for the citizens. To assist you in meeting the desires of the citizens, the government has designed a point system that indicates the value of the issues as accurately as they can be estimated. Your goal is to maximize the total number of points for the whole negotiations.

Security

The disclosure of TOP SECRET information from the "Goal" sections that follow is left to your discretion during the negotiations. The following Area discussions are divided into three sections: Descriptions, Goals, and Intelligence.

Descriptions: All descriptions are common knowledge.

> *Goals*: All goal sections are TOP SECRET. These are the intentions and priorities of Arak. They also provide additional information which is not available or known to Barkan.

> *Intelligence*: These sections are the result of espionage which has been conducted. Information about Barkan is presented that may be useful during negotiations.

Area I

Description: This is a choice food producing area, forest products resource area, and a potential source of bauxite (aluminum ore). The area is 50 miles wide and approximately 90 miles long.

> *Goal*: Ownership of this area can help overcome several major problems faced by Barkan. They are: insufficient food for Barkanians, a balance of payments deficit, and a diminishing supply of pulpwood for its paper mills. In addition, it could provide a source of raw material for the country's developing industrial base.

> There have been severe shortages in four of the last twelve years resulting in thousands of cases of rickets and anemia in preschool-age children. Naturally the solution to this problem is a high priority for Barkan. The second problem is the balance of payments deficit. Because of the recent food shortages Barkan has run up a large deficit and its credit rating is quite poor in the worldwide monetary market. It is crucial that Barkan overcome this deficit by developing an export business.

The townships in the central part of Area I are particularly well suited for wheat production, although wheat can be grown successfully anywhere in the valley. Wheat is central in the diet of Barkanians. Other food crops can be grown at various places throughout the area. It is very important to obtain as much land as possible to alleviate the threat of disease to Barkanian children.

Barkan is well known for its quality fruit preserves which it exports when Area I is in its possession. Export of these preserves brings in substantial revenue and adds immensely to the prestige of the country. Much of Area I is ideally suited for highly profitable production of strawberries, peaches, and various berries necessary for the production of preserves.

As a result of uncontrolled logging 50 years earlier, Barkan's own forests are presently being consumed faster than trees are being replaced. If you can gain control of most of the forest land in Area I, a steady supply of wood pulp can be obtained. This will keep the paper mills running while the traditional sources of pulpwood within the established border replenish themselves. Without a sufficient supply of pulpwood, the paper mills will close down and over 5,000 employees will be laid off.

The Ministry of Agriculture and Natural Resources has assigned a point value to each of the townships to indicate the relative value of each in solving Barkan's problems. These are indicated in the TOP SECRET map. The Ministry estimates that if you gain control of any combination of townships worth 140 to 160 of the 248 points, then Barkan will be free of food shortages, will be able to export preserves, and will have sufficient pulpwood.

Based on these estimates, the Prime Minister has instructed you to try to obtain the maximum number of points you can for your country.

Intelligence: Because of the highly productive and useful nature of this area, you can expect Arak to be very interested in this area, or at least very resistant to the idea of giving up all or part of this area.

Area II

Description: This is a very arid region which, until recently, was largely unknown. Because of the remoteness of this region, little development has taken place. The area is 50 miles wide and 90 miles long. Ten years ago Cordan erected Steeltown about 25 miles outside this region. Cordan has never made any move to take over this region and remains friendly to both Arak and Barkan.

Goal: Barkan has been put in a very difficult position in recent years. The need for steel has been acute in the past 10 years. Production of machine tools, trucks, heavy equipment for construction, and defense weapons have all depended on a steady supply of raw steel into Skill City, 50 miles south of Area II.

Since the erection of Steeltown in Cordan, Barkan has traded vigorously for the steel produced. This has been marginally satisfactory in the past but it presents Barkan with two problems: irregularity of delivery and a balance of payments deficit with Cordan.

Historically, approximately 10 percent of the orders of steel from Steeltown have arrived more than three months late. This occurs because Steeltown is operating over capacity and so incurs frequent breakdowns.

The trade has been secured primarily through the mining of a small coal deposit southeast of Skill City, about 75 miles from Steeltown. Coal is sold to Steeltown from this deposit at $5 per ton and steel is purchased for $25 per ton. This has caused a serious balance of payments problem and the rapid depletion of this small coal deposit. It is estimated by the Ministry of Agriculture and Natural Resources that at current rates of mining, this deposit will be depleted at the end of two years. Consequently, an intensive search was made for a new coal deposit. An extremely large deposit was located. However, it is 100 miles north of Skill City, right on the border of Arak. Knowledge of this deposit has been kept TOP SECRET and it is known that Arak is not aware of this important resource. If this deposit could be obtained, trade with Cordan would continue and the balance of payments problem could be resolved.

Barkan has long desired to produce its own steel, but it has not had all the necessary factors of production. It does have an iron ore deposit 700 miles south (not on map) but it can not exploit it because the iron ore and coal must be within 150 miles of each other to be economically useful. The Ministry of Industry advises that Barkan has the technical skills to build a steel mill, but that there are not enough skilled steel workers to fill all the positions in a steel mill.

The Ministry of Industry found it impossible to anticipate all the solutions you, the negotiator, might devise but to help you weight the issues in Area II the Ministry advises that:

1. A solution that *almost certainly* will provide for reliable delivery of steel for the long run (20 years) is worth 100 points.

2. A solution that probably will provide long-term reliable delivery of steel is worth 70 points.

3. A solution that reduces the deficit with Cordan is worth 40 points.

4. No solution is worth zero points.

Intelligence: The goals and priorities of Arak are not known. However, it is known that Arak receives at least some of its steel from Cordan. Also, it is estimated that steel is important to the welfare of Arak, as with most developing countries.

Time for the Conference

The conference is scheduled to last thirty minutes. A treaty must be completed and signed by both negotiators by the end of the conference to prevent war between Arak and Barkan. Failure to prevent this war will result in no points for you as a negotiator.

For Barkan Only

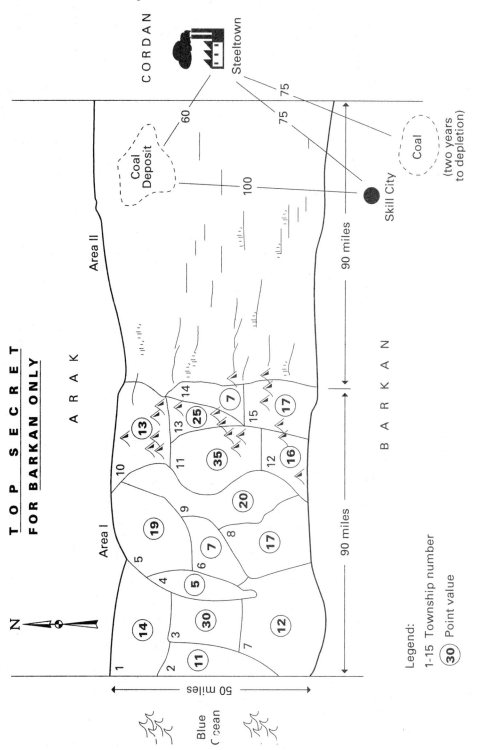

Appendix O

Treaty for "Border Dispute"

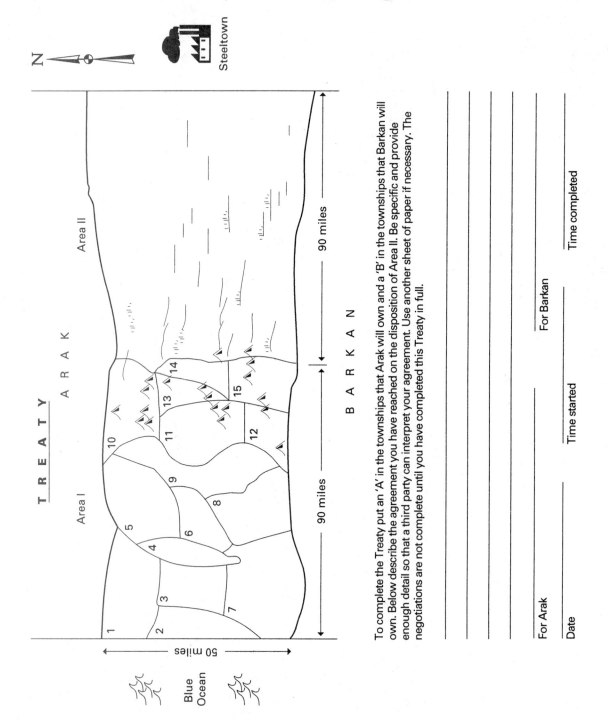

To complete the Treaty put an 'A' in the townships that Arak will own and a 'B' in the townships that Barkan will own. Below describe the agreement you have reached on the disposition of Area II. Be specific and provide enough detail so that a third party can interpret your agreement. Use another sheet of paper if necessary. The negotiations are not complete until you have completed this Treaty in full.

For Arak _____   For Barkan _____

Date _____   Time started _____   Time completed _____

Appendix P

Scoring Protocol for "Border Dispute"

Area I Scoring: Add the points for each negotiator.

Area II Scoring:

100 points   A solution that *almost certainly* solves the steel problem will include access to both of the mineral resources (coal and iron) in Area II, plus the use of Barkan's technological skills for building a steel mill and Arak's skilled workers to man the plant. (Although the chances are remote, it is possible for one negotiator to gain all of the resources and the opponent to end up with none.

70 points   A solution which *probably* solves the problem is one that falls short of the above but does better than simply gaining access to one resource (as below). This includes any solution which provides partial to full access to both mineral resources, but does not include the indication of plans to share technology and skilled labor. Some examples are:

      1. Full ownership of both iron and coal.

      2. Full ownership of one resource and half of the other.

      3. Partial ownership of both iron and coal.

      4. Sharing "rights" to both or "joint exploration" of the area.

40 points   A solution which eliminates the balance of payments deficit is full or part ownership of one resource. There is no indication of any sharing of resources or sharing of technology and manpower. Some examples are lines drawn in Area II like this:

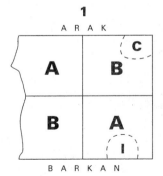
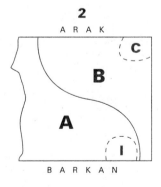
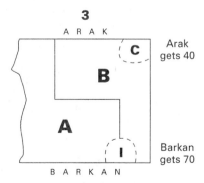

0 points   No solution. The negotiators reach no agreement or one negotiator relinquishes all rights in Area II.

Appendix Q

Case Study for "Chris Jamison"

Case Study: _____

Chris Jamison

Chris Jamison was sitting alone, deep in thought on Friday afternoon in June in the Phoenix branch office of the Big Six accounting firm, Arthur Andersen & Co. He has worked there in the tax audit division for the past six years and has done very well. He has worked hard in lower staff positions and has developed a strong reputation, both at the local office and recently, at Chicago headquarters, as a very competent professional who has great promise within the company.

Chris sat contemplating the conversation he had just had with his office manager and mentor, Jim Wilkins, about Chris' promotion to the position of tax audit manager within the firm. This promotion would involve Chris' relocating to a new branch office in Portland. The promotion would represent a personal and gratifying challenge Chris had wanted for some time now, and would serve as an outstanding opportunity leading to much higher management advancement within the firm.

Despite this very positive news, Chris felt quite perplexed and anxious about how this career opportunity would affect his family. His wife, Kim, was just finishing up her Ph.D. in English Literature at Arizona State University. Ever since their marriage eight years before, Kim had dreamed about teaching English literature at an Ivy League school back East. She also wanted to do professional writing on the side. University faculty positions in English Literature were very scarce throughout the country, and Kim had heretofore been looking for a position with very little success. Recently, however, she interviewed at Cornell University and was offered a one-year visiting assistant professor position beginning in September. Kim was very pleased with this opportunity which could possibly turn into a permanent position at Cornell. As Kim considered whether or not to accept the Cornell offer, she thought that even if a permanent position were not subsequently offered, she would have a much stronger chance at obtaining a permanent faculty position elsewhere with Cornell experience on her resume.

Chris initially felt very pleased for Kim, but now he was feeling torn between supporting Kim in her career dream pursuit by moving to Cornell in the small town of Ithaca, New York, or accepting the very attractive career opportunity recently presented to him. Jim Wilkins indicated that he understood Chris' dilemma, but that he should know that such a tremendous opportunity within the firm occurs rarely. Besides, his turning down this career advancement offer might even, in fact, hurt his prospects for significant future advancement within the firm.

Chris had majored in accounting in college and had a solid B grade point average. He was a good student, but wasn't very excited about his coursework. After graduation he accepted a job with a small firm which helped support Kim through graduate school. A year later they had a child, David. Soon, Chris joined Arthur Andersen & Co. with a considerable salary increase; but more importantly to him, he became very pleased and excited about his new work and career opportunity. David was placed in day care during the time when Kim was occupied with her studies. Chris was glad that Kim was able to spend much of her study time at home with David, but he had feelings of regret and even guilt that he himself had so little time to spend with his precious child.

Chris thought about the conversation that he would soon have with Kim when he returned home. His anxiety was heightened by Jim Wilkins' request for him to have a response to the promotion offer when he returned to work the following Monday morning.

Appendix R

Element B¹

Element B is designed to help me become more aware of how I behave toward other people, and how I think other people behave toward me. There are no "right" or "wrong" answers. The more honest I am, the more information I receive from Element B.

After I read these directions, I turn to the questionnaire. For the columns on the left of the items, I complete the section entitled

What I See

I describe the situation from my point of view.

For each statement, I circle one of the letters at the left of the item. The letters indicate how much I agree with the item. The more I agree, the farther to the right my selection is.

Disagree				Agree	
a	b	c	d	e	f

When I have completed the left-hand column for all items, I return to the top of the page and complete the section entitled

What I Want

Here, I describe the situation the way I want it to be.

For each statement, I circle one of the letters at the left of the item. The letters indicate how much I agree with the item. The more I agree, the farther to the left my selection is.

Want				Don't Want	
a	b	c	d	e	f

Definitions of the relevant terms may be helpful.

       include   = do things with, share

       control   = take charge, influence

       open   = disclose, tell true feelings

Now I turn to the questionnaire and begin.

---

¹ © 1987 by Will Schutz, Ph.D., author of *The Human Element: Productivity, Self-Esteem and the Bottom Line* (1994). Element B was first introduced in *The Truth Option* (1984). Publisher: WSA, 61 Camino Alto, Suite 100-C, Mill Valley CA 94941, (415)383-8275.

What I See   **What I Want**

Disagree   *Agree*   *Want*   *Don't Want*

a b c d e f   1. I seek out people to be with.   g h i j k l

a b c d e f   2. People decide what to do when we are together   g h i j k l

a b c d e f   3. I am totally honest with my close friends.   g h i j k l

a b c d e f   4. People invite me to do things.   g h i j k l

a b c d e f   5. I am the dominant person when I am with people.   g h i j k l

a b c d e f   6. My close friends tell me their real feelings.   g h i j k l

a b c d e f   7. I join social groups.   g h i j k l

a b c d e f   8. People strongly influence my actions.   g h i j k l

a b c d e f   9. I confide in my close friends.   g h i j k l

a b c d e f   10. People invite me to join their activities.   g h i j k l

a b c d e f   11. I get other people to do things I want done.   g h i j k l

a b c d e f   12. My close friends tell me about private matters.   g h i j k l

a b c d e f   13. I join social organizations.   g h i j k l

a b c d e f   14. People control my actions.   g h i j k l

a b c d e f   15. I am more comfortable when people do not get too close.   g h i j k l

a b c d e f   16. People include me in their activities.   g h i j k l

a b c d e f   17. I strongly influence other people's actions.   g h i j k l

a b c d e f   18. My close friends do not tell me all about themselves.   g h i j k l

a b c d e f   19. I am included in informal social activities.   g h i j k l

a b c d e f   20. I am easily led by people.   g h i j k l

a b c d e f   21. People should keep their private feelings to themselves.   g h i j k l

a b c d e f   22. People invite me to participate in their activities.   g h i j k l

a b c d e f   23. I take charge when I am with people socially.   g h i j k l

a b c d e f   24. My close friends let me know their real feelings.   g h i j k l

a b c d e f   25. I include other people in my plans.   g h i j k l

a b c d e f   26. People decide things for me.   g h i j k l

a b c d e f   27. There are some things I do not tell anyone.   g h i j k l

a b c d e f   28. People include me in their social affairs.   g h i j k l

a b c d e f   29. I get people to do things the way I want them done.   g h i j k l

a b c d e f   30. My closest friends keep secrets from me.   g h i j k l

a b c d e f   31. I have people around me.   g h i j k l

What I See

Disagree   *Agree*

Want *Don't Want*

a	b	c	d	e	f	32. People strongly influence my ideas.	g	h	i	j	k	l
a	b	c	d	e	f	33. There are some things I would not tell anyone.	g	h	i	j	k	l
a	b	c	d	e	f	34. People ask me to participate in their discussions.	g	h	i	j	k	l
a	b	c	d	e	f	35. I take charge when I am with people.	g	h	i	j	k	l
a	b	c	d	e	f	36. My friends confide in me.	g	h	i	j	k	l
a	b	c	d	e	f	37. When people are doing things together I join them.	g	h	i	j	k	l
a	b	c	d	e	f	38. I am strongly influenced by what people say.	g	h	i	j	k	l
a	b	c	d	e	f	39. I have at least one friend to whom I can tell anything.	g	h	i	j	k	l
a	b	c	d	e	f	40. People invite me to their parties.	g	h	i	j	k	l
a	b	c	d	e	f	41. I strongly influence other people's ideas.	g	h	i	j	k	l
a	b	c	d	e	f	42. My close friends keep their feelings a secret from me.	g	h	i	j	k	l
a	b	c	d	e	f	43. I look for people to be with.	g	h	i	j	k	l
a	b	c	d	e	f	44. Other people take charge when we work together.	g	h	i	j	k	l
a	b	c	d	e	f	45. There is a part of myself I keep private.	g	h	i	j	k	l
a	b	c	d	e	f	46. People invite me to join them when we have free time.	g	h	i	j	k	l
a	b	c	d	e	f	47. I take charge when I work with people.	g	h	i	j	k	l
a	b	c	d	e	f	48. At least two of my friends tell me their true feelings.	g	h	i	j	k	l
a	b	c	d	e	f	49. I participate in group activities.	g	h	i	j	k	l
a	b	c	d	e	f	50. People often cause me to change my mind.	g	h	i	j	k	l
a	b	c	d	e	f	51. I have close relationships with a few people.	g	h	i	j	k	l
a	b	c	d	e	f	52. People invite me to do things with them.	g	h	i	j	k	l
a	b	c	d	e	f	53. I see to it that people do things the way I want them to.	g	h	i	j	k	l
a	b	c	d	e	f	54. My friends tell me about their private lives.	g	h	i	j	k	l

Scoring Key

Circle each letter which you checked in the questionnaire and score one point for each, then transfer your scores to the summary sheet on the next page.

11	12	13	14
1. d e f	1. g h i	4. e f	4. g h
7. c d e f	7. g h i j	10. e f	10. g h
13. c d e f	13. g h i j	16. e f	16. g h
19. d e f	19. g h i	22. e f	22. g h
25. e f	25. g h	28. e f	28. g h
31. e f	31. g h	34. f	34. g
37. e f	37. g h	40. e f	40. g h
43. f	43. g	46. e f	46. g h
49. f	49. g	52. d e f	52. g h i
Total letters circled	Total letters circled	Total letters circled	Total letters circled
_____	_____	_____	_____

21	22	23	24
5. d e f	5. g h i	2. c d e f	2. g h i j
11. e f	11. g h	8. c d e f	8. g h i j
17. e f	17. g h	14. c d e f	14. g h i j
23. d e f	23. g h i	20. d e f	20. g h i
29. e f	29. g h	26. b c d e f	26. g h i j k
35. d e f	35. g h i	32. d e f	32. g h i
41. d e f	41. g h i	38. d e f	38. g h i
47. e f	47. g h	44. c d e f	44. g h i j
53. d e f	53. g h i	49. f	49. g
Total letters circled	Total letters circled	Total letters circled	Total letters circled
_____	_____	_____	_____

31	32	33	34
3. e f	3. g h	6. e f	6. g h
9. e f	9. g	12. e f	12. g h
15. a b c	15. j k l	18. a b	18. k l
21. a b c	21. j k l	24. f	24. g
27. a b c d	27. i j k l	30. a b c	30. j k l
33. a b c d	33. i j k l	36. e f	36. g h
39. f	39. g	42. a	42. l
45. a b c d	45. i j k l	48. e f	48. g h
51. f	51. g	54. d e f	54. g h i
Total letters circled	Total letters circled	Total letters circled	Total letters circled
_____	_____	_____	_____

Summary Sheet

	11
I include people.	
I want to include people.	

12

	13
People include me.	
I want people to include me.	

14

	21
I control people.	
I want to control people.	

22

	23
People control me.	
I want people to control me.	

24

	31
I am open with people.	
I want to be open with people.	

32

	33
People are open with me.	
I want people to be open with me.	

34

Principles of Interpretation

- Scores range from 0 to 9. Each score indicates the degree to which you agree with that scale name.

- *Element B* is not an evaluation. There is nothing good or bad about any score. Scores are opportunities to learn more about yourself.

- Your scores are a reflection of how you have chosen to be, up to now. You can change if you have the desire and the willingness to learn how to change.

- The primary value of this instrument is as a springboard. You learn from observing your responses to the scores. These responses may tell you more about yourself.

- When you find yourself responding angrily or defensively to one of the scores, consider the possibility that, deep down, you believe the score is accurate and you do not want it to be. Or consider that only one percent is accurate. Is there something you can learn from that one percent?

- If the scores do not fit the picture you have of yourself, you may assume (1) *Element B* is inaccurate, or (2) the part of you that responded to the items is telling you something about yourself you have not been paying attention to, or (3) there is some truth in both (1) and (2) above.

- In short, if you avoid seeing these scores as judgments, you may experience the joy that comes from getting to know yourself a little bit better.